EMPOWERING PROGRESSIVE THIRD PARTIES IN THE UNITED STATES

This groundbreaking collection of writings explores how progressive third parties in the United States can become more electorally successful and politically influential. It is the only recently published book that focuses exclusively on how such parties may advance. Their rise may be essential to countering the powerful, growing sway of wealth within the two major American parties and to creating a more just, democratic United States.

Contributors include key participants in and observers of the U.S. left third party movement. Nearly all have previously authored books or articles on progressive politics. Many have led effective left third party efforts, and some have held elected office on behalf of a progressive third party. Together, the writers reflect on a wide range of relevant parties, including the Green Party, the Vermont Progressive Party, the Labor Party, the Working Families Party, Socialist Alternative, and potential new parties on the American left. The writers highlight a variety of strategies and conditions that may facilitate electoral breakthroughs by such parties and their candidates. Overall, the collection suggests that U.S. progressive third parties may make more headway if they thoughtfully combine their idealism and sense of urgency with a flexible, pragmatic approach to gaining power.

Jonathan H. Martin is Professor of Sociology at Framingham State University and a long time political activist.

EMPOWERING PROGRESSIVE THIRD PARTIES IN THE UNITED STATES

Defeating Duopoly, Advancing Democracy

Edited by Jonathan H. Martin

Routledge
Taylor & Francis Group

NEW YORK AND LONDON

First published 2016
by Routledge
711 Third Avenue, New York, NY 10017

by Routledge
2 Park Square, Milton Park, Abingdon, Oxon OX14 4RN

Routledge is an imprint of the Taylor & Francis Group, an informa business

British Library Cataloguing in Publication Data
A catalogue record for this book is available from the British Library.

Library of Congress Cataloging-in-Publication Data
A catalog record for this book has been requested

ISBN: 978-1-138-02200-3 (hbk)
ISBN: 978-1-138-02201-0 (pbk)
ISBN: 978-1-315-77736-8 (ebk)

Typeset in Bembo
by Apex CoVantage, LLC

Printed and bound in the United States of America by Publishers Graphics, LLC on sustainably sourced paper.

CONTENTS

TABLES

CONTRIBUTORS

Sayeed Iftekhar Ahmed is adjunct faculty in the School of Security and Global Studies at the American Public University System in Charles Town, West Virginia. He received his PhD in political science from Northern Arizona University. His writing focuses on democratization, gender and development, water governance, and Islamism. He is the author of *Water for Poor Women: Quest for an Alternative Paradigm*, and he is working on another book with the tentative title *Islamism in Pakistan and Bangladesh*.

Theresa Amato was the national campaign manager and in-house counsel for both Nader for President 2000 and Nader for President 2004. She is the author of *Grand Illusion: The Myth of Voter Choice in a Two-Party Tyranny*.

Terry Bouricius is a founder of the Vermont Progressive Party and its predecessor, the Progressive Coalition. He was the first Progressive elected to the Burlington (Vermont) City Council and to the Vermont House of Representatives, in 1981 and 1990, respectively. After serving for 20 years in public office, he worked as a policy analyst on election reform issues. He earned his BA in political science from Middlebury College. He is the author of *Building Progressive Politics: The Vermont Story* and several journal articles about sortition, a nonelectoral method for implementing democracy. He recently completed a book manuscript about sortition. He lives with his family in Burlington, Vermont.

Daniel Cantor is the national director of the Working Families Party (WFP) and the founding director of the New York WFP. Previously, he was an organizer for and cofounder of the New Party, which was similar to the WFP. He also has worked as a union organizer and community organizer, as well as the Labor coordinator for Rev. Jesse Jackson's 1988 presidential campaign. He is the coauthor of a book on foreign policy entitled *Tunnel Vision*. He lives in Brooklyn, New York.

Mark Dudzic is a former Labor Party national organizer and president of OCAW Local 8–149 and OCAW District 8 (in the Oil, Chemical, and Atomic Workers Union). He currently is national coordinator of the Labor Campaign for Single-Payer Health Care.

Mike Feinstein is a former two-term Santa Monica City Council member (1996–2004) and mayor (2000–2002). He has been active with the Southern California Association of Governments, California League of Cities, and Local Government Commission. He has run many campaigns for public office and has over two decades of experience as a Green Party organizer at the local, state, national, and international levels.

John Halle is currently director of studies in music theory and practice at Bard College Conservatory of Music. Formerly on the faculty of Yale University, he also was a Green Party member of the New Haven Board of Alderman. He attained that office in a special election in 2001, and he was reelected later that year. His political writings have been published in *New Politics, Counterpunch, Jacobin*, the *New Haven Advocate*, the *New Haven Register*, and elsewhere. His scholarly work involves connections between the mental representations of musical and linguistic structure. He lives in the Hudson Valley with his wife and son.

Thomas Harrison is codirector of the Campaign for Peace and Democracy. He is also on the editorial board of the independent socialist journal *New Politics*. He works as a secondary school history teacher.

Katherine Isaac is the former secretary-treasurer of the Labor Party and the author of *Civics for Democracy*.

Ramy Khalil was the 2013 campaign manager for Kshama Sawant, who is a socialist city council member in Seattle. He is the editorial coordinator for www.SocialistAlternative.org, the website for Socialist Alternative.

Jonathan H. Martin is Professor of Sociology at Framingham State University and a longtime political activist. His teaching focuses on power and inequality. His articles on progressive politics and political consciousness in the United States have appeared in *New Political Science, Humanity and Society, Equity and Excellence in Education*, and other academic journals. In recent decades, he has assisted Green and left-independent candidates at the local, state, and national level.

Patrick Quinlan was a key player in the rise of the Portland (Maine) Greens from 2001 to 2006. He was the manager for the campaigns of former Green state representative John Eder in 2002 and again in 2004. He also served as Eder's legislative aide in 2004 and 2005. He volunteered on various other Portland Green campaigns during this period. Quinlan is the author of many books and ebooks. His crime thriller *Smoked*, which has been translated into four languages, received worldwide critical acclaim. *All Those Moments*, the memoir he cowrote with film legend Rutger Hauer, was a *Los Angeles Times* bestseller. His newest novel is called *Sexbot*. His website is www.patrickquinlan.com.

PREFACE

The story of how this book came to be offers a revealing first glimpse of the context, obstacles, and opportunities surrounding the contemporary progressive third party movement in the United States. By "progressive third parties" (also known as "minor parties on the left"), I am referring to those organizations that primarily (1) strongly advocate for greater social equality and other goals that further the collective good, and (2) try to get affiliated candidates elected to public office rather than those solely backed by either of the two major U.S. political parties. The efforts to build left minor parties and help their candidates compete in elections are what I am calling the larger "progressive third party movement." This movement is attempting to challenge, impact, and defeat a party system in which the Republicans and Democrats are so dominant that together they comprise what is sometimes called a "duopoly." As will be argued in subsequent chapters, it is a system that works to maintain an unjust, unpopular status quo on behalf of the wealthy few who largely control it. Therefore, in fighting against the duopoly and for the vast majority of people in the United States and elsewhere, the left third party movement may be seen as trying to advance democracy in a critical way.

Key to understanding the origin of this book on progressive third party empowerment is the account of how I, as the editor and a contributor, was inexorably drawn to the subject over the course of several decades. I've had an interest in left-leaning politics my whole life, galvanized in large part by my parents' involvement in the progressive social movements of the 1960s and early 1970s. As an adolescent in the 1970s during the Nixon–Ford era, it seemed to me that getting more Democrats elected might be the best hope for pushing the country in a more constructive (and leftward) direction. However, by the late 1970s and early 1980s, I felt a growing frustration with the increasing conservatism of the Democratic Party. It started to make me question the Democrats' priorities and even the workings of the whole two-party system. Democratic president Jimmy Carter had ended his second term by making deep social program cuts and proposing major increases in military spending. Then, on Carter's heels and soon after I entered college, came Republican Ronald Reagan. As president, Reagan continued and accelerated the conservatism of the late Carter years. And it appeared that the Democrats in Congress, who were in the majority at the time, did little to resist him. To a large extent, they actually helped him achieve his right-wing program of upward economic redistribution and increased militarism.

Reagan's relentless military buildup was so disturbing that by the time I graduated from college in 1985, I was intent on working for an arms control group in Washington, DC. As luck would have it, there were no job openings in such organizations, and I wound up getting hired to be a lower level assistant for my Democratic U.S. senator. Working for a prominent Democrat only increased my frustration with the Democratic Party, as I was able to see its true conservatism from the inside. For instance, although the senator was a public supporter of the movement to freeze the nuclear arms race with the Soviet Union, I learned that he privately was seeking funding for certain new, more advanced nuclear weapons systems (which would be produced at a military plant in our state). At that point, through reading in my free time, I began to learn more about what really had happened to the Democratic Party since the 1970s. I discovered that it had shifted to the right in order to appeal to increasingly conservative corporate elites who were allocating more and more resources to funding politicians' campaigns and influencing elections.

However, it wasn't until 1990, after Reagan had been replaced as president by George H. W. Bush and I had become a graduate student, that I had the opportunity to seriously consider the alternatives. At that time, I listened to a recorded speech by Bernie Sanders, who was the socialist former mayor of Burlington, Vermont, and an independent candidate for the state's lone congressional seat. One of my college professors previously had told me about Sanders's notable accomplishments in revitalizing the city. I had learned that Sanders was affiliated with the Progressive Coalition, later to become the Vermont Progressive Party. But I had never heard him speak before, and his recorded words transfixed me. To an enthusiastic audience, Sanders vividly spoke of how the wealthy controlled the government for their own benefit and at the expense of the vast majority of Americans. He lambasted both major parties for primarily serving the rich and corporations. Most importantly, he described in detail how he and others had won local offices as progressives operating outside of the two-party system. The breakthrough in Burlington that he described sounded like it wasn't mostly the result of an accident, good luck, or a miracle, but instead, was largely the product of persistent and clever organizing by a small group of insightful and committed activists.

The above facts concerning Sanders, as well as his historic congressional election victory months later, signaled to me that a viable progressive third party politics might be possible elsewhere in the United States, perhaps even in many parts of the country. And, if so, such a politics might be able to help stem and even reverse the bipartisan conservative tide that had been inundating the country for more than a decade—causing serious damage here and in the many parts of the world dominated by the United States. Yet, it was unclear to me exactly how left third party politics could grow and spread in the United States, especially in light of various huge obstacles that confronted it. So I was left with an important strategic puzzle.

Subsequently, while working on my doctoral dissertation, I tried to start putting the pieces of the puzzle together through activism. Bill Clinton, using a lot of left populist rhetoric, had been elected president in 1992. His turn to the right once in office also solidified my interest in directly supporting left third party alternatives, as it did for many other progressive activists at the time. In early 1994, I began attending some organizing events of a group called Labor Party Advocates, which later became the Labor Party. Later that year, I briefly traveled to Vermont to volunteer for Sanders's second and ultimately successful campaign for reelection to Congress. Next, in 1996, I helped out a bit with Ralph Nader's initial, limited presidential effort. My first more substantial foray into progressive third party politics came a couple of years later, when I joined a local chapter of the Green Party, and in 2000, when I got heavily involved in Nader's second, more serious presidential campaign. Then in 2002 and 2004, while starting to teach at the college level, I volunteered for two serious Green state representative campaigns in the Boston area.

Importantly though, none of the above efforts except for the victorious Sanders campaign seemed to amount to much, at least not at the time. The Labor Party never really got off the ground electorally by running its own candidates. Nader lost by huge margins in both presidential races. Also, his 2000 campaign was tarnished by the widespread allegation that some of his votes had helped Republican George W. Bush win. The two Green state legislative candidates also lost by large margins, and they didn't seem to leave any strong, enduring local Green organization in their wake.

Over the next few years I began to wonder, what does it really take for progressive third parties to avoid spending a lot of time and energy on efforts that dramatically fall short? How can they make electoral breakthroughs more often? Which strategies really have the potential to pay off? Answering these questions required more than just getting involved in left third party politics. It necessitated serious research and analysis. This insight led me to conduct, between 2009 and 2011, the investigation that eventually formed the basis for one of the chapters in this book. It focused on what enables left third party candidates to win seats in state legislatures. Yet this study only dealt with a small piece of the problem. More such work was needed from a variety of angles to really do the matter justice.

Thus, the idea for this book was born in 2012. I decided then that I would recruit other relevant political observers to help me present an assortment of analyses concerning how left third parties in the United States can advance electorally.

The audience for the anthology would be those likely to have a substantial interest in the subject, including progressive activists and intellectuals, political scholars, and students of American politics. The hope was (and still is) that the book not only could educate readers about progressive third party strategic options but also could help inspire and guide a new wave of left third party activism.

However, it turned out to be surprisingly difficult to find contributors for the collection. Certain individuals who had done prominent writing in this area in the past seemed to have lost interest in the topic or even run out of compelling new ideas. Others said that they were too busy—with projects that they apparently deemed to be more important. What did this say about the intellectual health of the progressive third party movement, I began to wonder. With persistence, in the end I was able to assemble a large enough core of inspired, well-qualified, and committed contributors to make a book proposal viable. Without their faith in the project and hard work, this book would not have been possible.

Trying to get a book contract became another illuminating hurdle. To my surprise, the editors of left trade presses that I approached were not interested in publishing an anthology on progressive third party politics. Some thought that the subject or multi-author format would be insufficiently appealing to their readership. Others were repelled by the popular misperception that third parties can't win, and still others had no use for electoral politics at all. To me, it was a sad commentary on the state of progressive book publishing. It was discouraging to think that these key disseminators of left thinking were unwilling or unable to provide a venue for strategic analysis that didn't fit into a very narrow political or commercial mold. It also was a rude awakening to learn of left trade publishers' effective disinterest in helping to build a vital grassroots progressive movement—especially one that actually had begun to demonstrate some potential in various places in recent decades. It reminded me of how broad and deep the acquiescence to major party dominance can be in the United States today.

I then decided to send proposals to certain academic publishers. I speculated that they might be more willing to take a chance on something that could be seen as somewhat ahead of its time politically or commercially, but still might be intellectually important enough to promote. Fortunately, I was right. To its credit, Routledge was one such publisher. I am thankful that it has editors who are forward thinking enough to support a project like this.

Other institutional support also helped me to complete this book. A few small grants from Framingham State University financed the research, editorial assistance (proficiently provided by undergraduate Dan Costello), and indexing. This demonstrates the university's democratic commitment to backing a wide range of scholarship, even if it challenges the political status quo. Successive chairs of the Sociology Department, Susan Dargan and Ben Alberti, enabled me to carve out the time I needed to work on the book.

Lastly, two other people deserve special acknowledgement. Gerry Martin, my mother, frequently offered strong encouragement regarding the political significance of this book, and her keen interest concerning my progress during the crucial final stages of editing and writing was especially appreciated. Meg Lovejoy provided the most critical assistance. A particularly perceptive fellow sociologist and my empathetic partner during the time that this book was being conceived and produced, she often supplied important editorial opinions and insights. She also regularly bolstered my belief that the project was vital and feasible, despite the obstacles.

In sum, this anthology sprouted from my own evolving awareness of the need and potential for viable left third party alternatives in the United States. But, like the progressive third party movement itself, the book clearly is the product of the aspirations and acts of a diverse collection of visionary individuals.

Jonathan H. Martin

INTRODUCTION

The Future Rise of Progressive Third Parties*

Jonathan H. Martin

> Those on the [American] Left who call for a third party are basing their choice on a prayer, not a plan.
>
> Michael Hirsch and Jason Schulman, "Beyond November," *Jacobin*, November 2012

What, if anything, can U.S. progressives do to build more electorally effective and politically influential third parties? Can they develop and implement viable strategies rather than operate on blind faith, contrary to what the above quote suggests? This collection of writings will address these questions, which have important implications for the future of the United States (and the larger world that is heavily affected by American policies).

Hypothetically, a strong partisan force that fights for the nonwealthy, vast majority of people could help create a more equal, just, healthy, and peaceful nation. However, wealthy campaign contributors critically shape the agenda of both major American parties today, and, in turn, the government consistently favors economic elites at the expense of ordinary citizens.[1] The modern Republican Party has aggressively advanced the interests of the privileged and opposed reforms that could directly benefit others, even minimally.[2] Accordingly, many progressives have looked to the Democratic Party, with its liberal rhetoric and

---

*The first half of this chapter was originally published in a slightly different form as "Hegemonic Duopoly at the Grassroots: Why Progressive Third Parties Rarely Win State House Elections," *New Political Science* 35, no. 2 (2013): 250–71. Reprinted by permission of the author and publisher.

New Deal past, as the only hope for meaningful change via electoral politics. Yet, this hope has become increasingly dubious in recent decades. As serious social, economic, and environmental problems have persisted and worsened, leading Democrats at the national level generally have proven unwilling or unable to assertively champion truly progressive solutions—those that unequivocally favor people in the middle and at the bottom of the social structure.[3] The Democrats' periodic populist oratory has not matched their actions. For instance, during the 2008 campaign, Barack Obama raised expectations that a bright new era for non-privileged Americans was at hand. Subsequently however, the dark reality—the close collaboration of the Obama administration with big business—became apparent. The following manifestations of Obama's procorporate bias, which reflect the dominant leaning of the Democratic Party, are especially illustrative:

- the staffing of top Obama cabinet positions with Wall Street insiders (whose earlier actions contributed to the financial crisis), big bank bailouts, and the failure to push for substantial reforms of the financial system;
- the passage of the Obama-backed Affordable Care Act, which appeared to be designed to satisfy the health industry much more than the advocates of universal and affordable health care (such as by failing to offer a new public insurance plan, creating many new private insurance customers, permitting private insurance plans to maintain substantial gaps in coverage, and still leaving tens of millions of people completely uncovered);
- the continuation in various forms of the "War on Terror," which seemed to be shaped much more by the imperative to enrich U.S.-based corporations (with valuable natural resources and lucrative military contracts) than by official pledges to spread democracy, bolster freedom, and enhance global security;
- the lack of sufficiently strong presidential leadership regarding global warming, which would require aggressively seeking large, mandatory reductions of carbon emissions and confronting an obstructionist energy industry; and
- the unprecedented amount of funds raised in the 2012 presidential campaign, much of it from large corporate donors, and the greatest amount for the Obama campaign.[4]

In sum, not only the Republicans but also the Democrats have allied with "the 1 percent." Plainly, from a progressive standpoint, there is good reason to consider what can be done *outside* of the major parties to at least create stronger leverage on behalf of ordinary people. Yet it is unclear whether any nonpartisan efforts can muster enough independent political clout to be effective. As described elsewhere in this book, large left-leaning nonparty organizations, such as national unions and other major liberal interest groups, seem unwilling or unable to effectively pressure the major parties to become much more responsive to the general public.

The U.S. Occupy movement aspired to create a society for "the 99 percent," and it succeeded in shifting public discourse. But it did not develop a sustainable political strategy for systemic change before it fizzled in the face of state repression. Much of what really may be required to influence government to create a substantially more egalitarian country is a *credible electoral threat*—by a viable third party with the same progressive goals as Occupy. In order to maximize its impact, such a party might need to regularly follow through on that threat and try to establish its own significant presence in government.

Possibilities

At present, given the obvious weakness of minor parties of the left, it may be hard to imagine how they ever can gain enough power to influence American politics on a large scale. According to a combination of sources, at least 168 political offices in the country were held by progressive third parties in 2014, and the vast majority of these positions were at the municipal and county level.[5] Left third parties have won very few seats in state legislatures. Individuals closely associated with these parties occupied just 12 out of 7,383 such seats in the entire nation as of mid-2015.[6] Only two people fundamentally linked to a progressive third party held statewide or federal office at this time.[7]

However, comparative and historical analysis of left politics suggests that there may be much hidden potential for progressive minor parties to impact U.S. politics. In modern times, left electoral parties in other advanced capitalist countries have helped create relatively strong social welfare states. They have done so by becoming a dominant force in national government for extended periods.[8] In the United States, of course, such parties have faced a particularly potent array of obstacles. The one most well known is the lack of proportional representation in elections, which enables all parties to gain political seats in proportion to the number of votes they receive, rather than based on their ability to win the most votes. Nevertheless, in past eras, U.S. left-wing third parties have used only modest electoral gains and influential ideas to bring about many important and enduring progressive reforms.

From the late nineteenth century to the mid-twentieth, American left third parties with just a modicum of state power helped make the U.S. political system significantly more responsive to the forgotten needs of ordinary citizens. The achievements of the Populists and the Socialists are particularly notable. In the 1892 leap that started their several-year electoral surge, the Populists won the presidential vote in five states and elected 5 U.S. senators, 10 congressmen, 3 governors, scores of state officials, and hundreds of state legislators as well as county officers. They also won enough seats to dominate the legislature in one state. Following the 1896 election, there were 22 members of Congress and 7 governors affiliated with the Populists.[9] In their first presidential election in 1900, Socialists won double digit shares of the presidential vote in a few states.[10] By 1911, they had elected at least 1,141 local officials in 324 municipalities, including majorities in the governments of 23 cities and towns. By 1918, they had elected a total of 80 state legislators and 2 congressmen.[11] Through their municipal victories that continued for several more decades, Socialists were able to implement reforms that substantially improved conditions for workers and the poor in various localities.[12] Additionally, at the state and national level the Socialists as well as the Populists electorally threatened the major parties and popularized their agenda enough to get many of their enlightened proposals adopted by government. They thereby contributed critically to the abolition of child labor, limitation of work hours, establishment of minimum wages and graduated income taxes, broadening of access to public education, expansion of suffrage to previously excluded groups, institution of direct election of U.S. senators, use of public referenda, and a variety of other changes beneficial to moderate and low income people.[13]

Despite their comparative lack of power today, minor parties of the left *are* having some of the above sort of impact in certain places in the United States, as will be noted in subsequent chapters. Likely, they could do more of this if they were just somewhat more effective in municipal and state elections again. Also, the history described above suggests that these parties could influence national policies once more if their effectiveness in federal races increased even moderately.

Moreover, even a series of relatively small advances by left third parties could be sufficient to energize the progressive third party movement with a pivotal new wave of public support. As discussed in later chapters, many Americans today already are sympathetic to third parties, progressive policies, and some left-wing ideology.[14] Much of what may be keeping this sentiment from empowering progressive third parties is the seemingly widespread belief (even among many progressives) that these parties cannot win or even make good electoral showings.[15] Such pervasive perceived powerlessness, irrespective of the political facts, may ensure the reality of a largely uncontested duopoly. Renowned social scientist Frances Fox Piven has observed: "People do not complain about the inevitable, and they certainly don't mobilize to change what they think is inevitable, but once new possibilities for change that are within reach of ordinary people become evident, or at least once people think they are evident and within reach, popular aspirations also expand."[16] Thus, several striking new demonstrations of progressive third party power (combined with the recent ones highlighted in this book) might inspire enough confidence in these parties to galvanize a critical mass of activism on their behalf. This in turn could stimulate more breakthroughs, greater hope, and so on. Such a dynamic could enable a more dramatic ascendancy of left third parties and a deeper progressive transformation of U.S. politics, despite the considerable impediments to their success. This especially could be the case if left third party gains are accompanied by a major national crisis (such as a sustained recession, government shutdown, military setback, or environmental disaster), along with a strong upsurge of progressive social movements.

But the above cycle of empowerment, whether more robust or mild, is unlikely to be sparked if the left third party movement doesn't first implement strategies that are capable of producing the initial catalyzing advances. This anthology aims to illuminate such strategies.

Goal and Summary of This Volume

In addition to offering encouragement and guidance to current or aspiring progressive third party activists, this book helps fill a significant gap in the literature on minor parties in the United States. Much already has been published that explores these parties' serious difficulties, their consequent failures, and their lesser known history of stimulating important reforms.[17] However, such work, produced largely by academics, is insufficient for addressing the questions posed here for two reasons. First, it does not focus primarily on *left* third parties, which may be both handicapped and advantaged in unique ways by their open, consistent opposition to the policies, interests, and ideology of dominant groups.[18] Second, this core literature on U.S. minor parties does not reflect much on how these parties can become more successful.

To a large extent the lack of scholarly interest in left third party empowerment may be purely disciplinary in nature. Many analysts of minor parties are political scientists, who often go to great lengths to appear politically neutral.

Yet much of the reluctance to strategize on behalf of any third parties may be the result of extreme pessimism about their prospects, given the serious institutional obstacles they face, especially in higher level races. Such impediments prominently include ballot access hurdles, a money-driven campaign system, media bias, and, as alluded to previously, the predominance of winner-take-all elections.

An emphasis on how much the above obstacles may hinder minor parties is factually justified. But the characterization of these parties as effectively blocked today doesn't sufficiently account for the occasional conspicuous breakthroughs they continue to achieve.[19] Like any system of dominance, the American duopoly may have contradictions, limits, gaps, weak points, and failures that can be effectively exploited by perceptive, skilled challengers. Strategic innovations, new issues and crises, and other changes in political conditions may enhance these opportunities. All of this points to the need for serious, sustained strategic analysis, which the central literature on minor parties does not provide.

Of course, there is a smaller body of modern work—mostly authored by left activists, writers, and thinkers—that does center mainly on progressive third parties and their candidates.[20] To varying degrees, some of this writing does evaluate the strategies of specific parties.[21] But it does not include much detail on how such parties generally might make more electoral breakthroughs. Moreover, it isn't sufficiently up-to-date, having been completed approximately one to two decades ago. As a result, this work doesn't cover more recent relevant developments in left politics or reflect on the pertinence of past efforts to our current and emerging political context. This anthology helps fill the above two holes. Looking backward and forward from the vantage point of the current period, it focuses specifically on how the contemporary U.S. progressive third party movement may advance politically, especially in the electoral arena.

The book's contributors are key participants in and analysts of the left third party movement in the United States. Virtually all have published books or articles on progressive politics. Nearly all have held elected office or have worked as key organizers for relevant campaigns and parties. A few of the authors are political scholars in academia. Based on experience, observation, or research, these writers share important insights about what type of progressive third party strategy has or has not worked, and by extension or implication, could work in the future—even in the face of serious obstacles. Many of the specific claims made or positions taken by respective authors reinforce or complement one another. Others appear to conflict with each other, at least on the surface. More abstractly, the collection as a whole suggests that the U.S. progressive third party movement is more likely to succeed if it channels its idealism and sense of urgency into an approach to gaining power that is pragmatic, yet is also farsighted and dynamic.

Chapters 1 through 5 focus on what it takes for progressive third parties to win first at the local level and only later try to advance to higher levels—known as a bottom-up strategy. The first four of these chapters stress the role of skillful, sustained, and extensive grassroots campaigning in an electoral context that appears to be favorable. The last of these chapters, by contrast, centers on how important a local candidate's bond to his or her community can be for creating the basic possibility of victory in the first place.

Chapters 1 and 2 highlight a pair of stunning successes by left third parties on the West Coast in the past several years. Perhaps the most striking of these cases, discussed in the first of these chapters, is the 2013 election of Kshama Sawant to the Seattle city council. Sawant is an openly self-identified socialist and member of Socialist Alternative, a revolutionary anticapitalist group. Such an event legitimately can be labeled "historic," since it would seem to have been impossible in the contemporary United States, the supposed ideological bastion of modern capitalism. How this breakthrough was accomplished certainly bears close attention for others on the left who hope to turn the "impossible" into reality. Ramy Khalil, Sawant's campaign manager and the author of this chapter, identifies several interconnected contributing factors—a committed socialist organization, a campaign that was both pragmatic and principled, an appealing and skilled candidate, intensive outreach and fund-raising, key union and media endorsements, and a larger context of growing public frustration with the political status quo.

Along the same lines, Chapter 2 reflects on an almost equally surprising event—the election in 2007 of Green Party candidate Gayle McLaughlin to be mayor of the city of Richmond, California. While Richmond is in the San Francisco Bay area, which has a progressive reputation, it is a racially and ethnically diverse community with a large working-class population. It is not some predominantly white, upper-middle-class college town, the supposedly typical breeding ground for leftist politics in the United States today. Longtime Green activist and writer Mike Feinstein, the author of this chapter and himself a former mayor (of Santa Monica), explains how this victory occurred. He attributes the win to two key factors—a hard-fought campaign and McLaughlin's strong reputation for being a very effective advocate for community needs during her first term on the city council. Notably, McLaughlin's breakthrough was not just a political fluke, since she was reelected three years later.

Chapter 3, which is much more extended, tells the story and considers the lessons of another remarkable Green Party breakthrough during the same decade, but on the opposite coast. Written by novelist and Green activist Patrick Quinlan, it recounts and analyzes how several primarily young, committed Greens changed the face of politics in Portland, Maine, between 2001 and 2006. They repeatedly got elected to the school committee and even to the statehouse during this period, and later to the city council. Quinlan was a campaign manager for John Eder, the only Green in the country at the time to be elected a state representative (in 2002 and again in 2004). Quinlan relates how a small group of Green activists, initially inspired by the 2000 Ralph Nader presidential campaign, won elections by learning and concertedly executing some very effective grassroots campaign techniques. He also suggests that the complacency of the local Democratic Party and other conducive elements of the political environment in Portland may have played a role. Last, Quinlan describes how a strong backlash by the local Democrats and a growing complacency by the Portland Greens themselves led to the latter's decline. Could a return to their earlier style and methods help the Greens to rise again in Portland? Could their initial path to success also be a model for other progressive third party activists? Quinlan leaves readers with some key questions about the transferability and sustainability of the breakthrough achieved by the Portland Greens.

Chapter 4 moves to another state within New England, one that has seen more sustained electoral success by a left third party than anywhere else in the United States in recent times. In Vermont from the 1980s onward, the Vermont Progressives became a significant force in the state's largest city, even a dominant one for two decades. The Progressives eventually also elected several members to the Vermont State House on a consistent basis, and perhaps more strikingly, the perceived father of their movement (Bernie Sanders) got elected to the U.S. House of Representatives in 1990 and to the U.S. Senate in 2006. Contributor Terry Bouricius, a former Progressive city councilor and state representative in

Burlington, focuses on how the Vermont Progressives were able to make and consolidate the initial breakthroughs that made them an established and influential presence in Vermont politics. He draws attention to a variety of factors, including the small-scale municipal context, a receptive media environment, participation in two-way races, a lot of door-knocking, mobilization of new voters, a highly appealing central candidate (Sanders), and a compelling populist message. Bouricius acknowledges that particular circumstances in Burlington and in Vermont were especially conducive to left third party victory. However, he concludes that key elements of the Progressives' bottom-up, popularly accessible approach are critical to making success possible elsewhere.

Chapter 5, which I authored, explores how progressive third parties can win more seats in state legislatures. It does so through an in-depth comparison of winning and losing state representative campaigns affiliated with the Greens and Vermont Progressives in New England during the first decade of the twenty-first century. It finds that the relative strength of candidates' social and cultural connections to their communities determines whether they have a chance of becoming winners—contrary to the popular belief that other factors primarily control the fate of left third party candidates. Thus, the chapter concludes that progressive third parties will be better equipped to win state legislative races if they recruit and run more locally well-connected candidates, and if they encourage party members to bond more strongly with their local communities.

Chapters 6 and 7 shift the focus from the local arena to the national stage. They address what it would mean and what it would take to run effective progressive third party presidential campaigns in the future. In Chapter 6, Theresa Amato, former presidential campaign manager for Ralph Nader, argues that Nader's races in the 2000s should inspire others to run similar campaigns. This directly challenges the widely held belief that Nader served as a bad example for electorally oriented progressives. As the Green Party presidential contender in the tight 2000 race, Nader allegedly enabled George W. Bush to defeat Al Gore by splitting the left-leaning vote in battleground states, particularly the pivotal state of Florida. Similarly, in 2004 and to a lesser extent in 2008, Nader's independent campaigns purportedly risked contributing to the loss of Democratic nominees. Yet, based on important but rarely considered electoral facts, Amato compellingly questions the popular assumption that Nader did function as an actual or potential spoiler. She also exposes the hidden antidemocratic logic that underlies recurrent strident warnings by Democrats that progressives' votes for left third party candidates like Nader are wasted or counterproductive votes. In fact, Amato notes how the Nader campaigns, energized by millions of votes, spawned intensified efforts not only to build the Green Party but also to democratize the electoral system (and thereby eventually make it easier to elect left third party candidates). She suggests that such impacts continue to reverberate in our politics today. Arguably, Amato presents a perspective on political change that is subtler and more long range than that of many progressives who reflexively oppose or dismiss left third party candidacies at higher levels.

In a complementary fashion, in Chapter 7, political scientist Sayeed Iftekhar Ahmed explores the factors that would allow the Green Party (or by implication, any other left third party) to run presidential campaigns that can achieve as much or more than the Nader 2000 campaign. Here, Ahmed primarily measures "success" in a narrower sense than Amato—by the percentage of the popular vote obtained and the position that a candidate finishes. However, he also suggests that such success is not only about immediate electoral achievement, since it can foster broader aims like party building and indirectly influencing government policies. Ahmed finds that the degree to which a progressive third party presidential candidate is well known, supported by a strong organization, and well financed is critical in determining how much his or her campaign can accomplish in both narrower and broader terms. Consequently, Ahmed argues that the Green Party, as the only national left-wing party, should do whatever is possible to run presidential candidates that are more advantaged in these three interconnected respects. In his view, this would require that the party become less ideologically driven, more candidate centered, and more culturally accessible and attractive to the majority of Americans. At the same time, Ahmed questions whether the Greens, with their countercultural orientation and intellectual style, are capable of making such a substantial shift. If they are not, then in his view a new progressive third party should be built that is willing and able to become more popularly appealing and electorally successful.

Chapters 8 to 11 actually do explore in some depth whether a new and potentially more effective third party of the left should be built, and if so, what type of party it should be and how it should be constructed. Chapters 8 and 9 reflect on the possible formation of a labor party, which could be empowered significantly by access to the organizational and financial resources of the labor movement. In Chapter 8, Mark Dudzic and Katherine Isaac consider the latest attempt to build such a party. Both authors were top party staffers. They describe how the party was founded with high hopes in the mid-1990s, and then how it declined and ultimately disbanded in the next decade. In explaining the Labor Party's demise, the authors stress its critical failure to gain enough support from labor unions, especially those at the national level; the unions essentially felt that they had to stick with the Democrats in order to survive and defend their members in the increasingly conservative, anti-union political economy of the early twenty-first century. Dudzic and Isaac conclude that it is not yet the right time to found the Labor Party again because of the lack of union support. However, they suggest that certain types of strategizing and organizing by labor activists could help create the basis for establishing such a party in the future, especially in light of growing labor disenchantment with the Democratic Party during the Obama era.

By contrast, in Chapter 9, John Halle, a former Green Party alderman in New Haven, Connecticut, who had sustained interactions with the local labor movement, offers a somewhat different analysis of labor party problems and prospects. He argues that the attempt to build such a party from the top down is *inherently doomed* by national labor leaders' long-standing attachment to working with the Democratic Party and, more deeply, to collaborating with rather than fundamentally challenging economic elites. Consequently, Halle maintains that a labor-oriented left third party only can be built independently of national labor heads and predominantly through the bottom-up approach. He gives a critical glimpse of a possible move in this direction in Lorain County, Ohio. There in 2013, local races were won by a renegade slate of thirteen candidates (including three independents) supported by local labor leaders. The slate unofficially is known as the Independent Labor Party.

Chapters 10 and 11 further address the matter of exactly how electorally independent progressive forces need to be, and how this should determine the orientation of a new party of the left. In a concise Chapter 10, Daniel Cantor, the executive director of the Working Families Party (WFP), which is active in several states, essentially calls for progressives to support the establishment of a nationwide left-leaning Tea Party. Such an organization, in the form of a geographically expanded WFP, would recruit and support more progressive Democratic candidates and push those who are elected to champion progressive legislation. Cantor suggests that WFP's record of helping to move the Democratic Party to the left on certain issues in particular states makes it a good vehicle for this strategy. This of course is an approach that unions *would* tend to support, and in fact, not surprisingly, they do provide much of the financial backing for the WFP.[22]

However, in Chapter 11, left writer Thomas Harrison presents a diametrically opposed vision for a new progressive party and the larger strategy that should shape it. He documents well the consistent, even increasing conservatism of leading Democrats in recent decades and years (actually including certain Democrats endorsed by the WFP). Correspondingly, Harrison argues that working within the Democratic Party to try to shift it to the left is a lost cause for progressives—largely a recipe for more betrayal, disappointment, and, ultimately, failure. He maintains that the only way for the broader Left to advance in the long run is to finally declare its electoral independence from what he finds to be an irreversibly corrupted Democratic Party. He calls on major left-leaning groups to found a completely new national political party. Such a party would unequivocally champion a bold progressive alternative in the electoral arena through its own uncompromised candidates. Unlike the Green Party, in Harrison's view this new party primarily would be rooted in well-organized, mass progressive constituencies and designed to appeal to a wide segment of discontented, non-elite Americans.

In the concluding Epilogue, I pose and respond to a series of lingering questions that the book may have evoked for readers. These questions and corresponding answers are intended to underscore the opportunities for progressive third party empowerment in the United States, facilitate the evaluation and application of the book's key strategic recommendations, and offer some concrete direction to aspiring left third party activists.

To many on the left, the call to activism can have a spiritual-like quality, since it pertains to the morally transcendent, epic struggle for social justice. However, actually building and competing for power is a much more down-to-earth endeavor. It requires developing and implementing political strategies that have the demonstrated or at least credible capacity to overcome or circumvent strong, entrenched obstacles. If this book persuades many readers that the desire to build left third parties in the United States can be based on workable plans rather than mere prayers, it will have achieved its main goal. If certain readers act upon such strategies, it may help move the U.S. progressive third party movement one step closer to winning its heroic fight against duopoly and for democracy.

Notes

1 Hacker and Pierson, *Winner-Take-All Politics*.
2 For a history and analysis of the contemporary rightward shift and orientation of the Republicans, see Hacker and Pierson, *Off Center*. It is important to acknowledge the Republicans' claim that what economically benefits the privileged will ultimately benefit everyone else. Objectively, this narrative has been discredited by the well-documented reality of class polarization, declining social mobility, widespread wage stagnation and decline, increasing work hours, mushrooming personal debt, and recurrent economic crises that have accompanied the conservative "trickle-down" economic policies of recent decades.
3 Hacker and Pierson, *Winner-Take-All Politics*. For a seminal early analysis of the Democrats' shift to the right, see Ferguson and Rogers, *Right Turn*.
4 Hodge, *The Mendacity of Hope*; St. Clair and Frank, *Hopeless*; Street, *The Empire's New Clothes*; *Why We Fight*, directed by Jarecki; and Center for Responsive Politics, "2012 Presidential Race."
5 Green Party of the United States, "Current Green Officeholders"; Vermont Progressive Party, "Elected Progressives"; Vermont Progressive Party, "Vermont Progressive Party Makes Gains"; Heintz and Hallenbeck, "Progressives Overtake Democrats on Council"; City of Burlington, "Statement of Votes"; Kelly Mangan, Executive Director, VT Progressive Party, e-mail message to author, May 21, 2015; Progressive Dane, "Our Elected Officials"; Progressive Dane, "Past Elections"; Marsha Rummel, Progressive Dane Alder (Madison, WI), e-mail messages to author, May 20–21, 2015; Jaffe, "The Third Party That's Winning"; Lockhart and Ocasio, "Working Families Party Claims Big Victory"; and Socialist Alternative, "What Socialists Say." The total of 168 is composed of the following tally: 131 Greens; 15 Vermont Progressives, and 1 Vermont Progressive–affiliated independent; 14 linked to Progressive Dane (Dane County, WI); 6 representing the Working Families Party; and 1 belonging to Socialist Alternative.

Only included are officeholders who are *primarily* associated with a left third party rather than a major party, or who are fundamentally associated with both. (The latter applies only to a small portion of the total.) Not included are those officials backed by a progressive third party but mainly associated with a major party. Such politicians commonly are described only with a major party label, despite their cross-endorsement from a minor party.

6 Council of State Governments, *Book of the States 2014*, 56–57, table 3.3; Green Party of the United States, "Current Green Officeholders"; Vermont Progressive Party, "Vermont Progressive Party Makes Gains"; Lockhart and Ocasio, "Working Families Party Claims Big Victory"; and Yee, "Working Families Candidate Wins." The total of 12 is composed of 10 state legislators affiliated with the Vermont Progressive Party and 2 affiliated with the Working Families Party. See note 5 for inclusion and exclusion criteria.

7 Vermont Progressive Party, "Statewide Officeholders: Doug Hoffer"; Galloway, "Progressives Announce Slate"; and Vermont Progressive Party, "Federal Officeholders: Bernie Sanders." This statement pertains to Auditor of Accounts Doug Hoffer and U.S. senator Bernie Sanders, both from Vermont and both associated with the Vermont Progressive Party. Hoffer is a Democrat/Progressive, yet his affiliation with Progressives appears to be as significant as that with the Democrats. Sanders is an independent who has a longtime affinity with the Progressives. Statewide and federal politicians elsewhere who have both Democratic and Working Families Party affiliations are not included here; this is because their Democratic affiliation is the core one.

8 Stephens, *The Transition from Capitalism to Socialism*; and Pontusson, *Inequality and Prosperity*.

9 Hacker and Kendrick, *The United States Since 1865*, 307–8; Hicks, "The Third Party Tradition in American Politics," 20; Reynolds, *Democracy Unbound*, 14; and Gillespie, *Challengers to Duopoly*, 93.

10 Isserman, "A Brief History of the American Left."

11 Weinstein. *The Decline of Socialism in America*, 116–18; and Reynolds, *Democracy Unbound*, 25, 34.

12 Reynolds, *Democracy Unbound*, 27–35.

13 Reynolds, *Democracy Unbound*, 13, 20, 47–48; Sifry, *Spoiling for a Fight*, 8–9; Gillespie, *Challengers to Duopoly*, 97, 101–2, 117, 209, 212; and Rosenstone, Behr, and Lazarus, *Third Parties in America*, 8–9, 105.

14 Collet, "Third Parties and the Two-Party System"; Jones, "In U.S., Perceived Need for Third Party Reaches New High"; Lotke et al. *The Progressive Majority*; Page and Jacobs, *Class War*; Halpin and Agne, *State of American Political Ideology*; Campaign for America's Future, "Populist Majority"; and Pew Research Center, "Public's Response to 'Capitalism,' 'Socialism.'"

15 The suggestion that many Americans, including plenty who lean to the left, think that left third parties can't win is not based on relevant survey or interview data (which to my knowledge does not exist). Rather, this impression of public opinion has been shaped by more than a decade and a half of the author's interaction with voters and fellow activists while working on behalf of various progressive third party electoral campaigns.

16 Piven, *Challenging Authority*, 141–2.

17 For contemporary examples of such work in ascending chronological order of publication, see Hazlett II, *The Libertarian Party and other Minor Parties*; Rosenstone, Behr,

and Lazarus, *Third Parties in America*; Herrnson and Green, *Multiparty Politics in America*; Lowi and Romance, *A Republic of Parties?*; Ness and Ciment, *The Encyclopedia of Third Parties*; Disch, *The Tyranny of the Two-Party System*; Bibby and Maisel, *Two Parties or More?*; Hirano and Snyder, "The Decline of Third-Party Voting"; Bennet, *Not Invited to the Party*; Bauer, "Third Party Candidates Face Long Odds"; Perry, *Duopoly: How the Republocrats Control*; Schraufnagel, *Third Party Blues*; Gillespie, *Challengers to Duopoly*; and Berg, "The Failure of the Minor-Party Movement."

18 For instance, *left-wing* third parties and candidates are less likely to receive large dona-tions, since such contributions overwhelmingly come from the economic elites that they openly challenge. At the same time, the unrestrained willingness of *leftist* minor parties and candidates to confront privileged groups has the potential to foster a rela-tively strong connection with many Americans who are upset about growing inequality.

19 For a clear example of the "blockage" perspective, see Berg, "The Failure of the Minor-Party Movement."

20 For contemporary examples of such work in ascending chronological order of publica-tion, see Bouricius, *Building Progressive Politics*; Reynolds, *Democracy Unbound*; Sanders, *Outsider in the House*; Rensenbrink, *Against All Odds*; Nader, *Crashing the Party*; Sifry, *Spoiling for a Fight*; Chester, *True Mission*; Hawkins, *Independent Politics*; Berg, "Greens in the USA"; and Amato, *Grand Illusion*.

21 See Bouricius, *Building Progressive Politics*; Reynolds, *Democracy Unbound*; Sifry, *Spoiling for a Fight*; Chester, *True Mission*; and Hawkins, *Independent Politics*.

22 Jaffe, "Will Cuomo Keep His Promises?"

Bibliography

Amato, Theresa. *Grand Illusion: The Myth of Voter Choice in a Two-Party Tyranny*. New York: New Press, 2009.

Bauer, Anne. "Third Party Candidates Face Long Odds." National Institute on Money in State Politics. Last modified May 18, 2010. www.followthemoney.org/press/Report View.phtml?r=4262010.

Bennet, James. *Not Invited to the Party: How the Demopublicans Have Rigged the System and Left Independents Out in the Cold*. New York: Springer, 2009.

Berg, John C. "The Failure of the Minor-Party Movement: Causes, Consequences, and the Way Ahead." Working paper, Government Department, Suffolk University, Boston, n.d., ca. 2013. www.uakron.edu/dotAsset/448aab74–6e5d-42b1-a999-e1d6769608a3.pdf.

———. "Greens in the USA." In *Green Parties in Transition: The End of Grass-roots Democ-racy?*, edited by Gene E. Frankland, Paul Lucardie, and Benoit Rihoux, 245–56. Farn-ham, England: Ashgate, 2008.

Bibby, John F., and Sandy L. Maisel. *Two Parties or More? The American Party System*, 2nd ed. Boulder, CO: Westview Press, 2003.

Bouricius, Terry. *Building Progressive Politics: The Vermont Story*. Madison, WI: Center for a New Democracy, 1993.

Campaign for America's Future. "Populist Majority: Exposing the Gulf between Ameri-can Opinion and Conventional Wisdom." Accessed February 16, 2015. http://populist majority.org/.

Center for Responsive Politics. "2012 Presidential Race." OpenSecrets.org. Accessed Sep-tember 14, 2014. www.opensecrets.org/pres12/#out.

Chester, Eric Thomas. *True Mission: Socialists and the Labor Party Question in the U.S.* London: Pluto Press, 2004.

City of Burlington. "Statement of Votes (Final): Annual City Election, March 4, 2014." Accessed April 7, 2015. www.burlingtonvt.gov/sites/default/files/CT/Election Results/20140304/election_summary_report_20140304.pdf.

Collet, Christian. "Third Parties and the Two-Party System," *Public Opinion Quarterly* 60, no. 3 (1996): 431.

Council of State Governments. *Book of the States 2014.* Lexington, KY: Council of State Governments, 2014.

Disch, Lisa Jane. *The Tyranny of the Two-Party System.* New York: Columbia University Press, 2002.

Ferguson, Thomas, and Joel Rogers. *Right Turn: The Decline of the Democrats and the Future of American Politics.* New York: Hill and Wang, 1986.

Galloway, Anne. "Progressives Announce Slate of 21 Candidates." VTDigger.org. June 1, 2014. http://vtdigger.org/2014/06/01/progressives-announce-slate-21-candidates/.

Gillespie, David J. *Challengers to Duopoly: Why Third Parties Matter in American Two-Party Politics.* Columbia: University of South Carolina Press, 2012.

Green Party of the United States. "Current Green Officeholders." Accessed January 9, 2015. http://www.gp.org/officeholders.

Hacker, Jacob S., and Paul Pierson. *Off Center: The Republican Revolution and the Erosion of American Democracy.* New Haven, CT: Yale University Press, 2005.

———. *Winner-Take-All Politics: How Washington Made the Rich Richer.* New York: Simon and Schuster, 2010.

Hacker, Louis Morton, and Benjamin B. Kendrick. *The United States Since 1865.* New York: Crofts, 1937.

Halpin, John, and Karl Agne. *State of American Political Ideology, 2009: A National Study of Political Values and Beliefs.* Washington, DC: Center for American Progress, 2009. Accessed February 17, 2015. https://cdn.americanprogress.org/wp-content/uploads/issues/2009/03/pdf/political_ideology.pdf.

Hawkins, Howie, ed. *Independent Politics: The Green Party Strategy Debate.* Boston: Haymarket Books, 2006.

Hazlett, Joseph M., II. *The Libertarian Party and Other Minor Political Parties in the United States.* Jefferson, NC: McFarland and Company, 1992.

Heintz, Paul, and Terri Hallenbeck. "Progressives Overtake Democrats on Burlington City Council." *Off Message: Vermont's Politics and News Blog. Seven Days,* March 3, 2015. www.sevendaysvt.com/OffMessage/archives/2015/03/03/progressives-overtake-democrats-on-burlington-city-council.

Herrnson, Paul S., and John C. Green, eds. *Multiparty Politics in America.* Lanham, MD: Rowman and Littlefield, 1997.

———. *Multiparty Politics in America: Prospect and Performance.* 2nd ed. Lanham, MD: Rowman and Littlefield, 2002.

Hicks, John D. "The Third Party Tradition in American Politics." *Mississippi Valley Historical Review* 20, no. 1 (1933): 3–28.

Hirano, Shigeo, and James Snyder, Jr. "The Decline of Third-Party Voting in the United States." *Journal of Politics* 69, no. 1 (2007): 1–16.

Hirsch, Michael, and Jason Shulman. "Beyond November." *Jacobin,* November 2012. www.jacobinmag.com/2012/11/beyond-november/.

Hodge, Roger D. *The Mendacity of Hope: Presidential Power, Corporate Money, and the Politics of Political Corruption*. New York: HarperCollins, 2010.

Isserman, Maurice. "A Brief History of the American Left." Democratic Socialists of America. Last modified February 6, 1998. www.dsausa.org/a_brief_history_of_the_american_left.

Jaffe, Sarah, "Will Cuomo Keep His Promises? The Working Families Party Went Out on a Limb When It Endorsed the Conservative Democrat." *In These Times*, June 2, 2014. http://inthesetimes.com/article/16767/will_cuomo_keep_his_promises.

———. "The Third Party That's Winning." *In These Times*, March 3, 2014. http://inthese times.com/article/16271/the_third_party_thats_winning1.

Jones, Jeffrey M. "In U.S., Perceived Need for Third Party Reaches New High." Gallup Politics. Last modified Oct. 11, 2013. www.gallup.com/poll/165392/perceivedneed-third-party-reaches-new-high.aspx.

Lockhart, Brian, and Keila Torres Ocasio. "Working Families Party Claims Big Victory." *Connecticut Post*, February 28, 2015. www.ctpost.com/local/article/Working-Families-Party-claims-big-victory-6108415.php.

Lotke, Eric, Robert Gerson, Paul Waldman, and Andrew Seifter. *The Progressive Majority: Why a Conservative America Is a Myth*. Washington, DC: Campaign for America's Future and Media Matters for America, 2007. Accessed February 17, 2015. http://cloudfront. mediamatters.org/static/pdf/progressive_majority.pdf.

Lowi, Theodore J., and Joseph Romance. *A Republic of Parties? Debating the Two-Party System*. Lanham, MD: Rowman and Littlefield, 1998.

Nader, Ralph. *Crashing the Party: Taking on the Corporate Government in an Age of Surrender*. New York: Dunne, 2002.

Ness, Immanuel, and James Ciment, eds. *The Encyclopedia of Third Parties in America*. Armonk, NY: M. E. Sharpe, 2000.

Page, Benjamin I., and Lawrence R. Jacobs. *Class War: What Americans Really Think about Economic Inequality*. Chicago: University of Chicago Press, 2009.

Perry, Darryl W. *Duopoly: How the Republocrats Control the Electoral Process*. San Francisco: Patriot Press, 2011.

Pew Research Center for the People and the Press. "Little Change in Public's Response to 'Capitalism,' 'Socialism.'" Last modified December 28, 2011. www.people-press.org/2011/12/28/little-change-in-publics-response-to-capitalism-socialism/.

Piven, Frances Fox. *Challenging Authority: How Ordinary People Change America*. Lanham, MD: Rowman and Littlefield, 2006.

Pontusson. Jonas. *Inequality and Prosperity*. Ithaca, NY: Cornell University Press. 2005.

Progressive Dane. "Our Elected Officials." Accessed May 20, 2015. www.prodane.org/our_elected_officials.

———. "Past Elections." Accessed May 20, 2015. www.prodane.org/past_elections.

Rensenbrink, John. *Against All Odds: The Green Transformation of American Politics*. Raymond, ME: Leopold Press, 1999.

Reynolds, David. *Democracy Unbound: Progressive Challenges to the Two Party System*. Boston: South End Press, 1997.

Rosenstone, Stephen J., Roy L. Behr, and Edward H. Lazarus. *Third Parties in America: Citizen Response to Major Party Failure*. Princeton, NJ: Princeton University Press, 1996.

Sanders, Bernie, with Huck Gutman. *Outsider in the House*. London: Verso, 1997.

Schraufnagel, Scot. *Third Party Blues: The Truth and Consequences of Two Party Dominance*. New York: Routledge, 2011.

Sifry, Micah. *Spoiling for a Fight: Third Party Politics in America*. New York: Routledge, 2002.

Socialist Alternative. "What Socialists Say: Elections and Political Parties." Last modified December 13, 2014. www.socialistalternative.org/2014/12/13/socialists-say-elections-political-parties/.

St. Clair, Jeffrey, and Joshua Frank, eds. *Hopeless: Barack Obama and the Politics of Illusion*. Oakland, CA: AK Press, 2012.

Stephens, John D. *The Transition from Capitalism to Socialism*. Urbana: University of Illinois Press, 1986.

Street, Paul. *The Empire's New Clothes: Barack Obama and the Real World of Power*. Boulder, CO: Paradigm Publishers, 2010.

Vermont Progressive Party. "Elected Progressives." Accessed April 6, 2015. www.progressiveparty.org/elected-progressives.

———. "Federal Officeholders: US Senator Bernie Sanders." www.progressiveparty.org/elected-progressives/federal-officeholders.

———. "Statewide Officeholders: Auditor of Accounts Doug Hoffer." Accessed April 5, 2015. www.progressiveparty.org/elected-progressives/state-officeholders/statewide.

———. "Vermont Progressive Party Makes Gains Despite National, Statewide Political Climate." VTDigger.org. Last modified November 10, 2014. http://vtdigger.org/2014/11/12/vermont-progressive-party-makes-modest-gains-despite-national-statewide-political-climate/.

Weinstein, James. *The Decline of Socialism in America, 1912–1925*. New York: Vintage Books, 1969.

Why We Fight (film). Directed by Eugene Jarecki. Culver City, CA: Sony Pictures Classics, 2005.

Yee, Vivian. "Working Families Candidate Diana Richardson Wins Brooklyn Assembly Post." *New York Times*, May 5, 2015. www.nytimes.com/2015/05/06/nyregion/working-families-candidate-diana-richardson-wins-brooklyn-assembly-post.html?_r=1.

1

HOW A SOCIALIST WON

Lessons from the Historic Victory of Seattle City Councilmember Kshama Sawant*

Ramy Khalil

Everybody knows you have to accept corporate money and work within the corporate-dominated two-party system to get elected, right? Not so with Kshama Sawant. In November 2013, nearly 100,000 voters elected her to the Seattle City Council—as an open socialist—and she didn't take a dime in corporate cash! In a huge political upset, Sawant's victory sent shock waves through the political establishment and even around the globe. Sawant is the first independent socialist elected in a major U.S. city in decades. Her historic breakthrough was covered by every major newspaper in the country, major TV stations, and newspapers around the world. In the months following her victory, Sawant and her Socialist Alternative political party led a successful movement to implement their main campaign pledge, raising Seattle's minimum wage to the highest in the country—$15 per hour.[1] And the movement is spreading nationally.[2]

How did Sawant and Socialist Alternative succeed in unseating a well-connected, 16-year incumbent Democrat? Is Seattle just a mecca of progressive politics? "Our campaign is not an isolated event," claims Sawant. "In fact, it's the bellwether for what's going to happen in the future."[3] Sounds nice. But is she dreaming?

The Times Have Changed

The success of other progressives in November 2013 suggests that Sawant's statement above isn't just a dream. Democratic candidate Bill de Blasio was elected by

* Originally published in a slightly different form on the website of Socialist Alternative, April 7, 2014, www.socialistalternative.org/2014/01/31/lessons-kshama-sawants-historic-victory/. Reprinted by permission of the author and SocialistAlternative.org

a landslide as New York City's mayor by promising to fight inequality and racist police brutality—much like Sawant, although he is by no means a socialist.[4] Ty Moore, another Socialist Alternative candidate, ran for Minneapolis City Council and came within just 230 votes of being elected. The labor movement in Lorain County, Ohio, was fed up with the Democrats' betrayals and succeeded in electing several "independent labor" candidates (though some maintained ties with the Democratic Party).[5]

"It's a sign of the times," argues Sawant. "The Great Recession has provoked a backlash from the 99 percent. People are fed up with losing their jobs, homes, and pensions."[6] A recent study found that the richest 1 percent captured 95 percent of the income gains of the economic "recovery" in the United States, while working-class people saw their incomes decline.[7] Student debt has surpassed $1 trillion, more than the total accumulated credit card debt in the country.[8] Meanwhile, corporate politicians continue their austerity agenda of tax breaks for corporations and the richest 1 percent while slashing social services and jobs for working people and the poor. In response to this growing inequality, a groundswell of resistance from working-class people keeps erupting across the globe: revolutions in the Middle East, general strikes across Europe, a labor uprising in Wisconsin, Occupy Wall Street, and protests in Turkey and Brazil. It's only a matter of time before the next mass struggle breaks out.

Transitional Method

Everyone is talking about inequality—and lots of people are eager to do something about it—but only a few activist movements in the United States have been able to give a popular expression to this burning desire. The Occupy Wall Street movement was extremely successful in thrusting the issue of inequality into the mainstream, but eventually the movement began dwindling with no clear way forward. As Occupy activists got drawn into the 2012 corporate-controlled elections, Socialist Alternative argued that the movement could be rebuilt by running 200 independent Occupy candidates across the country.[9] Unfortunately, very few activists took up this call, and discussions about challenging inequality were drowned out by the corporate media, which refocused political debates around Obama, Mitt Romney, and other corporate politicians' agendas.

One exception to this trend was the tremendous response Occupy activist Kshama Sawant received in her first election campaign in 2012. She won 29 percent of the vote against the Washington State House Speaker Frank Chopp, the most powerful state legislator in Washington. This demonstrated the potential that existed if Occupy had run more independent candidates.

Around the same time, fast-food and Walmart workers captured people's imaginations by organizing rolling one-day strikes across the country demanding a $15 per hour minimum wage and decent working conditions. In 2013, Sawant's next campaign linked up with the fast-food strike movement in Seattle, and we in Socialist Alternative recognized that the demand for a $15 minimum wage was gaining a tremendous resonance. After many meetings and discussions, we decided to focus our campaign around a call to "Make Seattle Affordable for All" and three specific, concrete demands: rent control and affordable housing, a tax on the superrich to fund mass transit and education, and, above all, a $15 minimum wage.

Socialist Alternative used what we call "the transitional method": We connect with the consciousness of everyday people, meet them where they are, and then point a way forward to help social justice movements achieve victory. The transitional method also entails linking demands for basic improvements in workers' day-to-day lives with the need for a fundamental restructuring of wealth and power in society along socialist lines.

Growing Openness to Socialism

Despite universal demonization of socialism by the corporate media and the political establishment, the Sawant and Moore campaigns demonstrated that "socialism" is no longer a dirty word. Multiple polls, including a recent Gallup poll, have found that a third of Americans react positively to the idea of socialism—a historic increase from decades ago and a 3 percent increase from 2010 to 2012.[10] Merriam-Webster declared the words "socialism" and "capitalism" together to be their Word of the Year in 2012 due to the high number of online dictionary searches for the words.[11]

The working class of the United States has not experienced being bitterly betrayed by Social Democratic or Communist political parties as in most other countries—parties that claimed to fight for socialism but ultimately sold out or even implemented austerity attacks on the working class. In the United States, socialism increasingly sounds like a new attractive idea, an appealing alternative to people suffering from unemployment, low wages, and growing debt under capitalism—despite much confusion about the real meaning of socialism. Among both African Americans and young people (ages 18–29) there is now more support for socialism than capitalism—a sign of things to come.[12] This helps explain in part why the results from both our 2012 and 2013 election campaigns revealed that of the demographic groups who voted for our candidate, most were low-income voters, youths, and people of color.

One of the secrets of our success was our analysis of the various levels of political consciousness of different sections of the population. Although we understood that only a small number of people consciously identify as socialists, we had concluded that there is quite a broad section of the population, especially young people, who are very open to socialist ideas, an even larger section who question capitalism, and a huge swathe of the population that is angry at Wall Street and corporate "politics as usual."

The Need for Political Leadership

Our electoral campaign tapped into the disgust with the political establishment (despite widespread political confusion), and we educated people, raised class consciousness and popularized socialist ideas. For example, Sawant popularized the idea that large corporations such as Boeing (which has plants near Seattle) should not be run for the profit of a few people, but instead should be taken into public ownership and democratically run by workers and the wider community.

However, the working-class anger at corporate politics simmering beneath the surface of society would never have been expressed in Seattle and channeled in a progressive direction in 2013 if we had not taken a bold electoral initiative. That is why it is vital that labor and other progressive movements not only organize rallies, strikes, and so on, but also follow Sawant and the Lorain County, Ohio, labor movement's example of running independent candidates. Otherwise, political discussions and debates throughout society will be controlled and limited by the two corporate parties. If working-class activists and progressive organizations do not build a strong left-wing political alternative, then the vacuum of growing anger in society will be filled either by right-wing demagogues or by populist Democrats who will attempt to contain our movements within the "safe" channels of the corporate Democratic Party.

To build on the momentum of Sawant's 29 percent of the vote in 2012, Socialist Alternative appealed to Occupy, labor, civil rights groups, and left-wing parties to join Sawant in running a slate of vigorous independent candidates for Seattle City Hall the following year.[13] Unfortunately, they failed to see the opportunity that existed and declined our requests, and many of them continued to bang their heads against the wall of the Democratic Party.

In Minnesota, by contrast, the state council of Service Employees International Union (SEIU) not only endorsed Ty Moore's Socialist Alternative campaign but contributed considerable financial and human resources. If more unions and progressive organizations would direct their resources to run and/or support independent candidates like this, there is no doubt we could run many successful campaigns and begin to build a new political party of the 99 percent.

Sawant's tremendous impact demonstrates how candidates and a political leadership are absolutely necessary to give a visible expression to the underlying anger and desire for change in society—and to channel that discontent around a clear agenda. The Seattle labor and progressive organizations' failure to recognize the huge opportunity they would miss by not participating in a coalition slate of independent candidates with Sawant largely stems from their lack of a class struggle, socialist perspective. Many on the left blame the country's conservatism on the confused consciousness of working-class people, often underestimating ordinary people's desire for progressive change. Marxists realize that there is a lot of political confusion among the working class, but we identify the source of the country's political conservatism in the ruling class and its media, as well as its political and other cultural institutions. Marxists believe that the majority of the working class wants progressive change, but that workers need fighting organizations and a political party to educate people and to harness and express the working class's latent power.

The missing ingredient in building a progressive movement is not primarily workers' consciousness, but rather the lack of a political leadership that can give voice to workers' interests. We believe that a workers' party and independent candidates will play an invaluable role in shifting the whole terms of debate, debunking the propaganda of the ruling elite, and educating workers about their real interests. We can already see how much having Kshama Sawant in office has been able to shift the Seattle political debate, and to some extent the national political debate, in favor of raising the minimum wage to $15 per hour.

How much more could be accomplished if we had hundreds of independent candidates and our own mass party fighting for workers and exposing the Republicans' and Democrats' corporate agenda? A new political party of workers, people of color, women, and environmentalists would shift the whole terms of debate in the country, unite various movements together, and significantly raise workers' consciousness about our real interests.

Despite the Citizens United Supreme Court ruling that legalized unlimited corporate spending on election campaigns, the Sawant, Moore, and Lorain County labor campaigns shattered the myth that candidates have to accept corporate money to run for office. When more labor, civil rights, and environmental organizations sever their ties with the Democratic Party and fund independent candidates, there is no question that we can definitely build a mass political alternative. Building such a party is an absolutely essential task today.

The Crucial Role of Socialist Alternative

Many progressive activists have argued that building a party such as Socialist Alternative is sectarian and a distraction from building a broader movement. Although Socialist Alternative is still a small, though rapidly growing, Marxist organization, it's clear that Sawant would not have won if we had not built up our socialist organization in the years before 2013. It was Socialist Alternative's political analysis that enabled us to identify the opportunity that existed for independent left-wing candidates. And it was only the existence of our activist organization that allowed us to implement our tactic and test this perspective in practice. Without an organization, our analysis and ideas would have remained untested, and a historic opportunity for the Left would have been lost.

While the Sawant campaign relied on much broader forces than Socialist Alternative alone, Socialist Alternative served as the backbone of the campaign, politically and organizationally. Without an organized core of experienced, dedicated socialist activists, it would not have been possible to build a grassroots campaign of approximately 450 volunteers and pull together a broader alliance of the following: *The Stranger* newspaper, six union locals, civil rights organizations, immigrant groups, progressive parties, and many others. Sawant definitely could not have won if we had not spent years in advance building Socialist Alternative, despite all the naysayers telling us we were utopian dreamers wasting our time. Against all odds, we swam against the stream and painstakingly built our organization practically from scratch.

For years, we organized and educated workers and young people around Karl Marx's ideas that the capitalist system is wracked by crises and increasingly unable to meet the basic needs of ordinary people, and that the working class is the revolutionary force that can build a new society. In addition, we benefited immensely from the contemporary Marxist perspectives, ideas, and experience of the Committee for a Workers International, a socialist organization in more than 45 countries around the world.[14]

A Bold Class Appeal

Another lesson from Sawant's success is that the majority of people don't want bland moderate candidates who compromise with big business. Most people are dying to see something different, a political leadership that will stand firm against the corporate onslaught. The Green Party has run some good left-wing candidates, but when third parties run middle-of-the-road candidates who are only marginally different from the corrupt establishment, they really limit their appeal. Sawant's popularity stemmed from her relentless attacks on the Republican and especially the Democratic politicians as tools of big business.

Sawant's pledge to live on only the average worker's wage and donate the rest of her salary to building social justice movements made her stand out. Sawant did not try to appeal to both the left and the right; she did not try to straddle the fence between the working class and the ruling elite; she stood completely on the side of the working class. And she inspired tremendous enthusiasm by not pulling any punches and arguing boldly (though also tactfully) for her principles.

We based our campaign on the logic of the class struggle. We did not moderate our demands to make them appear reasonable and acceptable to the corporate elite or upper-middle-class professionals. Rather, we fought for far-reaching reforms that spoke to the day-to-day needs of working-class people, even though it would put us into conflict with the corporate political establishment. Workers who are busy working and commuting will not make time to volunteer for a campaign that is not going to make a real difference in their lives. But approximately 450 people were inspired to volunteer thousands of hours to the Sawant campaign. This was because we were fighting for concrete reforms like a $15 per hour minimum wage that would dramatically improve their lives.

Principled but Not Sectarian

While our campaign argued clearly that progressive social change won't be initiated by either Republicans or Democrats, we also took a nonsectarian approach to voters who supported Sawant but had not yet fully broken with the Democratic Party. We welcomed many activists who were excited to volunteer for our campaign but were also volunteering for Democrats in other races. In October 2013, a group formed called Democrats for Sawant, expressing rank-and-file Democrats' discontent with their party leadership.

Unlike some ultra-left radicals, we did not put up artificial barriers that would obstruct people beginning to move in a positive direction from getting involved with the Sawant campaign. As long as people supported our core demands and our candidate who persistently critiqued the Democratic Party and capitalism, we welcomed their support. We worked together with these activists to build the Sawant campaign while also selling them our newspaper and pamphlets and trying to convince them to break with the Democratic Party and capitalism. But crucially, we used a friendly, patient tone to discuss our ideas with them. A condescending, impatient attitude would have been counterproductive. At the same time, we did not opportunistically bend to the intense pressure to lower our socialist banner or endorse Democratic candidates. We used our campaign to consistently advocate for the formation of a new independent party of the 99 percent and for democratic socialism.

This principled yet skillful approach was essential for convincing a number of unions to endorse our campaign. At first, practically all the labor leaders dismissed our electoral campaigns and endorsed our Democratic opponents—Frank Chopp in 2012 and Richard Conlin in 2013. But eventually our transitional approach and our bold class appeal kept winning more and more support among rank-and-file union activists. By October 2013, we experienced a surge in support for our campaign and won a strong majority for an endorsement in the King County Labor Council. Unfortunately, the 28–21 vote fell just shy of the two-thirds required for a formal endorsement.

Mass Fundraising and Outreach

We could not have won without taking a bold, serious approach to fundraising. Richard Conlin raised $242,000, and we built a powerful war chest of $141,000, over half of what Conlin raised. Yet our donations were overwhelmingly from working-class people and activists—1,400 donors with a median donation of only $40. Without these donations, we could not have afforded crucial necessities such as 50,000 glossy professional handbills, 140,000 mailers, 5 banners, robocalls, a few newspaper ads, and more than a dozen campaign organizers.

Throughout 2013, our campaign inspired about 450 volunteers to blanket the city with 7,000 posters and 1,350 yard signs, and to knock on more than 17,000 doors. We phone-banked thousands of voters, set up literature tables at farmers' markets, and participated in protests and parades. Our staff also worked tirelessly, gaining broad attention with around 150 media articles throughout the campaign.

We were extremely fortunate to have the support of *The Stranger*, a liberal weekly that is the second largest newspaper in Seattle. *The Stranger* was fed up with the inequality created by the Great Recession and by the complicity of the Democratic Party establishment in aggravating the social crisis (for example, by slashing billions of dollars from education and social services in Washington State, while handing corporations billions of dollars in tax breaks every year). This newspaper made the unusual decision to use its status as an influential liberal publication to publish story after story promoting a radical socialist challenger in hopes for once of tilting the balance of local politics away from corporate interests.

This doesn't mean that we cannot run successful campaigns by independent working-class candidates without a major corporate media outlet on our side. The labor, civil rights, and environmental organizations have plenty of money and resources that we can use to construct our own independent mass media—our own TV stations, radio shows, and newspapers. The key task is to build support within these mass organizations to break with the submissive approach to politics (that is, supporting the Democratic Party at all costs) and instead commit resources to creating our own media and independent electoral campaigns.

The support from *The Stranger* and liberal voters who make up the majority of Seattle's population was partially due to our strategic approach of carefully selecting the seat for which to run. A major factor in our success was selecting races both in 2012 and 2013 where there would likely be only one or at most two other opponents, and especially no Republican in the race. This prevented Democrats from scaring people into voting for the "lesser of two evils" because there was no Republican in our particular race that liberal voters might fear. (In most urban areas, the Democratic Party has a monopoly over local politics, so other independent candidates can definitely find similar races to run in across the country. However, it is worth running even if there are Republicans in the race.) In both 2012 and 2013 we also chose to run against incumbents who had been in office for at least 16 years—which meant they had had plenty of time to expose their corporate connections and anger their working-class supporters.

Join the Fight

Last but not least, we had Kshama Sawant—an intelligent, eloquent, passionate yet tactful immigrant woman of color—running against stale establishment white guys in both 2012 and 2013. Sawant is an impressive speaker and a determined fighter, no doubt. But she is also an ordinary person who happened to attend a couple of public forums in 2008 and was impressed with Socialist Alternative's political clarity. Through discussions with Socialist Alternative, she decided to dedicate her life to fighting for a socialist world.

We ordinary people often gravely underestimate our potential to play a role in changing the world. We should follow Sawant's shining example and commit ourselves to this cause for which there is no greater reward. Nothing in life is more meaningful than fighting alongside other working-class people to end inequality, oppression, and environmental devastation.

Notes

1 Sawant, "Seattle's Kshama Sawant Hails Vote for Minimum Wage."
2 15 Now, "15 Now."
3 Burkhalter, "Socialist Candidate Upends Politics as Usual."
4 Jones, "New York: Will De Blasio Deliver?"
5 For more information on these races, see Chapter 9 by John Halle in this book.
6 Kshama Sawant, in discussion with the author, January 2013.
7 Yousuf, "Obama Admits 95% of Gains Gone to Top 1%."
8 Rohit, "Student Debt Swells."
9 "Sawant, "Imagine 200 Occupy Candidates."
10 Newport, "Democrats, Republicans Diverge on Capitalism."
11 Merriam-Webster, "Words of the Year 2012."
12 Pew Research Center, "Little Change in Response to 'Capitalism,' Socialism.'"
13 Locker, "Socialist Wins 28% of the Vote."
14 Committee for a Workers' International, "Socialistworld.net."

Bibliography

15 Now. "15 Now." Accessed August 12, 2014. http://15now.org/.
Burkhalter, Aaron. "Socialist Candidate Upends Politics as Usual in Challenge to Longtime Liberal." *Real Change*, October 23, 2013. http://realchangenews.org/index.php/site/archives/8300.
Committee for a Workers' International. "Socialistworld.net." Socialistworld.net. Accessed August 12, 2014. www.socialistworld.net/.
Jones, Alan. "New York: Will De Blasio Deliver for Working People?" Socialist Alternative. Last modified October 24, 2013. www.socialistalternative.org/2013/10/24/new-york-will-de-blasio-deliver-for-working-people.
Locker, Phillip. "Socialist Wins 28% of the Vote in Seattle." Socialist Alternative.CA. Last modified November 12, 2012. http://socialistalternative.ca/posts/464.
Merriam-Webster. "Words of the Year 2012." Accessed November 7, 2014. www.merriam-webster.com/info/2012words.htm.
Newport, Frank. "Democrats, Republicans Diverge on Capitalism, Federal Gov't." Gallup Politics. Last modified November 29, 2012. www.gallup.com/poll/158978/democrats-republicans-diverge-capitalism-federal-gov.aspx.
Pew Research Center for the People and the Press. "Little Change in Public Response to 'Capitalism,' 'Socialism.'" Last modified December 28, 2011. www.people-press.org/2011/12/28/little-change-in-publics-response-to-capitalism-socialism.

Rohit, Chopra. "Student Debt Swells, Federal Loans Now Top a Trillion." Consumer Financial Protection Bureau. Last modified July 17, 2013. www.consumerfinance.gov/newsroom/student-debt-swells-federal-loans-now-top-a-trillion/.

Sawant, Kshama. "Imagine 200 Occupy Candidates." YouTube video, 3:17. Posted November 3, 2012. www.youtube.com/watch?v=KNrplWkPgnM.

———. "Seattle's Socialist City Council Member Kshama Sawant Hails Historic Vote for $15/Hour Minimum Wage." Interview by Amy Goodman. *Democracy Now*, June 5, 2014. www.democracynow.org/2014/6/5/seattle_s_socialist_city_council_member.

Yousuf, Hibah. "Obama Admits 95% of Income Gains Gone to Top 1%." Last modified September 15, 2013. http://money.cnn.com/2013/09/15/news/economy/income-inequality-obama.

2

A GREEN BECOMES MAYOR

The Election of Gayle McLaughlin in Richmond, California*

Mike Feinstein

Many voters rightfully see the Green Party as an environmental champion. But can Greens win elected office in racially diverse, crime-ridden, working-class cities that are in economic decline? Apparently the answer is yes according to voters in Richmond, California (with a population of over 100,000). On November 7, 2006, they elected Gayle McLaughlin as their mayor.

McLaughlin's victory in Richmond, which is among northern California's most important cities, came only two years after she was elected to the Richmond City Council. When she defeated Democratic Party incumbent Irma Anderson, the local Bay Area political establishment was stunned. Anderson—who brazenly accepted and spent $110,000 from Chevron Oil, Pacific Gas and Electric, and other corporate interests during her campaign—outspent McLaughlin by $82,000. The Green grassroots campaign "sent political shock waves across the Bay Area," according to McLaughlin, "as it highlighted the Green Party's organizational maturity and strong progressive values."[1] These values were a strong threat to the Chevron Corporation, which owns one of the largest refineries in California in Richmond (a storage capacity of 15 million barrels that occupies 25,000 acres on the city's western waterfront). It is also the city's largest local employer, although only a small percentage of Chevron employees are actually Richmond residents. The refinery is notorious for health and safety violations, and contributing to local pollution.

In the mayoral race, Chevron went far beyond simply supporting the incumbent and funded more than 20 hit pieces on McLaughlin. Lacking any dirt, they

* Originally published in a slightly different form in the Winter 2007 edition of Green Pages, the national newspaper of the Green Party of the United States. Reprinted with permission of the author and Green Pages.

accused her of irresponsibility for simply wanting to collect more tax revenue from Chevron. McLaughlin did support local Measure T, which would have generated $8 million a year in Chevron taxes for Richmond's many needs. One of the themes of her campaign was to get corporations such as Chevron to pay their fair share to the community, and to use this increased revenue to fund anti-violence programs, including a year-round, part-time jobs program that would employ 1,000 young people. In response, Chevron attacked both McLaughlin and Measure T (for which she was not the author) with fury, mailing three or four hit pieces a week. Chevron succeeded in defeating Measure T by 58 percent to 42 percent. With no organized campaign to counteract it, Chevron was able to create a general confusion about the measure among voters.

Despite Chevron's attacks, machinations, lies, and scare tactics, McLaughlin is now mayor. "We've learned in Richmond that one good way to defeat the flood of hit pieces against a Green (or progressive) candidate," McLaughlin said, "is to uphold our principles, and at the same time invest everything we have in time and people, developing a long grassroots campaign."[2]

Campaigners for McLaughlin started walking precincts nine months before the election. By early March, volunteers were spreading the "Gayle for Mayor" word every week until November. At the same time, true to her Green principles, McLaughlin refused corporate contributions. Yet she still raised $28,000, including $1,200 from the Green Party of California, which recognized the importance of her candidacy.

It was this hard work combined with McLaughlin's positive reputation in the community—her great standing on the city council, the respect of her colleagues, and the good policies advanced in her short time in office—that enabled McLaughlin to withstand the attacks and win the election. She finished first, with 37.5 percent in a three-way race, 242 votes ahead of the Democratic incumbent, who had 36.3 percent, followed by a third-place Democratic finisher at 25.7 percent.

As mayor, McLaughlin sees her biggest challenge and top priority as "stopping the endemic street violence of this city," she said.[3] The roots of this violence lie in part in the city's long-term economic downturn. Richmond is a classic working-class industrial city that has fallen upon hard times. During World War II, many African Americans migrated to Richmond to work building Liberty ships at the large shipyard. Many of them were women, which is why this is the site today for the Rosie the Riveter memorial. The shipyard has long since shut down, leaving Chevron as Richmond's largest employer. But with few locals hired and with limited opportunities overall for local jobs, violence and a torn community are a result. Statistically, Richmond is considered one of the most crime-ridden cities in the nation.

"Even though other cities with more resources and longer political experience have not been able to find a way out of this kind of urban decline," McLaughlin argues, "for Richmond, it is an imperative. We must lead the city away from this nightmare that literally bleeds its residents and frightens investors."[4] Seeking to reduce the city's street violence to half by 2010 is part of McLaughlin's Ten Point Plan for a Better Richmond. In addition to her jobs program, McLaughlin proposes community policing, a Richmond Youth Corps, more after-school programs, mentoring for parolees, support for high-school graduation, and support for local small business. To combat long-term recidivism, she also advocates increased regional cooperation with neighboring cities for making available support groups, mental health counseling services, educational opportunities, and housing assistance.

McLaughlin holds a bachelor of science degree in psychology, graduating summa cum laude, and her graduate studies include psychology and education. She has worked extensively in nonprofit organizations promoting literacy, social justice, and environmental health, and addressing the needs of disadvantaged youth.

A longtime activist from a Chicago union family, McLaughlin was the third of five daughters of a carpenter father and a housewife mother. Her political consciousness accelerated in the 1960s, especially being in Chicago during the violent response to demonstrators there at the Democratic National Convention in 1968. McLaughlin recalls how her mother was "really outraged that young people were mobilizing for a good cause, and there was such a harsh response from the Chicago police and the political structure in Chicago. It kind of alerted me that there was a different kind of value system."[5] In the 1980s, McLaughlin became involved with the Central American solidarity movement and also played an active role in national networking efforts to unite progressives, including coalition-building efforts with PUSH (People United to Save Humanity) and the Rainbow Coalition.

After moving to Richmond in 1998, McLaughlin quickly got involved with local community issues. By 2004, she was elected as a Green to the city council on a shoestring budget campaign. Her two years on the council were marked by significant achievements. She convinced the council to require proper environmental oversight for two toxic sites within Richmond—Zeneca and UC Field Station. She also championed the East Bay Regional Park District's purchase of Breuner Marsh to build a park for Richmond residents and cosponsored an initiative that repealed the 12-year practice of allowing Chevron to self-permit, self-inspect, and self-certify its own projects. During this time, she also served on the steering committee of the Richmond Greens. In 2004, she cofounded the Richmond Progressive Alliance, an alliance of Progressive Democrats, Greens, and independents.

Now that McLaughlin is mayor, she is getting considerable attention. The *Contra Costa Times*, *Oakland Tribune*, *Sacramento Bee*, and *San Francisco Chronicle* have all done follow-up stories covering McLaughlin's victory. In December 2006, Green Party members welcomed McLaughlin with thunderous applause at San Francisco's Roxie Cinema, where she was a featured speaker at a forum titled "Greening a Hopeful Moment: Progressive Politics After the Democrats' Election Victory." McLaughlin said that for the Green Party to become successful, it is not enough that the party's membership grows in numbers, but that its members grow in the strength of their commitment and solidarity with each other.

While she's happy that her campaign has helped build the Green Party, McLaughlin has made it clear that she is there first to govern for the community, and that she will bring a Green perspective appropriate for the community. Richmond is 35 percent white, 29 percent African American, 34 percent Latino, and 15 percent Asian American. "There are indeed many tones of Green," she said, "and the Green tone of the Richmond mayor will need to reflect the realities of our geography and people."[6]

Notes

1 Gayle McLaughlin, in an interview with the author, December 2006.
2 Ibid.
3 Ibid.
4 Ibid.
5 Ibid.
6 Ibid.

3

THE RISE OF THE PORTLAND GREENS

Patrick Quinlan

> The Democrats and Republicans are a paper tiger. When you get close to
> them, you see that they're not super-geniuses. You see that the system is
> vulnerable. It relies on the mystique of the process and the average citizen's
> belief that they don't have the special qualities necessary to run. I come
> across a lot of progressives who say, "I don't have what it takes." It isn't
> true. The only qualification you need is the ability to connect with other
> citizens.
>
> John Eder, Maine state representative (Green), 2002–2006

The Green Party chapter based in Portland, Maine, is one of the few local third
parties in the United States to achieve electoral success in a consistent way over
a long period of time. Since 2001, there has always been at least one Green in
elected office, and during certain years, there have been as many as six. At least
14 different Greens have held office in the past decade. The Greens are now the
de facto opposition party in the city. They have supplanted the Republicans, who
have held only a handful of seats during the same time period that the Greens
have been in office.

Moreover, during the period from 2001 through 2006, the Greens became a
serious threat to the Democratic Party's long dominance of city politics. During
those years, prominent Green officeholders like State Representative John Eder
and school committee members Stephen Spring and Ben Meiklejohn were at the
center of the city's political battles. They often waged high-profile campaigns to
enact policy in line with their Green values.

By 2006, Eder, who at the time was the highest ranking elected Green in the
United States, had inspired a new generation of Maine Green activists to pursue

elected office. Although he was the only Green in the State House (that is, the entire state legislature of Maine), he had his own legislative staff and office, with a parade of young interns who later sought office themselves.

Eder had secured a commitment from the governor of Maine to fund a new multicultural and multilingual center for the Portland public schools (a district where the many new immigrants speak literally dozens of languages). He had also cofounded Green Future, a small political action committee that had raised more than $10,000 to fund candidate recruitment, as well as campaign trainings for new candidates and their volunteers. He routinely won the city's Best Politician designation in annual voting held by the *Portland Phoenix*, the local arts and entertainment magazine. He also was a fixture in the local and statewide media.

Meanwhile, during the height of the wars in Iraq and Afghanistan, Spring and Meiklejohn led a fight to drastically curtail military recruitment in the public high schools, winning a stunning victory. They, along with fellow Greens Jason Toothaker and Susan Hopkins, had also lost contentious battles to put an end to student tracking and to change the name of the Columbus Day holiday to Indigenous Peoples' Day.

The Portland School Committee, formerly a sleepy chamber dedicated to rubber-stamping budgets, had become a place of intrigue, high drama, and hyperbolic media coverage. In 2006, the committee was nearly evenly divided, with five Democrats and four Greens. Even though school committee seats are nominally nonpartisan, votes often occurred exactly along party lines.

With all this momentum, it appeared that the Portland Greens were destined to make dramatic changes to city government. However, at the end of 2006, the Green wave seemed to break. In November, although Kevin Donoghue and David Marshall became the first Portland Greens to win city council seats, both John Eder and Stephen Spring lost their own seats by narrow margins.

The losses were devastating to the cause. Spring was the firebrand leader of the Greens on the school committee. Green Party member Rebecca Minnick was elected that fall, and had Spring retained his seat, the Greens would have achieved a majority on the committee. This would have cleared the way to move forward a host of new initiatives. Meanwhile, Eder was the statewide face of the Green Party, and his loss meant the closure of the Green Party office at the State House in Maine's capital city of Augusta.

In early 2007, more bad news struck the Greens. School committee member Toothaker (who had gotten his start in politics as an intern in Eder's State House office) was arrested for public drunkenness and attempting to run from a taxi fare. The resulting scandal, which was front page news for two weeks, turned public opinion against the Greens. Toothaker was forced to resign his seat.

Soon after, Ben Meiklejohn's driver's license was suspended by a computer glitch, and he was arrested for driving without a license. His mug shot was splashed across the front pages of local newspapers for days. "There was no crime,"

Meiklejohn says, "but I was tarred and feathered anyway." Although he was ultimately cleared of the charge, his innocence didn't gain much newspaper coverage, and he lost his reelection bid that fall. Within one year, all three of the early leaders of the Portland Greens were out of office.

Despite those losses, the Portland Greens regrouped and soldiered on. As of this writing, four Greens hold elected office in Portland, including City Councilors Marshall and Donoghue, who have each been reelected twice. In addition, longtime Green activist Ben Chipman, now registered as an independent, sits as a state representative.

However, the momentum the Greens once enjoyed has clearly dissipated. They are not as united as they once were, they are nowhere close to a majority on any elected body, and for the time being, they are no longer seen as much of a threat to the Democrats. The vicious battles of the early to mid-2000s are now just a faint memory. Greens in office keep a lower profile these days, and they are sometimes criticized for not acting on Green ideals or not clearly identifying themselves as Greens.

The first generation of Portland Greens took everyone by surprise, including itself. A group of eccentric people, outsiders, suddenly found themselves in positions of influence and responsibility. They also found themselves in a ferocious battle with an entrenched, much bigger and better funded opponent. Greens learned as they went along, and they were often surprised by the turns that events took.

What happened? How did the Portland Greens gain electoral success in the first place? And why did they lose momentum? The answers to these questions may help other progressive third party activist groups seeking to put a dent in their own local power structures.

On the following pages, I recount the history of the Portland Greens. I illuminate the factors that fostered their rise and later their stall. In discussing the Green's rise, I focus on the role of certain hyperenergetic individuals, their openness to learning how local politics works and to adopting successful campaign techniques, and their willingness to work long hours for uncertain reward. Later, I focus on how abandonment of previously successful practices, combined with pushback from the dominant Democrats, led to the sudden end of Portland's first Green surge. Last, I suggest that only a return to such methods could enable the Portland Greens to rise again. I propose that these tactics are essential to the sustained success of any antiestablishment candidates (including those in other places and from other progressive third parties).

My assessments come from my years as a Portland Green, my presence at many of the seminal events that shaped the Green movement in Portland, and interviews I conducted with key Portland political activists during the winter and early spring of 2014.

Certainly, Green political achievements stem, in part, from the peculiar characteristics of the city of Portland itself.

Portland, Maine: A City Ripe for Plucking

> I'd been out of school for a year or two and I was living in rural Harpswell. That winter, there was a terrible ice storm, everything was frozen over, and I went without power for more than a week. In the midst of this, I got a call from my friend Ben Meiklejohn. He was living in Portland. He said, "The lights are on here in the city. The bars are open. Why don't you move down here?" A short time later, I was living in Portland too.
>
> Ben Chipman, former Green activist and Maine state representative (Independent), 2010–present

Portland is a small, picturesque city located on the coast of Maine, about 100 miles north and east of Boston. With about 65,000 residents, it is tiny by the standards of many other cities. In some ways, it bears a closer resemblance to a giant college campus than an actual city.

Indeed, there is a large population of young people in Portland, many of whom attend the various local colleges, including the University of Southern Maine, the Maine College of Art, the University of New England, and Southern Maine Community College. There is a lively bar and café culture in Portland, and young people flock there from all over rural Maine because it is by far the largest, most cosmopolitan city in the state.

Geographically, the city's most obvious feature is a peninsula that juts out into Casco Bay. The peninsula is where the city's thriving downtown business and arts districts are located, as well as the hopping club scene, and the working waterfront. Extending south and west of the peninsula is a much larger semisuburban sprawl, made up primarily of single family homes and some multifamily dwellings, which gradually segues into strip malls and farmland the farther you get from downtown. When tourists say they are going to Portland, they mean they are going to the Portland peninsula.

Politically speaking, the peninsula is where the action is. It is the most densely populated area in Maine, with large numbers of new immigrants, poor people, homeless people, and people under 30 years old. It is the only place in the city where renters outnumber homeowners. The neighborhoods are easily walkable. It would take you an hour to walk from one end of the peninsula to the other.

In general, while all of Portland could be considered somewhat liberal-minded, the peninsula is where ideas like gay marriage, legalization of marijuana, repeal of corporate personhood, dedicated bike lanes, single-payer health care, and resistance to our country's various wars all find favor with large majorities of the population. Much of Portland is fine with the status quo. On the peninsula, there is constant agitation for change.

Because the districts are physically small, the voters on the peninsula are easier to reach than anywhere else in the city. It is possible for a candidate going
door-to-door on the peninsula to knock on every door in an electoral district
twice during the course of a campaign. Further, because there isn't a tradition of
massive spending on political campaigns in Maine, a candidate can run a reasonably competitive campaign without a lot of money. In state-level races, like those
for state representative and state senator, there is even public funding available.

The peninsula is where the early leaders of the Portland Greens lived when
they launched their first campaigns. They clearly benefited from the liberal, even
radical, outlook of the population and from the small size of the electoral districts.
They also benefited from the bloated and overconfident state of the Democratic
Party in Portland.

By the time the Greens arrived on the scene, the Democrats had dominated
Portland politics for several decades. Democratic Party control of the city was
more or less complete, and it had been for as long as anyone could remember.
Democratic candidates for office were easy shoo-ins, and they barely bothered
to run campaigns at all. Few young activists were excited by the establishment
Democrats, so the party itself was heavily skewed toward middle-aged and older
people.

Outside of a few vicious Democratic primaries, there hadn't been a culture of
closely contested campaigns in Portland for many years. It seems possible (from
their response to the initial appearance of the Greens) that the Portland Democrats hadn't had to run hard for office for so long that they didn't remember how
to do it.

The Democrats had let their defenses way down. As the years passed, a group
of ambitious Green activists had quietly gathered in the city. They came from disparate backgrounds, but one thing united them—a desire to incite change.

The Early Days

> I was never political. I wanted to recycle and to save the whales. I got myself
> elected to the student senate because every year the school threatened to
> close our dorm. We had to fight to keep it open. I represented Colvin Hall,
> which was a special place, and we were always trying to protect it. That's
> how I ended up in politics.
>
> Ben Meiklejohn, University of Maine student body president,
> 1995–1997, and Portland School Committee member, 2001–2007

The group that would eventually become the Portland Greens was born nearly
150 miles away, in the small college town of Orono.

In 1993, eight years before Ben Meiklejohn became the first Green elected to office in Portland, he arrived at the University of Maine at Orono, the largest school in the Maine state university system. Located just north of Bangor, the school has about 11,000 students. It is known for, among other things, its long cold winters, its successful hockey, baseball, and football teams, and being the alma mater of horror writer Stephen King.

Meiklejohn was a musician and went by the nickname "Zen Ben." He lived at Colvin Hall, an alternative residence hall. There the students, mainly artists, governed themselves, pooled their resources to buy food, cooked communal dinners, and in general lived a somewhat different and independent lifestyle from that of the mass of students.

Soon, Meiklejohn was Colvin Hall's representative to the student senate. On the senate, he met Ben Chipman, who had grown up on his grandparents' farm and whose uncle had been a successful politician in the Harpswell, Maine, area for many years. The two became friends, in part because they were the only student senators who didn't align themselves closely with either the Democratic or Republican parties.

One day, they were sitting in Chipman's dorm room, drinking beer. They saw an advertisement in the campus newspaper encouraging students to run for student body president and vice president. They thought it might be fun, so they decided to run as a ticket. Meiklejohn would run for president and Chipman for vice president.

The advertisement also encouraged candidates to seek endorsement from a political party. Since they didn't identify with the Democrats or Republicans, they tried to come up with another party that might endorse them. There wasn't much to choose from. The two decided they were interested in winning the endorsement of the Maine Greens, a group that didn't have ballot status as an official political party.

"We had a flyer of theirs," Meiklejohn says. "It outlined their Ten Key Values, and I couldn't disagree with any of it. Chipman felt the same way. We were both like, I guess we're Greens, and we just didn't know it."

They went to see the leaders of the Maine Greens, including Greg Garrett and Bowdoin College professor John Rensenbrink, who had been among the cofounders of the Green Party of the United States 10 years earlier. Also present was environmental activist Jonathan Carter, founder of the Forest Ecology Network. The previous year he had run for the U.S. Congress as a Maine Green and had gained almost 10 percent of the vote.

During the meeting, Meiklejohn pulled out his guitar and sang a song he had written for the occasion. The song was called "Radioactive Radiation Blues." When he was done, John Rensenbrink said, "You guys seem like a couple of candidates we can support." The two Bens went back to school, where they ran for the first time as Greens, and lost.

Despite the loss, the following year Meiklejohn ran for president again, this time without Chipman. He ran on a platform of unifying the opposing factions on campus—commuters, residents, and the various rival fraternity houses, which were often openly hostile to one another. He won, serving as a popular student body president for two terms, until he graduated. To gain his second term, he beat a player from the University of Maine Black Bears hockey team, which had just won the national championship.

John Eder Appears

> I had been reading the Beat poets—Kerouac, Ginsberg, Corso—when I was in college. Around that time, the early 1990s, Allen Ginsberg came to my school for a talk, and I met him. He had dinner with me and about ten other students. He told us, "Go out and see the world." So I did.
>
> John Eder

John Eder was a drifter. As a baby, he had been given up for adoption. Raised in Brooklyn, New York, in an adoptive family with an abusive, alcoholic father, he left home at the age of 15. He spent a short time living on the streets. Then he finished his high school years as a ward of the state at a boys' home in Port Jefferson, New York, on the eastern end of Long Island.

After high school, Eder spent one year at Daemen College in Buffalo, New York. When he left college, he worked for a while at the Greyhound bus station. Then he left Buffalo altogether. He spent the next several years traveling from place to place. At different times, he lived in New York City; Philadelphia; Athens, Georgia; New Orleans; and Austin, Texas. He crossed into Mexico, living mostly in Mexico City and in the tiny desert town of Real Catorce.

During his travels, Eder lived in abandoned buildings with other squatters. He stayed with anarchist groups. He stayed in homeless shelters. He stayed on the couches of friends. At times, he lived in a tent. In Texas, he joined the Hare Krishna, shaved his head, and lived in their residence. He rode the freight trains. He hitchhiked and bicycled thousands of miles. He worked dozens of short-term jobs, mostly as a laborer.

Wherever he went, driven perhaps by the injustice he experienced in his upbringing and a desire to set things right, Eder participated in political activism. In 1992, while still in Buffalo, he volunteered for Bill Clinton's first presidential campaign, putting up signs. Later, he escorted women into abortion clinics through crowds of antichoice protestors. He demonstrated for homeless rights and against the death sentence of Mumia Abu Jamal (an African American journalist who was widely believed to have been wrongly convicted of murdering a police officer).

By 1996, Eder and his first wife were living in a trailer in Alfred, Maine, on land owned by the Brothers of Christian Instruction, a Catholic missionary order dedicated to education. It was a quiet, rural life. They had very little money. That year, Green Party cofounder John Rensenbrink ran for Congress, the kind of top-of-the-ticket race that Greens always lost by giant margins. Eder recalled:

> There was a John Rensenbrink sign by the side of the road maybe half a mile up from us, one lonely green and white sign. It said, "Think Rensenbrink." At that time, I had no contact with the Greens at all. There was just this sign that no one maintained. Every week or so, someone would knock it down. Whenever I noticed it was down, I would go out there and put it back up. Finally, one day it was just gone. So I went to the hardware store, bought some wood, some paint, and a stencil, and remade the sign myself.

In 1997, Eder moved up to Portland for the first time. Now, between bouts of traveling, he made Portland his home base. He would leave on long trips south. He hitchhiked north one year and wintered over at a farmer's house on the isolated Gaspe Peninsula in Quebec. He spent some time living in a tent in a friend's backyard in Bar Harbor. But he would always return to Portland.

He began to put down something akin to roots. He volunteered regularly at a food co-op called the Good Day Market. He went back to school and became a licensed massage therapist. As the economy boomed in the late 1990s, his massage business flourished, and he rented an office. He painted houses and did odd jobs on the side. His marriage had broken up, but he moved into an apartment with his new girlfriend.

The year 2000 was a presidential election year. Eder decided he wanted to volunteer for a campaign again. The Al Gore campaign had an office in Portland. Eder says:

> I went to the Gore office one day, ready to volunteer. Everybody there was in suits and ties. They looked like little bankers and businessmen. They could have easily been the Republicans. I was a pretty scruffy dude, but neatly dressed, and respectful. Still, no one paid me any mind. Finally, an old bird came up to me and asked what I wanted. They made it clear that they didn't want me. So I walked over to the Ralph Nader office. I went in there, and the Greens put me to work in five minutes. They had me standing outside, corralling people to come in and register with the Green Party.

Nader 2000

> It was a super-exciting year—a thrilling year. A lot of young people, old people, just energized people were coming into our Monument Square

office, trying to reclaim their power. I don't know if politics within the Greens was ever as exciting as that year, before or since.

Ben Meiklejohn

Ben Meiklejohn had graduated from college and moved to Portland in 1997. He was busy during his first few years there.

In 1998, the Greens gained ballot status as an official party in Maine, under the name the Maine Green Independent Party. That year, Meiklejohn ran for state representative in the same district where John Eder would eventually win. He lost, but received 27 percent of the vote against incumbent Democrat Mike Saxl. It should have been a surprising result, though few people took note of it.

In early 1999, Meiklejohn went to city hall and obtained the list of people in Portland who had registered to vote as Greens. The list was already 80 or 90 names long. He formed a group he called the Portland Green Independent Committee and contacted everyone on the list. He began to hold monthly meetings, and at first a handful of people would show up.

In the fall of 1999, Meiklejohn ran for Portland School Committee, and lost. "Our campaigns were real primitive in those days," he says. "There weren't many Green campaigns going on anywhere, so I was able to raise a little money from Greens all over the state. Then it was basically me and my friends, sitting around my apartment, putting stamps on envelopes."

By then, Meiklejohn had started to do a basic version of door-to-door campaigning. He worked from the voter list. But he didn't segment the list, or target certain voter groups, or keep records of his interactions or his support levels, and he didn't do any follow-up with people he had met.

Meiklejohn says, "I didn't really put forward many ideas or policies right away. It was more like I was taking a survey than campaigning. I would go to someone's door, hand them a photocopied flyer, and say, 'Hi, I'm interested in knowing what's important to you.' Then we would talk about it."

In 2000, the legendary consumer advocate Ralph Nader ran for president of the United States. He ran with the endorsement of the Green Party, and his name was on the Green ballot line in states where the Greens had party status, though he never personally registered to vote as a Green. Even so, his run generated tremendous enthusiasm within the Green Party.

Ben Meiklejohn was hired by the Nader 2000 campaign as the campaign coordinator for Maine. His college friend Ben Chipman now held a part-time job as the statewide coordinator of the two-year-old Maine Green Independent Party. As the Nader campaign gained momentum, the two Bens thought that if they pooled their resources, they might be able to open an office.

They found an empty street-level storefront in Portland's downtown Monument Square, a large, European-style plaza which is really the heart of the city. The cost was $3,000 for the small space through the campaign season. Meiklejohn told the Nader national campaign that if they contributed $1,500 to the cost of the office, the Portland Greens would raise the other $1,500. The Nader campaign agreed, and the Greens raised $1,500 in less than a week.

Monument Square quickly became ground zero of the Nader campaign in Maine. Ralph Nader made three visits to Portland during his campaign, each visit more successful than the last, drawing new energy into the local party. The office was a bustling hive of activity, and more than 400 people registered there to vote as Greens.

As the election neared, Nader did a speaking event at Portland High School. A raucous capacity crowd packed the auditorium, with 1,600 people in attendance each paying $10 for the privilege. The national campaign split the proceeds with the local party. To illustrate the magnitude of all this, Al Gore visited Portland during that same campaign season, and barely 200 union members came out to hear him speak for free.

The day of the rally, a Green activist named John Eder picked Nader up at the airport in Manchester, New Hampshire. "Since I was a kid, Nader had always been a hero of mine," Eder says. "Now my girlfriend Suzanne and I were in this little rental van with him and his aide and a Secret Service guy. I drove them around town. Nader was very smart, but also unassuming and easy to talk to. The whole thing was a little bit surreal. I don't think it really sank in with me until much later."

In addition to the Nader campaign, Meiklejohn ran for office for the third time, again for school committee. Focused on his work for the Nader campaign, he lost again. Meanwhile, Derrick Grant, a student at the University of Southern Maine, ran as a Green for state representative. He ran against Democrat Mike Saxl, and he was the second Green to do so.

By now, Saxl was the majority leader of the Maine House of Representatives (subsequently referred to as the state house), and he would soon become Speaker of the House. He was also two years from being term-limited out of office. In 2002, the seat would become open, with no incumbent to defend it. Derrick Grant, who was juggling school and work, barely campaigned beyond putting up some signs and bundling his literature for coordinated distribution by Nader volunteers. Even so, he received 35 percent of the vote.

Greens took notice. For some reason, Democrats didn't.

Victory at Last

> Success consists of going from failure to failure without loss of enthusiasm.
> Winston Churchill

In 2001, 30-year-old Ben Meiklejohn ran for Portland School Committee as an at-large candidate. It was the fourth straight year that he had run for public office, and the third straight year that he had run for school committee. He had been losing races consistently since 1998.

At-large seats were different from district seats in the sense that at-large races were citywide. There was more ground to cover, by a lot. However, two seats were up for grabs instead of just one, and the top two vote-getters would win the seats. Meiklejohn continued his door-to-door approach of simply asking voters what was on their minds. Without much money in his campaign coffers, his literature was once again just photocopied handbills.

Ben Chipman served as his campaign manager, and because of the Nader campaign, both Meiklejohn and Chipman had a lot more organizing experience than they once did. Also, there were now five times as many registered Greens in Portland than there were just a couple of years before. There were more volunteers available to canvas the city, dropping Meiklejohn literature on doorsteps.

It was an off-year election, and most of the attention was drawn to a Portland voter referendum on the question of single-payer health care. Health insurance companies spent hundreds of thousands of dollars on advertising to defeat the measure. They did so even though it was a nonbinding referendum that, if it passed, would merely result in a public resolution stating that the city was in favor of single-payer. (In the end, the resolution passed by a wide margin, with more than 70 percent of the vote.)

Meanwhile, the school committee race was quiet by comparison, without any fanfare or excitement until the results came in. Incumbent Democrat Kim Matthews won the race easily. The surprise was that Ben Meiklejohn had come in second, which was enough to win a seat. He had gained just 17 more votes than Republican incumbent Jeffrey Peters.

Peters immediately requested a recount, which was his right because the race was so close. But on the morning of the recount, as observers from the various political parties gathered at city hall, and city workers prepared to hand count the ballots, Peters suddenly announced that he was withdrawing his request. He stated that he wanted to spend more time with his family.

Ben Meiklejohn had been elected to the school committee, the first Green elected to office in Portland. It was, by any definition, a tiny beachhead. The school committee was a minor elected body and nominally a nonpartisan committee.

"When I got on the committee, no one saw me as a threat," Meiklejohn says. "People were amicable and friendly. They seemed almost proud that a Green had been elected in Portland. It showed how progressive a town we were. Democrat Herb Adams took me under his wing. I was one committee member out of nine, and totally new to the job. I was like a little Green pet."

Even so, outside the committee, Meiklejohn was seen as a hero. He was a well-known Green, and closely associated in the public mind with the Nader campaign the year before. He had also received more than 5,000 votes. His election demonstrated to other Greens that winning was possible. One of those watching was John Eder.

The Michael Quint Campaign

> The Democrats abandoned Michael [Quint, 2002 Democratic primary candidate for state senate]. It was an ugly, bloody campaign, and Michael got slaughtered. In the end, we were under siege. I looked around, and just about the only people still there were Greens. I was mad at Democrats after that. I decided I wasn't going to support people just because of a party label. I was going to stand with the people who stood with us.
>
> Todd Ricker, Quint campaign manager and organizer for
> Service Employees International Union (SEIU)

Todd Ricker has never been a Green. When the Greens started their surge in Portland, Ricker was an organizer for the Maine State Employees Union (MSEU). He was also a Democrat. In early 2002, he took five weeks' vacation from his job to run the primary campaign of his friend Michael Quint. Quint, also a Democrat, was a state representative from Portland—the first openly gay state legislator in Maine's history.

Quint was running in the primary for state senate against relative Maine newcomer Ethan Strimling, the executive director of a local nonprofit organization who was born and raised in New York City. Strimling had gone to college at the University of Maine, and then he moved to Portland with obvious political aspirations. In a Portland state senate race, whoever won the Democratic primary would win the general election. In a sense, the primary, scheduled for June 11, was the general election.

No one remembers why the Greens first became involved with Michael Quint's campaign. Certainly, John Eder was acquainted and somewhat friendly with both Ricker and Quint. Also, Eder's fledgling campaign for state representative was just getting underway, and it being so early in the season, there wasn't much for people to do. But there was never any formal agreement that Eder's volunteers would work for Quint. It just happened.

Soon, between 6 and 10 Greens were at Quint's headquarters on an almost nightly basis, making phone calls to registered Democrats. The phone calls were the first of numerous eye-openers for the Greens. The Quint campaign was working from the city voter list, but they were using it in a way that Greens had not seen before.

The list was a gold mine of information about voter activity, and the Quint campaign had drilled down into the available data. Since this was a Democratic primary, naturally they were calling only Democrats. However, they were doing more than that. For example, the list showed the last times each voter had appeared at the polls, one of the most crucial things a campaign can know about a voter.

Many registered voters only show up for the high-profile races, such as those for president, governor, or Congress. They don't vote in the local elections, they don't vote during special elections, and they don't vote in primaries. Using this information, the Quint campaign had vetted the list, choosing only the "super-voters" who voted in every election no matter how unimportant. They discarded everyone else.

They managed to shrink the list to just the people who were likely to turn up at the polls on primary day. The group was not quite 15 percent of the registered Democrats in the city. Amazingly, these relatively few people would decide for everyone else who would be the next state senator from Portland.

Further, when the campaign called people, the phone interactions followed a rigid, typed-up script. It enumerated three of Quint's political achievements, asked the voter to describe their own concerns, allowed for a little give and take between voter and caller, and then finished with the question, "Can Michael count on your vote?"

It was a question with three possible answers: yes, no, or some variation of I don't know. Callers were then supposed to assign each voter a number from 1 to 5 based on the interaction. People with a 1 were clear supporters of Quint. People with a 5 were clear supporters of Ethan Strimling. People in the middle inhabited a gray area of uncertain support.

The technique gave the campaign a very good idea of how much support Quint was building. In theory, the campaign could go into primary day knowing whether they would win or lose. Also, if the race was close, they could station volunteers at the polls, keeping a record of which voters turned up. By the afternoon, they could begin calling supporters who hadn't appeared at the polls yet, urging them to go and vote.

It quickly became clear to the Green volunteers that the Democrats were much more sophisticated in their approach to campaigning. However, no sophisticated techniques could save Michael Quint, and his campaign suddenly went down in a fiery inferno similar to the crash of the *Hindenburg*.

Quint owned a house in the Parkside neighborhood of Portland. State representatives in Maine are not well paid, and like many people in Portland, he rented out bedrooms in his house to help make ends meet. In general, he rented rooms to friends and acquaintances, and often enough, his housemates were gay men.

At some point, a reporter for the local daily newspaper, the *Portland Press Herald*, began a brief sexual relationship with one of Quint's housemates. During that relationship, the reporter managed to extract some sensitive information from the housemate. The information included these tidbits:

- Early on, Quint's campaign had failed to pay a vendor for a number of T-shirts they had purchased.
- Quint's house was entering foreclosure.
- Quint had been saying for years that he had graduated from the University of Southern Maine and had indicated as much in his campaign literature. However, he had never actually finished college.

The reporter wrote articles revealing the information he had gathered. As the primary approached, he released the stories in sequence, from least to most damning. By the time the news came out that Quint hadn't graduated from college, the campaign was in disarray. Polling indicated that Quint's early lead in the race had disintegrated. Quint's longtime popularity in his own state house district remained strong, but in the wider state senate district he was losing people in droves.

In private, Quint insisted that he had graduated. As a result, Todd Ricker decided to hold a press conference on the steps of city hall to deny the latest allegations. It was a bad move. By the morning of the press conference, reporters from all the local newspapers and radio stations had been able to confirm with the university what everyone already knew: Michael hadn't graduated.

Overnight, Democratic Party activists deserted the campaign. At the press conference, Quint was left twisting in the wind, hammered by questions he couldn't reasonably answer. He just continued to say that he had a diploma, and that it was somewhere in his mother's attic. Quint's political career was all but over. In the 12 years since, he has never again run for public office. Standing behind him and with him outside city hall that day were about 15 Green Party activists.

"What was it about the collapse of our campaign that attracted Greens?" Todd Ricker says now. "Everyone else was repulsed." Whatever it was, it created a formidable new ally in Todd Ricker, and a shift in the way Greens ran their campaigns, especially how they went door-to-door.

The Eder Campaign Begins

I was just as inspired by Ben Meiklejohn as I was by Ralph Nader. Here was a guy who lost and lost and lost, and then won. When he and Chipman came to me and told me I could take Mike Saxl's seat, it didn't seem like a fantasy. I went to see Derrick Grant, who had run for the seat most recently, and he said to me, "There's no way in hell you'll win that seat." Somehow, that made it even clearer that I could win.

John Eder

The Eder campaign began with high hopes. Ben Meiklejohn had just won a school committee seat. The glow from the Nader campaign of 2000 was still on people's faces. And Eder was gearing up to run for the state representative seat being vacated by democratic speaker of the house Mike Saxl, who was stepping down because he had reached his term limit. Derrick Grant had received 35 percent of the vote barely campaigning against Saxl in 2000, and now it was an open seat.

Eder's campaign became the first highly organized, machinelike campaign run by Greens in the City of Portland. It was a winner-take-all race, and therefore on the surface, a much harder race to win than Meiklejohn's. It was also an officially partisan contest. As a result, Eder's name would appear on the ballot with "Green Independent" below it. That was something that Meiklejohn didn't have to deal with in his technically nonpartisan race.

Even so, there were factors in Eder's favor:

- The Greens had a lot of new young activists, inspired by Nader and Meiklejohn, and eager to work on a campaign.
- Races for state offices in Maine are subject to Maine's Clean Elections Law, which provides a set amount of state-sponsored money to each campaign (as long as the campaign jumps through a few administrative hoops and doesn't accept any outside money). In 2002, the amount for a state representative race was about $4,400.
- Although the Democrats were the largest single party affiliation in the district, they weren't the majority. About 45 percent of registered voters were Democrats. Another 40 percent were independent (or technically "unenrolled") voters. An additional 10 percent were Republicans, and 5 percent were registered Greens. This breakdown gave Eder a chance, if only a slim one.
- The Democrats ran a weak candidate to replace Mike Saxl. They had controlled city politics for so long that they must have assumed the seat was safe, and whomever they ran would simply win.

The candidate was David Garrity, a gay man in late middle age with an abrasive personality. He was a Democratic Party activist, but this seemed to mean that he pulled strings to get himself invitations to awards dinners and, in one case, a plum assignment as a superdelegate at the Democratic Party national convention. He had never held an elected office. Over the years, he had made many enemies, even among people in the gay rights movement.

In a district made up of nearly 75 percent renters, Garrity and his longtime partner were wealthy landlords who owned several buildings in the neighborhood. Many of their tenants did not like them. They lived in a beautiful brownstone in a row of restored historic homes, and they had made numerous enemies among their wealthy neighbors as well. Indeed, it was all too easy to find people who did not like David Garrity.

Last, yet very important, Garrity was past the age where he had the energy required for intensive door-to-door work meeting voters. Going door-to-door was the centerpiece of 33-year-old John Eder's campaign strategy.

of training

Todd Ricker was crucial to this effort. Ricker the Democrat came in and gave comprehensive door-to-door training to Eder and his volunteers. The techniques he shared are so effective that they are still used by many Portland Greens. A few of these techniques include the use of a navigator, the use of an opening, the use of a closing, and the use of clincher cards and double clincher cards.

The Use of a Navigator

The navigator is a volunteer who walks with the candidate while the candidate is going door-to-door, or "doing doors." The navigator carries the voter list on a clipboard, as well as a small map of the neighborhood, campaign literature, folded window signs, a small flashlight, and anything else that might be needed.

As they approach a door, the navigator tells the candidate a little about the person they are about to visit: "This is Jane Doe's house. She is a 37-year-old Democrat. Her husband's name is John." While the candidate interacts with the voter, the navigator takes a few notes about the issues important to that voter. At the end of the interaction, the navigator notes the level of support the voter had for the candidate.

More than anything, the navigator serves as a companion for the candidate. Knocking on doors is hard work. The navigator finds the addresses, so the candidate can focus solely on the next visit. The navigator can keep the candidate's energy up, keep him or her on track, and offer moral support when an interaction goes badly. An experienced navigator can even offer the candidate tips on improving interactions.

Using navigators requires tremendous commitment from the campaign. If a candidate is out on doors five evenings a week, that means someone in the campaign, usually the campaign manager, has to be on the phone lining up navigators ahead of time (and finding replacements when one falls through).

The Use of an Opening

An opening is a line that can be used again and again when beginning any voter interaction. It takes psychological pressure off the candidate because the opening is rote, and so requires no thought. It usually goes something like, "Hi Jane. My name is John Eder, and I'm running to become your state representative. Can you tell me what issues are important to you?"

Most people have issues that are important to them, and if asked, are eager to talk about them. Often enough, the issues are unrelated to the office the candidate is seeking. For example, a person might say, "My mother is losing her memory and

I can't afford a nursing home for her." If elected, the candidate can do nothing about this issue, but while at the door, the candidate can lend a sympathetic ear and maybe even help the voter think of a possible solution.

In most cases, the voter will talk about issues that are related to the candidate's office. These situations can lead to lively discussions. Even if the voter says, "I don't really know what the issues are," then the candidate can respond, "Well, if you don't mind, let me tell you about a few of the things I want to work on."

The Use of a Closing

In most voter interactions, the closing is the most important part, and often the hardest part for the candidate. It consists of the candidate shaking hands with the voter, smiling, looking the voter in the eye, and saying: "Can I count on your vote?"

The whole point of going door-to-door is to get people to vote for you. Asking for the vote is the logical endpoint in each interaction. It is a moment of shared intimacy. When a voter makes a commitment to the candidate in those circumstances, they remember it, and they are unlikely to change their mind later. It also allows the navigator to determine an accurate level of support for that voter.

Portland Greens use a 1 to 3 system, where 1 means the person has committed to voting for the candidate, 2 means the level of support is unknown or undecided, and 3 means the person has committed to vote for the opponent.

It can be difficult emotionally to shake hands with a person and then hear that they plan to vote for your opponent, or even that they're still undecided. Even so, it must be done. If a navigator is out with a candidate who consistently doesn't make "the ask" (for the vote), the navigator has to insist on it, or even end the doors session early and then take up the issue with the campaign manager. Closing the interaction with "the ask" is that important.

The Use of Clincher Cards and Double Clincher Cards

Clincher cards are short postcards that the candidate sends to the voter after an interaction on the doors. They are basically handwritten thank you notes, and it is important to write and send them as soon as possible after the interaction. The catch is that when writing each card, the candidate has access to the notes that the navigator took during the interaction. So, the candidate might write something like: "Dear Jane, it was great to meet you at your door on Tuesday evening. I was very sorry to hear about your mom, and I hope that things work out for you. Thank you for committing to vote for me in November. If there is any way I can help you, please don't hesitate to call me."

The postcards can be made inexpensively on card stock with the candidate's return address (and logo) in the top left corner. Usually, six or eight cards can fit on one page of card stock—two across and three or four down.

Clincher cards are a powerful way to strengthen a relationship started at the doorstep. Double clincher cards are the way to set it in cement. As soon as the candidate finishes the clincher card, he takes out another card, dates it for a week before Election Day, and writes almost the exact same message, except slightly altered to account for the passage of time. In this case, the candidate might write: "Dear Jane, it was great to meet with you at your door back in September. I hope everything is working out for you. Please remember to get out and vote for me on Election Day next week, Tuesday, November 8. Thank you."

The double clincher cards are put into a shoebox at the campaign office, and they are not used until a week before election day. You don't put stamps on double clincher cards right away because postage is expensive, and you may need that money for something more important. If a week before the election the campaign still has enough money, the double clinchers go in the mail.

The effect of the double clinchers is similar to the effect of a time bomb. If the campaign is going well, then the candidate has begun to receive media attention. The voters who met the candidate on the door may be following this closely, or it may be something happening well in the background of their lives, along with all kinds of other "noise." Suddenly, a few days before the election, that voter receives *another* handwritten card in the mail from the candidate. "Oh my God," the voter thinks. "He remembers me."

The Earth Quakes—John Eder Wins

The process of campaigning was transformational and empowering. I had been underground for years. I had lived on the fringe of society, without a bank account and a lot of times without even an address. I hated my own name. I wanted to finally get over the feeling of being alienated and ashamed. I wanted to go door-to-door and see if people would accept me. I felt that if people in Portland could like and accept me, then maybe I really had found my home.

John Eder

John Eder was a soldier "on doors." He began going door-to-door in early July, when most people's minds were on the beach or baseball or backyard barbecues. He started gradually, three evenings a week, then four, then five. The campaign kept him well-stocked with volunteer navigators.

He played around with different times and days. Early afternoons on weekdays were bad—no one was home except the elderly, who often wouldn't answer the door anyway. Early evenings were better. A long Saturday could garner dozens of voter interactions.

The summer was quiet and Eder gradually piled up the doors. Outside of his close inner circle, few people imagined he would win. Even so, he knocked on every voter's door in the district and then started again from the beginning. After going through the district twice, he started again a third time.

The campaign used other techniques as well. Todd Ricker came up with a catchy slogan: "New Ideas, Real Solutions." Eder commissioned a local artist to create an image of a head with a light bulb going on above it, and the campaign slogan along the bottom. Posters of the image became a sought-after piece of political art.

Eder, dressed in a business suit, appeared unannounced at an editorial board meeting of the large daily newspaper in Portland, the *Portland Press Herald*. He spent an hour describing his background and chatting with the editors about issues facing the city and state. He came across as knowledgeable and sincere. The *Press Herald*, which normally printed humorous or condescending stories about the local Greens, published a short, respectful article about the visit.

Mindful of the accusation that Greens were spoilers who threw races to Republicans, the campaign reached out to the Republican in the race. He was a multimillionaire businessman who had started a nonprofit animal rights organization. They showed him the data from recent elections in the district. The district was so liberal that the chance of a Republican winning there was near zero.

wow

The businessman admitted that the local Republican Party had cajoled him to run because they didn't want an empty ballot line. He and Eder connected on the question of animal rights. He agreed to drop out of the race and throw his support behind Eder. He hosted a coffee hour with Eder in the exclusive waterfront development where he lived. He also signed a letter endorsing Eder, which went to every Republican in the district in the week before election day.

As time passed, a sort of magic began to happen. Eder himself unveiled a winning, almost statesmanlike personality. Perhaps all those years of wandering and meeting strangers had given him a certain charisma. At the doors, he won voters over in almost every interaction. Sometimes the person would say, "I don't believe in a single thing you stand for. But you came here to see me, you're working hard, and I'm going to vote for you."

Bernie

People invited him in for lemonade on hot days, tea and cookies in the evenings, even for dinner. Like a political pied piper, he accumulated volunteers of every stripe. John Eder signs began to appear everywhere. As election day approached, the campaign took on an almost joyous tone. Phone polling suggested that he was ahead by a margin of nearly two-to-one. In the week before the election, the local newspapers released their endorsements. All three newspapers in the city endorsed Eder.

On election night, when the results came in, Eder had taken 65 percent of the vote to Garrity's 35 percent, exactly as the polling had predicted. The proprietress of the Danforth Inn, a beautiful Victorian era hotel, hosted a victory party for the campaign. More than a hundred people packed the hotel's great room. Eder was now the only state representative in the United States who was a member of the Green Party.

Early the next morning, at the Green Party office, the phone started ringing and didn't stop. One of the many callers was Ralph Nader, offering his congratulations. Overnight, Eder had become a minor political celebrity, and his victory would soon lead to dozens of people joining the Greens and running for office in Maine. One of those people was a man named Stephen Spring.

Stephen Spring

In the back of my mind, I had actually considered running for office for a long time. I just didn't know how to go about it. I didn't know there were resources available. I didn't know that there were these progressive people around who seemed to know exactly what they were doing.

Stephen Spring, Portland School Committee member, 2003–2006

Stephen Spring was different from the other Greens. Nearly 40 years old when he first ran for office, Spring was more established than many Green activists. He owned a house just off the Portland peninsula. He had a career as a public school teacher, and in early 2003, he was just finishing two years in a research position at an education think tank affiliated with Northeastern University in Boston. "Stephen was very qualified for the position, probably the most qualified person to serve on the school committee in the past thirty years," says Ben Meiklejohn.

Spring's domestic partner Gustavo Caldas worked as an airline flight attendant. Because of the airline's generous travel allowances for employees, Stephen and Gustavo often traveled abroad during their vacation time. Stephen had visited dozens of countries, and he was a fluent Spanish speaker.

Stephen had registered to vote as a Green while living in Boston, but he had never participated in any political activism. He was back in Portland full-time for about two weeks when he noticed a small event announcement in a local weekly newspaper. The announcement described a Green Party barbecue being held one weekend in a backyard not far from his house.

For no other reason than the fact that he didn't have much else to do that day, Spring decided to attend. While mingling with the people at the barbecue, he met a young man named Ben Chipman. Somewhat oddly upon meeting a stranger, Chipman quickly started pressing him for specific details about his life: "Where do you live? What do you do? Are you registered Green?" Then Chipman said something even odder: "You know, you're eligible to run for the District 2 school committee seat. Herb Adams has that seat, and he's vulnerable. I think you could win."

Herb Adams was a longtime Democratic Party politician and a fixture on the Portland scene. He was a state representative. He had been the Cumberland County register of deeds. He had served numerous terms on the school committee. In his spare time, he lectured on history and political science at the University of Southern Maine. He had won so many elections in his career, and he had such an encyclopedic knowledge of local politics, that there was a widespread perception that he was unbeatable.

However, the Greens had been watching him. During 2002, while John Eder was winning his race, a Green named Jeff Spencer had run against Adams for his state house seat. Spencer lost, but Adams hadn't campaigned particularly hard. In fact, other than showing up for public meetings, sending a couple of mailers, and putting up some signs *the day before the election*, Adams hadn't campaigned at all.

Further, Adams was now holding two elected seats simultaneously—a state house seat and a school committee seat. Greens thought holding two seats at once would be distracting to Adams. It would also make a good argument on the doors as to why he should be voted off the school committee. How could one man hold two seats and do a good job at both?

At the barbecue, Stephen Spring told Chipman he would think about running. Stephen went home and talked it over with Gustavo. The fact that there was an established Green Party, which had already won seats, made his decision easier. By the next morning he had decided that he would run for office. He went to see Chipman at the Green Party office in Portland. It was 18 hours after they had first talked about it, and Stephen was ready to throw his hat in the ring.

This being a municipal election, no public funding was available. To pay for the campaign, Stephen was able to raise a few hundred dollars from friends and family. He also applied for an endorsement from the Victory Fund, a political action committee that seeks to help openly gay men and women get elected. He became the first Green candidate in the United States to be endorsed and funded by the Victory Fund.

Finally, Stephen and Gustavo held a party at their house that raised several hundred dollars. By then, the Greens were evolving a new house party fundraising technique. A couple of Greens would make a big show of locking the door to the house or apartment. John Eder would make a pitch for the candidate to the assembled crowd, and say, "No one's leaving here until we've raised five hundred dollars. Who's going to pledge the first hundred?"

A few awkward moments would pass. "Come on, let's get this thing rolling," Eder would say. Then a plant who had already committed to contribute a hundred dollars would tentatively raise his or her hand and say, "I'll do it. I'll give a hundred dollars."

Of course, a cheer would go up. After that, the ice was broken, and the rest of the crowd would start offering their fives, tens, twenties, and fifties. It seemed to work every time.

In retrospect, the victory itself was easy. Spring received endorsements from two popular local officials—John Eder and Ben Meiklejohn. Unlike Eder, who put 60 to 80 hours a week into his first campaign, Stephen worked 30 hours a week on his campaign, while juggling other commitments. He spent most of that time going door-to-door, employing the same techniques Eder had used. Eder, who had knocked on thousands of doors and was well known to Spring's constituents, served as Spring's first volunteer navigator. He did doors with him many times after that.

"I was commuting to Boston a couple of days a week, finishing up my work down there," Spring says. "In the evenings, I would do doors. I had a navigator 80 or 90 percent of the time, and I probably knocked on a thousand doors. In the mornings, I would relax with my coffee on the train and write my clincher cards all the way down."

Herb Adams continued his baffling pattern of behavior. He encouraged Spring while barely campaigning himself. It was almost as if he wanted to lose. He went to a few neighborhood meetings. He put up a few signs near polling places the day before the election. And by all accounts, he was stunned and angry when Stephen Spring took 55 percent of the vote on Election Day.

Spring's appearance on the school committee ushered in a new era in Portland politics. He had ousted an incumbent Democrat, the first Green to do so. Greens had won a campaign race in Portland for three straight years. There were now Greens in two out of nine seats on the committee, and Spring was naturally outspoken. "I'll admit I was pretty quiet on the committee until Stephen got there," Meiklejohn says. "He embraced his Green Party enrollment as intrinsic to what he was doing. His spirit showed me how our values impacted and were not separate from our work. He didn't shy away from expressing his beliefs, to put it mildly."

The Battle for Portland

You put your head out there, and they beat you about the head and neck. They lie. They cheat. They wheel old men and ladies on oxygen into a courtroom and bully them into lying. Their own people see how ugly it is, and for a little while that makes you even more popular. But then it begins to stick to you. Somehow you get painted with the ugly stick.

John Eder

John Eder was becoming a threat. He was enormously popular within his district, and in early 2004, it seemed unlikely he would face a serious challenge in the upcoming election. Further, he was something of a celebrity among Greens throughout Maine, the United States, and to some degree internationally. Inspired by his victory in 2002, 24 Greens announced their intention to run for state representative in districts across Maine. Eder took the new candidates on a walking tour of the State House building in Augusta, shepherding them into the legislative chamber and showing them where they would sit if they took office. Now the Democrats were watching Eder. They didn't like what they saw.

Every 10 years in Maine, the state legislature redraws the district lines. On the face of it, the process has to do with changes in population distribution, and certainly that plays a role. However, the process is also highly political, and the party in power tends to draw the lines in ways that are advantageous to keeping themselves in power.

In the spring of 2004, it was time to redraw the lines. Eder's state house district was known as District 31. It encompassed most of the West End of the Portland peninsula and much of the downtown area where the office towers and the Old Port bar scene were, but where few people lived.

When the new districts were announced, it turned out that Eder's district had shifted west, and his apartment was two blocks outside of his old district. Somehow, Eder now lived in the district that encompassed the eastern end of the peninsula, a neighborhood called Munjoy Hill, the stronghold of Democratic state representative and future speaker of the house Ben Dudley. Eder lived all the way across town from Munjoy Hill, now in an area with just a handful of voters from his previous district.

It was an old-fashioned case of gerrymandering. Eder had effectively zero chance of defeating incumbent Dudley in his own neighborhood, but he did have one thing in his favor. He was a renter, and since his lease had expired months before, he was now renting month-to-month.

So Eder moved six blocks west, back into his old district. Furthermore, he issued a press release and held a small press conference in which he chatted with reporters from the local TV stations and newspapers; meanwhile, in the background, Green volunteers unloaded a rental truck into his new apartment. The coverage made Eder more popular than ever, and many Democrats voiced anger at their own party in letters to the editor of the *Portland Press Herald*.

amazing

The move put Eder into a district that he now shared with incumbent Democrat Ed Suslovic. The difference was that the district was made up of 75 percent of Eder's old district and 25 percent of Suslovic's. Now it was Suslovic who faced an uphill battle in alien territory.

The campaign proceeded quietly through the dog days of summer. Eder did a thousand doors. Suslovic went on vacation, and he was out of town most of the time. When Suslovic returned in the fall, he ventured out on doors. Greens did drive-bys and hung out on street corners, watching him.

Even though Suslovic was months behind the preferred campaign schedule, he only went out on doors a few days a week. There didn't seem to be any logic or pattern to the doors he knocked on. He was always by himself. He didn't take notes following his interactions. From the outside, it looked like an ineffective and half-hearted door-to-door effort. Either Suslovic didn't know how to do doors, or he felt that the outcome of the campaign wouldn't hinge on what he did.

In late September, shocking news arrived. It concerned Green activist Ben Chipman. Eder's position as a state representative had meant that just like the Democrats and the Republicans, the Greens were entitled to an office at the State House. The legislature also had provided a salary for a part-time legislative aide to staff the office, one day a week. Greens had raised money from across the country to fund an extra day a week, making the aide a two-day-a-week job. Ben Chipman had served as Eder's aide, doing research, supporting bills, carrying out constituent service work, and supervising interns. However, without warning toward the end of September, the Maine attorney general's office indicted Chipman on charges of voter fraud. Moments after he was indicted, he was suspended without pay from his job as legislative aide.

"I had no idea this was happening," Chipman says. "The legislature wasn't even in session. I was at home that day. No one from the State House told me I was indicted or suspended. I got a call from a reporter who wanted a statement. A statement about what? About my indictment."

Chipman had participated in a special election race earlier that year in the city of Biddeford, Maine. He had organized the campaign of Green activist Dorothy Lafortune, who was running for a state house seat that had become empty. After the campaign, allegations arose that Chipman and three others had manipulated and bullied voters at a nursing home into voting for Lafortune.

These were serious charges. Chipman was facing jail time. He could no longer work at the State House, and prominent Democrats began calling for Eder to publicly disavow him and promise not to work with him again. Instead, learning from the Michael Quint press conference fiasco, Eder refused interviews and released a simple statement reminding the public that Chipman hadn't been convicted of a crime. He did state that Chipman was playing no role in his current campaign.

By then, Chipman was one of the most effective organizers in the state of Maine, regardless of party. He was a high-energy, tireless activist who had been on the ground in every successful campaign the Greens had run. Nearly a year would pass before he was acquitted of the charge against him and was reinstated as Eder's aide with full back pay. Now, however, he was out of work, and no campaign could touch him in public.

Eder pressed on, but after the gerrymandering, and with his legislative aide under indictment, his campaign took on a siege mentality. He recalls, "It's a lonely feeling, sitting in the bunker, waiting for the next attack. You don't know when it will happen or what shape it will take. You just know that it's coming."

In mid-October, Eder was well ahead in the polls. Then, a couple of weeks before election day, he got a call in the middle of the night. The caller was Ed

King, proprietor of the *West End News*, a popular weekly newspaper available throughout the city. King wanted Eder to come to his apartment, saying only that it was important. When Eder arrived, King laid out some paperwork on a desk. The paperwork was records of some of Eder's financial peccadillos. Eder had bounced a few checks in the past year. He was behind in payments to the company that owned the Augusta Go bus, the commuter van in which he often rode the 50 miles to the State House. Some years before, nearly broke, he had applied to the city for general assistance and had been rejected.

"A man came here tonight and brought me these," Ed King said. "He said he thought a good storyline would be that if Eder can't manage his own money, why is he up in Augusta managing ours?" Eder and King stared at each other for a long minute. "Do you want to give me a statement?" King said. "Here's my statement," Eder said. "Don't print this, Ed. You see what they're doing. This isn't a story. It's a hatchet job. This is them trying to put a bullet in my head."

wow

King decided not to run the story. In the next two weeks, Eder received the endorsements of all the local newspapers, as well as most of the unions and environmental organizations. Once again, he won handily, dispatching Ed Suslovic, who became the second Democratic Party incumbent to fall to a Green. However, the exhausting dirty war for his reelection, coupled with the fact that no other Green had won a state house seat anywhere in Maine, meant that Eder's victory celebration was far more muted this time.

The Battle for Portland, Part 2

> Okay, we're Greens and we were against the war. But the military recruitment thing was really about equalizing post-secondary opportunities. Why should military recruiters be in the students' faces all the time when a representative from Harvard can only come twice a year, and it has to be scheduled beforehand?
>
> Ben Meiklejohn

The school committee operated on three-year terms, which meant that in 2004, Ben Meiklejohn was also up for reelection. Like Eder, he won handily, this time coming in first of three candidates, and receiving almost 17,000 votes citywide.

Joining Meiklejohn and Spring on the school committee was Jason Toothaker, a 21-year-old college student who had interned for John Eder at the State House. Toothaker squeaked onto the committee, in a race so close that the ballots were recounted by hand. When the dust settled, Toothaker had won by a single vote.

Having three Greens on the school committee led to pitched battles between the Greens and the Democrats. Much of this played out in the newspapers. Word spread, and residents of Portland began to watch the school committee meetings on the local cable access TV station. Soon, people were throwing school committee parties. "It was like boxing on pay-per-view," Spring said. "People would invite their friends over, serve beer, and watch the action. Afterwards, people would come up to me on the street and tell me they were rooting for me on TV."

Toothaker came up with the idea of changing the Columbus Day holiday to Indigenous Peoples' Day. It became a media sensation. The idea was to remind students that Christopher Columbus didn't discover America. In fact, when he arrived, there were already people living here. The measure was defeated 6–3.

Meanwhile, Stephen Spring and Ben Meiklejohn were quietly nurturing another idea. The wars in Afghanistan and Iraq were at their height. The military had a voracious need for new recruits, and military recruiters were constantly at Portland High School, the city high school with the highest concentration of low-income and minority students.

The rules for military recruiters were lax, to say the least. Recruiters could show up at the school any number of times they chose—in 2005, they showed up 28 times. They could come into the cafeteria and talk with students for any length of time they chose. They could walk the hallways, chatting with students between classes. They frequently played loud rock music outside the school to bring students to their recruiting table. They gave away T-shirts and ball caps. "It was like a rock concert when they showed up," Spring said. "And it seemed like they were showing up every other day."

Moreover, recruiters had unfettered access to student demographic information. Information such as grades, family makeup, and whether the student was eligible for free or reduced-price meals all was given to recruiters. Recruiters were using this information to target specific students. Who wasn't likely to be college bound? Who came from a poor or broken family, and therefore likely needed a good income immediately upon graduation?

Few people knew this, but on the emergency contact cards students filled out at the beginning of every year, families could choose to opt out of sharing private information with military recruiters. Only about 2 percent of families chose to do this in any given year. Spring and Meiklejohn wanted to change this. They wanted military recruiters to be treated like employment and college recruiters. This meant that they would have access to the school a limited number of days per year, and their behavior would be severely curtailed. They would have to schedule their appearances in advance. They couldn't simply wander the halls or enter the cafeteria.

The Greens also wanted to block recruiter access to student demographic information. They wanted to change the sharing of information with military recruiters from an opt out to an opt in. This meant that instead of checking a box if they didn't want their information shared, families would have to check a box if they did want the information shared.

In 2005, attorney Susan Hopkins, another Green, was running for an at-large school committee seat. To call attention to the recruitment issues, she, Meiklejohn, Toothaker, and Spring appeared on the steps of Portland High School on the first day of school. They held oversized demonstration copies of the emergency contact card and handed out pencils with the inscription "Welcome Back to School Portland High Bulldogs. Opt-Out or Opt-In. It's YOUR Decision!"

Hopkins ran specifically on her opposition to military recruiting and came in first in a three-way race. Greens now had four votes on the committee, and two Democrats on the committee were very liberal. The military recruitment issue was gaining a lot of media attention, and one Democrat decided to join the Greens on the issue early on.

For months, Stephen Spring worked on Ellen Alcorn, the second Democrat, cajoling her to vote for it, but he couldn't get a commitment from her. Although they already had a 5–4 majority, Spring felt that they needed that second Democrat as a buffer vote. As chair of the policy subcommittee, he took a chance and scheduled a vote on the issue anyway.

The proposed rule, called the Equitable Recruitment Access Policy, included the following provisions: (1) Military recruiters were barred from cafeterias and hallways, and they were required to meet with students in the guidance office (like college recruiters); (2) military recruiters were limited to seven visits per year; and (3) all emergency contact cards were required to have opt-in instead of opt-out language.

The measure passed, six votes to three, and at the time it was one of the most comprehensive policies limiting military recruitment in the country. Recruiters saw their access to Portland's children suddenly and drastically curtailed. In the year after the new rules were adopted, and with the new opt-in feature on the emergency contact card, the percentage of families who chose not to share information with military recruiters jumped from 2 percent to 65 percent.

"Afterwards, I talked with Ellen Alcorn to thank her," Spring said. "She told me that she mostly voted for it because she wanted the controversy to stop. She wanted the media attention to stop. She wanted the whole thing to go away."

The Greens Recede

There's a burnout factor. It takes a lot more work to run and serve as a Green, because you have a lot more to overcome, and there is no network. There's no machine behind you. You just have to keep working harder. You get pooped out. It's hard to sustain that energy. You're constantly building support, and as soon as you blink, as soon as you stop for a second, it goes away.

Ben Meiklejohn

By 2006, the Greens had solidified into Portland's major opposition party. In 2005, local attorney and Green activist Susan Hopkins had joined Meiklejohn, Spring, and Toothaker on the school committee. However, party lines had hardened and votes routinely went 5–4 in favor of the Democrats. Meanwhile, young Green activists David Marshall and Kevin Donoghue, both of whom had volunteered on earlier John Eder campaigns, were gearing up to run for city council. Rebecca Minnick was running for the open school committee seat on Munjoy Hill. A Green majority on the school committee was in sight.

A small political action committee called Green Future, cofounded by Eder, was pouring money into training new candidates and their volunteers on effective campaign techniques. It was also contributing the $250 limit to Green municipal campaigns.

Eder's life was changing, however. He had bought a house in his West End district. He and his longtime girlfriend Suzanne had married. He was up for reelection, but state representatives in Maine only made about $16,000 a year. Eder's expenses were higher than they had ever been, and he needed money.

In the summer of 2006, Eder took a job working for Pat LaMarche's campaign for governor of Maine. LaMarche, who had run as the Green Party candidate for vice president of the United States in 2004, was running for governor simply to help maintain the Greens' party status in Maine. She needed to gain 5 percent of the vote statewide for the Greens to keep their ballot line. In the end, she would get 9 percent, a respectable showing.

Eder's position on the LaMarche campaign meant he had little time to work on his own reelection. His original plan had been to leave the LaMarche campaign after Labor Day, then spend two months on the doors. As a still-popular incumbent running against a relatively unknown Democrat, two months of hard campaigning seemed like it would be enough. But when Labor Day came, he didn't leave the LaMarche campaign. Indeed, despite the increasingly desperate pleas from other Greens, he stayed with LaMarche until the end, and he never went out on doors.

"You can never let your guard down, or your energy," Eder says. "I guess I didn't realize that. I thought I had all this capital, and all this support. I had been working nonstop for that district for four years. I was tired. I had dragged myself along, banging on countless thousands of doors. Thousands. It's not an exaggeration. Everyone knew me. People constantly stopped me in the street to talk politics. Did I really need to come to their door again? I guess so."

At the same time, Stephen Spring had enrolled at the University of Maine Law School in September. Inundated by the demands of his freshman year, a similar train of thought occurred to him. He was a popular politician. Everyone knew him. Did he really need to go out on doors? In his mind, the answer was no.

Eder lost by 97 votes. Spring lost by 213. In electoral math, every vote for a candidate subtracts a vote from his opponent. If Eder had won over 49 more voters, he would have won. If Spring had attracted 107 more voters, he would have won.

On the doors, you can have 15 or 20 voter interactions a night. A month of hard work on the doors probably would have won either campaign. Instead, the first Green surge in Portland abruptly ended. While the Greens continued to hold local offices in subsequent years, they did so in smaller numbers and with greatly reduced overall political impact. Moreover, they lost their three most dynamic and inspiring leaders.

By early 2007, Stephen Spring had sold his house and moved to Austin, Texas. Later, he received a PhD in education. John Eder went back to college as an undergraduate and spent a semester in Ireland as an exchange student. He has returned to politics in recent years, but more effectively as a behind the scenes organizer of ballot initiatives than as a candidate or public figure. Ben Meiklejohn also returned to college—to pursue a degree in music performance, specifically for the oboe. He is out of politics as of this writing, with no firm plans to return.

Last Words

How do we make sense of the experiences described above? Before formal conclusions are offered, here are some final reactions by various Greens described in this chapter:

> I was under this assumption that everybody was motivated by good impulses, or pure ideals. It was a shock for me to discover that some people are there to feather their nests. A lot of Democratic and Republican politicians are not passionate about what they're doing. They don't care. They're just putting in a couple of terms in office, being good soldiers, so they'll be rewarded with twenty-year desk jobs at the end of it. Meanwhile, Greens are bloodying themselves, trying to change the world.
>
> John Eder

> It gets me excited just talking about it with you. We were fighting for what we believed in, and we were throwing everything we had into it. And what's more, we were right. I hope that I get to do it again one day. I miss it. I really do.
>
> Stephen Spring

> Close to a hundred Greens have run for State House seats in Maine. Only one has ever won, and that's John Eder. Will another Green ever win a State House seat? I don't know. I do know this. I ran as an independent and won the first time. Then I won again. I'll win again this year. Mainers like independents. There's a long history of independents holding office in Maine.

And the Democrats don't see me as a threat anymore. They could have ger-rymandered me this year, and they didn't. I can work with them now. They tried to put me in jail ten years ago.

Ben Chipman

We tapped into a populace that was apolitical, disenfranchised, and had hatred toward the two parties and politics in general. But people get excited when they see convictions in action from officeholders. That's what gets me excited. What's the point of sitting in office if you're not trying to challenge the status quo, and if you're not a threat to the system? I'll tell you this: If I come back, I'm more equipped to be a politician than I was previously. I'm more thick-skinned. I've been through some harsh shit.

Ben Meiklejohn

Data wins elections. We know that. But what also wins is commitment. In any given campaign, the side that's the most insanely driven, the most single-minded, the most obsessed . . . that's the side that usually wins.

Todd Ricker

Conclusion

The Portland Greens experienced a meteoric rise to prominence in the early 2000s. They never controlled a single legislative body, but they injected Portland politics with a vitality and excitement that had been missing previously. Arguably, they helped make local government somewhat more responsive to the public, at least for a while. Their appearance seemed sudden, but was actually the result of years of effort. For a time, their momentum seemed unstoppable, but as soon as two of their leaders stopped doing the arduous, door-to-door campaigning that was the main source of their success, the wheels quickly came off the movement.

To my mind, for any "outsider" political group, the most critical way to gain relevance, the most vital way to win, is to go out and meet the people you seek to represent. John Eder often refers to it as "retail politics," and it is the hardest and most important work a politician can do. You talk to hundreds and eventually thousands of people, one by one, door by door, day after day after day.

This is how you build the people's trust and keep it. The trouble is, if your mes-sage is at all controversial, you typically can't afford to stop building that trust after you've won, nor to make mistakes or suffer mishaps that erode it. You normally also can't afford to get tired, or at least not to stay that way for long. You probably won in the first place largely because of how close you were to the voters. If you ever allow yourself to become distant, you likely will lose.

So, if you are a controversial outsider politician at the local level, *what does it take to sustain your ability to connect to voters, election after election?* To keep up the intensive person-to-person contact, do you require extraordinary stamina and focus, an unusual amount of free time, or a special type of help from your supporters and allies? To make connecting with constituents more manageable, do you need a certain kind of district, a particular bond with your community, a political office requiring more public interaction (such as mayor), or some especially memorable political accomplishments? To avoid being fatally tainted by a minor scandal, do you have to have a certain degree of personal maturity and good luck? Or does your ability to keep bonding with voters (despite your antiestablishment orientation) demand some other asset?

The precise answers to these questions are beyond the scope of this author's political experience and knowledge. Yet such answers are critical to understanding how a local left third party can not only gain but also *maintain and expand* power in government. The Portland Greens of the last decade have shown us how to begin that process, and their story has raised pivotal questions for those who hope to go further in the future.

4

LESSONS OF THE VERMONT PROGRESSIVE PARTY*

Terry Bouricius

The most successful third party effort in any state over the past several decades has been the Vermont Progressive Party. It traces its roots to an unlikely victory in Burlington, Vermont, in 1981. For most of the past three decades its supporters have held the mayor's office and a significant number of city council seats. At least three dozen different members have been elected to the city council during that time. But its success is not limited to Burlington. Between 1991 and 2012, 14 different members were elected to the Vermont House of Representatives from around the state, with as many as 6 holding seats at one time. As of 2014, 3 members were serving as state senators. Party members have also been elected (in nonpartisan races) to a wide variety of municipal offices across Vermont, and Bernie Sanders, though always running as an independent, has been repeatedly elected to the U.S. Congress.[1]

This chapter will recount some of this history, with special attention to the circumstances surrounding the various breakthrough events at the municipal, state, and federal levels. Correspondingly, it will suggest how and to what extent electoral achievements by Vermont Progressives may be a model for similar such successes by progressive third parties elsewhere. Specifically, I argue that there are several interrelated obstacles to the rise of successful third parties in the United States that, thanks to a convergence of fortuitous circumstances, were avoided or overcome by Progressives in Burlington, Vermont, starting in 1981. Most of these

---

* Various observations in this chapter are consistent with those made earlier in the author's book *Building Progressive Politics: The Vermont Story*, Madison, WI: Center for a New Democracy, 1993.

impediments reemerged as Progressives sought to expand their efforts statewide. I discuss how Progressives dealt with these problems at the state level with mixed success. The circumstances that allowed the various Progressive breakthroughs are not unique to Vermont. It is feasible to find other jurisdictions that are ripe for a new progressive third party. The issues that I address are media access, scale, money, the "spoiler" dynamic, and electoral credibility.

Although the term "spoiler" has a negative connotation, I am using it as short-hand for a constellation of issues related to the problems that can occur when more than just two candidates contend in a plurality winner-take-all election (that is, one in which a candidate wins by getting the largest share of votes, even if that is less than a majority). Third party candidates are often accused of "taking" votes from major candidates closest to them on the political spectrum, both "spoiling" their chances and possibly throwing the race to the major candidate furthest away from them on the political spectrum. Plurality election rules discourage third party candidacies. This is because voting for a more-favored minor party candidate instead of a less-favored major party candidate can help the other, least favored major party candidate win the most votes, and thereby, the election. Consequently, many voters feel that a vote for a candidate who is deemed to have little chance of winning is a "wasted" vote. Thus, whether a candidate is perceived as having a realistic chance of winning can become a self-fulfilling prophecy (causing candidates who are thought of as unlikely to win being deprived of the votes needed to have any chance of winning).

The spoiler dynamic is unique to plurality winner-take-all election systems common in the United States. It is not a problem in most representative democracies, which generally use proportional representation when electing legislative bodies, and some sort of majoritarian runoff system when electing an executive office. Proportional representation allots a share of seats to all political parties based on the percentage of votes they receive, while a majoritarian runoff system requires a second round of voting among the top two candidates if no candidate receives more than half or close to half of the total votes in the first round. The result is that voters are able to choose among candidates from multiple parties without constantly feeling the pressure to select the "lesser of two evils."

In the United States, the spoiler dynamic and the other obstacles mentioned above reinforce each other. Their interconnectedness means that seeking to solve just one or two of them is not sufficient. However, I am not arguing that these are the only impediments faced by would-be third party initiatives across America. For example, some jurisdictions have severe ballot access restrictions, which Vermont does not.

Based on the experience of Vermont Progressives, I also argue that some commonly pursued efforts of aspiring third parties, such as platform and policy development, are all but irrelevant to electoral prospects. This is frustrating for activists who enter politics themselves, specifically because of philosophical and policy concerns, but electoral politics unfortunately is shaped by factors other than ideology and issues. Such factors prominently include voters' general impressions of candidates based on simple political, cultural, and psychological cues and related biases.

I will not be focusing on Vermont Progressives' policy proposals or accomplishments, such as the establishment of the first municipal housing land trust, tax reform, or efforts to enact single-payer health care. The purpose of this chapter is to tell the story of how a third party grew and achieved the level of electoral success it did within the U.S. political environment. However, it should be noted that this bit of history, like all history, was shaped by countless unrecognized factors and elements of chance. I will do my best to relay those factors of which I am aware that appear to me to have been especially significant, but I make no pretense of providing a comprehensive analysis. While every jurisdiction in the United States faces many unique obstacles and opportunities, there may be some lessons to be learned by third party activists from the Vermont story.

First, a few words about my biography are in order. I got involved in third party politics in 1972 after hearing Bernie Sanders speak at an event at Middlebury College. Sanders was clearly intelligent, with a class analysis that matched my own. Beyond merely being against the war in Vietnam and supporting the rights of racial minorities and women, he spoke about a generally unacknowledged ruling oligarchy in the country—a rich elite that had established the "rules of the game" to its benefit and against the interests of the vast majority of working people. Perhaps more significantly, he was completely up-front—lacking any of a typical politician's pretense or phoniness. Although Sanders later became a U.S. senator, at that time he was a fringe candidate running under the Liberty Union Party label for governor of Vermont. I joined the Liberty Union Party and ran for state senate a couple of times. I briefly served as state party chair before giving up on the Liberty Union around 1978. Soon after, I was an organizer of the Vermont chapter of the Citizens Party and was a delegate to the national convention that nominated environmentalist Barry Commoner to run for U.S. president in 1980. In 1981 I was elected to the Burlington city council,[2] becoming the first Citizens Party candidate elected in the United States. This was the same election in which Bernie Sanders was elected mayor as an independent. I served a decade as a city councilor, and then another decade as a member of the Vermont House of Representatives as a Progressive. After leaving the legislature in 2001, I worked for another decade with FairVote: The Center for Voting and Democracy on policy analysis and advocacy of election reforms such as proportional representation and instant runoff voting. As of this writing, having become more interested in nonelectoral tools for democracy, I am working on a book about sortition (the use of random lottery selection of representative bodies in lieu of elections).[3]

The Burlington Context

The center of left politics in Vermont in the 1970s was the Liberty Union Party. In addition to Bernie Sanders's runs for governor and the U.S. Senate, nearly all statewide offices and a number of local legislative elections were contested by the party. Martha Abbot, who later became the long-term chair of the Progressive Party, won 5 percent of the vote for governor in 1974 under the Liberty Union label, allowing the party to gain major party status. Sanders got 6 percent in 1976, but concluded that the Liberty Union had lost its momentum and didn't have a future. Bernie dropped out of the party in 1977. The Liberty Union Party still exists, with a handful of supporters mainly in the Brattleboro area, but generally gets a small percentage of the vote.[4]

For some years prior to the watershed Burlington municipal election of March 1981, leftist politics had been channeled into several distinct streams. The antiwar Liberty Union Party had passed its zenith. A small but active Maoist-oriented Communist Party (Marxist-Leninist), or CPML, was waning. Filling this vacuum, a number of political activists helped launch the Vermont chapter of the new Citizens Party in 1980. In the November election for U.S. Congress, the incumbent moderate Republican Jim Jeffords was running without any Democratic opponent. Robin Lloyd, the Citizens Party candidate garnered 13 percent and Peter Diamondstone, the Liberty Union candidate got around 8 percent. I ran a token race for state senate in Chittenden County, but I campaigned primarily just within Burlington.

I realized that I had done reasonably well within my own neighborhood and decided to run for the city council in the March city election. Bernie Sanders had made a parallel assessment, after friends pointed out that in his last statewide election he had gotten over 20 percent in some Burlington wards. Bernie decided to run for mayor as an independent. Meanwhile, Citizens Party activists also had decided to run a candidate for mayor, with local journalist Greg Guma being the likely candidate. We instantly recognized that for a left candidate to win against the incumbent Democrat, there would have to be just one leftist candidate to avoid splitting the left vote. After a meeting at a coffee shop, where Sanders made clear he was going to run regardless, Greg Guma agreed to withdraw, leaving Sanders a clear shot.

A couple of aspects of the local political context helped make conditions conducive to a challenge to the status quo. First, for years, resentment had been building against the incumbent Democratic mayor Gordon Paquette in various quarters. Some people were upset about the massive urban renewal demolition of a largely Italian low-income neighborhood to make way for a downtown shopping mall and hotel. Others were critical of what they perceived as "old boy network" cronyism within the mayor's office and Democratic city council. All but one or two of the 13 city council seats were held by Democrats. Many observers felt they served as a rubber stamp for the mayor's policies.[5] Second, there were several left-leaning, Saul Alinsky-style community organizing groups active in Burlington.[6] These groups, such as the North End Community Organization (NECO), People Acting for Change Together (PACT), and the King Street Youth Center, were involved in low-income rental neighborhoods doing grassroots organizing around such issues as tenants' rights and rent control.

The 1981 Burlington Elections

In 1981 the Republicans tacitly supported Mayor Paquette and didn't put up a candidate of their own. Burlington, unlike most of Vermont at this time, was seen as a Democratic stronghold. Republicans had a hard time finding candidates willing to invest the time and money to run an obviously hopeless race. In addition, Paquette was seen as business and developer friendly. There were two other independent candidates running in addition to Sanders—a compassionate but inarticulate low-income retiree, Joseph McGrath, (who was not taken seriously and received only a handful of votes), and Dickie Bove, an owner of a well-known Italian family restaurant in town. Bove had challenged Paquette in the Democratic caucus, and decided to bolt the Democratic Party to run as an independent when the caucus nominated Paquette for a fifth term. Thus, despite Guma's decision to step aside, there still ended up being a split in the anti-Paquette vote. However, Bove, as a business owner, appealed to more conservative voters than Guma would have and, in the absence of a Republican candidate, probably "took" more votes from Paquette than Sanders.

Both Sanders and I campaigned mainly by knocking on doors and handing out leaflets. Our campaigns were not coordinated beyond the fact that I handed out Sanders leaflets as well as my own at doors. Paquette apparently assumed that he would have an easy time winning reelection, and so he chose this time to put a rather substantial property tax increase on the ballot. My Democratic opponent also seemed to assume that she would win reelection and did little campaigning in the city council race. When NECO, which was centered in my ward, invited us to a candidate debate, she declined. NECO then endorsed my candidacy and distributed a flyer criticizing her unwillingness to debate. The above mistakes by the Democrats, born of overconfidence, clearly benefitted our campaigns.

A candidate debate also figured prominently in the mayor's race. A coalition of neighborhood organizations decided to hold a mayoral debate at a local church. PACT had been agitating for rent control, and tenant issues became a big focus of the debate. On the night of the debate the church was packed, primarily with low-income renters. It was obvious that the crowd disapproved of Paquette and quickly warmed up to Sanders. His thick Brooklyn accent made it obvious he was a transplant, but combined with his messy hair and refusal to wear a tie, it also gave him a genuineness that distinguished him from the typical polished politician.

By the end, Paquette was getting boos, Bove was treated politely, and Sanders was receiving loud cheers and ovations. Until that event, I don't think most people thought anybody had a chance to defeat the long-term incumbent. In many people's minds the race became a two-person contest catapulting Sanders into the contender role. However, most experienced political observers still assumed Paquette, as a repeatedly reelected incumbent, would win comfortably. The safest bet is almost always that whatever happened yesterday will happen again tomorrow. It is primarily hindsight that allows us to laugh about how wrong these experts were.

In politics, perceptions of reality help generate reality. Once Sanders was seen as a contender by the news media, and this view was spread through the community, it became true. If news reporters were going to report on the mayor's race, they had to discuss Sanders.

The media environment of Burlington in 1981 was not typical of most other communities in the United States. Burlington was the quintessential big fish in the small pond. Burlington was the largest "city" in Vermont but had a population under 40,000. Significantly, Burlington was not a suburb of some larger metropolis. Hardly any other community of that size in the United States had comparable attention from the local news media. There were three major television stations (CBS, ABC and NBC), as well as two newspapers (the daily *Burlington Free Press* and the alternative weekly *Vermont Vanguard Press*), for whom Burlington was the center of the universe.

The mayor's race was a regular element of news coverage, which it would not have been if Burlington had been a suburb, overshadowed by a larger neighboring community. The race was small enough that it was below the threshold for buying TV advertising. If Burlington had been a larger-sized U.S. city, the sheer cost of running a campaign, with the necessity of purchasing media ads, would have assured Sanders would never be known by most voters. Sanders's media exposure was almost exclusively free "earned" media news coverage.

The collapse of local news media throughout the country since that time, and the rise of the Internet have created a very different media environment than existed in 1981. It is beyond the scope of this chapter to suggest how the current media environment might be effectively used by a new third party, but the core concept that the new party must find a way to be a nearly equal player with the establishment parties remains vital.

The Sanders campaign did not raise or spend much money, but that was not essential in this unique media environment and small scale. The Sanders campaign only had a few campaign pieces, including leaflets, "Sanders for Mayor" buttons, and shopping bags that were handed out downtown. There was no voter preference identification phone calling, though that would become a mainstay in future campaigns. The core of his campaign organization consisted of residents of a low-income housing project, some former Liberty Union allies, and personal friends. His campaign manager, Linda Niedweski, was a nutritionist with no significant prior campaign experience, but she had a natural sense of organization.

Yet, Bernie always has been very much a micromanager. He has met with advisors to get input and bounce around ideas, but he always has relied on his own gut instincts when making the final strategic calls.

The themes of the Sanders campaign were class-based but general in nature, as were those of my campaign. Sanders was a democratic socialist, who knew very little about the nitty-gritty of municipal governance. Sanders did not campaign as a socialist, and Paquette did not bother to make an issue of the widely known fact in the campaign. One theme that caught on was Sanders's core message that "the waterfront is not for sale." This referred to a proposal that had been floating around for several years to redevelop the city's Lake Champlain waterfront as, what Sanders called, an "enclave for the rich." This was land that had been created in the previous century by the railroad filling in the lake shore to create industrial warehouse space where lake transportation and rail met. By the mid-twentieth century this piece of land, with beautiful views of sunsets over the lake, was woefully underused and in fact all but abandoned, with rusting oil tanks and old railroad cars. In 1980, a wealthy Burlington developer, Antonio Pomerleau, was proposing the construction of a marina, high-cost condos, and a high-rise luxury hotel. The potential benefits to the city's property tax base made this an inviting proposal to many establishment politicians. However, Sanders tapped a significant wellspring of class-based resentment among many Burlingtonians by challenging this proposal as an attempt to turn the waterfront into a playland for the rich. Sanders also questioned the need for Paquette's large property tax increase, and supported the call for flexible rent control that PACT was advocating through a charter change to establish a Fair Housing Commission. While hardly any voters knew the details of the Fair Housing Commission proposal, they understood that candidates were either on the side of tenants or landlords.

The next momentous news event of the campaign was when Sanders received the endorsement of the Burlington police union (the Burlington Patrolmen's Association). There had been significant friction between the union and Mayor Paquette. It was basic union concerns, animosity toward Paquette, and support for youth programs, which Sanders favored, that paved the way for the endorsement. As soon as union leader Joe Crepeau, a blue-collar corporal, made the announcement, any residual worries about Sanders being a socialist seemed to evaporate. If the police supported him, he must not be a bomb-throwing radical.

Since there were no detectable spoiler concerns in the race, if there was a perceived contest, it was seen as essentially a two-person contest. Insider Democrats still assumed Paquette would win easily. By contrast, by Election Day Sanders insiders had a sense that Sanders actually might win, but few other observers thought that was likely. To my knowledge, no opinion polls had been conducted.

Largely due to interest in this unique mayoral race, voter turnout jumped 30 percent over the previous mayoral election. Burlington used old lever-style voting machines combined with hand-counted paper absentee ballots at each of the city's six ward polling stations. The preliminary results indicated that I had won a seat on the council with a clear majority, and other Citizens Party candidates across the city had come reasonably close as well. But the big story was that Bernie Sanders had a lead over Gordon Paquette, 43.2 percent to 43.1 percent, with the remainder going mostly to Dickie Bove. Burlington's city charter required a runoff if no candidate had at least 40 percent of the vote (rather than the more customary 50 percent plus majority threshold). Thus, if the results stood up in a recount, Sanders would become mayor.[7]

Sanders's key advisors, such as University of Vermont religion professor Richard Sugarman, were worried about the possibility of overnight vote rigging by Paquette's political appointees. A 3 a.m. visit to the home of Superior Court Judge Ed Amidon succeeded in getting an order to impound the voting machines and ballots. The recount, some days later, was tense. As part of the court-appointed recount team, I discovered a transcription error that reduced Sanders's total by 10 votes, but that was not enough to lose his lead. In the end, he won by just 10 votes.

The Progressive Breakthrough

In a March 8, 1981, *New York Times* story, headlined "Vermont Socialist Plans Mayoralty with a Bias toward the Poor," Sanders acknowledged "there is little I can do from City Hall to accomplish my dreams for society." Yet he also stated, "We're coming in with a definite class analysis and a belief that the trickle-down theory of economic growth, the 'what's good for General Motors is good for America' theory, doesn't work."[8] The Burlington political establishment was in shock. They assumed the election had been a fluke, and quickly decided to stonewall until the "fungus," as one Democratic president of the city council termed it, could be removed at the next mayoral election. But the first test of whether this had been a fluke came very quickly, because no candidate in the Ward 3 city council race had topped the 40 percent threshold. In that race, a Citizens Party candidate had earned enough votes to force a runoff between the nominee of the Democratic Party and the former Democratic state legislator from that neighborhood, Sadie White, who was running as an independent under the "Tax-payers' Advocate" label. Sadie White was then a 79-year-old blue-collar Roosevelt Democrat, who had been sidelined by the local Democratic Party. She and Sanders saw eye to eye on many class-based city issues, and they became strong allies. She won the runoff—with the endorsements of Sanders and the Citizens Party in a low-income ward where Sanders had won by an overwhelming majority.

Governing and Growing

The first year of the Sanders administration was essentially a siege. The Democrats and Republicans on the city council were united against Sanders, Sadie White, and me.[9] The council refused to ratify the mayor's appointments of city officials, such as city clerk and city attorney. It even fired his secretary, who would replace the one who retired when Paquette left, citing a hiring freeze that it had imposed after Paquette's proposed tax-increase had been voted down. So, the executive branch officials were virtually all Paquette holdovers, eager to see Sanders fail.

Sanders pulled together an unofficial and unpaid cabinet to advise him and analyze the city's budget. We held our meetings outside of city hall because of concerns about the possibility of hidden microphones. Although that may seem paranoid, it was later revealed that the city clerk had been opening the new mayor's mail, which even the city council found outrageous, leading to his suspension. The public reaction to this stonewalling strategy of the council was dramatic. People felt that the fundamental principles of fair play were being violated. Calls to "let the mayor be mayor" were common. A genuinely grassroots group, Citizens for Fair Play, was formed and bitterly criticized the city council.

In March of the following year, 7 of the city council's 13 seats came up for election. The Citizens Party candidates won 3 of those seats, bringing the total Sanders supporters (with the consistent support of Sadie White) to 5. In 1982, the mayor's appointments were approved for a change. Sanders brought in bright and competent people. The city's finances were a mess; the friend Paquette had appointed as city treasurer had no financial training. It soon was discovered that the city had an unrecognized $1.9 million fund balance surplus, and that the huge tax increase Paquette and the council had requested was unnecessary. There were other examples of past financial mismanagement. Under Paquette, the city had established a committee of insurance agents that decided what insurance the city needed and divvied up the city's business. This self-dealing was costing the city dearly. By simply putting the insurance out to bid in a normal manner, the city saved roughly $300,000. So, in addition to being seen as a friend of average working people, Sanders developed a reputation for competent governance.

Solidifying the Gains

In the 1983 mayor's race there was some red-baiting that sought to generate fear of Sanders's socialist ideology. Today, the term "socialist" has probably lost much of its bogeyman impact due to its incessant misuse by Republicans, tagging pro-capitalists such as Obama with the appellation. But this was during the Cold War, when the Soviet Union and the United States were perpetually on the brink of nuclear war, and labels like "socialist" and "communist" were frightening to most Americans.[10] Burlington voters, however, had firsthand experience with a socialist mayor, and most agreed he was competent, trustworthy, and on their side.

Registering new voters in low-income neighborhoods was a campaign priority.[11] We entered the new world of computerized campaigns with a portable Kaypro computer, on which we maintained records of registered voters and their political leanings as identified from mass phone calling. In 1983, computers were not yet a common part of political campaigns, and no other party in Burlington was using them.

With low-income citizens and university students having particularly low voter registration rates combined with the high mobility and turnover of renters, door-to-door efforts to register new voters became a central element of Progressive campaigns. College students had played virtually no role in the 1981 election, but now Progressives actively sought to register them. Later, this led to an attempt by the Burlington Board of Voter Registration to restrict student voting by requiring students to present themselves personally before the board. The city attorney refused to defend the board, noting this was discriminatory and illegal, and the process was stopped.

Door-to-door voter registration drives were often combined with filling out absentee ballot request forms, so that the voters would get a ballot by mail. Providing this service to the voter seemed to create a psychological inclination toward reciprocity in many voters' minds, and thus a likelihood of voting for the candidate. We would make daily checks of which absentee ballots were being mailed out by city hall, so that we could mail a piece of campaign literature to recipients the same day. We then followed up to verify which voters' ballots had been mailed back to city hall, so that near the deadline we could contact voters who had not yet returned their ballots to get them in on time.

The voter registration effort was integrated into an intense voter-identification phone calling operation. The voter-ID campaign fed data to the get-out-the-vote effort, which included side-checking at the polls on Election Day to identify which supporters had not yet voted by mid-afternoon, so they could be called and offered rides.

There was intense interest in Burlington politics now. The Democrats pulled out all the stops in hopes of exterminating this alternative politics. A powerful Democratic state senator, Esther Sorrell announced she would run against me for the lowly city council seat. The Democratic leader in the Vermont House of Representatives, Judy Stephany, announced she would run for mayor.

Voter turnout in 1983 jumped another 43 percent above the 1981 level (nearly double the pre-Sanders rate). By the close of polls on Eelection Day, we were feeling pretty good. While Sanders and I were greeting voters at the Ward 2 polling place, we noted the depressed look on Esther Sorrell's face as the poll closing time approached. She hardly knew any of the people coming to vote, who were eagerly greeting Sanders and me. There had been almost a total demographic turnover in this renter district since her previous electoral successes.

I won by a healthy margin and Sanders won reelection with 52 percent of the vote. He defeated Representative Judy Stephany, who received 31 percent, and the Republican chair of the school board, Jim Gilson, who trailed with 17 percent. Sanders's popularity stemmed from a combination of a common-man style and a general sense that he was on the side of working people, rather than "the rich." Most supporters probably couldn't have named any specific Sanders campaign proposals, but simply felt an affinity for Bernie (as he was universally called). The politics of personality trumped old party label politics. It was not uncommon to hear voters say, "I may not agree with everything Bernie says, but he speaks his mind, and I trust him." It was this gut-level impression by voters that Progressives were on the side of the "little guy," rather than any specific policies, that underlay the Progressive's success.

Following the 1983 elections, the Citizens Party evaporated on the national and local levels, and the Burlington party members and other Sanders supporters united under the label the "Progressive Coalition." For all intents and purposes the Progressive Coalition was a political party. It endorsed candidates, many of whom ran with the Progressive Coalition label on the ballot. However, some candidates of the Progressive Coalition, including Sanders himself, ran using the "independent" label.

In the 1984 municipal elections, the Progressive Coalition climbed to a total of six seats on the city council, and the Democratic caucus, which had once had complete hegemony, had been reduced to just two members. One of those Democrats resigned for personal reasons shortly after the election, but before the council reorganization day. This left just 12 councilors. So, when it came time to elect the council president, the lone Democrat and five Republicans voted as a block, and the Progressives voted for me, creating a 6 to 6 tie. After 30 ballots, going late into the night, I was finally elected council president, and the Progressives also got a majority on the powerful finance committee.

City council races in this period tended to be one-on-one contests, rather than three-way races. The spoiler concern under plurality rules encouraged the weaker major party in a particular ward to sit out a race if there was a Progressive candidate. Over time, the city wards settled into a series of two-party battlegrounds; Wards 1, 2 and 3, for example, featured contests between Democrats and Progressives, while Ward 4 typically had only Democratic and Republican contenders. When there were 3 candidates, more common in Wards 5 and 6, often no candidate exceeded the 40 percent threshold, thereby triggering a runoff election. Burlington did not become a normal multiparty democracy, nor solve the spoiler problem, but rather accommodated it in the same manner that some Canadian provinces did, by evolving a series of distinct two-party duopolies in different provinces.

Early Attempts to Go Statewide

In 1986, following a couple of reelections by Sanders and a steady stream of reelected and new Progressive city councilors, Sanders decided to challenge the incumbent Democratic governor of Vermont, Madeline Kunin. He was frustrated with the limited scope of municipal government. Again, he chose to run as an independent. Sanders was fairly well known in many parts of Vermont because his political history was considered to be newsworthy outside of Burlington and because the news media from Burlington penetrated much of northern Vermont. While Sanders had an experienced campaign "machine" in Burlington, there was no statewide equivalent. The remnants of the Vermont Rainbow Coalition and the allied 1984 Jesse Jackson presidential campaign in Vermont along with some of Sanders's old Liberty Union friends provided a leg up, but the statewide campaign organization had to be built almost from scratch. Many progressives in the state rallied around his campaign, but with a Republican, Peter Smith, also in the race, the classic spoiler concern returned with a vengeance, and Sanders only received 14 percent of the vote statewide.

Sanders won reelection as mayor for the last time in 1987. When Vermont's lone member of the U.S. House of Representatives, James Jeffords, opted to run for an open seat in the U.S. Senate, Sanders decided to run for the open House seat in 1988. Building on the contacts and campaign organization started in the governor's race, Sanders did much better this time, though spoiler concerns were a constant drain. Ironically, Sanders was facing Peter Smith again, the same Republican he had faced in the governor's race. The early returns on election night showed Sanders in the lead, but by morning it was clear that Smith would win the seat with 41 percent of the vote. However, Sanders trounced the Democrat, a former Democratic leader in the Vermont House, Paul Poirier, by 38 percent to 19 percent.

Sanders did not seek reelection as mayor in 1989. The big question on everyone's mind was whether the Progressive Coalition had staying power or would evaporate with Sanders's departure. The Progressives ran Peter Clavelle, director of the city's Community and Economic Development Office and a key member of the Sanders administration. The Republicans sat out the race so as not to split the anti-Progressive vote. Clavelle defeated the Democrat, Nancy Chioffi, by 56 percent to 44 percent.[12] This successful passing of the torch demonstrated the Progressives' long-term viability.

Statewide Breakthrough

In 1990 Sanders again challenged Peter Smith, now the incumbent congressman. But this time the "spoiler" shoe was on the other foot. If a Democratic-leaning voter was worried that a split left voting block would allow the Republican to win reelection with less than a majority, it made sense to vote for Sanders, rather than the Democrat, since the 1988 results indicated that Sanders had the best chance of defeating Smith. So, it was the Democratic candidate, Dolores Sandoval, who was abandoned by the campaign donors, unions, and voters, receiving just 3 percent of the vote. Sanders won election with an impressive 56 percent majority, becoming the first self-described socialist in Congress in several generations.

Sanders had always been reliant on a high volume of small campaign contributions. But now he also received substantial contributions from organized labor.
The Sanders campaign in subsequent House and Senate races was able to develop
a vast network of leftist small donors across the country, such that Sanders generally has been able to outspend his opponents. This feature of Sanders's success is
probably not replicable for more than a few candidates at the federal scale, since in
the nation as a whole, there is nowhere near as much radical Left money as there
is establishment and corporate money (which maintains both the Democratic and
Republican party candidates). It is doubtful if the national funding base Sanders
has developed could finance a large number of candidates, who all would be competing for the same piece of the pie. Some sort of public campaign finance reform
seems to be essential for wider success.

In that same November 1990 election year, I and some other Progressives ran
for the Vermont House of Representatives. Two of us won our elections in neighboring low-income districts of Burlington. I defeated an incumbent Democrat,
who I had narrowly lost to in a race four years earlier. Tom Smith, once a member
of the tiny Communist Workers' Party, but since moving to Burlington a member
of the Progressive Coalition, also won a seat. Like me, Smith was then serving as
a Progressive on the city council.

Vermont, with a population not much more than 560,000 in 1990, had 150
seats in its House of Representatives, so the districts were quite small. This allowed
us to run relatively low-budget campaigns that relied mainly on door-knocking
and voter registration efforts. However, because the scale of both the city council
and legislative races was so small, money was never a deciding factor. Big money
interests essentially didn't care about the outcome of such races. In fact, Progressive candidates frequently outspent their major party opponents.

Linking ourselves to Sanders's popularity was also an important campaign
strategy. The specific issues in a state legislative race were virtually irrelevant; it
was the general sense that we were on the same side as Bernie, for ordinary people
and against the powerful establishment, which seemed to matter to voters.

Formalizing the Vermont Progressive Party

In Vermont, Sanders was universally seen as the godfather of the Progressive Party,
and he always received its endorsements. However, he never formally joined the
Progressive Party, nor used its label on the ballot. From his first race for mayor
until he entered the 2016 Democratic presidential primary, he always has run
as an independent (and in fact, he is the longest serving such member of
Congress in U.S. history). While in Congress, Sanders has caucused with the
Democrats, endorsed a number of Democratic candidates for federal offices, and
finally become a Democratic presidential candidate himself. But he has steadfastly
refused to identify as a congressional Democrat. In any case, in the 1990s Progressives hoped to build off Sanders's congressional victories and create a party that

could elect legislators from outside Burlington, and to statewide offices. It was not obvious if this would be possible. Sanders was widely seen as a unique character with a special charisma that allowed him to win a statewide election.[13] The same issues discussed above that typically frustrate third parties in the United States, which had been avoided or overcome in Burlington, reemerged as a challenge in this effort to go statewide.

In the 1990s more Progressives were added to the legislature, but only from Burlington.[14] However, in 1999 the Progressive Coalition, which had grown statewide, decided to take the formal step of becoming a statewide political party by organizing under the state's political party statutes, with town-level committees, state convention, bylaws, and platform. Thereafter, the party ran candidates from all over the state for the Vermont House. It also engaged in numerous (often token) statewide campaigns, in which scale was an overwhelming obstacle in terms of money, media visibility, and credibility.

While Vermont is an extremely small state, it is of sufficient size that expensive television ads are a central element of any successful statewide campaign. The Progressive Party has sought to deal with the challenge of scale by focusing primarily on legislative races around the state. However, Vermont's public finance campaign law (written by Progressive and Democratic Party legislators) seemed to offer a way around these obstacles for certain statewide races encompassed by the law.

Progressive Party candidate Anthony Pollina became the first candidate to qualify for public financing in his 2000 campaign for governor against the Democratic incumbent, Howard Dean. The public funding made Pollina a "credible" candidate in the eyes of the media, and he was included in all candidate debates, surveys, and so on. While somewhat outspent, Pollina was able to purchase a respectable number of TV ads. Although the issue of scale had been successfully addressed, the spoiler issue had not. With a right-wing Republican candidate, Ruth Dwyer, in the race, the spoiler issue reared its head once again, and appeared to substantially suppress Pollina's vote total. In the end, he garnered only 9.5 percent of the vote to Dean's 50.4 percent and Dwyer's 38 percent.

Pollina ran again in 2002, but this time for lieutenant governor. He did not seek public financing for this race because an early public opinion poll conducted by the Progressive Party was alleged to be an in-kind donation that would have disqualified him. Pollina's heightened name recognition from his gubernatorial race and AFL-CIO endorsement[15] enabled him to raise a reasonable amount of money. Perhaps because the office was not seen as all that important by most voters, or the Republican was seen as moderate, the spoiler issue, though still a factor, seemed less significant in many voters' minds. However, the spoiler dynamic seemed to come to fruition with the election of Republican Brian Dubie with just 41.2 percent of the vote to Pollina's 24.8 percent and Democrat Peter Shumlin's 32.2 percent.[16]

The need to resolve the spoiler problem was now quite palpable. This firsthand experience by Vermont Democrats of a spoiler scenario (on the heels of the 2000 U.S. presidential election, in which some people blamed Nader's campaign as "spoiling" Gore's chances against Bush), intensified interest in a corrective election reform pushed by Progressives. Known as instant runoff voting (IRV), it determines the winner of an election in a manner similar to a runoff election, but without a separate round of voting used in a traditional runoff election. It allows voters to indicate their runoff choices by ranking candidates in order of preference. If one candidate gets a majority of first choices, that candidate is elected. If no candidate gets an initial majority, the candidates with the fewest votes are eliminated sequentially until just two remain. The candidate who is elected is whichever finalist is ranked higher by a majority of voters who have indicated a preference.[17] Since the Democrats were seen as the party at risk from the ill-effects of spoiler dynamics, the IRV issue took on a partisan flavor, with Republicans opposing the reform. At this point, I had left public office and was working with FairVote: The Center for Voting and Democracy, promoting IRV in Vermont. We eventually managed to get a bill through the legislature to implement IRV for certain statewide races, but the proposed law was vetoed by the Republican governor, James Douglas, who himself had won with a plurality vote of just 44.9 percent. We were subsequently able to get a charter amendment passed in Burlington to use IRV in mayoral elections.[18]

Without instant runoff voting or proportional representation,[19] the spoiler dynamic is a common obstacle for Progressive candidates beyond Burlington. An alternative strategy for dealing with the spoiler problem is known as fusion, in which a small third party co-nominates selected candidates with one of the establishment parties. Only eight states permit this practice.[20] In 2003, the Progressive Party's bylaws were amended to allow fusion, which had been expressly disallowed initially. A number of Progressive candidates (particularly those outside of Burlington) resorted to seeking nominations from both the Progressive Party and Democratic Party as a means of assuring a one-on-one race to avoid spoiler concerns. This could be accomplished by formally running and winning in one party's primary while winning the nomination in the other party's primary through write-in votes, or by receiving the nomination from the local party committee in situations where no candidate had filed to run in that primary.[21] In any case, in the 2000s up to the present day, a handful of Progressive legislators from all around the state regularly were elected running with both a "P" and "D" by their names. These fusion Progressives comprised most though not all the Progressives who won State House seats outside of Burlington. In 2012 the first Progressive to win a statewide office (auditor of accounts), Doug Hoffer, also ran with both party labels.

Whether fusion was an intentional strategy of the Progressive Party or was not, Vermont election law compelled Progressives to deal with the issue. Since the Progressive Party regularly gets more than 5 percent of the vote in statewide elections, it qualifies as a major party under state law. This also means it must have a primary election to nominate its own candidates. This creates the opportunity for candidates of other parties to run under the Progressive Party label, even if they do not support the party platform, simply by getting some of their supporters to write in the candidate's name in the Progressive primary. This allows candidates of the Democratic Party to "raid" the Progressive primary to either shut out a genuine Progressive opponent, or run as fusion candidates.

While the fusion strategy initially may have enabled Progressives to sidestep the spoiler problem in specific situations, and increase the number of Progressives in office, this author actually considers fusion to be extremely dangerous to the long-term future of the Progressives as a genuine and viable left third party. Fusion (also promoted by quasi-third party groups such as the Working Families Party) not only can encourage hostile takeovers by Democrats but also can cause progressive third parties to blur or even erase the distinction between their candidates and Democrats in order to attract liberal Democratic support. The eventual result can be a party that no longer has the ability or desire to present a coherent, distinctive, and appealing left alternative.

Vermont Lessons

In summary, Progressives in Burlington and Vermont overcame or avoided the obstacles to third party development primarily by the luck of circumstances rather than strategic planning. However, those who hope to emulate what was accomplished in Vermont should consider the lessons of the experience.

The initial breakthroughs were at a rather small municipal scale. This meant that money was not a determining factor in the election outcomes. Sheer volunteer hours made the difference. Before the Progressives, it was uncommon for candidates in Burlington to do substantial door-knocking or voter registration. By 1983 the ante had been upped, such that for a candidate to win an election at a ward or legislative district level, it was expected that he or she would knock on every door in the district, and even the mayoral candidate would do plenty of door-knocking.

Sanders and the Citizens Party were able to avoid the spoiler issue at the outset by running in races against incumbent Democrats, in which there was no Republican candidate. Nobody was worried about a need to vote for some "lesser evil" candidate. The fact that the incumbent Democrats were overconfident and had built up a certain amount of popular resentment was also crucial. Once we had won office, the spoiler label no longer could be employed against us and in fact might be applied to a Democrat. The psychological barrier to being a credible candidate, faced by most third party candidates, had been eliminated. Once in office in 1981, we were helped dramatically by the old guard's violation of residents' sense of fair play. If there is one ideology that seems to trump all others in America, it is the need for everybody to play fair. The voters severely punished the incumbent Democrats in subsequent elections, not due to any thought-through policy considerations, but due to anger and disgust.

Rather than merely seeking realignment of existing voters, the Progressives largely relied on bringing new voters into the process. Initially these were almost exclusively low-income residents, but later they included college students. Since voter turnout in municipal elections is generally low, identifying supporters through phone-calling and turning them out to vote was a central element of the early campaigns. The steady decline of landlines and phone book entries has changed the nature of this task, so a substitute methodology needs to be employed.[22]

Burlington's unique media environment within Vermont (being a big fish in a tiny pond) was also important for the Burlington breakthrough. Burlington was the center of the world for the local newspapers and television network news programs. When a viewer saw Sanders on the evening news, he was put in the same mental category with any other "credible" candidate. However, Sanders's unique personal style and forthrightness made him stand out and remain memorable. It is possible, though not at all certain, that the Progressive Party could have developed in Vermont's relatively accommodating environment even without Sanders. But Sanders definitely made the successes of the party much easier to achieve. Sanders's initial victories opened the door a crack, but riding his coattails was not enough to automatically overcome the issues that create the obstacles for third parties discussed in this chapter.

Last, the ability to develop and deliver a simple, engaging message with which voters could easily and strongly identify was an important element of the Progressives' success. This appeal in Burlington and in statewide campaigns was ideological only in the broadest sense of the term, in that it was class-based—on the side of the "little guy" and against the rich. It of course was best crystalized and articulated by Bernie Sanders. Other progressive third parties could benefit from formulating a similarly appealing message as well as applying the other lessons of the Vermont Progressive Party.

Lessons and Prospects for Future Progressive Third Parties

How might it be possible to start building a successful progressive third party in the United States, especially in light of the analysis above? To begin with, it is essential to solve in some way the problems associated with the spoiler issue, and those associated with scale, media access, money, and electoral credibility. Many progressives are pursuing obvious election reforms to address these obstacles, including public campaign financing, instant runoff voting and proportional representation election methods, and democratic media alternatives.

Finding ways around these obstacles within the current environment (prior to winning these needed reforms) requires careful evaluation of unique circumstances in a given jurisdiction. For example, since gerrymandering and demographic trends have created a huge number of de facto one-party jurisdictions in the United States, in which incumbents go unchallenged, it is likely that non-spoiler toehold opportunities exist somewhere in nearly every state. Rather than starting with statewide races, beginning with local races (in which door-to-door campaigning may substitute for paid advertising) can overcome the money and media obstacles. This strategy, key to the success of the Vermont Progressive Party, can be applied elsewhere in the country.

Of course, there still may be some fundamental difficulties with trying to build a third party that remains true to progressive or socialist ideals. Some political scholars such as Anthony Downs claim that it is structurally impossible in the United States. They argue that the winner-take-all election system not only strongly favors two-party dominance due to the spoiler dynamic but also pushes those parties toward the middle, or the median voter. Their model presumes that the median voter is centrist. Thus, in their view, without ongoing political education that moves large numbers of people to the left (shifting the median) and keeps them there, it is unlikely that a left party can gain and hold power.[23] This argument about party convergence would appear to have some merit, given the wide distribution of voters across the spectrum of political self-identification, in combination with the well-established tendency of major parties to moderate their positions in general elections in pursuit of electoral majorities.

However, in addition to ignoring the inclinations of many alienated nonvoters, the Downs perspective overlooks a simple fact: Americans' political opinions often are internally contradictory.[24] Indeed, most voters that this author encountered as a political candidate seemed to have no consistent political ideology, left or right. What's more, there is not just a single left–right political spectrum. Ideology can be differentiated along countless other dimensions as well. The concept of a median voter is an analytical construct for a theoretical two-dimensional world that cannot be applied too literally to our messy reality. Thus, a party similar to the Vermont Progressive Party may not necessarily be too far to the left for many voters.

In fact, much opinion polling of recent decades suggests that a majority of the U.S. public is to the left of the government on a wide range of policy issues, from health care to taxation and more.[25] This may indicate a potential opening for progressive third parties, if the obstacles discussed in this chapter can be overcome. Still, it is important to recognize that poll responses are somewhat dependent on wording and framing,[26] and they usually are gathered without giving respondents an opportunity to deliberate or consider an array of alternatives.[27] Rather than thinking of voters as having pre-established preferences that lie along some ideological spectrum, it may be just as valid to think of them as being open to going in very different policy directions depending on the context.[28] For this reason, progressive third parties need to be flexible in how they perceive and address voters, as Vermont Progressives have realized.

In deciding how to vote, people generally rely on simple cues or heuristics, such as the advice of trusted figures, party labels, or superficial impressions of candidates.[29] Voters' gut-level impressions of a candidate may even shape their lasting attitudes toward both that candidate and his or her party.[30] This reality is dismaying for those focused on policy but cannot be ignored. Electoral politics is a game of psychological manipulation, more than anything else.[31] I am not arguing that voters are mindless dupes, but simply that it is not realistic to expect most people to invest the time and energy necessary to critically evaluate the myriad of policy and candidate alternatives. Since a voter's individual vote is extremely unlikely to change the outcome of an election, it just isn't worth the effort to become well informed. Economists refer to this as "rational ignorance."[32] Urging voters to inform themselves about policy details and candidates' specific positions on issues is a fool's errand. Thinking of voting as an act of group solidarity on behalf of one's team, class, or political party is more fruitful. This may help us to understand why, for example, ordinary Vermonters of seemingly different political stripes often say that the reason they come out to vote for Bernie Sanders is simply because he represents the "common person." U.S. progressives must understand this in order to have any chance of building an effective and lasting third party, even if the obstacles discussed in this chapter did not exist.

Conclusion

To recap the above observations and conclude, the specific details regarding why Progressives have been somewhat successful in Burlington and Vermont may result from unique circumstances; yet for this success, the principal (and near-universal) obstacles facing third party development in the United States needed to be avoided or overcome. In a nutshell, much of the approach might be summarized as "start small with nearly inconsequential offices, flying below the radar of big money opposition, and build on these small successes to lay the groundwork for larger ones." It also entails running at first in one-party jurisdictions, trying to mobilize new voters, and crafting a core message that appeals to voters with limited interest in policy detail.

Modeling other left third party projects specifically on the apparent lessons of Vermont seems to be a practical strategy, though this should not preclude consideration of other relevant experiences and approaches. On the state level, the phenomenal success of the Minnesota Farmer-Labor Party in the first part of the twentieth century deserves study as well.[33] Also, while there are good reasons to remain skeptical of grand strategies that seek to leapfrog local and state efforts, such as focusing on presidential campaigns, it is possible that overarching economic or cultural factors ignored by the major parties may open the door to completely different strategies for launching a progressive third party.[34] Nevertheless, it is important to not overlook the path taken by the Vermont Progressive Party, given its exceptional contemporary record of electoral achievement.

Notes

1 Vermont Progressive Party, "A Legacy of Progressive Leadership."

2 The city council then was called the board of aldermen, but the name was changed some years later. For consistency, I will use the term "city council" throughout this chapter.

3 It may be that third party politics is the best way to advance progressive policy. However, after 20 years' experience as an elected third party public official and more decades as an election reform activist, I have come to the startling conclusion that elections are simply not the best tool for running a democracy. In my view, elected bodies are inherently *elite* bodies that fail to represent the diversity of the represented population. Rather than picking from among competing teams of would-be rulers, I believe that democracy should be a system of *self*-government. I have come to be an advocate for the jury model of democracy, in which representative samples of randomly selected citizens are charged with deliberating over and adopting laws, rather than relying on competitive elections to form legislatures. There is a growing body of scholarly literature on this approach, known as *sortition*, and even some real world applications in places like British Columbia, Australia, and Iceland. But such a fundamental restructuring of democracy, away from competitive elections and toward deliberative juries, is probably even more unlikely than reforms for proportional representation, instant run-off voting, and public campaign finance. One starting point for those curious about this approach to democracy can be found in Bouricius, "Democracy through Multi-Body Sortition." There also is a wealth of information at the Australian New Democracy Foundation website.

4 These Vermont state election results and others mentioned in this chapter can be found in the election database on the Vermont Secretary of State's website.

5 The top city Democrats tended to be the descendants of working-class Irish and French Canadian immigrants, some of whom had become financially successful in fields that don't require advanced degrees, such as real estate. The Republican Party politicians more often were WASP business executives, lawyers, or stockbroker types.

6 Alinsky, *Reveille for Radicals* and *Rules for Radicals*. For much of his life, mid-twentieth century left activist Saul Alinsky advocated organizing low income people around local issues. He felt that relatively small initial victories at the community level by those who were the most dispossessed would lead to the empowerment of the oppressed on a larger scale.

7 These Burlington municipal election results and others referred to in this chapter can be found in the records of the Burlington city clerk and in various editions of the *Burlington Free Press*.

8 Knight, "Vermont Socialist Plans Mayoralty."

9 Bernie Sanders, Sadie White, and I all became close friends. White's loyalty to the Sanders "revolution" was largely a personal and emotional loyalty, with policy being secondary.

10 During the 1980s, Burlington established sister-city relationships with Yaroslavl, in the Soviet Union, and Puerto Cabezas, in Sandinista-controlled Nicaragua. These connections provided a lot of fodder for right-wing opponents, but such people-to-people diplomacy efforts were well received by most Burlingtonians.

11 A particularly memorable "new voter" I registered was an elderly woman in her eighties who had never voted before. When she turned 21, women weren't legally allowed

to vote, since the Nineteenth Amendment to the U.S. Constitution had not yet been ratified. Convincing her to register and vote for the first time was gratifying.

12 Clavelle went on to be the longest serving mayor in Burlington's history. He served until 2006, except for one term, when a Republican won the office. By the end of Clavelle's service, however, he sought fusion with the Democratic Party and ultimately ran as a Democrat in an unsuccessful campaign for governor. He was succeeded as mayor by yet another Progressive, Bob Kiss.

13 "Charisma" is a vague and nonexplanatory term with no predictive value; it is almost always applied only after a person's success.

14 Dean Corren, David Zuckerman, and Steve Hingtgen were elected from neighboring districts in Burlington.

15 Unions in Vermont are not very strong. However, Sanders and other Progressives started receiving union endorsements early on, and that continues to this day.

16 Actually, the Vermont constitution declares there to be no winner for certain statewide offices if no candidate gets a majority. In these cases, the legislature picks a winner from among the top three finishers. In this case, Shumlin urged legislators to elect the plurality leader, Brian Dubie, which they did.

17 IRV sharply mitigates spoiler concerns, though there are possible IRV election scenarios in which the spoiler dynamic still can occur.

18 Instant runoff voting was used in two mayoral elections (in 2006 and 2009). In both of them, Progressive candidate Bob Kiss was elected. However, a financial scandal involving the city's telecom enterprise put Kiss in such a bad light that the charter was amended again to repeal IRV, and Kiss was replaced by a Democratic mayor, Miro Weinberger (in a 2012 race with no Progressive Party candidate).

19 It is important that we not conflate instant runoff voting and proportional representation. IRV is a majoritarian, winner-take-all voting method that still favors two-party domination. Proportional representation, on the other hand, is a system that accommodates multiple parties being elected to a legislature in proportion to their strength. IRV is far more likely to be seen as acceptable to the existing major parties, while proportional representation is a much greater threat.

20 Gillispie, *Challengers to Duopoly*, 29. Vermont's election laws allow a limited form of fusion. The candidate does not get a separate spot on the ballot for multiple nominations, but rather has all party affiliations listed after the candidate's name. Also, state law does not allow an individual to appear on the primary ballot of more than one party in a given year. Therefore, in order to receive more than one party nomination the candidate either must win one of the nominations as a write-in candidate or get nominated by a party committee authorized to fill a "vacancy" on the party's list of nominees.

21 Vermont has an open primary system. Voters are not registered into political parties, so any voter is allowed to select any party's primary ballot. This encourages cross-party mischief, such as voting for the weakest candidate in a party primary of a party the voter doesn't actually support.

22 In Vermont, voter registration application forms ask for phone numbers, so campaign volunteers can wade through the applications on file in city hall to transcribe voters' cell phone numbers.

23 Downs, *An Economic Theory of Democracy*.

24 Page and Jacobs, *Class War*.

25 Page and Jacobs, *Class War*, and Lotke et al. "The Progressive Majority."

26 Moore, *The Opinion Makers*, 152–58.

27 Fishkin and Luskin, "Experimenting with a Democratic Ideal," 287.

28 Zaller, *The Nature and Origins of Mass Opinion*, 1, 266.

29 Concerning the role of superficial impressions in voting, a number of studies actually have found that the winners of elections can be predicted with approximately 70 percent accuracy by merely doing the following: (1) showing photographs of the candidates to any random group of people who are unfamiliar with the candidates for one second or less, and then (2) asking which person looks more competent. See Todorov et al., "Inferences of Competence from Faces Predict Election Outcomes." For a brief overview of the use of heuristics in voting and other political decisions, see Glynn et al., *Public Opinion*, 284–86.

30 I know many Burlingtonians who strongly admired Sanders in the 1980s and attached that emotional connection to his Progressive Coalition, and then to the Progressive Party. Indeed, like family Democrats and Republicans, there are now second-generation Progressive voters who grew up in a Progressive voting family.

31 Westen, *The Political Brain*.

32 Caplan, *The Myth of the Rational Voter*.

33 During its peak in the 1920s and 1930s, the Minnesota Farmer-Labor Party managed to elect three governors, a majority of the state legislature, four U.S. senators, and eight U.S. representatives. The extension of federal power during the New Deal substantially narrowed the prospects for state level radicalism, however. In modern America, with federalism and globalization, it is not clear if the successes of the Minnesota Farmer-Labor Party are in any way replicable, but they definitely deserve careful study. For an incisive history and analysis of the party, see Valley, *Radicalism in the States*.

34 A prominent illustration of how such officially disregarded factors can generate a viable third party happened in the 1850s, when governmental unresponsiveness on the slavery issue led to the successful establishment of the third party known as the Republican Party.

Bibliography

Alinsky, Saul David. *Reveille for Radicals*. New York: Vintage, 1969.

———. *Rules for Radicals*. New York: Vintage, 1989.

Bouricius, Terrill G. "Democracy through Multi-Body Sortition: Athenian Lessons for the Modern Day." *Journal of Public Deliberation* 9, no. 1 (2013): 1–19. www.public deliberation.net/jpd/vol9/iss1/art11.

Caplan, Bryan Douglas. *The Myth of the Rational Voter: Why Democracies Choose Bad Policies*. Princeton: Princeton University Press, 2007.

Downs, Anthony. *An Economic Theory of Democracy*. New York: Harper, 1957.

Fiskin, James S., and Luskin, Robert C. "Experimenting with a Democratic Ideal: Deliberative Polling and Public Opinion." *Acta Politica* 40 (2005): 284–98. www.uvm.edu/~dguber/POLS234/articles/fishkin.pdf.

Gillispie, David J. *Challengers to Duopoly: Why Third Parties Matter in American Two-Party Politics*. Columbia: University of South Carolina Press, 2012.

Glynn, Caroll J., Susan Herbst, Garret J. O'Keefe, Robert Y. Shapiro, and Mark Lindeman. "Public Opinion and Democratic Competence." In *Public Opinion*, Caroll J. Glynn, Susan Herbst, Garret J. O'Keefe, and Robert Y. Shapiro, 249–98. Boulder, CO: Westview Press, 1999.

Knight, Michael. "Vermont Socialist Plans Mayoralty with a Bias toward the Poor." *New York Times*, March 8, 2001. www.nytimes.com/1981/03/08/us/vermont-socialist-plans-mayoralty-with-bias-toward-poor.html.

Lotke, Eric, Robert Gerson, Paul Waldman, and Andrew Seifter. *The Progressive Majority: Why a Conservative America Is a Myth.* Washington, DC: Campaign for America's Future and Media Matters for America, 2007. Accessed March 8, 2014. http://cloudfront.mediamatters.org/static/pdf/progressive_majority.pdf.

Moore, David W. *The Opinion Makers: An Insider Exposes the Truth Behind the Polls.* Boston: Beacon Press, 2008.

Page, Benjamin I., and Lawrence R. Jacobs. *Class War: What Americans Really Think about Economic Inequality.* Chicago: University of Chicago Press, 2009.

Todorov, Alexander, Anesu N. Mandisodza, Amir Goren, and Crystal C. Hall. "Inferences of Competence from Faces Predict Election Outcomes." *Science* 308, no. 5728 (2005) 1623–26.

Valley, Richard M. *Radicalism in the States: The Minnesota Farmer-Labor Party and the American Political Economy.* Chicago: University of Chicago Press, 1989.

Vermont Progressive Party. "A Legacy of Progressive Leadership." Accessed August 3, 2014. www.progressiveparty.org/organize/legacy.

Westen, Drew. *The Political Brain: The Role of Emotion in Deciding the Fate of the Nation.* New York: Public Affairs, 2007.

Zaller, John. *The Nature and Origins of Mass Opinion.* New York: Cambridge University Press, 1992.

5

COMMUNITY CONNECTIONS

How Progressive Third Parties Can Win More State Legislative Elections[*]

Jonathan H. Martin

How can progressive third parties win more seats in U.S. state legislatures? As of this writing, these parties hold only 12 out of more than 7,000 such positions in the United States.[1] This failure transcends state politics, since statehouse seats are the common springboard for political parties to obtain federal office and shape national policy. By getting elected to state legislatures, politicians typically gain the experience needed to run for higher office and advance their party's agenda across the country.[2] Thus, unless progressive third parties can learn how to shatter the statehouse glass ceiling more often, they may have little chance of influencing nationwide politics in the future.

Existing scholarship does not adequately address this problem. As mentioned in the Introduction, there is a substantial literature on the electoral politics of contemporary American third parties, including several studies that cover particular progressive third parties or consider them as a group.[3] This body of work identifies various obstacles to progressive third party electoral success, but it doesn't clearly show which impediments are more critical and yet possibly surmountable at lower electoral levels.

The focus by most of the literature on large external obstacles—including American public opinion and political institutions—falls short. Some observers

[*] Originally published in a slightly different form as "Hegemonic Duopoly at the Grassroots: Why Progressive Third Parties Rarely Win State House Elections," *New Political Science* 35, no. 2 (2013): 250–71. Reprinted by permission of the author and publisher. The author thanks approximately 50 interns and assistants for their significant contributions to the research. Alyssa Baldassini and Phillip Cosmos deserve special mention for their extended efforts.

suggest that most Americans have an ingrained aversion to progressive and third party politics,[4] which would certainly make difficult the effort to elect progressive third party state legislators. But the merit of such claims is dubious. Public opinion polls actually indicate that for the past few decades, most Americans have been supportive of many aspects of a progressive agenda and often of third parties.[5] More significantly, much of the existing analysis of minor party and progressive third party weakness focuses heavily on well-known, deeply embedded structural barriers. These include stiff ballot access requirements for non-major party candidates; a mostly privately funded campaign finance system that advantages candidates who can raise a lot of money; winner-take-all election rules that strongly encourage voters to choose "the lesser of two evils"; and mainstream media bias against third parties and the Left.[6] However, such obstacles do not appear to be quite so impenetrable and decisive in many lower level races, including those for state legislature. In order to become eligible and potentially competitive, non-major party candidates for state representative in most states require zero to several hundred ballot petition signatures and several thousand to tens of thousands of dollars—amounts that are not necessarily prohibitive.[7] Also, in roughly 40 percent of state legislative elections, there is only one major party candidate running; in such races, voters' fear of spoiling the candidacy of a "lesser evil" Democrat or Republican is not a relevant factor.[8] Last, given the comparatively scant and inconspicuous media coverage of candidacies for lower level political offices in general, regardless of their party or ideological affiliation, it seems unlikely that media prejudice against progressive third party candidates in particular could be a crucial impediment to their success in state legislative elections. In sum, while external obstacles may be important, they do not sufficiently explain why these candidates do not win statehouse races at least somewhat more often. Moreover, a preoccupation with such impediments, which are very hard to dismantle, tends to result in a disabling pessimism about such candidates' prospects.

A more constructive approach to the problem also would need to address primarily internal obstacles—the qualities of left third parties themselves that may reduce their competitiveness in statehouse races—which may be more subject to change. The minimal contemporary research along these lines, which is survey-based, finds that most minor party candidates, including those running for state legislature, tend to be too politically inexperienced and nonpragmatic (that is, ideologically driven) to be electorally competitive.[9] This work represents a good start, but some investigation of actual campaigns is needed to determine whether and how these or other factors are really at play in relevant elections.

Here I address the above gap by presenting results of an in-depth study of campaigns involving progressive third party candidates for state legislature. Specifically, I find that progressive third party candidates' common lack of strong social connections to their local communities is a pivotal underlying reason that they do not win statehouse elections more frequently. Correspondingly, I suggest that the two major parties often dominate these races because their solid bond to local social and cultural life enables them to build strong community relationships. Last, I consider how in the future this dominance could be contested more effectively by left-wing minor parties and their candidates.

Method

In-depth comparative analysis of relevant campaign cases is needed to get to the bottom of the hidden dynamics in question here. Between 2009 and 2011, I collected data on 17 illustrative races for state representative held between 2002 and 2008. These 17 cases provide sufficient diversity for making analytic generalizations[10] about the reasons for the lack of success by progressive third parties in state legislative elections.

All of my cases include candidates affiliated with two prominent progressive third parties, the Green Party of the United States (GPUS) and the Vermont Progressive Party (VPP). Both of these parties clearly qualify as "progressive" by virtue of their egalitarian ideology and policy positions. I selected them because they are the only two progressive third parties in the country that routinely run their own candidates for state legislature and thereby directly compete with the major parties in this context. They have other characteristics that also make them worthy of study. The GPUS is national in scope, runs many state legislative candidates throughout the country, and yet very rarely wins these races. Since they founded their party in 1984, U.S. Greens have conducted more than 700 campaigns for state representative or an equivalent office across the vast majority of states. By 2015, they had won only five times. As of this writing, they do not occupy a single state legislative seat in the country.[11] By contrast, the VPP, based entirely in Vermont, is noteworthy for its comparative (though still quite limited) electoral success at the statehouse level. Established as the Progressive Coalition in Burlington in 1981 and then officially as a statewide party in 1999, it is the only third party, left-wing or otherwise, that consistently has won a small number of state legislative races in recent decades. It presently holds 7 (out of 150) seats in the Vermont House of Representatives, as well as 3 (out of 30) seats in the Vermont Senate.[12] Consequently, studying candidates from both the GPUS and the VPP potentially can facilitate an illuminating analysis of differences in progressive third parties' electoral effectiveness.

Specifically, my 17 cases include both of the following two types of nonincumbent progressive third party candidates for state representative, defined by campaign outcome and/or capacity:

1. *Winners.* These candidates won, despite the pitfalls that apparently derail most other progressive third party candidates at the same level.

2. *Viable Losers.* These candidates lost. However, they appear to have had a credible chance of winning. This is because they not only sought to win, but they also demonstrated a strong electoral potential—by running a high-intensity campaign, having a significant reputation in their district, and/or coming somewhat close (within 10 percentage points) to winning the same seat in a prior election.

By analyzing what produced these viable losers in comparison to what produced winners, I would be able to reveal which factors really can make the difference between winning for the first time and losing for progressive third party candidates for state representative. I chose not to study "sure losers," who do not seriously pursue victory or show that they are capable of achieving it.[13] Instead, by selecting races with viable loser candidates, I could learn why winning tends to be so difficult for even many of the best progressive third party statehouse campaigns.

I found all of my cases in New England, the only region where a comparison between viable losers and winners was possible. While there have been viable losers throughout the country in recent years, only New England has had at least a tiny cluster of winners.[14] Though a transregional or national sample would be desirable, multiple winners in other regions also would be needed in order to adequately control for differences in political context between regions. Nevertheless, a study of campaign cases just from New England can illuminate a significant part of the national story and enable informed speculation about the United States as a whole.

I chose my 7 specific winners because they were the only such candidates in New England during the period in question, 2002–2008. They included 6 Progressives and 1 Green. I uncovered 14 viable losers in the region during this same time frame. I selected 10 of them so as to attain substantial representation from both parties studied here, variety with respect to candidates' apparent campaign strengths, and diversity with respect to the location and character of their districts. These 10 were comprised of 4 Greens and 6 Progressives. My 17 case districts were located in four out of six New England states (Connecticut, Massachusetts, Maine, and Vermont), and together they included a fairly wide range of community types, from large cities to small rural towns.[15] Tables 5.1 and 5.2 provide basic details on each case.

In the end, I was confident that my sample strongly reflected the larger group being studied. Despite the fact that my goal was not representativeness, the cases I chose actually included for the period in question, virtually all of the statehouse winners and viable losers from the Green Party in New England, and the vast majority of those from the Vermont Progressive Party.

In order to uncover that which enabled the candidates in my sample to win or that which kept them from winning, I applied an appropriately limited yet

TABLE 5.1 Progressive Third Party Candidates for State Representative: Winners

P3P Candidate Party	Election Year	Location district	Setting	Party of other candidate(s)	Vote for P3P candidate	Margin of victory
John Eder *Green*	2002	Portland (ME) *District 31*	Medium urban	D	**65%**	+30%
Sarah Edwards *Progressive[d]*	2002	Brattleboro (VT) *Windham 3–3*	Small urban	I[i]	**54%**	+7%
Dexter Randall *Progressive[d]*	2004	Northwestern Northeast Kingdom (VT) *Orleans-Franklin 1*	Rural	R	**52%**	+5%
Winston Dowland *Progressive*	2004	Central-northern Northeast Kingdom (VT) *Orleans-1[t]*	Rural	R[i], R[i], D	**27%**	+0.14%
Sandy Haas *Progressive[d]*	2004	Central Green Mtns. (VT) *Windsor-Rutland 2*	Rural	R	**55%**	+10%
Susan Hatch Davis *Progressive[d]*	2006	Central-eastern (VT) *Orange 1[t]*	Rural	R[i], R[i], I	**28%**	+0.36%
Mollie Burke *Progressive[d]*	2008	Brattleboro (VT) *Windham 3–2*	Small urban	NA unopposed	**100%**	+100%

P3P = progressive third party

R = Republican; D = Democrat; I = Independent

[d] = also listed as a Democrat via write-in win in Democratic primary, but not candidate's main affiliation

[i] = incumbent

[t] = two-seat district

focused version of the "qualitative comparative method"[16] as I gathered and evaluated data on each of their campaigns. To begin with, so as to learn more about campaign conditions and their possible effect on campaign outcomes, for every case I collected and reviewed relevant campaign literature, news articles, and any other pertinent electoral information available. For the same purpose, I also conducted one to two hour interviews with critical campaign participants and observers. They included the candidate or the campaign manager; the opponent(s) or a representative of the opponent(s) campaign; and usually a key outside political observer, such as a local journalist who covered the race. Next, I determined which condition(s) if any consistently were present for winners and absent for viable losers. Last, I re-evaluated the interview data for compelling common explanations of the role of any such factor(s) in affecting campaign outcomes.

TABLE 5.2 Progressive Third Party Candidates for State Representative: Viable Losers

P3P Candidate Party	Election Year	Location district	Setting	Party of other candidate(s)	Vote for P3P candidate	Margin of loss	Why Viable
Michael Aleo Green	2002[s]	Greater Northampton (MA) 1st Hampshire	Small urban, suburban-rural	D	**38%**	−25%	OW, HI
Paul Lachelier Green	2002	Cambridge-Somerville (MA) 26th Middlesex	Large urban	D[i]	**37%**	−25%	OW, HI
John Battista Green	2002	New Milford (CT) District 67	Suburban-rural	R[i]	**31%**	−38%	OW, HI, SR
Jill Stein Green	2004	Waltham-Lexington (MA) 9th Middlesex	Small urban-suburban	R, D[i]	**21%**	−38%	OW, HI
Joyce Chen Green	2004	New Haven (CT) District 93	Medium urban	D[i]	**27%**	−45%	OW, HI, SR
Ben Meiklejohn Green	2006	Portland (ME) District 120	Small urban	D	**43%**	−14%	OW, HI, SR
Jean Szilva Progressive	2006	Winooski (VT) Chittenden 3–6[t]	Small urban	D[i], D[i], P	**26%**	−8%	OW, HI, SR
Heather Riemer Progressive	2006	Burlington (VT) Chittenden 3–3[t]	Small urban	D[i], D, P	**19%**	−13%	OW, HI, SR
Cindy Weed Progressive	2008	Northwestern (VT) Franklin 4	Rural	R, D	**32%**	−10%	OW, HI, SR
Nancy Potak Progressive	2008	Southern Northeast Kingdom (VT) Orleans-Caledonia 1[t]	Rural	R[i], D[i], L	**28%**	−5%	OW, HI, NV

P3P = progressive third party
R = Republican; D = Democrat; L = Libertarian; P = Vermont Progressive
[i] = incumbent
[s] = special election in April 2002
[t] = two-seat district
OW = oriented toward winning; HI = high-intensity campaign
SR = significant reputation in district; NV = near victory in last election

Findings

Weaker Predictors of Campaign Outcomes

Contrary to what one might expect, progressive third party winners were not consistently more advantaged than viable losers regarding almost all common campaign advantages. This can be seen as follows (with the affiliation of Green and Progressive candidates signified on first mention by "G" and "P," respectively, along with the state abbreviation and specific location of the district).

Ease of ballot access. Neither winners nor viable losers had any trouble getting on the ballot. Requirements ranged only from 16 to 150 voter signatures, depending on the state and population of the district. These were obtained in a matter of a few weeks at the most.

Money. While all progressive third party winners had similar or greater campaign funds than their main major party opponents, so did more than half of viable losers. One of the largest financial gaps between candidates actually *favored* a viable loser, John Battista (G-CT, New Milford). He had four times the money of his opponent, a one-term Republican incumbent, yet he lost in the end by a whopping 38 percent margin. Thus, while the relative amount of money progressive third party candidates raised may have been important, it did not necessarily determine their electoral fate.

Media bias. An in-depth, systematic review of news coverage in each race revealed no clear, consistent leaning in favor of or against virtually all progressive third party winners and viable losers. This was judged in terms of frequency of coverage, amount of emphasis on candidates, and the substance and tone of commentary about candidates. In eight cases, including three of which were viable losers, there was not even an aggregate leaning one way or the other. In eight other cases, only subtle, slight differences in overall coverage could be detected. Yet in five of these cases, only one of which was a winner, press coverage actually leaned toward the progressive third party candidate. Likewise, the one exception to the pattern of relatively fair local news coverage was a leaning decidedly in favor of viable loser Paul Lachelier (G-MA, Cambridge-Somerville). A 30-year-old sociology graduate student, he repeatedly was portrayed in newspaper articles (especially in the local alternative press) as the young, energetic, independent challenger to the establishment-oriented, entrenched, longtime Democratic incumbent. Nevertheless, Lachelier lost by a 25 percent margin. Perhaps media tends to be rather receptive to local third party candidates because they are perceived to be at least somewhat capable of winning at the local level, in contrast to its more discriminatory approach to minor party candidates for much less attainable higher level offices. In any case, for the lower level races in question here, I found no evidence that viable losers generally were more disadvantaged by media coverage than winners.

Endorsements. All progressive third party candidates studied here received endorsements from progressive organizations and/or leaders in their district or state. While the number and apparent quality of endorsements varied somewhat among candidates, there was no pattern that generally distinguished winners from viable losers. Candidates with relatively more endorsements included a combination of the former and the latter, as did those with comparatively fewer endorsements. Several candidates received the prized statement of support or effective support from one or more local newspapers, but these candidates included not only three winners, Dexter Randall (P-VT, Northeast Kingdom), Winston Dowland (P-VT, Northeast Kingdom), and John Eder (G-ME, Portland), but also two losers, Paul Lachelier and Michael Aleo (G-MA, Greater Northampton). All Vermont Progressives in contested races were endorsed by Vermont U.S. senator Bernie Sanders, one of the most popular politicians in the state, but only slightly more than half of them won. Overall, winners did not have an endorsement edge over viable losers.

Number, incumbency, and political orientation of opponent(s). Progressive third parties may perceive that their candidates are much more likely to win against certain types of opponents—*a singular adversary* (rather than multiple opponents), *a non-incumbent* (rather than an incumbent), and *a candidate who is politically very different* (rather than more similar with respect to partisan and policy orientation). Under the former (italicized) conditions, respectively, the serious threat of being perceived as a spoiler is absent, the opponent does not have the reservoir of support and connections associated with being in office, and it is easier for the minor party candidate to make a case for himself or herself to voters. However, in contrast to the above expectations, as indicated in Tables 5.1 and 5.2, my sample of progressive third party winners *and* viable losers both were comprised of candidates who challenged one opponent and multiple opponents; incumbents and non-incumbents; and Republicans, Democrats, and non-major party candidates. Likewise, my interviews also revealed that opponents of winners *and* viable losers included a fairly even mixture of policy conservatives, moderates, liberals, and progressives. Thus, winners as a whole did not have opponents who seemed to be inherently easier to beat in the common ways just discussed.

Experience in municipal office. Among the progressive third party candidates in my sample, having served in municipal office was not strongly associated with winning a seat in the state legislature. Three out of seven winners had served on a select board and other local boards. These included Winston Dowland, Sarah Edwards (P-VT, Brattleboro), and Sandy Haas (P-VT, central Green Mountains). One of the other winners, Molly Burke (P-VT, Brattleboro), had served as a town meeting representative. However, three viable losers also had municipal government experience. They included alderman Joyce Chen (G-CT, New Haven) and school board members Ben Meiklejohn (G-ME, Portland) and Jean Szilva (P-VT, Winooski). Tellingly, all of the above candidates who had served in municipal office except Burke, who ran unopposed, faced principal major party opponents with even more substantial political experience as a state legislator or a mayor. Some of these progressive third party challengers were able to surmount this obstacle while others were not, apparently for reasons that transcended their experience in local government. Meanwhile, three winners—Eder, Randall, and Susan Hatch Davis (P-VT, central-eastern)—had no experience in municipal government at all.

Candidate effort. Virtually all of the progressive third party candidates selected for this study, both winners and viable losers, worked hard—campaigning for several months at least half-time and sometimes full-time. The one notable exception, of course, was Mollie Burke, the Progressive from Brattleboro who did not have to campaign because she was unopposed. All of the other candidates spent most of their campaign time door-knocking, as serious challengers at the state and local level typically are advised to do. There was no indication from my interviews that those progressive third party candidates who won generally worked harder than those who lost. The average campaign duration for both winners (excluding Burke) and viable losers was five months. Notably, only one winner (Sarah Edwards) consistently campaigned full-time, while half of the viable losers did so! One of these viable losers, Jill Stein (G-MA, Waltham-Lexington), campaigned for an entire year, which was at least twice as long as any other candidate. Clearly, candidate effort did not necessarily make the critical difference between winning and losing.

Campaign organization. The sophistication and size of the progressive third party campaign organizations varied considerably from well-oiled machines with multiple staff and scores of volunteers to loose, candidate-managed operations with a handful of helpers. (To some extent, this range reflected differences in campaign demands that corresponded to the variation in population size among districts in different states.) Not surprisingly, the campaigns of winners tended to be at the more organized end of the spectrum, relative to local campaign norms. Clearly, organization matters, as my interviews with campaign personnel and observers confirmed time after time. This was most graphically illustrated by the campaign of Green John Eder in Portland, Maine. Its stunning landslide win (by a 30 percent margin) over the Democratic opponent in 2002 was widely attributed in large part to Eder's "army" of volunteers that easily overwhelmed the Democrat's virtual one-man, minimalist effort. Still, most of the viable loser campaigns also were well organized, especially those of Michael Aleo, Jill Stein, Paul Lachelier, Cindy Weed (P-VT, northwestern), Heather Riemer (P-VT, Burlington), and Jean Szilva. Arguably, one of the best organized of the entire sample (of winning and losing campaigns) was the Green campaign of Michael Aleo. A progressive activist in his late twenties, Aleo ran for a seat in a district that included Northampton, Massachusetts, and certain towns nearby. His campaign developed rapidly in the wake of a sitting Democratic representative's resignation and the delayed scheduling of a special election. It not only had a dedicated core of volunteer staffers but also actually appeared to develop the characteristics of a social movement—with large numbers of volunteers intensely devoted to a common cause (as likewise occurred for the campaigns of three winners—Eder, Edwards, and Haas). Aleo himself claimed that his superenergized, three-month operation "squeezed every vote possible out of the district," and one of his Democratic opponent's campaign staff even admitted being "out campaigned" by Aleo. However, Aleo lost by a 25 percent margin. In sum, progressive third party winners and viable losers were not necessarily distinguishable by their level of campaign organization.[17]

Substantive appeal. Hypothetically, progressive third party campaigns may present a more or less compelling message to voters, and this could affect how well they do on election day. However, I found no discernible overall difference between winners and viable losers with respect to what kind of case they made to their voters. In their literature and public statements, both types of candidates took common progressive stands on issues. These included calls for several of the following, in descending order of frequency: more funding for public education, mass transportation, and other infrastructural improvements; universal and affordable health care; job creation and more support for local economies and small businesses; stronger environmental protection and greater development of renewable energy; equitable taxation; affordable housing and tenants' rights; living wages; campaign finance and other electoral reforms; marriage and reproductive rights; an end to standardized educational testing; and greater corporate and governmental accountability. To varying extents, winners and viable losers alike combined these proposals with criticism of prevailing policies and with one or more popular progressive themes, including democratic, economic populist, antiestablishment, and communitarian motifs. Likewise, in different measures, both types of candidates drew attention to what they felt were their own noteworthy personal strengths, such as their innovativeness, commitment, energy, relevant experience, or political effectiveness. Sometimes they also highlighted alleged negative aspects of their opponent(s) or those in power in their state. While certain of the above messages may have helped or hurt the progressive third party candidates, none consistently was associated with their victory or defeat.

Candidate personality. A candidate's personal style obviously could affect his or her ability to win. For the sake of appealing to ordinary voters, a warmer (more engaging or down-to-earth) manner could be a significant campaign asset, while a cooler (more reserved, serious, or even abrasive) style could be a considerable liability. However, my interviews with campaign observers and participants, including the progressive third party candidates themselves, did not reveal a consistent gap between the winners and viable losers in this regard. Candidates who clearly appeared to have the warmer persona included several winners (Eder, Edwards, Randall, and Dowland) as well as a number of viable losers (Aleo, Lachelier, Stein, and Weed). Similarly, candidates who seemed to have a cooler presentation included not only a bunch of viable losers (Battista, Meiklejohn,

Szilva, Riemer, and Potak [P-VT, Northeast Kingdom]), but also a couple of winners (Haas and Davis). One of the "warmest" candidates was viable loser Cindy Weed, a Progressive from the town of Enosburg in rural central Franklin County, Vermont. A part-time jewelry maker and local bluegrass musician, she had an amiable, animated, folksy, interactive way of talking that probably would put most people at ease. Conversely, one of the "coolest" candidates was winner Susan Hatch Davis, another Progressive. A former state of Vermont security specialist from rustic Orange County, she spoke in a minimalist fashion with a nonemotional, barely audible voice (despite the fact that the content of her statements reflected a very strong commitment to economic justice). In brief, progressive third party candidates who won did not generally seem to have a more popularly appealing personal style than those who lost.

Ideological and partisan orientation of district. One might imagine that progressive third party candidates' electoral results would correspond closely to the ideological or partisan leanings of their districts. However, in my sample this was not the case. Some winners did run in urban districts that were known for being progressive or solidly Democratic. They included John Eder (in Portland, ME), and Sarah Edwards and Molly Burke (both in Brattleboro, VT). Yet, other winners ran in rural districts known to be conservative or firmly Republican, specifically Progressives Dexter Randall and Winston Dowland (in Vermont's bucolic Northeast Kingdom), and Susan Hatch Davis.[18] Dowland's case was the most striking in this group; it featured a district that reportedly had elected only conservative Republicans for the past several decades! Viable losers also could be found in ideologically disparate districts. Some ran in more conservative-leaning places, such as Progressive Nancy Potak (also in the Northeast Kingdom) and Green John Battista (in semi-rural New Milford, CT). Similar to Dowland's case, Battista's district had elected only Republicans to the state legislature for decades. However, other viable losers ran and lost in much more progressive places with a history of electing Democrats, including Green Ben Meiklejohn (in Portland, ME), Progressive Heather Riemer (in Burlington, VT), and Green Joyce Chen (in New Haven, CT). Overall, district ideology and partisanship did not appear to favor the winners over the viable losers.

Partisan coattails. Related to the above, some of my campaign interviewees in heavily Democratic districts in which the progressive third party candidate lost to a Democrat speculated that the outcome may have been facilitated by a partisan surge that year in favor of Democrats on the ballot for much higher level offices (such as president or governor). This occurred in the cases of viable losers Chen and Stein (in 2004), and Riemer (in 2006). However, another progressive third party candidate who faced such a Democratic up-ticket tide (in 2002), Green John Eder, still defeated his Democratic opponent by a 30-point margin. This casts doubt on how decisive partisan coattails necessarily are in separating viable losers from winners.

Size of district. One might expect that progressive third party candidates in districts with smaller populations are a lot more likely to win than those in districts with larger populations. Unlike many major party candidates, minor party candidates often lack the resources and organizational connections to reach larger numbers of voters. However, in a district with fewer voters, it still is possible to communicate with much of the electorate in person via a serious door-to-door effort. Accordingly, all of the winners in this study in fact came from the less populous states of Vermont and Maine that have house districts with about 4,000 to 8,000 people. By contrast, five viable losers came from the more populous states of Connecticut and Massachusetts that have house districts with 20,000 to 40,000 constituents. The latter group of candidates clearly faced much more of a challenge for that reason. However, the other five viable losers did not have this problem because they also ran in the smaller Maine and Vermont districts. These patterns suggest that district size may matter, but it is not enough to consistently differentiate winners from viable losers.

While various common campaign variables described above may have made an important difference in some or even many of the races under consideration, none *regularly* distinguished the winning from the losing progressive third party campaigns. On this basis, without further information, one might conclude that the divergent outcomes of these campaigns can be understood only in terms of the unique constellation of factors at play in each particular race. However, one critical finding robustly suggests otherwise.

Stronger Predictor of Campaign Outcomes

The data showed that progressive third party winners did have one constant advantage over viable losers—*community connectedness*. By this, I mean a candidate's degree of social ties and social similarity to voters. In this sense, winners consistently were in a better position than viable losers.

Social Ties. Winners' stronger social ties to voters typically were reflected by their longer residency in their districts, which tended to make them more familiar and seemingly more committed to their communities. Almost all winners had been district residents from a few decades to their whole life, and some also had family that had lived in the district for generations. Six out of seven winners fit this long-timer description (Randall, Dowland, Davis, Haas, Edwards, and Burke). By contrast, eight out of ten viable losers had lived in their districts for less than 20 years, and thereby could be considered relative newcomers. One of them, Paul Lachelier, had done so for only two years. In the one case in which the progressive third party winner was a relative newcomer too (Eder), his opponent also was such, and importantly, the district itself largely was populated by newcomers. In the two cases in which viable losers actually were long-timers (Stein and Weed), neither was a lifelong resident, and both were up against a principal major party opponent who not only had lived in the district his whole life but also had come from a politically prominent family that had resided in the district for generations (and even had its name attached to a local road or public building). Notably, in 14 out of the 16 cases in which the progressive third party candidate faced an opponent, the main opponent was a lifelong resident.

Another marker of winners' greater social ties to voters was the fact that they had engaged in work or other activities that involved more association with larger numbers of ordinary citizens. This occurred before they ran for state representative or any other government office, and it enabled these candidates to become more widely and deeply known and respected in their districts. Such popularizing, locally oriented actions in the community included the following:

- delivering the daily mail, operating a welding business heavily used by local farmers, and serving as the statewide "Commander of Disabled American Veterans" (Dowland);
- owning and operating a dairy farm in a largely agricultural area and being a prominent activist on behalf of issues affecting dairy farmers (Randall);
- managing a large, popular food cooperative (which is one of the two major downtown supermarkets) and serving on a number of boards of directors for local social service organizations (Edwards);
- directing the community theater and maintaining one of the few law practices in the district (Haas);
- regularly organizing major church-sponsored charitable events (Davis);
- over many years, being the primary ice skating coach for youths in town and an art teacher in a local private school (Burke); and
- founding a tenant's union and an organization opposed to pesticide use on city sidewalks, and actively meeting and getting acquainted with many district residents in the course of daily neighborhood walks (Eder).

The fact that all of the above things were done in fairly small districts (with several thousand people at most) undoubtedly accentuated their perceived impact and significance. Correspondingly, winners often were described by other campaign interviewees as having been well known in much of their district prior to running for any elected office. In several such cases (Burke, Dowland, Edwards, and Haas), the aforementioned popularizing actions may have contributed to candidates' prior election or appointment to municipal government (boards, commissions, committees, or meetings). Holding municipal positions undoubtedly enhanced their social ties among those in the district interested or involved in local politics, and it certainly boosted their perceived qualifications for statehouse office. Yet, it was clear from not only the campaign interviews but also the campaign news coverage that much of these candidates' original broad popular appeal had stemmed from their high-profile nongovernmental efforts.

By comparison, viable losers' primary work and activities before any foray into electoral politics had involved a more limited association with people in the community. Most had been occupied in one or more types of progressive activism that tend to directly engage with a small minority of people. Viable losers' other pre-electoral pursuits, as follows, also entailed comparatively less interaction with ordinary citizens in their district:

- teaching elementary school for a couple of years and then being unemployed (Aleo);
- working on a sociology dissertation, catering part-time, and doing recreational weightlifting (Lachelier);
- practicing psychotherapy as a psychologist and leading an organization focusing on local environmental conservation (Battista);
- practicing medicine in nearby communities outside of the district and publishing a book on environmental health (Stein);
- attending a university that bordered the district and regularly going to a local church (Chen);
- doing a variety of odd jobs and playing in a local avant-garde rock band (Meiklejohn);
- working as a medical researcher at a university bordering the district (Szilva);
- working as an organizer for an electrical workers' union and being involved in activities in schools that her children were attending (Riemer);
- attending college part-time, making jewelry, and playing in a local bluegrass band (Weed); and
- working as a consultant for environmental engineering projects in the northeast United States (Potak).

While some of the above activities might make one known in part of one's community, they probably would not make one well known in most of the district—unlike most winners' pre-electoral pursuits that involved broader community engagement, leadership, and exposure. This difference was important because virtually all of the main major party opponents for viable losers and winners were broadly known nonelectorally—via some potent combination of local high-profile employment or business, charitable work, social service, social activism, recreational activity, religious participation, association membership, or respected family name. In various instances, opponents already had converted this "community capital" into elected office (in the state legislature or at the municipal level), thereby giving them more recognition in their districts and further potential electoral advantages.

Of course, a few viable losers (Chen, Meiklejohn, and Szilva) did manage to get more public exposure via local governmental service prior to their statehouse run, specifically by being elected to municipal boards, as mentioned earlier. This not only improved their perceived qualifications but also established their reputations among people who followed local politics. However, it still did not appear to be an adequate substitute for broader and deeper nongovernmental social ties. As an alderman representing just one ward in a multiward house district in New Haven, Chen did not become known to most voters in the district through her official functions or campaigning. As members of the school board in their respective cities of Portland (ME) and Winooski (VT), Meiklejohn and Szilva only would have been personally familiar mostly to voters who were interested in local educational policies. Meanwhile, all three of these candidates were up against an opponent who had become very well known throughout much of the district. These opponents included a sitting mayor who had overseen a multiyear downtown redevelopment project and previously had chaired several municipal boards and agencies (versus Szilva); a current state representative who had worked for many years in the district as a social worker and whose father was the influential minister of a popular local church (versus Chen); and a former state senator for the district who, along with her family, had owned and operated a popular print shop in the district for several decades (versus Meiklejohn).

Similarly, it would seem that merely campaigning previously in the district was not a sufficient substitute for becoming widely known and liked via popular, nonelectoral local actions. The fact that viable loser Nancy Potak had run and come within one percentage point of winning in the same district two years earlier (2006)—against an incumbent who had barely campaigned for reelection—did not negate the fact that she continued to be someone who was not broadly involved in local affairs. As a regional environmental consultant and a single-payer health care activist for several years, her local reputation in her two-seat house district still lagged behind the two major party incumbents, who had been active in the local business community for decades. Thus, it was more difficult for her to win in the next race studied here (2008), when the previously lazy incumbent conducted a more serious campaign. Likewise, Jill Stein's minor reputation as a former Green gubernatorial candidate (who had received 3.49 percent of the vote in 2002) did not outweigh the fact that she had not been highly active in the local community in her Waltham-Lexington (MA) district, especially in comparison to her opponent. He was an incumbent Democrat and son of a well-liked former Waltham mayor, and he had been deeply involved in Waltham's social and political activities for his whole life.

Had the five governmentally and electorally experienced viable losers above been more locally active, like the winners, they likely would have been stronger challengers to their more locally engaged incumbent opponents. Indeed, as noted above, winners who had challenged yet actually defeated socially entrenched, well-known incumbents had themselves become much better known via their everyday activities.

Social similarity. In addition to having stronger social ties to voters than viable losers, winners were more connected to their communities because they were socially similar to more voters. Social similarity is an important electoral asset because it may foster voters' identification with and trust for a candidate. Specifically, winners were more like the voting majority or plurality in the district with respect to residential location, social class, race, ethnicity, age, education, and/or culture. They had the following such commonalities with many or most voters:

- living in a town, ward, or neighborhood with a large share of the total district vote (Eder, Edwards, and Haas);
- being working class in a largely working-class district (Dowland and Davis);
- being a farmer in a rural identified district (Randall);
- being well-educated and cosmopolitan in a district with many urban transplants (Edwards, Burke, and Haas); and
- being a young (30-year-old), lower-middle-class renter in a district with many such residents (Eder).

By contrast, viable losers were socially *dissimilar* to many or most voters as follows:

- living in a town or neighborhood with a relatively small share of the total district votes (Stein, Lachelier, Meiklejohn, and Potak);
- being Chinese American in a predominantly African American district (Chen);
- being highly educated and professionally oriented in a district with a working-class majority or plurality (Aleo, Lachelier, Stein, Szilva, Battista, and Potak);
- being a single, young, countercultural renter in a part of the city with many family-oriented homeowners and more middle-aged and elderly residents (Meiklejohn);
- being an out-of-state transplant in a dominant local culture that values being born in-state (Weed and Potak); and
- being a working person in her thirties in a district with a significant number of university students and recent graduates in their late teens to early twenties (Riemer).

The importance of the above difference between winners and viable losers becomes more apparent when considered in relation to the social characteristics of the candidates' main opponents. All of the viable losers had principal opponents who did not share their social dissimilarity with the district. Joyce Chen's opponent was black, like most residents from her district in New Haven, Connecticut. The main opponents of Lachelier, Stein, Szilva, Battista, and Potak appeared to be part of a local old-boy network that overlapped strongly with a parochially oriented working-class culture, and some of them lived in a part of the district with a relatively large share of likely voters from that culture. Opponents of Potak and Weed were native Vermonters in rural districts that privileged that status culturally, like most rural areas of Vermont. Lastly, Heather Riemer's main opponent was a recent graduate and student government leader at the University of Vermont (UVM), in a Burlington district with a significant bloc of UVM students and recent graduates. Most of the winners also had opponents who had important social similarities with voters, yet the winners themselves did likewise, as detailed earlier. John Eder was the only winner who challenged a principal opponent who obviously was socially dissimilar to most of the district. In this case, the opponent was a well-to-do landlord, which according to campaign interviewees had negative connotations for the low- to moderate-income renters who comprised the majority of voters in Portland, Maine's District 31.

Campaign Informants' Confirmation

In sum, with respect to community connectedness, winners had an edge over viable losers, and this was the *only* constant disparity between the two groups of candidates. This apparently was not a mere coincidence. In their interview accounts of the election outcomes, key campaign participants and observers themselves frequently highlighted the importance of this consistent gap. They often depicted community connectedness as a critical mediator of a candidate's chances from the beginning of the campaign. They repeatedly suggested that in their district, it largely determined one's ability to become well known, liked, and trusted, to thereby build a big base of strong supporters, and ultimately, to appeal to the electorate as a whole. Such commentary was compelling because it came from individuals who knew voters, the district, and the race very well from the inside. Of course, on its own it didn't prove that relatively strong community connections were vital. But it was persuasive when combined with the one consistent association in all the campaigns between those connections and winning.

Key players and watchers in races with a winner regularly suggested that this candidate was *competitive from the outset* because of relatively strong community connections. In some cases, they mainly emphasized the pivotal role of candidate involvement in the everyday social or political life of the district. For example, Progressive Sarah Edwards identified her own "rich experience as a community person" in Brattleboro as the foundation of her victory. A reporter who covered the race explained further that "it makes a difference that she had roots in the community" through her local activities because this was how "she acquired a base of support" large enough to make it possible to win. The focus was the same in campaign interviewee accounts of why Progressive winners Sandy Haas and Winston Dowland were especially competitive in their districts elsewhere in Vermont. Back in Brattleboro, unopposed Progressive winner Molly Burke suggested that having "all of these personal connections" in town "on different levels" gave her a clear "advantage" in her district, especially when she became the first candidate to enter the race over a year before the election. This may have dissuaded other prospective candidates from entering the race subsequently. In any case, Burke explained that being socially well acquainted with the one known potential Democratic rival actually helped her to gain his eventual backing.[19]

For other winner cases, major campaign participants and observers also emphasized the significance of longtime residency, social similarity, or both. For instance, a Democratic candidate who ran in the same race as Progressive Susan Hatch Davis stressed that "lifetime residency in the district was important" in enabling Davis to appeal to enough voters to win, as was the fact that she was "working class in a working-class district." Similarly, various campaign interviewees in the Randall case noted that Progressive Dexter Randall started his winning race with a substantial core of likely supporters because he was a dairy farmer in a largely dairy farming area of Vermont. Likewise, key actors in the winning race of John Eder mentioned that the Green's having been relatively young and less established made him naturally appealing to the largely youthful and more transient voters in his Portland, Maine, district. This especially was the case when Eder was compared to his middle-aged Democratic opponent who, in the words of one of Eder's campaign managers, was "badly matched to his district as a rich landlord."

By contrast, campaign interviewees often depicted progressive third party viable losers as having been critically handicapped from the start by an inadequate base and popular appeal due to relatively weak community connections. For instance, it was commonly observed in the case of Green viable loser Paul Lachelier that the candidate's hard fought campaign was doomed by his "outsider" image in his east Cambridge-Somerville (MA) district—combined with the incumbent Democratic opponent's lifelong "salt of the neighborhood" status and consequent "rock solid base" in east Cambridge. Similar assessments regularly were made about the pitched yet seemingly ill-fated battles waged by almost all (eight out of nine) other viable losers. They were used to explain the losses of Stein, Aleo, Battista, Potak, Szilva, Chen, Meiklejohn, and Weed. All of these candidates' races essentially were described as mismatched fights between disadvantaged relative outsiders and advantaged relative insiders.

In some of the above cases, the persistence of the "outsider" label was surprising. It stayed stuck to Progressive Nancy Potak despite the fact that she had come very close to winning before, and it remained affixed to Jean Szilva, Joyce Chen, and Ben Meiklejohn, even though they previously had been elected to municipal office.[20] Even Progressive viable loser Cindy Weed—who had married into a family that had lived in her rural northwestern Vermont district for generations and had become well known locally over the course of several decades—was portrayed by campaign interviewees as being disadvantaged by originally having come from out-of-state and therefore still being a comparative outsider. According to a local reporter who had followed Weed's grueling three-way race, the victorious

Republican opponent had a decisive edge because he was "from a farming family" that had lived in the still primarily agricultural district since the colonial era. As a result, many district residents, who themselves were longtimers, felt that the Republican could "identify with their concerns," that he "spoke what they were feeling," was that someone "who they would trust" to "resolve problems" about which they cared most.[21] Apparently, because of a lack of sufficiently strong community connections relative to their opponents and the composition of their districts, viable losers were not really as "viable" as they initially seemed to be.

For one race with an "outsider" viable loser, a rare district benchmark poll verified the common account of the problem. It was conducted for Green Jill Stein nearly eight months before she lost the 2004 election. It showed that 59 percent of likely voters in her Waltham-Lexington (MA) district agreed that "since Waltham makes up a larger part of our house district, it's better for our representative to come from Waltham than from Lexington."[22] Both Stein and the Republican challenger in the three-way contest were from Lexington (a mostly upper-middle-class suburb). Meanwhile, the incumbent Democrat was a lifelong resident of Waltham (a largely working-class city). Not surprisingly, he won the race with 60 percent of the vote.

Of course, campaign factors other than community connections may have been more decisive in the final outcome of certain races, yet this did not necessarily negate the underlying importance of those bonds. For instance, Progressive Molly Burke obviously won because she had no opponent. However, when interviewed, she suggested that her potent community connections in Brattleboro actually enabled her to dissuade potential opponents from entering the race. Somewhat differently, campaign interviewees in districts with other winners consistently claimed that much of what put these candidates over the top on election day was their having had a stronger campaign organization and doing more door-knocking than their opponent(s). Yet, as discussed above, other comments by these same respondents suggest that this could not have happened if these winners had not been at least as well-connected to their communities as their opponents in the first place—and thereby able to mobilize a large enough base of supportive and receptive voters. Conversely, in the case of one of the viable losers, Progressive Heather Riemer, statements by campaign interviewees, and an audiovisual recording of a televised candidate debate suggest that Riemer may have been defeated in part because her main Democratic opponent door-knocked more and had a more engaging public persona.[23] However, campaign effort and candidate style may have assumed a greater importance in the outcome of this viable loser case precisely because the community connectedness gap between Riemer and her opponent was smaller than in other such cases. (Riemer's union organizer job and her involvement in local schools bonded her to her district only somewhat less strongly than her main Democratic opponent, a former student senate president at the University of Vermont—a dominant institution in Burlington.)

Generally then, relative community connectedness seemed to function as an *essential gateway* to making loss quite likely or victory truly possible for progressive third party state legislative candidates. Regardless of how viable they were in other respects, when they were less connected to their community than their main opponent to begin with, they appeared in all likelihood to be headed for a loss. In such cases, other campaign factors could affect the percentage of the vote obtained to some extent, but seemingly not enough to produce a victory. Conversely, when progressive third party candidates were at least as well-connected to their community as their main opponent (or even potential opponents) at the start, they apparently were aimed toward a possible win. Then, other campaign variables could determine whether this possibility was actualized in the end. It appears that viable losers followed the former trajectory, while winners took the latter course. In brief, having a relatively strong connection to one's community was not enough to win, but it clearly seemed to be essential for victory.

Conclusion

National Relevance

This research has found that a community connectedness gap is critical to explaining why certain serious progressive third party candidates for statehouse in New England have been able to win and others have not. An obvious implication is that insufficient community connection is a key reason that left-wing minor party candidates have not been elected more often in the region in recent years. Such a conclusion raises more doubt about the prevailing belief that external obstacles are the primary reason that candidates from progressive third parties win so rarely.[24] Yet, the result reported here actually is consistent with the longstanding observation that positive name recognition and the community connections that usually create it are crucial for getting elected at lower electoral levels throughout the United States.[25] In this respect, the challenge of being a competitive progressive third party candidate for state legislature in New England really is not so different from that of being a more viable state legislative candidate of any ideology or party affiliation anywhere in the country. Thus, we can infer that left third party candidates for statehouse throughout the country stand little chance of winning without being well-bonded to their communities (both relative to their likely opponents and to local norms concerning social bondedness).

If more left third party state legislative candidates in New England were relatively well-connected to their communities, it seems likely that more of them would win. However, this also could apply to such candidates in other regions, particularly in states in which financial and other logistical obstacles to third party candidacies are weaker. Left-wing (and other) minor party candidates throughout the country usually are not as well known in their communities as their major party opponents.[26] Starting to rectify this imbalance at the local level might begin to allow more of the former to win state legislative elections in various regions.

Admittedly, New England has a concentration of certain features that may be more conducive to the development and success of progressive third parties. Several of these conditions that pertain to the northern states in the region include lesser-sized districts with relatively small populations, a culture of public participation in local politics, and relatively low budget races—all of which may make door-to-door efforts by partisan outsiders easier to carry out and ultimately more effective.[27] Meanwhile, states in southern New England have a union density that is higher than the national average,[28] which hypothetically can provide for progressive politics a larger base, more organizational support, and a more receptive political culture than elsewhere. Likewise, the region as a whole has quite a few cities and towns that are populated substantially by intellectuals, students, artists, and assorted counterculture types, who may shift the local culture enough to provide a stronger springboard for left-wing and third party politics.[29] Lastly, most of the states in New England do rate high in policy and public opinion liberalism, an obvious plus for progressive candidates.[30]

However, one or more of the above propitious conditions also exist in various states or parts thereof in other regions of the country.[31] Therefore, arguably, significant untapped potential for the success of progressive third party state legislative candidates can be found across the United States. Thus, even if there is a greater overall possibility for such success in New England, if it increasingly becomes actualized there, it could inspire other winning efforts elsewhere. Historically, New England often has functioned as a national breeding ground for dissident and reformist politics.[32]

Likely, if more locally well-connected progressive third party candidates start to run for state legislature and win, regardless of where they do so, they may motivate similar candidates to step out of the political woodwork, run, and win. To some extent, this dynamic already appears to have unfolded for Progressives in Vermont in the form of a minor statewide proliferation of victories in races for state legislative seats since 2002.[33] The same process has not yet occurred in any state for the Green Party, which runs most of the progressive third party candidates for state legislature in the country. Its few statehouse victories, which have occurred since 1999, have remained isolated as well as ephemeral.[34] Very few of its state legislative candidates seem to be both oriented toward winning *and locally well-connected*—and therefore capable of winning.[35] Meanwhile, Republicans and Democrats everywhere appear to run statehouse candidates with this essential quality against third party opponents, as well as each other, routinely. Until this partisan balance of grassroots social influence starts to shift, it is hard to see how the major parties can be challenged effectively at the state legislative level much more often.

Hegemony and Counter-hegemony

The preceding analysis enables us to identify a characteristic of major party supremacy in the United States that is central to understanding the challenge facing progressive third parties. Two-party dominance seems to be more *hegemonic* in local elections than it is with respect to races for statewide and national office. Hegemony, as conceived by Italian social theorist Antonio Gramsci, pertains to dominant groups' rule or leadership that is maintained through active popular consent rather than coercion. Hegemony is secured not only through material rewards, politics, and ideology, but also through influence over everyday culture and social relationships. Via these means people may be convinced that consent is in their interest.[36]

We have seen here how two-party hegemony at the local level may be sustained through superior community connections. The campaign cases in this study illustrate how critical a role these social bonds may play in the defeat and aggregate marginalization of minor party candidates. Essentially, the typically stronger community connections of major party candidates often may convince most voters that these candidates are better able to understand, represent, and help them than usually less well-connected minor party candidates. In other words, much of the reason that progressive third party candidates do not win more seats for state legislature seems to be that voters do not fully trust them personally and actively reject them in favor of more individually trusted major party opponents. This voluntary individual discrimination contrasts with the mandatory institutional exclusion more prevalent at higher levels (via the combination of winner-take-all elections, strong barriers to ballot and media access, and the need for huge amounts of campaign money). Because local voting decisions are mediated much more by direct, shared daily experience than by information from large institutions, control of local election outcomes by major parties requires a strong community connection by its candidates. Also, the fact that the political stakes are much lower at the local level enables the major parties to put more stress on dominating via social influence than through overt institutional discrimination.

The observation above suggests that progressive third parties are unlikely to win state legislative races more often unless they can build more local counter-hegemony—by increasing their number of candidates and potential candidates with strong community connections. Obviously, trying to recruit locally well-connected members and sympathizers to be candidates would have to be a top priority. However, in order to make running with a left-wing minor party appealing to such typically politically prudent individuals, it first might be necessary to try to win municipal races in their districts. This would demonstrate to them the party's local electoral viability. Of course, strong community connections also may be a prerequisite for winning many of these races. However, it would appear from the candidate biographies in this chapter and elsewhere in this book that such a requirement is somewhat less uniform and stringent at the municipal level.[37] Last, encouraging existing party members to get more involved in influential activities within their communities, particularly in leadership roles, also might expand a left third party's pool of socially well-connected members—with the potential to become good state legislative (and municipal) candidates. Examples of what such activities might entail have been illustrated above in the description of winners' local doings. Some of these efforts would require a willingness to mesh with a local cultural "mainstream." Others that are more clearly political, issue-oriented, or (in certain communities) embedded in popular local "alternative" institutions might not.

Prospects

Despite progressive third parties' longstanding marginality and even absence in communities throughout much of the United States, there are a couple of reasons to believe that they are capable of starting to change that status via the steps outlined above—should they choose to do so. First, the very existence of the winners described here demonstrates that it is possible to attract well-connected, highly viable local candidates in these ways, even in some seemingly nonprogressive communities. The experience of Vermont Progressives in particular illustrates how the combination of municipal success (epitomized by the decades of city council and mayoral victories in Burlington), a willingness to routinely invite locally well-established people to run for state legislature, and an organizational culture of local involvement can be effective. The more Progressives apply this proven formula, the more likely they may be to expand their presence in the state legislature. This also applies to Greens in other states. They not only have the example of Progressives to follow but also their own somewhat similar model in John Eder and the Portland (Maine) Green Independent Party, which has been able to establish a significant presence in lower level government.

Second, some of what prevents progressive third parties from doing what is necessary to win more state legislative races may be a certain ignorance of what it really takes to win, but that presumably should not be hard to rectify. The fact that many of the viable losers in this study initially were surprised, disappointed, and sometimes even embittered by their loss appears to reflect lack of knowledge about the determinants of electoral competitiveness, especially the critical role of community connectedness. Over time, they generally came to understand what had happened more clearly. Yet, it should not be difficult for aspiring candidates to gain more insight about their true prospects *before* the decision to launch their campaign is made. Having to repeatedly recreate this awareness one campaign at a time seems unnecessary if not wasteful. Any state progressive third party organization with a coherent electoral planning committee and some basic institutional memory easily should be able to access and disseminate this knowledge, as well as consistently use it to recruit, screen, and develop more competitive candidates. This could facilitate the concentration of limited time and resources either on those locally well-connected candidates who truly are able to win or on the creation of the conditions for such candidates to emerge in the future.

Still, just because progressive third parties are capable of focusing on identifying, developing, and otherwise supporting more well-connected and viable statehouse candidates, it does not necessarily mean that they are willing to do so. Many Green Party activists do not seem to mind devoting themselves to continually running unwinnable yet heroic-feeling campaigns (including those in which the candidate seems unlikely to even make a "good showing"). These efforts supposedly function to educate voters, shift public discourse, recruit new members, form new local chapters, and ultimately build a base for future, stronger campaigns. Of course, it is not clear how often and to what extent this actually happens. Nor is it evident that the predominant enduring result is not activist burnout and reinforcement of the debilitating public perception that progressive third parties cannot win. Arguably, only one of the losing (and relatively less well-connected) campaigns studied here may have resulted in a heightened capability for victory in a later election.[38] For the sake of future electoral competitiveness, it would appear that the enthusiasm and solidarity that candidates generate among their strong supporters during campaigns normally is not a sufficient substitute for ongoing, deep connections to the larger community. Yet, the persistent lure of running almost any candidates for any offices, regardless of their true viability, may be potent enough to prevent some progressive third party activists from taking the need for community connectedness more seriously. On a deeper level, this quixotic reflex seems to be an understandable though counterproductive reaction to the marked difficulty of recruiting candidates—when a party lacks grassroots counter-hegemony.

In order to advance electorally, progressive third parties must be able to react more thoughtfully to their disempowerment. Not doing so may yield many more losing, ineffectual campaigns and possibly cause certain rare, winnable (locally well-connected) campaigns to go unrecognized and flop. The 2010 Green state representative campaign of Mark Miller in Pittsfield, Massachusetts, provides a particularly vivid illustration of the latter pitfall. Miller shocked himself and other Greens in the state by getting 45 percent of the vote and coming within 5 percent of defeating the longtime Democratic incumbent in a two-way race. What was so surprising about it was that Miller had barely campaigned and had raised only a few thousand dollars, roughly a quarter of what his opponent had raised. Miller didn't think he had a real chance of winning, and the Massachusetts chapter of the Green Party didn't focus on his race. At the time, the organization largely was engaged in promoting its 2010 gubernatorial candidate (who got 1.43 percent of the vote in the end).[39]

Why had Miller done so well, better than any Green state legislative candidate in Massachusetts to date? Community connections! He was a well-liked former reporter, editor, and co-owner of the city's major newspaper, the *Berk-shire Eagle*. Miller's family had owned and operated the paper for decades up until the mid-1990s, making "Miller" something of a household name in the city. Locally, Mark Miller himself had become widely admired for his integrity. One of his few key campaign volunteers, who had interacted extensively with Pittsfield voters, bluntly stated that they didn't care what Miller's party affiliation was. This activist observed that it didn't matter that Miller actually represented the "Green-Rainbow Party," the Massachusetts Greens' odd-sounding name since their 2002 fusion with the African American based Rainbow Coalition Party in the state. The volunteer explained further that Miller was so well known and well respected in Pittsfield that people there would have voted for him "even if he belonged to the Polka Dot Party."[40]

If Miller and the Greens in Massachusetts had known that community con-nections could make such a difference, they may have taken the race much more seriously and done things that could have enabled Miller to win. Thus, Greens may have missed a historic opportunity for a first-time breakthrough into the Massachusetts state legislature, an event that could have been a critical catalyst for the growth and success of the Green Party in the state and possibly elsewhere.[41]

However, in Massachusetts and across the United States, progressive third par-ties can choose to learn from their frequent election losses, in addition to their rare, stunning wins. The lesson about the importance of community connec-tions is something that they must absorb well in order to mount a more effective democratic challenge to the hegemonic duopoly. Any partisan struggle to build government that, in Lincoln's words, is really "by the people" and "for the people" cannot succeed unless it is joined by candidates who are widely perceived to be "of the people."

Notes

1 See Introduction, note 6. This number pertains to state legislators who are fundamen-tally associated with a progressive third party. It does not include those who receive some backing from such a party yet have a core affinity only for a major party. For instance, it excludes politicians who are commonly perceived and identified solely as Democrats, even if they are supported or endorsed by a third party of the left.
2 Berkman, "State Legislators in Congress"; Manning, "Membership of the 113th Con-gress," 2–4; and Karch, "States as Policy Testing Grounds."
3 See Introduction, note 17 and note 20.
4 For example, see Herrnson, "Two-Party Dominance," 16–17; and Gillespie, *Challengers to Duopoly*, 19.
5 See Introduction, note 14.
6 See Introduction, note 17 and note 20. All of the works cited highlight one or more structural obstacles to a greater or lesser extent.

7 Weigel, "Signing Your Way onto the Ballot"; Kasniunas and Shea, *Campaign Rules;* and National Institute on Money in State Politics, "Political Contribution Logarithmic Scatterplot Profile."

8 Sifry, *Spoiling for a Fight*, 6; Winger, "No Dem-Rep Contest in 40%"; and Winger, "Legislative Candidates on the Ballot."

9 Collet, "Taking the Abnormal Route"; and Francia and Herrnson, "Running against the Odds," 83–85. In the same piece, Francia and Herrnson also spotlight other internal disadvantages of minor party campaigns (pertaining to finances, budget, organization, and strategy), but these all largely seem to be effects of major external constraints.

10 Glaser and Strauss, *The Discovery of Grounded Theory*, 21–24. Analytic generalizations are qualitative claims about the underlying *form and dynamics* of aspects of social life. For the sake of analytic generalizations, a sample need not be large enough to be representative—only varied enough to illustrate however many dimensions are critical to the subject matter and research question.

11 Green Party of the United States, "Election Database." These five victories include Audie Boch (state assembly, Oakland, CA, 1999), John Eder (state representative, Portland, ME, 2002 and 2004), Richard Carroll (state representative, North Little Rock, AR, 2008), and Fredrick Smith (state representative, West Memphis, AR, 2012). Not included are independent representatives who may associate with the Greens but are not officially endorsed or nominated by them. The Eder case is discussed later in this chapter and in considerable depth in Chapter 3. Boch, Carroll, and Smith all benefited critically from having opponents who were severely tainted or effectively disqualified by serious scandals. Within months of being elected, Boch and Carroll switched their party affiliations to independent and Democrat, respectively. Both were defeated in the next election. In 2014 Smith sought reelection as a Democrat by running in the Democratic primary. He lost.

12 Vermont Progressive Party, "A Legacy of Progressive Leadership"; and Vermont Progressive Party, "Vermont Progressive Party Makes Gains."

13 Sure losers appear to be very common among third party candidates. See Collet, "Taking the Abnormal Route"; and Francia and Herrnson, "Running against the Odds."

14 Green Party of the United States, "Election Database"; and Vermont Progressive Party, "A Legacy of Progressive Leadership."

15 With respect to racial-ethnic composition, some of my case districts were rather homogeneous and others were fairly heterogeneous.

16 Rihoux and Ragin, eds., *Configurational Comparative Methods*; and Schutt, *Investigating the Social World*, 343–44. The qualitative comparative method essentially entails explaining causality by first, determining which configuration of factors across divergent cases consistently are present when a particular outcome occurs, and second, using qualitative data from within those cases to interpret why this might be so. It is a useful way of assessing causality under the following constraints: when the number of cases under consideration is too small for a valid statistical analysis; when the presence of multiple factors that potentially could shape the outcome under consideration might make a coherent understanding of the causal process difficult; and when it could be important to distinguish conditions that are *necessary* for an outcome from those that are *sufficient*. Analyzing why my 17 campaign cases turned out as they did presented all of these challenges.

17 Peter Francia and Paul Herrnson find that insufficient campaign organization, defined as a lack of paid professionals among campaign staff, is a key obstacle to the success of minor party candidates for state legislature. See Francia and Herrnson, "Running

against the Odds," 92–93. However, none of the winners in my sample had paid professional campaign staff, while three of the viable losers did.

18 Sandy Haas also won in a rural district (in the central Green Mountains), but it included what seemed to be a fairly even mixture of ideological conservatives and progressives.

19 Burke noted that Republicans, who rarely run a candidate in Brattleboro, were not known to have considered running someone against her.

20 In Potak's case, it would appear that she nearly transcended her "outsider" label and almost won in the prior election in 2006 because her "insider" main opponent didn't take her seriously enough. He didn't make this mistake again in 2008, Potak's losing race studied here. It would seem that for certain municipal races, such as those won by Szilva, Chen, and Meiklejohn, the "outsider" label is not as salient as it is for statehouse races. This may be due to the fact that the former races can be less competitive—since in some cases more seats may be available, the district may be smaller, or the pay for the seat may be lower than for state representative races in the same area.

21 The extent of the Republican's connection with the district may have been even more apparent in his 2010 two-way rematch with Weed, which he won again (narrowly), despite having been convicted of driving drunk only months before the election!

22 Cohen, "Jill Stein Survey Results and Analysis."

23 Channel 17 Town Meeting Television, "Burlington House Candidate Forums."

24 Of course, the importance of having broad community connections in many lower level races is fostered by winner-take-all election rules that push candidates to appeal to majorities or pluralities of voters in their districts. But this does not mean that candidates' lack of community connections in general is a primarily external problem.

25 See Scott, *How to Go into Politics*, 36; and Moncrief, Squire, and Jewell, *Who Runs for the Legislature?*, 119–20.

26 Collet, "Taking the Abnormal Route," 108.

27 National Conference of State Legislatures, "2010 Constituents Per State Legislative District"; Gray, "The Socioeconomic and Political Context of the States," 20–22; Jewell and Morehouse, *Political Parties and Elections*, 208–209, 216; and National Institute on Money in State Politics, "Political Contribution Logarithmic Scatterplot Profile."

28 U.S. Department of Labor, "Union Members Summary"; and U.S. Department of Labor, "Table 5. Union Affiliation by State."

29 Chinni and Gimpel, *Our Patchwork Nation*, 25–31, 65–72.

30 Gray, "The Socioeconomic and Political Context of the States," 2–5, 23–24.

31 See notes 27–30.

32 Palmer, "The Northeast," 34.

33 Vermont Progressive Party, "A Legacy of Progressive Leadership."

34 Green Party of the United States, "Election Database." See note 11.

35 This statement is based on the author's own participation in the Green Party for more than a decade and a half.

36 Gramsci, *Selections from the Prison Notebooks*; and Artz and Murphy, *Cultural Hegemony in the United States*, 1–46, 246–55.

37 See note 20.

38 In 2008, Progressive (and non-native Vermonter) Cindy Weed lost by a 10 percent margin to a Republican (and lifelong district resident) in the three-way northwestern Vermont race studied here. She lost to him again in 2010, by about 2 percentage points, but then she defeated him in 2012 by nearly an 8-point margin. It may be that Weed's campaign in 2008 initially helped set the stage for the 2012 triumph. However,

the lack of a Democrat in the post-2008 races and especially the Republican's 2010 pre-election conviction for drunk driving (which likely weakened his connection to the community) may have helped make Weed more competitive than she would have been otherwise. Of course, in 2014, Weed as the incumbent lost by nearly 10 percentage points in a hard fought two-way race against another Republican and lifelong district resident. Thus, Weed's longer story still may underscore the importance of community connections.

39 Martin, "A Tale of Two Campaigns"; and Mark Miller and members of his campaign, in discussion with the author, January 2011.

40 See note 39.

41 Luckily for the Greens, Miller's victorious opponent resigned several months after Election Day, giving Miller a chance to run again in a four-way special election in October 2011. This time, Miller, having realized that he could win, campaigned harder. Yet, it still was not hard enough, according to him and his campaign manager (in discussion with the author, November 2011). Miller lost the race to another Democrat by a 3 percent margin.

Bibliography

Amato, Theresa. *Grand Illusion: The Myth of Voter Choice in a Two-Party Tyranny*. New York: New Press, 2009.

Artz, Lee, and Bren Ortega Murphy. *Cultural Hegemony in the United States*. Thousand Oaks, CA: Sage, 2000.

Berkman, Michael B. "State Legislators in Congress: Strategies Politicians, Professional Legislatures and the Party Nexus." *American Journal of Political Science* 38, no. 4 (1994): 1025–55.

Bouricius, Terry. *Building Progressive Politics: The Vermont Story*. Madison, WI: Center for a New Democracy, 1993.

Channel 17 Town Meeting Television. "Burlington House Candidate Forums (3–1, 3–3)." CCTV, October 9, 2006. www.cctv.org/watch-tv/programs/burlington-house-candidate-forums-3–1–3–3.

Chinni, Dante, and James Gimpel. *Our Patchwork Nation: The Surprising Truth about the "Real America."* New York: Gotham Books, 2010.

Cohen, Dan. "Jill Stein Survey Results and Analysis." Unpublished report, last modified February 17, 2004.

Collet, Christian. "Taking the Abnormal Route: Backgrounds, Beliefs and Political Activities of Minor Party Candidates." In *Multiparty Politics in America*. Edited by Paul S. Herrnson and John C. Green, 103–24. Lanham, MD: Rowman and Littlefield, 1997.

Francia, Peter L., and Paul S. Herrnson. "Running against the Odds: Minor-Party Campaigns in Congressional and State Legislative Elections." In *Multiparty Politics in America: Prospect and Performance*, 2nd ed. Edited by Peter L. Francia and Paul S. Herrnson, 79–124. Lanham, MD: Rowman and Littlefield, 2002.

Gillespie, David J. *Challengers to Duopoly: Why Third Parties Matter in American Two-Party Politics*. Columbia: University of South Carolina Press, 2012.

Glaser, Barney and Anselm Strauss. *The Discovery of Grounded Theory*. Chicago: Adeline, 1967.

Gramsci, Antonio. *Selections from the Prison Notebooks of Antonio Gramsci*. Edited and translated by Q. Hoare and G. N. Smith. New York: International Publishers, 1971.

Gray, Virginia. "The Socioeconomic and Political Context of the States." In *Politics in the American States: A Comparative Analysis*, 9th ed. Edited by Virginia Gray and Russell Hanson, 1–29. Washington, DC: CQ Press, 2008.

Green Party of the United States. "Election Database." Accessed February 19, 2015. www.gp.org/elections/candidates/index.php.

Herrnson, Paul S. "Two-Party Dominance and Minor-Party Forays in American Politics." In *Multiparty Politics in America: Prospect and Performance*, 2nd ed. Edited by Peter L. Francia and Paul S. Herrnson, 9–29. Lanham, MD: Rowman and Littlefield, 2002.

Jewell, Malcolm E., and Sarah M. Morehouse. *Political Parties and Elections in the American States*, 4th ed. Washington, DC: CQ Press, 2001.

Karch, Andrew. "States as Policy Testing Grounds." In *Political Encyclopedia of U.S. States and Regions*. Edited by Donald P. Haider-Markel, 23–29. Washington, DC: CQ Press, 2009.

Kasniunas, Nina, and Daniel M. Shea. *Campaign Rules: A 50-State Guide to Campaigns and Elections in America*. Lanham, MD: Rowman and Littlefield, 2010.

Manning, Jennifer E. "Membership of the 113th Congress: A Profile." Congressional Research Service. Last modified November 24, 2014. https://fas.org/sgp/crs/misc/R42964.pdf.

Martin, Jonathan H. "A Tale of Two Campaigns: 2010 Massachusetts Green-Rainbow Party State House Campaigns." Unpublished report, last modified January 11, 2011.

Moncrief, Gary F., Peverill Squire, and Malcolm Jewell. *Who Runs for the Legislature?* Upper Saddle River, NJ: Prentice Hall, 2001.

National Conference of State Legislatures. "2010 Constituents Per State Legislative District." Accessed February 19, 2015. www.ncsl.org/legislatures-elections/legislatures/2010-constituents-per-state-legislative-district.aspx.

National Institute on Money in State Politics. "Political Contribution Logarithmic Scatterplot Profile." Last modified July 12, 2014. http://classic.followthemoney.org/database/graphs/meta/meta.phtml.

Palmer, Kenneth T. "The Northeast." In *Political Encyclopedia of U.S. States and Regions*. Edited by Donald P. Haider-Markel, 23–29. Washington, DC: CQ Press, 2009.

Reynolds, David. *Democracy Unbound: Progressive Challenges to the Two Party System*. Boston: South End Press, 1997.

Rihoux, Benoit, and Charles C. Ragin, eds. *Configurational Comparative Methods: Qualitative Comparative Analysis (QCA) and Related Techniques*. London and Thousand Oaks, CA: Sage, 2008.

Schutt, Russell K. *Investigating the Social World: The Practice and Process of Research*, 7th ed. Thousand Oaks, CA: Sage, 2012.

Scott, Hugh D., Jr. *How to Go into Politics*. New York: John Day, 1949.

Sifry, Micah. *Spoiling for a Fight: Third Party Politics in America*. New York: Routledge, 2002.

U.S. Department of Labor–Bureau of Labor Statistics. "Table 5. Union Affiliation of Employed Wage and Salary Workers by State." Last modified January 23, 2015. http://stats.bls.gov/news.release/union2.t05.htm.

———. "Union Members Summary." Last modified January 23, 2015. http://stats.bls.gov/news.release/union2.nr0.htm.

Vermont Progressive Party. "A Legacy of Progressive Leadership." Accessed February 19, 2015. www.progressiveparty.org/organize/legacy.

————. "Vermont Progressive Party Makes Gains Despite National, Statewide Political Climate." VTDigger.org. Last modified November 10, 2014. http://vtdigger.org/2014/11/12/vermont-progressive-party-makes-modest-gains-despite-national-statewide-political-climate/.

Weigel, David. "Signing Your Way onto the Ballot." *Campaigns and Elections* 23, no. 10 (2002): 34–39.

Winger, Richard. "Legislative Candidates on the Ballot: Dems, Reps Fail to Run in Many Legislative Races." *Ballot Access News*, October 1, 2014. www.ballot-access.org/2014/10/october-2014-ballot-access-news-print-edition/.

————. "No Dem-Rep Contest in 40% of State Legislative Races." *Ballot Access News*, November 1, 2012. www.ballot-access.org/2012/11/november-2012-ballot-access-news-print-edition/.

6

BEYOND THE "SPOILER" MYTH

Exploring the Real Lessons of the Nader Campaigns for Progressive Politics

Theresa Amato

Ralph Nader. His name invariably provokes reaction—both positive and negative. Long heralded for his five decades of daily advocacy for consumers, workers, voters, taxpayers, and citizens, he is considered among the most influential Americans of all time.[1] His work has yielded several major pieces of federal legislation, dozens of public interest organizations, and thousands of public interest advocates.

Yet there are some who only know Nader for one part of his activism—his campaigns for president of the United States, particularly that in 2000 and to a lesser extent, those in 2004 and 2008.[2] Many Americans, including some admirers, supporters, and allies, view his electoral forays with utter disdain.[3] These divergent reactions result mainly from the debate over whether Nader's candidacy in the 2000 presidential election "caused" Texas Republican governor George W. Bush's electoral victory. The "spoiler" claim is that by running, Nader as a progressive "took votes away" from Democratic vice president Al Gore. Allegedly, this "caused" Gore to lose the razor-thin close election in Florida and tipped the election overall to Bush.[4] This claim is used not only to discredit Nader but also the progressive third party movement as a whole.[5]

In this chapter I contend that the "spoiler" argument is both limiting and limited. The anti-democratic implications of this position will be exposed. Whether Nader's run really made a decisive difference in the 2000 election outcome will be questioned. Regardless of the answer, I maintain that the Nader 2000 campaign and the ensuing Nader presidential campaigns should embolden progressives to participate in independent and third party electoral politics rather than frighten them into submission to the two-party system. Toward that end, the hidden contributions of these campaigns to the strengthening of American democracy will be highlighted. In sum, I contend that the true legacy of the Nader campaigns is not the short-term "spoiling" of progressive politics, but rather, its long-term cultivation. The analysis begins by considering the problems that the "spoiler" argument poses for one of the most important American political ideals.

Spoiler Logic as Anti-Democratic

In the United States, third party and independent campaigns keep voter choice and alternative candidacies alive outside of the two major parties. Our antiquated electoral system features none of the modern attributes of those multiparty countries that maximize voter preferences with proportional representation, instant run-off voting, and the absence of an electoral college. Here in the United States, minor parties and independents must fight to preserve political diversity, remove barriers to entry, and strengthen electoral competition by providing alternative ballot choices and agendas. [6] Irrespective of the consequences of their participation in any one election, the preservation of the right for minor parties to participate in democratic elections serves a broader, greater good.

The alternative to voter choice (the flip side of candidate diversity) is a ballot whose contents are dictated exclusively by the state. There are few proponents of the spoiler argument who would take the extreme position that the state should only permit the two major parties to be on the ballot. So why do citizens who value freedom of speech and political association, as well as electoral choice and a more responsive politics, espouse a spoiler argument?

A system of candidates seeking to maximize their vote totals by trying to gain political support is what we call a competitive democracy. If one parses the spoiler argument, what is being said? That only some candidates are spoilers but others—the Democrats and Republicans alone—are non-spoilers presumptively entitled to a voter base. If all candidates must earn their votes, how can anyone be a spoiler? Are they all not competitors in an open election? Nader himself has repeatedly said that, which he stated in a June 2014 interview: "Everybody has an equal right to run for election. We're either all spoilers of one another, trying to get votes from one another, or none of us are spoilers. We're not second-class citizens because we're a Green Party candidate or a Libertarian candidate. . . . The brass of these two parties is they control the election machinery so they keep you off the ballot, harass you, file a lawsuit, delay you, exhaust you."[7] In this excerpt, Nader refers to the way in which minor party candidates are often suppressed outright by burdensome ballot access requirements and legal challenges to ballot status, or they are so drained from just trying to be heard (given their routine exclusion from debates), that their ability to campaign is severely limited.[8] The result is that many citizens who would like to vote for third party candidates cannot or will not do so (rightly sensing the unfavorable odds or uphill struggle facing candidacies outside of the two major parties).

Spoiler logic is rooted in an insidious assumption—that the two major parties own the votes and voters. Based on this assumption, including any third party or independent is invariably a zero-sum proposition. It is intruding on the major parties' playing field, rather than expanding the electorate by motivating the 50 percent of eligible voters who don't bother to vote in presidential elections and giving the ones who do greater choice. A party that is interested in gaining adherents and engaging the electorate for the public good would focus on how to attract those who are not part of a democratic contract (in which the represented choose their representatives). It would not simply claim all current voters and discourage others by eliminating or suppressing diverse ballot choices.

By promulgating the spoiler narrative, it's easier for the major parties to declare all the existing voters for themselves and anyone outside of the two parties as the interlopers, second-class citizens, or spoilers of "their" presumed vote totals in a two-horse horse race. If non-major party candidates are stopped from getting on the ballot or gaining voter support, then nonvoters may remain ignored and their nonparticipation may be taken for granted. Moreover, reluctant voters may have their choices limited to the "lesser evil" of the major party choices. If third parties and independents are allowed into the debate, introducing uncertainty into the electoral map and polling, then the major parties can face more variables and unknowns. This unpredictability, which introduces risk for the major parties, should be motive enough for minor parties and independent candidates to run—to provide a competitive democracy.

The tendency to denigrate and dismiss third party candidates as spoilers is part of a larger pattern of anti-democratic institutionalized discrimination against them, and against ordinary voters and disenchanted nonvoters. Support for or acceptance of this dynamic thereby contradicts core, widely held progressive principles. As discussed below, the factual basis of the spoiler argument itself is dubious at best, but assessing this part of the argument should not be the end of the analysis. Our flawed electoral process allows for that possible "spoiler" outcome, and it is a price we pay for open competition until we fix the electoral system. In the meantime, we must move beyond the endless spoiler obsession into concrete action to reform the structural problems, and into scholarship that addresses the substantive features of Nader's historic campaigns.

The Folly of the Spoiler Narrative

Some basic elements of the 2000 presidential election outcome set the stage for the development of the spoiler argument. The Nader campaign in 2000 received the greatest percentage of the vote for a progressive third party candidacy since "Fighting Bob" La Follette's Progressive Party run in the 1924 presidential election. Ralph Nader received 2,882,955 votes or 2.74 percent of the popular vote nationwide.[9] The Democratic nominee, Al Gore Jr., won the popular election. He received 50,999,897 votes nationwide, while the Republican nominee, George W. Bush, received 50,456,002.[10] The State of Florida through its Republican-dominated legislature, however, awarded its 25 electoral votes to Bush.[11] This allowed Bush to win the Electoral College vote with 271 total votes compared to 266 for Gore (with one elector abstaining), and it enabled him to claim the presidency of the United States. The final decision occurred after the following:

- a protracted examination of various ballots from different counties and overseas (sent by mail);
- expedited, fierce legal battles that resulted in the Florida Supreme Court ordering a manual recount; and
- split U.S. Supreme Court decisions that the recount should be stopped, an equal protection violation should be declared (because of the differing vote counting methods of the Florida counties), and no valid recount could be conducted (in sufficient time for the electors to participate in the state's federal electoral process).[12]

In Florida, 10 candidates were on the presidential ballot. The official vote totals before the blocked recount were 2,912,253 for Gore and 2,912,790 for Bush, a difference of 537 votes.[13] Ralph Nader and all seven other minor party candidates on the ballot received more than the 537 vote difference. Nader received 97,488 votes in Florida, the most votes not cast for either Bush or Gore, but by no means the only ones. For example, Libertarian Harry Browne received 16,415 votes and Reform Party candidate Pat Buchanan received 17,484.[14] However, no one suggests that these other candidates and their voters spoiled a clear-cut election for Bush or sent Florida into its electoral tailspin. Instead, the popular narrative became that Nader, who ran a 50-state campaign, was the spoiler who deprived Gore of victory in Florida.

The 2000 election was the first one since 1888 in which the winner of the popular vote did not win the electoral vote.[15] This, coupled with the narrow margin between the two major party candidates, set the stage for nonstop media attention. For 36 days while the vote counting, recounting, and legal wrangling ensued, political commentators and journalists attempted to assign blame for the fiasco.[16] Numerous critical variables contributed to the Florida outcome, including the following:

- the voter registration process, in which tens of thousands of voters' names were erroneously purged as felons or ineligible ex-felons by order of Secretary of State Katherine Harris (who, as the state chair for the Bush election campaign, served in a dual and thus arguably partisan capacity);[17]
- anecdotal reports of a variety of electoral dirty tricks, such as modern-day voter suppression tactics (including intimidating voters and misinforming people of color about voter ID requirements) that dissuaded voters from going to or staying at the polls;[18]

- numerous instances of reported voting machinery dysfunctions that, for example, assigned negative vote totals to various candidates in Volusia County;[19]
- the ballot design (approved by the Democrats) that confused Palm Beach County Gore supporters so much so that thousands "over-voted" erroneously for both Gore and Reform Party candidate Pat Buchanan);[20]
- instructions to Duval County voters to vote on every page, even though the presidential list spread over two pages, thus generating thousands of spoiled "over-votes"; [21]
- failure to recount 1.25 million votes (based on optical scans);[22]
- difficulty in determining what votes in which counties and areas overseas would be recounted;[23] and
- differing standards on what to count as a "vote" when more than one choice was indicated—or when it was difficult to determine if a paper ballot with a punched in fragment called a "chad" constituted a fully formed or indicated "vote" (based on whether the chad was perceived to be dimpled or to be hanging by a certain number of corners).[24]

Other Florida-based factors had the potential to alter the outcome of the race. These included the substance and positions of the major party candidates on such local topics as the drama of kidnapped Cuban child Elian Gonzalez (after the Democratic U.S. attorney general Janet Reno ordered him returned to his father in Cuba); Gore's straddling on development issues in the Everglades (which may have cost him environmentally based votes); and various other sore spots concerning the implications of Gore's candidacy for Florida.[25] Also, the media possibly played a role in dampening voter turnout, as five major stations erroneously and prematurely went on air to discuss the election results in Florida while some polls were still open in the state.[26] Last, the Bush campaign, by hiring a variety of law firms, managed to tie up with conflicts of interest the business of several of the Florida law firms that could have provided election law attorneys to the Gore campaign during the recount. Ethical rules would preclude the firms from representing both sides of the dispute.[27]

Despite the many election "irregularities" in Florida and the partisan taint of the decisions that settled the outcome there, the national Democratic leadership ultimately chose to accept the results. Gore conceded the election to Bush five days before the Electoral College cast their votes on December 18, 2000. When it was time for the U.S. Congress to officially tally the Electoral College vote, not one Democratic senator joined the 13 Democratic House members in their January 6, 2001, objection to the Electoral College report. This precluded a discussion that could only be had if a member of both houses of Congress requested it.[28]

Nationally, a host of factors affected the Electoral College race itself and Gore's loss. Gore, the sitting two-term incumbent vice president in relatively good economic times, would have won his home state of Tennessee or President Bill

Clinton's home state of Arkansas if he were a strong candidate. Either would have given him the presidency. He won neither, thereby largely indicating a fatally weak candidacy.[29] Likewise, a different Al Gore seemed to show up for each of the three presidential debates—confusing the voters and failing to meet expectations that the expert debater Gore would demolish the bumbling, barely verbal governor from Texas.

In some ways, the presence of Nader in the race and the tightness of the contest may have helped Gore. The Democrats and the media megaphone they had were also able to use Nader's candidacy nationally as a mobilization device. In the last weeks of the campaign, they sent various speakers around the country, including Florida, to caution their base against voting for Nader and to stimulate it to vote for Gore.[30] The election was broadcast as "too close to call" for days, and this may have mobilized even more voters for Gore than those 97,488 Florida voters who chose Nader.

Though Nader voters were commonly assumed to be likely "Gore voters," the relevant evidence suggests otherwise. Nader voters were in fact widely split across the political spectrum.[31] According to Al From, a prominent centrist Democrat of the Democratic Leadership Council, "The assertion that Nader's marginal vote hurt Gore is not borne out by polling data. When exit pollsters asked voters how they would have voted in a two-way race, Bush actually won by a point. That was better than he did with Nader in the race."[32] The Voter News Service exit polls showed that without Nader in the race, 47 percent of Nader voters would have voted for Gore, 21 percent would have voted for Bush, and the rest, 32 percent, would not have voted.[33] Nader cites a Stanley Greenberg poll showing that 38 percent of Nader's voters would have voted for Gore, 25 percent for Bush, and the rest would have stayed home.[34] Still other polls and analysis indicate that only about 60 percent or less of Nader's votes would have gone to Gore in a Gore-Bush matchup.[35]

Given the above complexities and a long list of possible contributors to the outcome of the 2000 election, only a simplistic analysis would attribute the result to Nader's candidacy.[36] According to its crude logic, if Nader is responsible for the closeness of the race between Bush and Gore, then so are all the other candidates. Patrick Buchanan and Harry Browne, who lean in a more conservative direction, would have to be seen as having "taken away" votes from Bush. More strikingly, George Bush would have to be viewed as having "taken away" registered Democrats who voted for him instead of Al Gore. Nader's vote, merely because he was a third party candidate with the most votes, received far more attention in the media's preset narrative of a two-party horse race than the fact that 13 percent of registered Florida Democrats voted for George W. Bush in Florida.[37] The 308,000 registered Democrats who voted for Bush—including a substantial number of union members and 191,000 self-described "liberals"—greatly outnumbered those who voted for Nader.[38] Finally, 52 percent of Florida's eligible voters either did not vote or voted for third-party candidates.[39] According to the spoiler logic, these nonvoters "took away" Bush *and* Gore's votes—by not showing up or by explicitly voting for someone other than the major party candidates.

A decade and a half after the 2000 election, and even with all this historically documented hindsight, many people continue to hold the Green Party presidential ticket responsible for the election of George W. Bush. Though Nader has not run since 2008, the Nader campaigns, in particular the 2000 campaign, still to this day ignite wildly passionate spoiler accusations. Some attribute the 2000 election result specifically to Ralph Nader's participation and campaigning in Florida. Others resent the fact that Nader highlighted the common failures of both major parties. He stated that "there are few major differences between the two parties," for which they are willing to fight (not the often misattributed "there is no difference between Mr. Gore and Mr. Bush").[40] Still others believe that third parties don't work and that electoral reformers should operate within the Democratic Party instead of squandering enormous energy and political capital on an electoral system that favors the major parties.[41] Others claim that Nader was a "Marxist," "Leninist," an agent or puppet of the Republicans, and so forth.[42] Some even blame Nader for Bush's win in 2004, when in no state was Nader's vote total the margin of difference between the two major candidates, and despite the fact that Bush beat Democratic senator John Kerry by more than 3 million popular votes.[43]

Wielding the Spoiler Club

During the 2000 election and its aftermath, prominent Democratic pundits promoted a vitriolic response that became a viral narrative to demonize Ralph Nader for causing Al Gore's defeat.[44] In the public eye, perhaps this helped to absolve Al Gore, the Democratic Party, and Democratic political operatives of their own failures in that election and the post-election outcome. Yet Al Gore himself actually did take personal responsibility for the fiasco.[45]

The "Nader as spoiler" story nonetheless continues to function as a widely told and potent cautionary tale to this day. It has been used, at least rhetorically, to degrade, deflate, and dissuade third parties and independents from running, especially in races anticipated to be close. Some forms of "Don't be a spoiler like Nader," "Remember 2000," or "Remember Ralph Nader" are repeatedly used as slogans when races are close. The intention is to scare progressives, idealists, activists, and others condescendingly deemed to be on the "lonely left." The purpose is to frighten them into not voting for whom they really support (based on their conscience) and into voting defensively instead (based on their fears).[46]

The spoiler blame heaped on Nader's participation in the 2000 election spilled over to both subsequent Nader campaigns in 2004 and 2008.[47] In 2004, part of the national Democratic strategy was to remove Nader from the ballot and drain the campaign of its resources by making it fend off ballot disputes and collect more signatures as insurance against those disputes. The Democratic Party and its allies thus brought 29 legal proceedings against the Nader 2004 campaign, including two dozen lawsuits.[48] Anti-spoiler attempts to keep Nader off the ballot were not limited to the Democratic Party. Even some forces within the national Green Party in 2004 (having been subject to endless recriminations for 2000) called for Nader to only run in states in which the race between the major party candidates was not perceived to be close.[49]

The vitriol arguably hit the high water mark in 2004 after Ralph Nader announced his candidacy. During the 2004 campaign, Scott Maddox, then the state chairman of the Florida Democratic Party, said that "Ralph Nader is the Benedict Arnold of Modern Democracy."[50] Terry McAuliffe, the Democratic National Committee Chairman in 2004 and known to be attentive to big corporate funders declared: "In state after state, Nader has become an extension of the Republican Party and their corporate backers."[51] In March 2004 columnist Robin Acarian wrote a literally damning *Los Angeles Times* piece, "Nader's Nadir," shortly after Nader's February 22 announcement to run. She claimed that, "To many Democrats, Nader represents an election-stealing evil just this side of the anti-Christ."[52] At least 14 websites were published during the 2004 election to dissuade Nader's run and discourage any voters from casting their ballots for him. They included statements by "repentant" Nader voters, prominent Greens, and former colleagues and supporters of Nader.[53]

With this hysteria as backdrop, is it any wonder that Nader's 2004 campaign office received tens of thousands of e-mails and letters urging him not to run? These communiqués stressed similar themes of abject fear, apocalyptic ruin of the country, and how "anybody but Bush" (including "Genghis Khan") was better than another four years of Bush.[54] Some were so vicious and aggressively threatening that I, as Nader's campaign manager, felt compelled to visit Homeland Security, call law enforcement to respond in some cases, and keep the headquarters of the campaign in a low profile office building with no identifiers.

The Nader campaign's petition circulators were also subjected to vicious and hostile treatment by people on the street—merely for exercising their First Amendment rights to collect signatures to get the Nader ticket on the ballot. The campaign even had to train people in nonviolence and de-escalation tactics to gather these signatures.

The treatment of Nader and his supporters by the Democratic Party and its allies was brutal. Even high-profile celebrity supporters, as well as Nader's 2000 vice presidential nominee, Winona LaDuke, were disgracefully shamed, shunned, asked to recant, or urged to endorse John Kerry, the Democratic nominee in 2004. Republicans have also used similar tactics to dissuade Tea Party or Libertarian candidates seeking to enter races outside of the party. (They've even used such methods against outsiders in Republican primaries, such as when they smeared

John McCain's upstart presidential candidacy in the South Carolina Republican primary of 2000).[55]

The major parties engage in these activities precisely to discourage minor parties or independents, and to stifle competition. The major parties want to diminish the chance that any competitors could build a significant following that could detract from their voter base. By keeping third parties and independents tied up in the minutiae of draconian ballot access procedures, by harassing or punishing prospective non-major party candidates, by removing them from the ballot as a potential political choice, or by dissuading or shaming their prospective supporters and voters—the major parties reduce the possibility that any challengers may gain a foothold that could threaten major party hegemony.

The major parties thus use this intimidation to preserve and solidify their electoral position. If minor parties and independents respond by succumbing to major party harassment and suppression—by refusing to rise to the challenge of running—the major parties win at the outset! They don't have to earn their votes against a true competitor; they just have to be "less worse" than the other major party that remains standing (in the form of a candidate) in the general election.

Demonizing rhetoric and the accompanying doomsday scenarios that major parties invoke are not only showered on the electoral swing states but also disseminated nationally—to reinforce the countrywide two-party exclusion of minor parties. When the national media reports that a presidential election will be "close," it often does not bother to explain that it is close in a national poll, but not in most of the states. In most states there usually is a landslide anticipated for one or the other major party candidate. Only a limited number of states generally are "in play," or will have an outcome that is not essentially predetermined. (The same is true for congressional races, a small fraction of which actually are competitive.)[56]

Goaded by the conservative rhetoric of the major parties and drama-seeking press alike, voters (who are all too unfamiliar with the intricacies of how the Electoral College works) become convinced that they cannot select the candidate of their choice. This happens even in states that almost certainly will be swept by the Republican or Democrat. Rarely does the media try to explain the structural causes of this predicament. They fail to note how our country is constrained by eighteenth-century electoral mechanisms. Such hindrances include the Electoral College; winner-take-all rules; and voting only on Tuesdays. They also entail the lack of proportional representation, instant runoff voting, same day or universal registration, and other means of avoiding the spoiler dynamic and expanding the participating electorate (employed in other countries).

To clear the field of all other viable competitors, the major parties deploy the classic rhetoric of reaction. They begin from a posture of entitlement, encouraging the horse-race scenario that the media is willing to magnify all too often. This allows them to avoid discussing the substantive platforms that the minor parties and independents bring to the table. Then they put non-major party candidates in a defensive position through the classic reactionary rhetoric of "futility" (that defeat is inevitable), "perversion" (that the pursuit of change will backfire), and "jeopardy" (that change is too risky to attempt right now). Such rhetoric was brilliantly explained in Albert O. Hirschman's classic book, *The Rhetoric of Reaction*. Hirschman argued that it is a typical conservative defense against progressive change in particular (used for example, to resist such transformations as the French Revolution, universal suffrage, and the construction of the social welfare state). [57] This rhetoric can be seen in the dominant discourse that protects the hegemony of the two major parties as follows: Futility discourse on third parties and independents includes statements such as "You will never win. Why bother?" Perversion discourse consists of comments such as "You will only hurt the party that has views with which you agree most" and "How will you feel if you help elect XYZ?" And jeopardy discourse is exemplified by the warnings "Not this year, when the stakes are so high," "This election is too close to have a third party," and then the related narcissistic appeal, "Think of what you will do to your legacy."

In this case, as in other historical exercises of political dominance, discourses of hopelessness and fear work, but not necessarily forever. Against all odds and bit by bit, those who are suppressed often do find a way to start breaking free of that which binds them. The hidden achievements of the Nader 2000 campaign, discussed below, are illustrative.

Accomplishments of a Progressive Candidacy Outside the Two-Party System

Regardless of whether or even if Nader is to "blame" for Gore's loss—a conclusion I equate to the notion that a startup in the garage with almost no financing is responsible for the relative market share of the technology behemoths Apple or Microsoft—it is time to reassess the Nader 2000 campaign. Now, 15 years later, it is time for academics, the media, and others to study the substantive results of the Nader 2000 candidacy beyond the spoiler narrative to which they have fallen prey. In 2000 and subsequently, what did Nader the candidate contribute to the national political discourse and landscape?

Wouldn't it be refreshing to posit whether without Ralph Nader's 2000 anti-establishment run, there would have been an antiwar Howard Dean frontrunner in 2004, or a population ready to "vote their consciences, not their fears" for Barack Obama in 2008, instead of the overtly prowar, all-but-coroneted front runner Hillary Clinton? Would there be a Bernie Sanders who at least pondered a 2016 presidential run outside the two parties with a "not for sale" campaign (stressing not being beholden to campaign contributors)—before he entered the Democratic primary with a similar message.? In the form of Senator Elizabeth Warren, would there be a firebrand populist roaring against corporations "cheating people" and possibly waiting in the electoral shadows? Would there have been an Occupy movement, fueled by the likeminded anticorporate group Adbusters; or the 2011 Madison, Wisconsin, State Capitol takeover and subsequent recall attempt of Republican governor Scott Walker? Would there have been all the other counterculture, culture-jamming campaigns of recent years (for example, by net neutrality advocates, defenders of civil liberties, and protectors of whistleblowers)?

Most of the ink spilled on the Nader campaigns has been critical of the outcome of the 2000 election, as well as the failures of Nader and the Green Party to build a sufficiently large and successful electoral alternative. It's time to study new and additional ramifications.[58] From the types of candidates running to the election reforms and political ideas percolating, I believe that the Nader campaigns' contributions have been grossly underanalyzed and underappreciated. For the major parties, the endless fascination with the spoiler narrative has operated conveniently to minimize further analysis of Nader's impact. I suggest at least three main areas to consider. They include the Nader campaigns' effect on the pursuit of electoral reforms, the expansion of electoral participation, and renewed attention to the problems of excessive corporate power. These changes have—at least in part—been propelled by the motivated adherents of Nader's campaigns, if not organized and led by the actual supporters of those campaigns. Since the Nader campaigns had a strong antiwar message from the beginning, their effect on subsequent antiwar efforts and candidacies is also worth considering—though the in-depth analysis required to illuminate that complex influence sufficiently is beyond the scope of this chapter.

Certainly, I do not contend that what has happened (or will happen) even in the three principal areas above is solely because of the Nader campaigns. There are myriad causes, events, and contributory effects. But the DNA of the Nader campaigns is embedded in many aspects of our politics today. For those trying to break through the two-party tyranny, the entrenched duopoly, there are more than enough potential outcomes in the past 15 years to study and expand upon. This not only pertains to purely electoral events, but also to the critical, epic battles between democratic rule and corporate greed (especially regarding whom our government favors in its taxation and spending policies).

Of course, I am not the person to undertake an objective study of these events, since I managed two of the Nader campaigns and participated in many subsequent, related civic and political endeavors. Indeed, I realize that it may even appear self-serving to call on others to reevaluate the legacy of the Nader campaigns. Yet the endless spoiler narrative has had its 15 years of fame, and objective studies of the substantive ramifications of these historic campaigns are long overdue.

The takeaway from the 2000 election is not just that the Supreme Court essentially had to intervene to pick a president—due to the complete incompetence of a broken election system that favored the two major parties and disenfranchised voters. The import of that election could also be the greatly underevaluated impact of the Nader campaign, one that actually may encourage the participation of minor parties and independents. The new narrative of the 2000 election could be how a small and energized startup of a campaign with a dynamic, iconic candidate—whose credible, progressive message appealed across the political spectrum and addressed long-ignored majoritarian concerns—could advance the struggle for a stronger democracy in the United States. This narrative might further note that the pivotal effect of the campaign was not on one election, but on the nature and focus of future elections, and the policies addressed between them. The starting point for the possible construction of such a new narrative can be found in several specific political ripples of the Nader 2000 campaign, including an intensifying movement to scrutinize and improve the electoral rules.

Electoral Reforms

In February 2001, in the immediate aftermath of the 2000 election, Ralph Nader and I attended the National Association of Secretaries of State meeting in Washington, DC. We went to present an agenda for electoral reform, designed to improve the process by which we choose our leaders. We proposed several steps, including:

1. End legalized bribery and support publicly financed campaigns.
2. Take back the public's airwaves and provide free time for ballot-qualified candidates.
3. Adopt same-day voter registration.
4. Work to open state and local debates to non-major party candidates.
5. Open up the two-party system by adopting proportional representation.
6. Gauge public opinion at the polls by initiating a national nonbinding advisory referendum.
7. Make every vote count by allowing instant runoff voting.[59]
8. Adopt a binding none-of-the-above option on every ballot line.
9. Demand strict enforcement of the Voting Rights Act with adequate sanctions.[60]
10. Accept a standardized national ballot.
11. Make elections officials nonpartisan (not bipartisan) on the local, state, and national levels.
12. Streamline and democratize the ballot-access process with uniform ballot access laws.
13. Count write-in ballots in all states.
14. Provide public disclosure of vote totals by precinct on the Internet.
15. Provide access to voter registration forms on the Internet.
16. Provide voter information pamphlets on-line, at polling places, and by mail to voters.
17. Provide nonpolitical assignment of ballot lines.[61]

With a few exceptions, these reforms are now highly visible on the public agenda and are routinely discussed. They are advanced not just by a few prominent voting reform groups, as was the case prior to 2000, but now by an entire cottage industry of electoral reform activists and academics inspired or reinvigorated by the 2000 election outcome.[62]

Also following the 2000 election results came the rapid growth in election law as a study and discipline in academia. After 2000, election law blogs, online weeklies, listservs, and more proliferated. For example, Daniel Lowenstein and Rick Hasen cofounded *The Election Law Journal*, and Rick Hasen started the *Election Law Blog*. Law schools started offering more election law classes and seminars. By 2014, at least 86 professors taught some form of election law—a phenomenon significantly attributable to the 2000 election.[63]

Beyond voting rights and some perennial voting topics, election laws themselves and the long overdue attention to improvement of the election process (that is, regarding who is eligible to vote, what counts as a vote, what circumstances trigger a recount, how we register and vote, the machinery of elections, and so forth) all received much greater attention in the aftermath of Florida. This was facilitated by the burgeoning scholarship and popular books about the 2000 election, and by the Carter-Ford and Carter-Baker Commissions' investigations of problems in the 2000 and 2004 elections, respectively.

The 2002 passage of the Help America Vote Act (HAVA) was another direct response to the 2000 election crisis—prompted by the subterfuge and extremely close outcome in Florida, and by the millions of votes lost nationwide through distortions of the election process.[64] HAVA was the official Washington response to the Florida fiasco. The tight Florida race had brought to light the decrepit, dysfunctional electoral machinery and processes that existed not only in Florida, but also nationwide—though the larger problem initially had escaped the national media glare while it was focused on the election outcome in Florida. Through HAVA, the federal government gave up to $3.9 billion over three years for the states to update their voter registration systems and voting machines (though compliance was not necessarily rigorous or uniform, and multiple extensions often were granted).[65] Voting machinery companies wined and dined low level public officials, who then spent money on their new machines—often comprised of multiple vote counting systems (some of dubious integrity).[66]

A voter fraud witch hunt also ensued, with numerous disputes erupting in several states concerning whether ID must be produced to vote, and what kind it should be. HAVA required the creation of provisional ballots to allow people to vote while their registration status is in contention. Such a situation could be the result of any number of factors, including improper purging of voter rolls; voter disqualification due to the failure to reregister (often due to a lack of awareness of the need in most states to register again after moving); or voter confusion about where to vote. How to properly validate mail-in votes and overseas mail-in votes received more belated attention. In sum, for every election after 2000, election officials and the media discussed and scrutinized the preparedness of our election systems.

Another fundamental outgrowth of the 2000 election outcome and its problems (as well as similar vote counting, election machinery, and voter registration troubles in the 2004 election) has been a greater awareness of minor parties and independents, and a more prominent discussion of ballot access and ballot reforms.[67] This shift has been fostered in part by more legal action on the part of non-major party candidates, and especially Ralph Nader. I documented such action in my book, *Grand Illusion: The Myth of Voter Choice in a Two-Party Tyranny*:

> In 2004 third-party and independent candidates for federal or state offices were involved in at least fifty-one lawsuits to get on the ballot in a record number of states. Thirty-nine of these cases involved our [the Nader] campaign; twenty-five were brought against us or our interests by the Democrats or parties in interest aligned with them in eighteen states . . . [and] our campaign filed fourteen challenges proactively, during the elections and after, in an effort to assert our rights to be candidates in the political process and to ensure better access for third-party or independent candidates.[68]

Nader sought redress for the harassment of his 2004 candidacy in the federal courts in the District of Columbia, in the Maine state courts, and before the Federal Election Commission—though the courts dismissed each case on procedural grounds, without allowing Nader a hearing on the merits of his claims and evidence. Yet, the Nader litigation (pertaining to 2000 and 2004) that involved multiple legal cases to open up the ballot and to spotlight unfair exclusions from debates had numerous positive effects. These included, for example:

- improved ballot access laws, which made it easier for candidates to get on and remain on the ballot as a choice for voters;[69]
- a revised interpretation of Maine's Strategic Lawsuit Against Public Participation law (SLAPP law), which made it more difficult to dismiss lawsuits against attempts to stifle electoral participation;[70]
- an apology from the Commission on Presidential Debates for its treatment of Nader outside of the first presidential debate in Boston in 2000—when agents of the commission threatened him with arrest for merely attempting to view the debate from a remote hall with a live television feed;[71]
- a major copyright/trademark decision that supported Nader's parody of MasterCard's "priceless campaign" for political speech purposes (a ruling in response to MasterCard's lawsuit against Nader for his 2000 campaign ad that contrasted him with candidates who chase campaign finance dollars);[72] and

- documentaries highlighting some of these cases, and generally more media attention on the relevant electoral processes and institutionalized barriers faced by third party and independent candidates.[73]

Expanded Electoral Participation

Nader's presidential runs have not only helped raise awareness of problems in the electoral system but also (along with parallel efforts) arguably have contributed to a shift in Americans' identity and behavior in a more democratic direction. The Nader campaigns may have fostered the increase in the proportion of the public that self-identifies as politically independent. A 2014 article by the Gallup Poll observes that "Americans are increasingly declaring independence from the political parties." It reports that "Forty-two percent of Americans, on average, identified as political independents in 2013, the highest Gallup has measured since it began conducting interviews by telephone 25 years ago."[74] Consider how Ralph Nader as part of a larger trend may have encouraged this development. In the span of less than two decades, from 1992 to 2008, first Ross Perot then Ralph Nader demonstrated how to run outside the two major parties and put previously ignored issues on the national agenda. Perot's independent and Reform Party presidential runs garnered major airtime, an invitation to the presidential debates, 19,741,065 votes (18.9 percent) in 1992, and 8,085,402 votes (8.4 percent) in 1996. Nader picked up the torch in 2000 with his own high-profile third party presidential campaign. These two candidates and others who ran outside of the two major parties in recent decades offered courage to those who wanted to introduce more choice in the electoral process. Any non-major party candidates who broke through the mainstream media firewall and escaped being completely cast as fringe challengers, as both Perot and Nader did, may have helped embolden others to self-identify outside of the two major parties.

Nader the candidate—whose reputation as the country's most accomplished consumer advocate enabled him to gain popular attention—inspired many outside the two parties. As Jason Netek wrote in the *Socialist Worker*, "Nader's bid in 2000, giving political expression to the broader global justice movement, had another element to the campaign that the modern left isn't very used to; it had widespread popular appeal."[75] In addition to elevating the Green Party of the United States from obscurity, Nader's campaign in 2000 helped recruit and energize thousands of Green Party members, many more of whom entered the electoral arena and won lower level offices in various parts of the country in subsequent years.[76] The Greens as of this writing have approximately 130 local officeholders.[77] Since Ralph Nader ran, they have continued to run candidates at the federal level, including presidential candidates. The Green who ran for president in 2012, Dr. Jill Stein, received federal matching funds, the first such Green candidate to do so since Nader in 2000.[78]

Nader has often said that "I start with the premise that the function of leadership is to produce more leaders, not more followers."[79] He styled his campaigns as "running with the people," not leading parades for spectators and onlookers. The campaign chant was not "Go, Ralph, Go!" but "Go, We, Go!"[80] He was keenly aware of and sensitive to party leaders' clearly expressed desire to not become known as the "Nader Party." Instead of dominating nascent efforts to organize and build the infrastructure of the Greens from inside the party, Nader continued to help support the Greens in a variety of ways from the outside. Nader was and always has been a registered independent, not a Green. Nonetheless, in his writings he touted the Green Party platform. He also attended or sent representatives (usually me) to their national and international meetings. In the aftermath of 2000, he supported the Greens at his own expense by appearing at multiple fundraisers for their party and candidates. He continues to do so.[81]

The New York State Greens wrote in 2004, "Ralph Nader has done more to grow the Green Party than any other individual in this country. He has run as our presidential candidate twice, and has helped the Green Party tremendously in raising funds in between campaigns. He has supported numerous local Green Party candidates, and has attracted media attention that the Green Party would not have received otherwise. Green Party enrollment surged after both of his presidential bids."[82] In their recitation of Nader's contributions to the party, the New York Greens noted that Ralph helped local Greens start 450 new local Green chapters across the country; achieved ballot lines for several states; supported state and local candidates; helped the party grow from an association of states into a national party; recruited and shared lists of tens of thousands of volunteers; and sparked the establishment of 900 Green chapters on college campuses.[83] With Nader running as their presidential candidate in 2000, and the Greens hosting the nominating convention for the Nader ticket, the Association of State Green Parties was then able to meet the criteria to apply successfully for and obtain recognition from the Federal Election Commission as the Green Party of the United States in August of 2001.[84]

Today, 30 years after its founding by a small group of concerned citizens in 1984, after the Nader 2000 campaign put the U.S. Green Party in the national spotlight and on the international map, the Green Party is the fourth largest party in the United States in terms of the extent of ballot access and party registration. For the 2012 presidential election, the Green Party had ballot lines in 36 states and Washington, DC. As of September 2014 for the midterm elections, it had statewide ballot access lines in 24 states.[85] By March 2014, the Green Party had 248,189 registered voters.[86]

Moreover, several influential progressives appear to have been inspired, fueled, or prepared by their participation in the Nader campaigns to make related political contributions. One example is Gayle McLaughlin, two-term Green Party mayor of Richmond, California (highlighted in Chapter 2 in this book).

In 2006 she was elected to be the first Green mayor of a large American city, with a population of more than 100,000. She credits her inspiration to run to Nader's 2000 campaign, where she was a volunteer.[87] Another instance is David Cobb, who became the 2004 Green Party nominee for president. He credits Ralph Nader for getting him back into politics after his prior disenchantment with the Democratic Party. Still another example is Kevin Zeese, an activist and public interest lawyer before serving as Nader's 2004 spokesperson. His work on many Nader position statements inspired him to become a third party U.S. Senate candidate (endorsed by the state's Green, Libertarian, and Populist parties) in Maryland in 2006. It also expanded the breadth of his activism. In the past decade, Zeese has assumed a variety of catalytic roles in a number of advocacy groups that challenge corporate power and complicit government behavior. A last illustration is Ben Manksi. In the 1990s, he already had been a skilled progressive organizer and in one local race, a Green candidate. In the years after he served as an organizer for the Nader 2000 campaign, his involvement in Green electoral politics intensified. He became the interim national director of the Campus Greens, cochaired the U.S. Greens, ran as a Green for state assembly in Wisconsin, and became the campaign manager for Jill Stein's 2012 Green presidential campaign.

Another legacy of the Nader runs has been to encourage the formation of organizations that challenge the duopoly to open up political debates and expand the democratic process. George Farah was a campaign staffer from the Nader 2000 effort and then the author of a groundbreaking book that exposes the Commission on Presidential Debates (which excluded Nader from the 2000 debate in a dramatic way).[88] He created the related nonprofit organization called Open Debates.[89] Christina Tobin, a 2004 and 2008 Nader campaign worker and a skilled ballot access defender from Illinois, started the Free and Equal Foundation. It supports greater voter education and more frequent debates with third party candidates. It uses the slogan of the Nader campaigns: "More Voices, More Choices."[90] A third individual, Oliver Hall, went to work for the Nader litigation efforts pertaining to the 2004 race (specifically concerning the retaliation faced by Nader for seeking ballot access).[91] Hall then started an organization called the Center for Competitive Democracy. It litigates cases on behalf of minor parties and independents across the political spectrum, in an attempt to reform draconian ballot access laws and other forms of unfair treatment.[92]

Of course, this representative sampling does not begin to address the broader tide of those who got turned onto politics by the Nader campaigns—and thereby became engaged in their communities, ran for office, went to law school to redress political injustices, or perhaps worked or simply voted for some alternative to the status quo. Illustrating the campaigns' important effect on the civic spirit are the words of one 21-year-old who wrote to Ralph: "When I was unhappy with all candidates from the two major parties, I did some research, and cannot begin to tell you how blown away I was. . . . You're the only person I can feel good about voting for."[93] This was one among many such positive, often heartwarming personal stories. When considering the full positive impact of the Nader campaigns, it is important to take into account not only the visible short-to-medium-term effects discussed here and above, but also the potential longer range contribution to far-reaching progressive goals—the subject to which we turn next.

The Marathon Message of the Nader Campaigns: Shifting Power

On October 28, 2000, the *New York Times* published a profile featuring my role as the national campaign manager of the Nader/LaDuke ticket.[94] A small exchange embedded in that article presages this essay 15 years later. It helps to place—as I tried to do for the reporter of the piece—my perspective on the Nader 2000 campaign efforts. (This view only was sharpened by the autocratic treatment we faced throughout the 2004 campaign). I told the interviewer, Somini Sengupta, who repeatedly asked me about the potential hazards of tipping the election to Bush, "You're coming at it [the 2000 campaign] from a horse race perspective," and "I'm looking at it as a marathon." I then said: "It's about building the civic movement so that fundamentally, there's a shift in power from corporations to citizens who want to take back their government. That's the real kernel of it, that shift in power."[95]

Essentially that was and is the thrust of Ralph Nader's life's work—subordinating corporate power to civic imperatives.[96] In his book *Crashing the Party*, Nader explains this most clearly, noting that, "The corporate quest for sovereignty over the sovereignty of the people is an affront to our Constitution and our democracy."[97] And that of course was the focus of his presidential campaigns. They emphasized the need for electoral and corporate reforms, and a realignment of national priorities. The latter entailed a shift from bloated defense budgets and imperial foreign policies to proactive domestic policies—including a living wage, better health and safety laws for consumers and workers, improved public infrastructures, Medicare for all, and a reduction of poverty and inequality, amongst other necessary changes.[98] By bringing these concerns to light on a national campaign stage three times, Nader helped carry and pass the torch of an invigorated civic empowerment and corporate reform message.

Following the 1999 Seattle protests against corporate globalization, Nader 2000 helped usher in the dominant progressive theme of the first decade of the twenty-first century by opposing excessive corporate power. Corporate America proved him prescient. Within two years of the 2000 election, the scandals of Enron, World Com, Global Crossing, and many others unfolded daily in the media; they brought attention to excessive CEO compensation and rampant corporate crime, fraud, and abuse. The Great Recession followed five years later with the burst of the housing bubble, record Wall Street bank bailouts, Main Street foreclosures, unemployment, underemployment, and consumer debt that ensued. Certain legislative reforms were implemented in response to these crises, though they were far from what was really needed to rein in corporations to the extent that Nader had suggested was necessary.

The 2010 Supreme Court decision that condoned virtually unlimited corporate contributions in *Citizens United* v. *Federal Election Commission* was followed in 2014 with the *McCutcheon* v. *FEC* decision lifting cumulative individual contribution limits. These actions cemented the urgency of the Nader campaigns' message that a properly functioning democracy is "not for sale." Among a growing public resistance to excessive money in politics, the comparable idea that "corporations are not people" continued to spread, along with the corollary that companies should not be afforded the right to purchase national elections. Numerous calls for amending the Constitution, involving all kinds of nonprofit educational and advocacy efforts, have taken up the cause that our elections should not be a commodity. Though other political candidates have carried this message, certainly the Nader campaigns headlined it and primed a generation of activists to embrace it.

Nader's campaigns helped usher in a prism for critiquing the above massive corporate failures in ethics and the shifting of resources and power from Main Street to Wall Street (all while the people on Main Street saw their retirements shrinking, jobs evaporating, and staggering credit card and student loan debt piling high). Is it any wonder after this decade that the Occupy movement was able to popularize the "1 percent versus the 99 percent" mantra? Destructive economic policies—with the prominent global backdrop of constant war and increasing governmental favoritism toward domestic and global corporate interests—have defined the zeitgeist thus far of the American twenty-first century. Nader's campaigns highlighted this condition long before it became the focus of a well-publicized cause. In so doing, they helped prepare the ground for the resistance that followed and, by extension, the resistance yet to come.

Conclusion

In the bitter February 2011 cold, I looked at the tens of thousands marching outside around the Wisconsin Capitol to support public employees' protests (against the proposed elimination of their unions by state government). I couldn't help but hear echoes of the Nader campaigns everywhere. Activists were camped in every cranny inside of the Wisconsin State Capitol's elegant rotunda, and famed guitarist Tom Morello was rocking the rafters and the outside streets with pro-labor songs. Signs hung from the statehouse banisters—declaring "We are the real Citizens United," "Walk like an Egyptian" (referring to the revolution in Egypt), "Power to the People," and "Stop Corporate Greed."

From Zuccotti Park's (Wall Street) occupation to the anti-eviction housing foreclosure campaigns, to the protests against the wars and new gas pipelines, to the movement to support the actions of Bradley Manning and Edward Snowden, to the net neutrality and single-payer health care campaigns of recent years, I see not only many of the principles of the Nader electoral platforms but also many of the principals instigating and contributing to the national discourse. Nader campaign supporters have advanced many of the frontiers of progressive advocacy. In so doing, they have significantly overlapped with the efforts of others in addition to Greens—including certain progressive independents, Democrats, and Socialists, and even some Libertarians and Tea Partiers (on issues of privacy, civil liberties, Internet freedom, empire-building, peace, and international trade).

Nader campaign DNA is present in many of these organizing efforts. Why have there been no serious studies of the political, economic, and social ramifications of Nader's campaigns and the many people he has drawn into politics and political activities? It indeed would be difficult to measure his impact on all those who have associated with or supported his campaigns. But to date there has only been silence, along with the limited (and limiting) two-party oriented focus on the spoiler argument.

Creating alternative candidacies, achieving ballot access, and presenting voters with different choices—the hard work of independent and minor party candidates—can help plant the seeds of progressive social change. In other times in the history of the United States, when we have had robust participation from parties across the political spectrum, third parties helped seed popular movements with critical ideas, farsighted activists, and important points of political leverage. They did so for the abolition movement, the suffrage movement, the populist movement, the labor movement, the civil rights movement, and other democratic movements. It is incumbent upon us today to plant more such seeds if we want to foster the long-term evolution of a healthy, well-nourished political "ecosystem."

Our political diversity is worthy of protection as a goal in itself, regardless of electoral or policy outcomes. It alone saves true voter choice—beyond the narrow range offered by the major parties—from extinction. The Nader campaigns, like others outside of the two-party system since the nineteenth century, have helped keep political diversity alive in our partisan monoculture.

Third parties and independents should take heart from the Nader campaigns. Instead of being repressed by reactionary spoilerist rhetoric (and backpedaling with apologies or timidly tiptoeing in repentance), they should go out and run, run, run for political office at all levels—to offer alternative ballot choices *and* build a better world. Someday scholarship and public opinion will catch up to Nader's visionary leadership. Meanwhile, those who follow his example will be on the progressive side of history.

Notes

1 Ross Douthat, "They Made America"; and Deseret News, "Life Lists Most Influential Americans."

2 Nader was on the New Hampshire ballot in 1992 as the "none of the above" candidate. In 1996 he lent his name to embryonic state Green Parties to help them get on the ballot. However, he did not raise or spend more than $5,000, which would have meant, under federal law, that he was a "candidate" for president that year. His 2000 campaign was his first serious effort to run for president. He did so as the Green Party nominee (on Green ballot lines) in states where the Greens had ballot access or could get it, and as an independent or other minor party candidate in those states where such designations would facilitate ballot access. In 2004 and 2008, Nader ran as an independent and on various minor party lines as needed to overcome burdensome ballot access laws.

3 *An Unreasonable Man*, directed by Mantel and Skrovan.

4 For example, see Cook, "The Next Nader Effect"; and Zuesse, "Ralph Nader Was Indispensable."

5 For example, see Zuesse, "Ralph Nader Was Indispensable"; and Domhoff, "Third Parties Don't Work."

6 Rosenstone, Behr, and Lazarus, *Third Parties*, 5.

7 Gillespie and Swain, "Ralph Nader Q & A."

8 Amato, "The Two Party Ballot Suppresses Third-Party Change"; and Scheuler, "The War on Libertarians and Independents."

9 Federal Election Commission, "2000 Official Presidential Results." Of course, we will never know about the write-in votes not properly counted or thrown away.

10 Ibid.

11 Brownstein, "GOP in Legislature Seeks Way." Seemingly, the leaders of the Florida legislature were intent on casting their state's electoral votes for Bush no matter what the Florida Supreme Court did.

12 *Bush v. Gore*, 531 U.S. 98 (2000).

13 Federal Election Commission, "2000 Official Presidential Results."

14 Ibid.

15 In 1888, Benjamin Harrison received 233 electoral votes to Grover Cleveland's 168 and thereby won the presidency, even though Cleveland had won the popular vote by more than 90,000 votes. Cleveland had been elected president in 1884, and he ran and won again in 1892. The anomaly of winning the popular vote but not the electoral vote has only happened four times in U.S. history—in 2000, 1888, 1876 (Rutherford Hayes versus Samuel Tilden), and 1824 (Andrew Jackson versus John Quincy Adams).

16 For example, see Toobin, *Too Close to Call*; Palast, *The Best Democracy*; and Tapper, *Down and Dirty*.

17 Palast, *The Best Democracy*, 11–12.

18 Brazile, *Cooking with Grease*, 279.

19 Information security specialist and writer Bruce Schneier observed, "In Volusia County, FL in 2000, an electronic voting machine gave Al Gore a final vote count of negative 16,022 votes." Schneier, "The Problem with Electronic Voting Machines."

20 Van Natta and Canedy, "The Palm Beach Ballot: Florida Democrats Say Ballot's Design Hurt Gore."

21 Tapper, *Down and Dirty*, chapter 1.

22 CNN, "Jeffrey Toobin: Election 2000 Anniversary."

23 Jackson, "Factcheck: The Florida Recount of 2000."

24 Ibid.

25 Van Natta and Filkins, "Contesting the Votes: Miami-Dade County: Mayor's Role a Riddle in Decision to Halt Recount."

26 Rendall, "Election Night Meltdown." The Voter News Service called the state of Florida for Gore 11 minutes before the polls were closed in the western Panhandle.

27 Jest, "Debunking Pathological Myths: Part 1"; "Debunking Pathological Myths: Part 2"; "Debunking Pathological Myths: Part 3"; and erpowers to Democratic Underground discussion list, June 25, 2013, www.democraticunderground.com/ 10023091107.

28 Al Gore conceded before the Electoral College report, thus signaling no desire to challenge the Electoral College outcome.

29 Federal Election Commission, "Distribution of Electoral Votes." Arkansas and Tennessee had 6 and 11 electoral votes, respectively, either of which would have given Gore the election in 2000 if he had won them.

30 Dao, "Democrats Hear Thunder."

31 Shinella, "Debunking the Myth"; and Allen and Brox, "Roots of Third Party Voting," 636.

32 From, "Building a New Progressive Majority."

33 Pomper, "The 2000 Presidential Election," 203, note 4.

34 Nader, *Crashing the Party*, 261.

35 Herron and Lewis, "Did Ralph Nader Spoil?," 24–25; Smith, "Poll Analysis: Nader Not Responsible"; and Fellmeth, "Nader Actually Helped Gore/Dems." Moreover, Nader had no intention of spoiling the election. Ralph Burden, who did a study of Nader's travel schedules and their implication for the vote in different states, concludes, "I find no evidence for a spoiler strategy. . . . Apparently, the Democrats' sour grapes were misplaced, as Nader appears to have been sincere about his motivations." "Ralph Nader's Campaign Strategy," 673.

36 Under the same zero-sum thinking, Reform Party candidate Pat Buchanan "cost" Bush the states of Iowa, New Mexico, Oregon, and Wisconsin. In these four states Buchanan's vote totals were greater than the number of votes by which candidate George Bush lost.

37 Wise, "No More Mister Fall Guy."

38 Ibid.

39 Ibid.; Jest, "Debunking Pathological Myths: Part 2"; and Hightower, "How Florida Democrats Torpedoed Gore."

40 Ralph Nader, letter to the editor, *New York Times*.

41 Domhoff, "Third Parties Don't Work."

42 Zuesse, "Ralph Nader Was Indispensable."

43 Suellentrop, "Blame Nader." The claim is that "undecideds" disproportionately broke for Nader rather than Kerry after deciding against Bush.

44 For example, see the statements by Todd Gitlin and Eric Alterman in the documentary *An Unreasonable Man*, directed by Mantel and Skrovan. Democratic strategist James Carville said, "Don't you think Ralph Nader has done enough damage to the country? I mean, he was probably singlehandedly responsible for electing George Bush." Stephanopoulus, "Carville on Possible Primary Challenge."

45 Jay, "Ralph Nader on Florida 2000." However, Joseph Lieberman, who himself ran as a third party candidate after failing to win his party nomination as an incumbent U.S.

senator, still blamed Nader as recently as June 2014. See McQuaid, "Lieberman Points to 2000."

46 For example, see zappadog0, "Why You Shouldn't 'Vote Your Conscience.'"

47 There were no ballot access litigation suits brought against Nader in 2008, but merely the thought of Nader participating in the election was enough to provoke an outsized emotional response.

48 Amato, *Grand Illusion*, 76, note 3.

49 Glick, "Green Party 'Safe States' Strategy."

50 Martin, "Florida Court Rejects Democratic Party Suit."

51 Ibid.

52 Acarian, "Nader's Nadir."

53 Pearce, "U.S. Nader Faces Vicious Smear Campaign." For example, these sites included NotNader.com; StopNader.com; TheNaderFactor.com; RepentantNaderVoter.com; Vote2StopBush.com; NoNader.org; ChangeIn04.com (aka "Greens for Kerry"); TheUnityCampaign.org (aka "Progressives UNITED to Beat Bush"); BlameItOn-Nader.com; SayNoToNader.com; No2Nader.com; RalphDontRun.net; DontVote-Ralph.net; and RalphNadir.com.

54 CNN Crossfire, "Transcripts: Interview with Ralph Nader."

55 Gooding, "The Trashing of John McCain."

56 Fair Vote, "Monopoly Politics 2014." Only 47 of 435 House seats for example are competitive—not firmly in the grasp of either major party and essentially up for grabs.

57 Hirschman, *The Rhetoric of Reaction.*

58 Gallagher, "Those Still Going on about Ralph Nader."

59 Instant runoff voting is an electoral system in which voters rank the candidates by preference. If no candidate receives the majority of votes, the candidate with the least votes is eliminated and the votes are again counted, with the process repeating until a majority winner is obtained. The system can avoid vote splitting among closely preferred and similar candidates.

60 The Voting Rights Act of 1965 prohibits the government from abridging or denying any citizen of the United States the right to vote in any federal, state, or local election on the basis of race or color.

61 The purpose of nonpolitical assignment of ballot lines is to prohibit major parties in power and in control of the ballot design from always designating preferential ballot space placement for themselves. Most of the actions on this list were first proposed by the Appleseed Center for Electoral Reform and the Harvard Legislative Research Bureau, and set forth in the Model Act for the Democratization of Ballot Access. See Harvard Legislative Research Bureau, "A Model Act for the Democratization of Ballot Access."

62 Lind, "Tea Party Should Divorce the Republicans." In the aftermath of the 2000 election voting and vote-counting fiasco, our electoral system still suffers from technical failures, systemic defects, and the continued discrimination against minor party candidates.

63 Hasen, *Election Law Blog.*

64 CalTech/MIT Voting Technology Project, "What Is, What Could Be."

65 Amato, *Grand Illusion*, chapter 9.

66 Rapoport, "Beyond Voting Machines."

67 For example, see Commission on Federal Election Reform, *Building Confidence in U.S. Elections.* It discusses the strengths and limitations of HAVA and work still required to achieve a properly functioning electoral system.

68 Amato, *Grand Illusion*, 76, notes 2–3.

69 See, for example, *Nader v. Blackwell*, 545 F.3d 459 (6th Cir. 2008), which struck down Ohio's requirement that circulators of candidates' petitions be state residents who are registered to vote. See also Amato, *Grand Illusion*, 76, note 3. Beyond the Nader 2004 campaign's nine state supreme court wins that resulted in greater ballot access for Nader's own candidacy, major victories in multiple jurisdictions were achieved that created improved ballot access for others. Even major party candidates benefited. For example, Representative John Conyers (D-MI), was able to secure a spot on the Democratic primary ballot for the Michigan primary in 2014 (even though his nominating petitions fell short of the requisite 1,000 signatures) because of *Nader v. Blackwell*. See Gray, "Conyers Camp Celebrates Judge's Ruling Putting Him on the Ballot"; and Sullivan, "Judge Puts Rep. John Conyers Back on the Ballot in Michigan."

70 *Nader v. Maine Democratic Party*, 41 A.3d 551 (Me. 2012).

71 See Farah, *No Debate*; and Open Debates, "Open Debates." Several lawsuits have been filed against the Commission on Presidential Debates both before and after the Nader campaigns by minor and independent candidates. Nader filed two relevant lawsuits—an unsuccessful one that challenged the commission's ability to host corporate-funded debates (based on an exception to the Federal Election Commission regulations), and another one launched against the commission for ejecting him from the grounds of the presidential debate at the University of Massachusetts in October 2000. The latter suit opened up the commission to scrutiny and obtained priceless information about how the two parties collude to exclude minor parties.

72 *MasterCard Int'l Inc. v. Nader 2000 Primary Comm. Inc.*, No. 00–6068-CV, 2004 WL 434404 (S.D.N.Y. Mar. 8, 2004).

73 At least three election documentaries have been produced explicitly discussing the Nader campaigns and its push for electoral reforms. See *100 Signatures*, directed by Greco and Greco; *An Unreasonable Man*, directed by Mantel and Skrovan; and *I'm Paying for This Microphone*, directed by Richmond.

74 Jones, "Record-High 42% Identify as Independents."

75 Netek, "Electoral Opening for the Left."

76 See Berg, "Greens in the USA," 250, 252; and Green Party of the United States, "All Candidates for Office."

77 Green Party of the United States, "Current Green Officeholders."

78 Winger, "Primary Season Matching $." During the 2012 election, Jill Stein received $333,331 in matching funds.

79 I have personally heard Ralph Nader say this often both on the campaign trail and elsewhere.

80 When audiences would chant "Go, Ralph, Go!" Nader would often turn the challenge onto them. "Go, We, Go!" he'd chant back.

81 See, for example, Metzger, "Nader Stumps for Funiciello, Hawkins."

82 Votenader.org, "Ralph Nader: Anti-Bush to the Core." Votenader.org is the website of the Nader presidential campaigns.

83 Ibid. For more on Nader's critical contribution to the Green Party's growth, see Berg, "Greens in the USA," 250, 252.

84 Green Party of the United States, "FEC Recognizes Green Party."

85 Winger, "2012 Presidential Ballot Status for President"; and Winger, "2014 Statewide Petitioning for Statewide Office."

86 Winger, "Libertarian Registration Up By 11%." These registration totals were calculated from individual state figures as of March 2014, except for the states of Connecticut, Massachusetts, and New York, for which the totals come from 2013. It should be noted that some states do not permit people to register as a Green Party member. Instead, they categorize non-major party registrants as "Independent" or some other nonpartisan label.

87 Nader et al., "Ralph Nader and the Greens."

88 See Farah, *No Debate*.

89 See Open Debates, "Open Debates."

90 Free and Equal, "About Free and Equal." Also, in 2010 Tobin ran for secretary of state in California as a Libertarian and came in fourth with 214,347 votes.

91 No court ever granted a hearing on the merits of the suits challenging the retaliation (instead dismissing them on procedural grounds). But Hall was responsible for changing the interpretation of the Maine SLAPP law statute through the litigation he brought to address the 2004 Democratic retaliatory onslaught against Nader's candidacy.

92 Center for Competitive Democracy, "About Us." I serve on the Center for Competitive Democracy's board of directors.

93 Letter from a college senior to Ralph Nader, undated but received in 2009 (after the 2008 presidential election). It urged Ralph Nader to run again for president in 2012.

94 Sengupta, "An Experienced Hand Leads Nader's Youthful Legions."

95 Ibid.

96 Nader, *Crashing the Party*.

97 Ibid, xxv.

98 Ibid, 319.

Bibliography

Acarian, Robin. "Nader's Nadir." *Los Angeles Times*, March 5, 2004.

Allen, Neal, and Brian J. Brox. "The Roots of Third Party Voting: The 2000 Nader Campaign in Historical Perspective." *Party Politics* 11, no. 5 (2005): 623–37.

Amato, Theresa. *Grand Illusion: The Myth of Voter Choice in a Two-Party Tyranny*. New York: New Press, 2009.

———. "The Two Party Ballot Suppresses Third-Party Change." *Harvard Law Record*, December 4, 2009. http://hlrecord.org/?p=10575.

Berg, John C. "Greens in the USA." In *Green Parties in Transition: The End of Grass-roots Democracy?* Edited by Gene E. Frankland, Paul Lucardie, and Benoit Rihoux, 245–56. Farnham, England: Ashgate, 2008.

Brazile, Donna. *Cooking with Grease: Stirring the Pots in American Politics*. New York: Simon & Schuster, 2004.

Brownstein, Ronald. "GOP in Legislature Seeks Way to Give Bush Electoral Votes, Politics: Florida's Republican Leaders, Outraged by State Supreme Court Ruling, Weigh Naming a Rival Set of Electors—Even if Gore Is Ahead in the Tally." *Los Angeles Times*, November 23, 2000. http://articles.latimes.com/2000/nov/23/news/mn-56410.

Burden, Barry C. "Ralph Nader's Campaign Strategy in the 2000 U.S. Presidential Election." *American Politics Research* 33, no. 5 (2005): 672–99.

Caltech/MIT Voting Technology Project. "What Is, What Could Be." Last modified July 1, 2001. http://vote.caltech.edu/content/voting-what-what-could-be.

Center for Competitive Democracy. "About Us." Accessed December 28, 2014. www.competitivedemocracy.org/about-us/.

CNN, "Jeffrey Toobin: Election 2000 Anniversary." CNN.com. Last modified November 7, 2001. http://edition.cnn.com/2001/COMMUNITY/11/07/toobin/index.html.

CNN Crossfire. "Transcripts: Interview with Ralph Nader." CNN.com. Last modified March 30, 2004. http://transcripts.cnn.com/TRANSCRIPTS/0403/30/cf.00.html.

Commission on Federal Election Reform. *Building Confidence in U.S. Elections: Report of the Commission on Federal Election Reform.* Washington, DC: Center for Democracy and Election Management, 2005.

Cook, Charlie. "The Next Nader Effect." *New York Times*, March 9, 2004. www.nytimes.com/2004/03/09/opinion/the-next-nader-effect.html.

Dao, James. "Democrats Hear Thunder on Left, and Try to Steal Some of Nader's." *New York Times*, October 25, 2000. www.nytimes.com/2000/10/25/us/2000-campaign-green-party-democrats-hear-thunder-left-try-steal-some-nader-s.html.

Deseret News. "Life Lists 20th Century's Most Influential Americans." Sept. 1, 1990. www.deseretnews.com/article/119956/LIFE-LISTS-20TH-CENTURYS-MOST-INFLUENTIAL-AMERICANS.html?pg=all.

Domhoff, William G. "Third Parties Don't Work: Why and How Egalitarians Should Transform the Democratic Party." Who Rules America.net. Accessed December 4, 2014. http://whorulesamerica.net/change/science_egalitarians.html.

Douthat, Ross. "They Made America: 100 Most Influential Americans." *Atlantic Online*, December 2006. Last accessed December 3, 2014. http://mail.google.com/mail/u/0/?hl=en&utm_source=en-et-more&utm_medium=et&utm_campaign=en&shva=1#search/jrichard/149e96e2d1d67dd7?projector=1.

Fair Vote. "Monopoly Politics 2014 and the Fair Voting Solution." Last modified November 7, 2013. www.fairvote.org/research-and-analysis/congressional-elections/monopoly-politics-2014-and-the-fair-voting-solution/.

Farah, George. *No Debate: How the Republican and Democratic Parties Secretly Control the Presidential Debates.* New York: Seven Stories Press, 2004.

Federal Election Commission. "Distribution of Electoral Votes." Last accessed December 3, 2014. www.fec.gov/pubrec/fe2000/elecvotemap.htm#search=distribution%20of%20electoral%20votes.

———. "2000 Official Presidential General Election Results." Last modified December 2001. www.fec.gov/pubrec/2000presgeresults.htm.

Fellmeth, Robert C. "Nader Actually Helped Gore/Dems." *Harvard Law Record*, March 24, 2003. Last accessed December 3, 2014, http://hlrecord.org/?p=10066.

Free and Equal. "About Free and Equal." Accessed December 29, 2014. www.freeandequal.org/about/.

From, Al. "Building a New Progressive Majority: How the Democrats Can Learn from 2000." *Blueprint Magazine*, January 24, 2001. Accessed December 3, 2014. www.dlc.org/ndol_cia014.html?kaid=86&subid=84&contentid=2919.

Gallagher, Tom. "Those Still Going on about Ralph Nader Electing Bush in 2000 Should Desist." *Los Angeles Review of Books*, January 10, 2014. http://lareviewofbooks.org/essay/still-going-ralph-nader-electing-bush-2000-desist.

Gillespie, Nick, and Jonathan Swain. "Ralph Nader Q&A: How Progressives and Libertarians Are Taking on Crony Capitalism and Corrupt Dems and Reps." *Reason.com*, June 11, 2014. http://reason.com/reasontv/2014/06/11/ralph-nader.

Glick, Ted. "A Green Party 'Safe States' Strategy." ZNet. Last modified July 1, 2003. http://archive.today/W3wh3.

Gooding, Richard. "The Trashing of John McCain." *Vanity Fair*, November 2004. www.vanityfair.com/politics/features/2004/11/mccain200411.

Gray, Kathleen. "Conyers Camp Celebrates Judge's Ruling Putting Him on the Ballot." *Detroit Free Press*, May 23, 2014. www.freep.com/article/20140523/NEWS01/305230097/John-Conyers-challenge-primary-ballot.

Green Party of the United States. "All Candidates for Office." Accessed November 23, 2014. http://gp.org/elections/candidates/index.php.

———. "Current Green Officeholders." Accessed November 1, 2014. http://www.gp.org/officeholders.

———. "Federal Election Commission Recognizes Green Party." Last modified November 8, 2001. http://www.wholeithaca.info/tcgp/2001/11/09-0539-Federal_Election_Commission_Recognizes_Green_Party.html.

Harvard Legislative Research Bureau. "A Model Act for the Democratization of Ballot Access." *Harvard Journal on Legislation* 36 (2) 1999: 451–478.

Hasen, Rick. *Election Law Blog*, July 1, 2014. http://electionlawblog.org/?p=62922&utm_source=feedburner&utm_medium=email&utm_campaign=Feed%3A+electionlawblog%2FuqCP+%28Election+Law%29.

Herron, Michael C., and Jeffrey B. Lewis. "Did Ralph Nader Spoil a Gore Presidency? A Ballot-Level Study of Green and Reform Party Voters in the 2000 Presidential Election." Working paper, April 24, 2006. www.sscnet.ucla.edu/polisci/faculty/lewis/pdf/greenreform9.pdf.

Hightower, Jim. "How Florida Democrats Torpedoed Gore: If the Vice President Had Locked Up His Party's Traditional Base in the Sunshine State, the Election Wouldn't Be Tied Up in the Courts." *Salon*, November 27, 2000. www.salon.com/2000/11/28/hightower/.

Hirschman, Albert O. *The Rhetoric of Reaction*. Cambridge: Harvard University Press, 1991.

I'm Paying for this Microphone: The Inside Story of America's Televised Presidential Debates. Directed by Christopher Richmond. MFA thesis, American University, 2012.

Jackson, Brooks. "Factcheck: The Florida Recount of 2000." Factcheck.org (A Project of the Annenberg Foundation). Last modified January 22, 2008. www.factcheck.org/2008/01/the-florida-recount-of-2000/.

Jay, John. "Ralph Nader on Florida 2000 and What to Do Next." *Truth-Out*, December 20, 2013. www.truth-out.org/news/item/20768-ralph-nader-on-florida-in-2000-and-what-to-do-next.

Jest. "Debunking Pathological Myths of the 2000 Election: Part 1—CNN Exit Polls Prove That Nader Did Not Cost Gore FL." Firedoglake.com. Last modified August 26, 2012. http://my.firedoglake.com/jest/2012/08/26/debunking-pathological-myths-of-the-2000-election-part-1-cnn-exit-polls-prove-that-nader-did-not-cost-gore-fl/.

———. "Debunking Pathological Myths of the 2000 Election: Part 2—Democrat Defections to Bush (Blue Dogs & Bush Democrats) Caused Gore to Lose FL." Firedoglake.com. Last modified August 27, 2012. http://my.firedoglake.com/jest/2012/08/27/debunking-pathological-myths-of-the-2000-election-part-2-democrat-defections-to-bush-blue-dogs-bush-democrats-caused-gore-to-lose-fl/.

———. "Debunking Pathological Myths of the 2000 Election: Part 3—Polling Data Proves That Nader Voters Did Not 'Switch Sides' During the Campaign." Firedoglake.com. Last modified August 29, 2012. http://my.firedoglake.com/jest/2012/08/29/

debunking-pathological-myths-of-the-2000-election-part-3-polling-data-proves-that-nader-voters-did-not-switch-sides-during-the-campaign/.

Jones, Jeffrey M. "Record-High 42% of Americans Identify as Independents." Gallup Politics. Last modified January 8, 2014. www.gallup.com/poll/166763/record-high-americans-identify-independents.aspx.

Lind, Michael. "Tea Party Should Divorce the Republicans: Why America Needs More Political Parties." *Salon*, July 2, 2014. www.salon.com/2014/07/02/tea_party_should_divorce_the_republicans_why_america_needs_more_political_parties/.

Martin, Patrick. "Florida Court Rejects Democratic Party Suit to Keep Nader Off the Ballot." World Socialist Web Site. September 20, 2004. www.wsws.org/en/articles/2004/09/nadr-s20.html.

McQuaid, Hugh. "Lieberman Points to 2000:Third Party Candidates Can Affect the Outcome of Elections." *CT News Junkie*, June 24, 2014. www.ctnewsjunkie.com/archives/entry/lieberman_points_to_2000_third_party_candidates_can_affect_the_outcome_of_e/.

Metzger, Amanda May. "Nader Stumps for Funiciello, Hawkins." *Poststar.com*, September 14, 2014. http://poststar.com/news/local/nader-stumps-for-funiciello-hawkins/article_ed7f68cc-3c72-11e4-b3f2-1f478eef6421.html.

Nader, Ralph. *Crashing the Party: Taking on the Corporate Government in an Age of Surrender*. New York: Dunne, 2002.

———. Letter to the editor. *New York Times*, August 12, 2000. www.nytimes.com/2000/08/12/opinion/l-nader-on-nader-627860.html.

Nader, Ralph, Gayle McLaughlin, Ross Mirkarimi, and Matt Gonzales. "Ralph Nader and the Greens: Progressive Politics After the Democrats' Election Victory." The A-Infos Radio Project. Podcast audio. December 28, 2006. www.radio4all.net/index.php/program/22014.

Netek, Jason. "Electoral Opening for the Left." *Socialist Worker.org*, December 16, 2013. http://socialistworker.org/2013/12/16/electoral-opening-for-the-left.

100 Signatures. Directed by Dean Greco and Nicole Greco. Flemington, NJ: Focus on the Good, LLC, 2013.

Open Debates. "Open Debates." Accessed December 4, 2014. opendebates.org.

Palast, Greg. *The Best Democracy Money Can Buy*. London: Pluto Press, 2002.

Pearce, Rohan. "U.S. Nader Faces Vicious Smear Campaign." *Green Left Weekly*, November 3, 2004. www.greenleft.org.au/node/31100.

Pomper, Gerald M. "The 2000 Presidential Election:Why Gore Lost." *Political Science Quarterly* 116, no. 2 (2001): 201–223.

Rapoport, Miles. "Beyond Voting Machines: HAVA and Real Election Reform." *Alternet.org*, July 29, 2003. www.alternet.org/story/16490/beyond_voting_machines%3A_hava_and_real_election_reform.

Rendall, Steve. "Election Night Meltdown: Media Monopoly Contributed to Exit-poll Errors." *Fairness and Accuracy in Reporting, Extra!* January 1, 2001. http://fair.org/extra-online-articles/election-night-meltdown/.

Rosenstone, Steven J., Roy L. Behr, and Edward H. Lazarus. *Third Parties in America*. 2nd ed. Princeton, NJ: Princeton University Press, 1996.

Scheuler, Jason. "The War on Libertarians and Independents." Breitbart.com. Last modified October 28, 2014. www.breitbart.com/Big-Government/2014/10/28/The-War-on-Libertarians-and-Independents.

Schneier, Bruce. "The Problem with Electronic Voting Machines." *Schneier on Security Blog*, November 10, 2004. www.schneier.com/blog/archives/2004/11/the_problem_wit.html.

Sengupta, Somini. "An Experienced Hand Leads Nader's Youthful Legions." *New York Times*, October 28, 2000.

Shinella, Anthony. "Debunking the Myth: Ralph Nader Didn't Cost Al Gore the Presidency in 2000." *Politizine.com* (blog). February 25, 2004. http://politizine.blogspot.com/2004/02/debunking-myth-ralph-nader-didnt-cost.html.

Smith, Sam. "Poll Analysis: Nader Not Responsible for Gore's Loss." *Progressive Review Undernews*, July 2002. http://prorev.com/green2000.html.

Stephanopoulus, George. "Carville on Possible Primary Challenge: Nader Has Done Enough Damage." *ABC News Politics Blog*, Sept. 20, 2011. http://abcnews.go.com/blogs/politics/2011/09/carville-on-possible-primary-challenge-nader-has-done-enough-damage/.

Suellentrop, Chris. "Blame Nader: The Undecideds Broke for the Other Challenger." *Slate*, November 3, 2004. www.slate.com/articles/news_and_politics/on_the_trail/2004/11/blame_nader.htm.

Sullivan, Sean. "Judge Puts Rep. John Conyers Back on the Ballot in Michigan." *Washington Post, Post Politics* (blog), May 23, 2014. www.washingtonpost.com/blogs/post-politics/wp/2014/05/23/michigan-rejects-rep-conyers-appeal-to-appear-on-the-ballot/.

Tapper, Jake. *Down and Dirty: The Plot to Steal the Presidency.* New York: Little, Brown, 2001.

Toobin, Jeffrey. *Too Close to Call: The Thirty-Six-Day Battle to Decide the 2000 Election.* New York: Random House, 2001.

An Unreasonable Man. Directed by Henriette Mantel and Steven Skrovan. La Cresenta, CA: Two Left Legs, LLC, 2006.

Van Natta, Don, Jr., and Dana Canedy. "The 2000 Elections: The Palm Beach Ballot: Florida Democrats Say Ballot's Design Hurt Gore." *New York Times*, November 9, 2000.

Van Natta, Don, Jr., and Dexter Filkins. "Contesting the Votes: Miami-Dade County: Mayor's Role a Riddle in Decision to Halt Recount." *New York Times*, December 1, 2000.

Votenader.org. "Ralph Nader: Anti-Bush to the Core, Bush Will Win Without These Issues Raised." Germantown for Nader. Accessed December 5, 2014. http://germantownnader.tripod.com/bkralphblk.pdf.

Winger, Richard. "Libertarian Registration Up By 11% Since 2012." *Ballot Access News*, April 2014.

———. "Primary Season Matching $." *Ballot Access News*, December 2012.

———. "2014 Statewide Petitioning for Statewide Office." *Ballot Access News*, September 2014.

———. "2012 Presidential Ballot Status for President." *Ballot Access News*, October 2012.

Wise, Tim. "No More Mister Fall Guy: Why Ralph Nader Is Not to Blame for 'President' Bush." Last modified November 9, 2000. www.timwise.org/2000/11/no-more-mister-fall-guy-why-ralph-nader-is-not-to-blame-for-president-bush/.

zappadog0. "Why You Shouldn't 'Vote Your Conscience': An Open Letter to the Lonely Left." *Daily Kos* (blog), October 30, 2012. www.dailykos.com/story/2012/10/30/1152687/-Why-You-Shouldn-t-Vote-Your-Conscience-An-open-letter-to-the-lonely-left#.

Zuesse, Eric. "Ralph Nader Was Indispensable to the Republican Party." *Huffington Post*, November 11, 2013. www.huffingtonpost.com/eric-zuesse/ralph-nader-was-indispens_b_4235065.html?view=screen.

7

THE U.S. GREENS IN PRESIDENTIAL ELECTIONS

Losing Their Mojo and Getting It Back*

Sayeed Iftekhar Ahmed

Generally, in Western democracies, left political parties have played a significant role in national politics by securing representation in federal electoral bodies, including the executive branch of government. Thus, such parties have acquired enough direct power or leverage to help create relatively strong welfare states.[1] However, in the United States, genuinely progressive parties have been much less successful in federal electoral politics. Uniquely, they have not become major parties at the national level capable of competing for control of the executive branch of government, though they have secured several third-place finishes in presidential elections. Even such minor successes at times have played an important part in pressuring the major parties to adopt progressive reforms (in order to keep the Left from advancing even further politically),[2] as noted elsewhere in this book. Furthermore, progressive third party presidential campaigns have been strong enough on occasion to facilitate or inspire a substantial wave of allied candidacies and party building at the grassroots level around the country.[3] The above significant achievements are suggestive of what could be accomplished if American left third parties were able to do better at the presidential level more consistently. Therefore, understanding why such parties haven't been more successful in recent presidential elections can help explain their general lack of political impact, as well as identify what they might do to become more politically effective.

The Green Party, which loosely was formed in the mid-1980s and then officially founded in several stages between 1991 and 2001, is one such progressive

* Originally published in a somewhat different form in *The Journal of Social Studies* 114 (April–June, 2007). Reprinted by permission of the author and publisher.

third party. In fact, it is the only such party that routinely has competed in U.S. presidential elections in recent years. For that reason, its involvement in these elections will be the focus of this chapter.

The Greens have run candidates in every presidential election since 1996. They nominated Ralph Nader, the famous consumer advocate, as their candidate for the presidential election in in 1996 and 2000. Nader garnered 0.71 percent and 2.74 percent of the popular vote, respectively. At the time, the latter result was somewhat higher than the median percentage (1.73 percent) received by all non-major party presidential candidates known to have secured at least third place up to that point in U.S. history.[4] Today, it remains the highest percentage ever gotten by a Green Party presidential candidate (see Table 7.1). It also enabled Nader to finish third in 2000. However, the Green Party was unable to retain this ranking in subsequent elections.[5] Additionally, no Green candidate has received a higher percentage of total votes than Nader did when he ran as an independent candidate in the 2004 and 2008 elections. What explains the Green's diminished results in recent presidential elections, and what would it take for them to do better in future races?

Before addressing the above question in depth, it is important to appreciate the broader context of two-party dominance and third-party resistance. Historian John D. Hicks once commented that "one formidable third party has succeeded another with bewildering rapidity" in U.S. presidential elections, that sometimes "these third parties seriously have affected the results of presidential elections," and that they also have "frequently had a hand in the determination of important national policies."[6] Yet, Daniel Mazmanian has observed that since 1828, when the electoral system assumed its contemporary form, "there has been no serious breach in the two-party pattern."[7] Other than the mid-nineteenth century, when the Republicans quickly ascended from a third party into one of the two major parties, and in 1912, when the Progressive (Bull Moose) Party secured second place (with former president Theodore Roosevelt as the candidate), no other

TABLE 7.1 Green Party's Presidential Election Results

Election Year	Presidential Candidate	Vice Presidential Candidate	Popular Votes	Percent of Popular Vote
1996	Ralph Nader	Winona LaDuke	685,435	0.71%
2000	Ralph Nader	Winona LaDuke	2,883,443	2.74%
2004	David Cobb	Pat LaMarche	119,859	0.10%
2008	Cynthia McKinney	Rosa Clemente	161,603	0.12%
2012	Jill Stein	Cheri Honkala	469,016	0.36%

Sources: Leip, "United States Presidential Election Results"; Federal Election Commission, "Federal Elections 2004"; and Federal Election Commission, "Federal Elections 2008."

minor parties in presidential elections have been able to mount such successful challenges to either of the dominant two parties.[8] Clearly, it is very difficult for minor parties or candidates to succeed in the U.S. electoral system, which Lisa Jane Disch has defined as the two-party "doctrine."[9] Single-member districts and winner-take-all systems severely limit minor parties in U.S. politics.[10] In contrast, proportional representation and parliamentary systems in most of the Western Europe democracies create space for the minor parties to play much more active roles in the state.

Despite the institutionalization of the two-party system, more than a thousand minor parties have emerged throughout U.S. history.[11] In about one out of five of the presidential elections since 1828, third party and independent candidates together have obtained at least 10 percent of the popular vote, and in roughly one out of seven of these elections, just one of these candidates has gotten more than 10 percent.[12] Yet, most third parties have been short-lived, and relatively few seem to have been able to make a substantial impact on the political process.[13] In fact, no minor parties except the Socialist Party and the Libertarian Party have achieved third place at the national level at least three times.[14] Many of them could not even maintain their organization's national activities past one election, and only a few minor parties have been able to do so for more than a decade.[15] Therefore, the question arises as to whether it is possible to make the Green Party more electorally effective and politically influential on a national level, or whether it will fade away from that arena like other third parties. This of course evokes a more specific strategic question: What would it take to build the Green Party into a stronger, more sustainable third party in presidential elections?

The Green Party has been hindered in several ways from maintaining third place in presidential elections after 2000. Along with various minor influences that are not discussed here, the most significant factors have been the Greens' inabilities to nominate relatively well-known candidates and raise sufficient election funds. Also, strong organizational networks clearly play a significant role in national elections, and minor parties tend to have extremely weak networks. The Green Party is no exception. Since it began to be officially established in 1991, the party never has been able to expand its organization sufficiently or attract another well-known candidate like Nader in 2000.

These three major and interconnected factors—candidates who are not well known, insufficient funds, and weak organization—are not exclusive to the Green Party; other minor parties in the United States also have faced the same obstacles in organizing successful election campaigns. However, the focus here is on the Green Party and its participation in various presidential elections. Below I show how these factors severely have hindered its success in such elections (and by implication, its influence in national politics). Correspondingly, I also argue that that the party will have to find a way to effectively address these factors in order to be more successful in presidential races and in general. Last, I propose that a partial strategic reorientation of the party may enable this to happen.

Value-Centered Party in Candidate-Centered Elections

The Green Party of the United States cannot do well in a presidential election if it does not run a well-known candidate. Nominating a well-known candidate is very important to success in any election, whether national or local. The advantage of such candidates is that their reputation, popularity, and sheer name recognition can attract more media attention, funding, activist support, and public interest than those candidates who are lesser known. This is not unique to the U.S. political system. Among observers of democratic elections around the world, it is a well-established fact that those candidates who are relatively well known generally have a better chance of winning than those who are not. Modern U.S. elections have become much more candidate oriented than party centric, though this trend actually began to develop in the nineteenth century. Since the election of John F. Kennedy in 1960, the weakening of party identification and the emergence of candidate-centered politics has changed the essence of U.S. politics, labeled by Anthony King as "the new American political system."[16] Many political scientists—such as Gerald Pomper, Walter Dean Burnham, Jack Dennis, and Thomas E. Patterson—have observed the trend toward weakened party identification.[17] Paul S. Herrnson stated that "the rise of the participatory primary; the enactment of the 1974 Federal Election Campaign Act (FECA); the introduction of polling, the electronic media, and modern marketing techniques into the political arena; and the decline of partisanship in the electorate helped foster the emergence of candidate-centered elections."[18] Thus, along with other factors (such as support for a popular issue, strong organization, and adequate finances), the ability to nominate well-known candidates has played a very significant role in winning more votes for the minor parties.

The trend of contemporary presidential candidates is toward more independence; they may play a more important role than their party in their campaigns and other election activities. The candidates, not the parties, now are taking the initiative in collecting funds and setting up campaign strategies. In the past, partisanship played a more vital role in the political process, and voters more often made their decisions based not only on candidates' performance but also on parties' policies.[19]

Some modern presidential primary candidates have taken strikingly independent positions. For example, in the 2008 Republican primary campaign, self-labeled libertarian Ron Paul took stands on various issues that were completely different from the eventual nominee, John McCain, and other contenders. Likewise in the 2004 Democratic primary, self-identified progressive Dennis Kucinich and the ultimate winner, John Kerry, addressed important issues from completely different points of view. Such independent positions on national and international affairs have presented difficulty for the electorate when using party identification as the guideline for selecting their candidates. Hence, at present, relatively fewer people feel a "steady and strong" psychological attachment to a particular party.[20] Contemporary voting behaviors—that is, candidate-centric voting—reflects the weakening of party identification and the prominence of candidate-centered politics.

Strong organizational networks, consisting of a far-flung, tight web of stable, well-funded party committees and allied nonprofit groups at various levels advantage the major parties in terms of their ability to attract strong candidates to run on their behalf. Such robust organizational structures (often referred to as "political machines") also help the candidates to fund and organize electoral campaigns. However, minor parties face extreme difficulties in attracting well-known personalities to compete from their relatively weak organizational platforms. These platforms typically consist of a widely dispersed, loosely knit collection of local party chapters, many of which are small, resource poor, and unstable—along with similarly feeble state and national bodies. Despite such limitations, these parties sometimes have been able to attract relatively well-known candidates, and this at least has helped them to do better than other such parties and secure third place in presidential elections. In fact, most of the more successful minor parties in the United States have been highly candidate-centered, which has made them largely "extensions of individual candidates."[21] Some minor parties' existence has depended solely on the candidates. For example, the three different versions of the Progressive Party (formed in 1904, 1924, and 1948, respectively) and the Union Party (formed in 1936) all disappeared soon after their presidential candidates were defeated.[22]

However, there is an important distinction between candidate-centered and ideologically based minor parties. Electoral success is the major goal and means of survival for the candidate-centered parties. By contrast, ideologically based parties usually exploit elections to promote their policies and programs; also, in the words of Paul Herrnson, they try to "influence the political debate and the issue positions of major party contenders, raise funds and recruit new members."[23]

A set of ideologically based minor parties formed at the turn of the last century were identified by V.O. Key as the "doctrinal parties" because instead of election success, their main aims were to propagate "a particular set of economic and ideological doctrines" in order to transform economic, political, and social systems on the basis of their ideologically based beliefs.[24] In this vein, the main objective of the Green Party is to uphold their Ten Key Values in state and civil society.[25] These values are grassroots democracy, social justice, ecological wisdom, nonviolence, decentralization, community-based economics, feminism, diversity, global responsibility, and a focus on the future.[26] Like other doctrinal parties, election is not the ultimate goal for the Greens; instead, they want to use elections as an opportunity to promote their policies and programs. For them, the electoral process is "a vehicle for publicity, education, and influence."[27] According to John Rensenbrink, cofounder of the U.S. Green Party, "the Green goal is to strive to be far more than . . . an electoral group aiming to put people in office." Also, he states that "running candidates [is] part of Green action, but Green action and the meaning of being Green is not limited" to election activities.[28] Herrnson notes that the Green Party is different than most minor parties today because "it has maintained a strong grassroots activist agenda," that includes, for instance, service and educational work on a variety of local environmental concerns.[29]

The Greens rely on a "two-legged approach"—that is, both electoral campaigns and movement activism—to try to disseminate their ideals and expand their organization.[30] This strategy has helped them to survive longer than typical candidate-centered minor parties, whose existence depends solely on the campaigns of specific candidates. At the same time, in comparison to other doctrinal parties in the United States, the Greens have been in a relatively good position politically because of their significant nationwide organization. While most U.S. doctrinal parties have not had much grassroots organization, the Greens at least have had party chapters in most states and in various parts of different states.[31] This has helped them to put forth their agenda and recruit members, as well as compete in national, state, and local elections. Consequently, as of this writing the Green Party was documented as having 248,189 registered voters and about 130 local officeholders.[32]

The Green Party's organizational foundation nevertheless has not been strong enough to ensure better results in presidential elections consistently. In order to accomplish this, the party would need to expand its base by recruiting more members into local chapters, as well as establishing more chapters in counties and municipalities where it currently has no party organization. The Greens also would need to be able run well-known candidates more regularly at all levels. Because election campaigns revolve around candidates and member recruitment often revolves around these campaigns, any party that cannot nominate a relatively well-known candidate will have difficulty attracting the electorate's attention and building party organization.

The serious problems that result from being unable to recruit well-known candidates are not uniquely experienced by the Green Party. Failure to nominate such candidates may result in the demise not only of weakly organized minor parties but also those that are well organized. One of the best examples of the latter is the Socialist Party of America, formed in 1901. By 1912, it had 118,000 dues-paying members. By 1918, it was able to elect a representative to the U.S. Congress, as well as 80 state legislators and over a thousand local officials.[33] Eugene V. Debs, a well-known labor leader, one of the founders of the Socialist Party, and the main orator and icon of the U.S. socialist movement, competed in the presidential elections of 1904, 1908, 1912, and 1920 on the Socialist Party ticket. He secured about 3 percent of the vote and third place in 1904 and 1908. He got nearly 6 percent and fourth place in 1912, a year in which Theodore Roosevelt was running as a Progressive. Debs's activist reputation, his skill in orating the socialist message, and his party's relatively strong organization helped him to attract votes. However, in 1916 Debs refused to run again because of his age and health. The party instead nominated a comparatively less well-known but still eminent newspaper editor and antiwar, socialist writer, Allan Benson. This decreased the party's total popular vote to about 3 percent, though combined with a third-place finish. When Debs ran again in 1920, despite his physical limitations, he got 3.4 percent and third place.[34]

Among the doctrinal parties in the United States, the Socialist Party is the only one that secured the significant third place in a presidential election at least five times, with a total of seven such finishes. This included getting more than 2.8 percent of the popular vote in three of these instances described above.[35] The Socialist Party also is the only party of its kind to have gotten more than 5 percent in a presidential race. These accomplishments demonstrate the party's relative strength, at least until 1920.

However, without better known candidates like Debs or Benson, the Socialists failed to win as many votes in presidential elections in later years, even though they still had a significant party organization into the 1930s. In 1924, the party didn't even run its own presidential candidate, but instead supported the Progressive candidacy of Robert La Follette. From 1928 to 1948, the Socialist Party's candidate was Norman Thomas, who previously was a socialist activist and unrenowned pacifist minister, though also a skilled orator. Thomas's popular vote ranged between only 0.17 percent and 0.76 percent in these elections, except in 1932, when he receive 2.2 percent.[36] His even lesser known successor in 1952 and 1956 (a lawyer, state party chapter leader, and former running mate named Darlington Hoopes) got only 0.03 percent and less than 0.01 percent of the vote, respectively.[37] The party ceased running presidential candidates altogether after 1956.[38]

Generally, the Socialist Party deteriorated over several post-Debs decades; it shrank and repeatedly split. Of course, factors other than the lack of well-known presidential candidates contributed to the party's long-term demise. They included factional conflict within the party; competition from other radical groups; government repression of leftists; waves of anti-socialist propaganda; progressive reforms that partially satisfied socialist demands; and relatedly, the declining popular appeal of the party's socialist ideology (which never had resonated well with most Americans).[39] Yet, the Socialist Party likely would have been better able to sustain itself and perhaps even advance nationally if it could have continued to nominate better known candidates for president. The same could be said of the Green Party today.

Trouble recruiting well-known candidates is a chronic problem for contemporary minor parties, including the Green Party. A striking difference between major and minor party candidates is that most major party candidates have had prior experience holding elected offices, whereas very few minor party candidates have had such experience.[40] Yet, as Herrnson notes, in the nineteenth century, the Greenbacks, the Populists, and several other minor parties were able to recruit better known candidates from the major parties. This was possible because these minor parties not only had survived for more than a decade but also "were in a position to distribute patronage and influence public policy."[41] Therefore, mainstream political leaders who wanted to change party affiliation found them to be "attractive vehicles" through which to compete in elections.[42]

In contrast, for well-known candidates who want to pursue their political agendas through third parties, the Green Party is not an attractive platform. Greens haven't had very much success in state and local elections in most parts of the country. Nor have they had enough organizational strength to influence national and state policies, or even local policies except in isolated instances. Because of their inherent organizational weakness, firm ideological commitment, and relative lack of electoral success, it is very difficult for ideologically centered parties like the Green Party to attract candidates from the mainstream parties or allied groups. Although the Greens have active party chapters in 42 states, these chapters typically are not strong enough to organize effective political campaigns.[43] Further, in order to get the nomination from the Greens, a candidate must accept the party's ideology and program. This requirement adds to the difficulty of attracting a well-known presidential candidate because very few public figures who have a strong national reputation (and who might aspire to the presidential nomination) are known to be followers of the Green philosophy and agenda.

The Green Party was able to attract the already renowned Ralph Nader as their candidate in 1996 and 2000, although he was a registered independent, because his political and social outlooks already were close to the Greens. According to Kevin Graham, "the two share a common passion for grass-roots organization and consumer-focused politics."[44] Through the 1980s and 1990s, Nader, like the Greens, was highly critical of the increasingly close relationship between big business and government, including leading politicians from both major parties.[45]

In the 2000 presidential election, Nader's positive reputation as a long-time consumer activist combined with the organizational aid of the Green Party played a significant role in attaining third place. However, that same reputation may not have been as influential a factor in his 2004 and 2008 campaigns. Running as an independent, without the support of a significant minor political party, Nader saw his vote count drop from 2.74 percent in 2000 to 0.38 percent in 2004 and 0.56 percent in 2008.[46] Besides being impacted by the loss of organizational help from the Greens, Nader likely was hurt by his "spoiler" image, acquired in the wake of the 2000 election. This newer and more negative reputation, whether or not it was deserved, probably turned away many progressive and other voters who were frustrated by the election and presidency of George W. Bush (for which they may have blamed Nader).

At their 2004 national convention in Milwaukee, Wisconsin, instead of Nader, most Green delegates endorsed David Cobb—a national Green party activist who was unknown to most Americans. They apparently did so because of Cobb's promise to only run in non-swing states, where there was perceived to be no danger of helping to reelect President Bush, and because of Cobb's commitment to build the Green Party from the grassroots. Also, Nader supporters claimed that Cobb benefited greatly from what they perceived to be an undemocratic delegate selection process. In any case, whereas the major parties started their electoral campaigns much earlier, the Greens took until the last week of June to declare Cobb as their candidate.[47] This reflected the weakness of Green presidential campaign strategy. Cobb was not as well known as Nader, which likely further contributed to shifting the Greens from third to sixth place, with only 0.10 percent of the popular vote.[48]

In 2008, the Green Party was able to attract former Democrat representative Cynthia McKinney, an African American, to run for president on their ticket. Despite coming from the mainstream of U.S. politics, McKinney did not do well in the election. She received only 0.12 percent of the popular vote, placing her sixth behind Nader and Chuck Baldwin of the Constitution Party.[49] Although McKinney had more name recognition than Cobb, she definitely was not as well known or popular as Nader.

In 2012 the Greens nominated physician and environmental health advocate Jill Stein. She was not well known outside of her state of Massachusetts, where she had run for state offices as a Green repeatedly and had lost by large margins each time. In her presidential race, she was able to secure 0.36 percent of the popular vote, placing fourth in the election behind Gary Johnson, the Libertarian candidate.[50] To put this in perspective, among all the elections he entered, Nader received his lowest percentage of the popular vote (0.38 percent) when he ran as an independent candidate in 2004. Nevertheless, this was still higher than Stein, who among all the subsequent Green presidential candidates received the highest percentage of the vote.

It therefore is clear that for electoral success, the Greens need to nominate a person who not only is an ardent follower of Green values, but who also is well known. In the last three elections, they have endorsed candidates who were Green activists or who were accepting of Green policies and programs, but who were not well known. Hence, their place in the election outcome and the percentage of the popular vote that they received both declined. Of course, the ability to recruit well-known candidates is not the only core determinant of Green Party success in presidential elections.

Elections Are Expensive

All over the world, including in the United States, the ability to raise large sums of money is central to electoral success. In comparison to other Western countries, contesting elections is an even more expensive venture in the United States because of the longer period of campaigning. In some parliamentary democracies, the election campaign cycle generally lasts for several weeks, but in the United States it can be a yearlong or multiyear process. Moreover, in some democracies political parties have opportunities to use government-sponsored free broadcast time on national radio and television, whereas candidates in the United States generally do not enjoy free access to these media. Last, while many other countries limit campaign spending, the United States only limits campaign contributions. These factors help to make U.S. election campaigns more expensive than those in other democracies.[51] It is almost impossible for candidates to do well in U.S. presidential elections without extensive financial resources. This has been a limiting factor for minor parties and independent candidates throughout U.S. history.

Minor parties and independent candidates can do relatively well in presidential elections when they can raise adequate funds, although as Alexander Heard observes, "no neat correlation is found between campaign expenditures and campaign results."[52] For example, in 1992 billionaire Ross Perot spent $60 million for his election campaign, which greatly helped him to become one of the most successful independent candidates, with 19 percent of the popular vote. One of the reasons that the Green Party could not attract enough popular votes in past presidential elections could be attributed to its inability to raise sufficient funds for its campaigns.

Minor party (and often independent) candidates generally have appeared to have had less ability to raise and spend money for elections, especially for higher level races. According to Paul Herrnson, "minor party congressional and presidential candidates [are] starved for resources."[53] For example in 2008, the campaigns of presidential contenders Barack Obama and John McCain spent about $730 million and $309 million, respectively. In 2012, the Obama campaign spent roughly $722 million, and the Mitt Romney campaign spent around $448 million. By contrast, Green Party presidential candidates spent about a quarter of a million dollars in 2008 and around a million dollars in 2012.[54] Further in the past, the major parties' expenditures also were much higher than those of minor parties, such as the Abolitionists in 1840, the Free Soilers in 1848, or the Populists in 1892.[55] Even the most successful third-party candidates in U.S. history have spent only a fraction of the money disbursed by the major party contenders. The best-financed minor party candidate, former president Theodore Roosevelt, spent only 60 percent of the average spent by his major party opponents in 1912. Likewise, in their presidential campaigns, 1968 American Independent Party candidate George Wallace and 1980 independent candidate John Anderson respectively spent 39 percent and 49 percent of what their major party opponents spent on average.[56]

Why have non-major party candidates often been relatively "starved" for money? Big donors usually make large contributions only to Republicans and Democrats for two simple reasons. First, major party candidates generally are perceived to be more capable of winning, given their typically superior reputation and organization, their more extensive and favorable media coverage, and their greater standing in public opinion polls. Second, Republicans and Democrats are seen as more capable of serving big donor interests. Their policy stands or actions tend to be more sympathetic to those with a lot of resources. Also, once in office, their many partisan political connections can allow them to impact policy more effectively.

In any election, of course, whether local or national, political campaigns play a crucial role in determining election success. Only through strong campaigns can candidates connect with voters, as well as publicize their policies and programs. For that reason, many if not most successful campaigns today absolutely require plenty of money. In this regard, as explained well by Benjamin Ginsburg, there is a significant difference between modern-day and nineteenth-century campaigns.[57] In the modern day, many campaigns, especially those at higher levels, primarily are "capital intensive," because they mainly are technologically based (with heavy reliance on television and advertisements, mass mailings, mass-produced literature, and automated calls).[58] These types of campaigns clearly are a lot more expensive.

By contrast, in the nineteenth century, campaigns were more "labor intensive." In these campaigns, political parties engaged a good number of individuals in election activities. Political parties' success mainly depended on the number of people they could employ, as well as their ability to connect with the voters. For example, in the 1880s, there were approximately 2.5 million people engaged in election campaigns.[59] In order to do well, political parties tried to gain support "from groups nearer the bottom of the social scale to use the numerical superiority of their forces," Ginsburg notes.[60]

Now, in technologically based, capital-intensive campaigns, the candidates', political parties' and allied groups' ability to spend much money on radio and television ads largely determines success in elections. Ginsberg argues that the shift from a labor-intensive to capital-intensive campaign "has meant that the balance of political power has shifted—perhaps decisively—in favor of the right."[61] He explains that rightist electoral actors have "superior access to the massive financial resources" because (given their more probusiness orientation) they always receive larger corporate donations than leftist electoral actors. This places the right in a better position to use various forms of electronic media. According to Ginsburg, "the expanding role of the new electoral techniques means that over the coming decades, groups closer to the political left will increasingly find themselves engaged in a species of political warfare that they are poorly equipped to win."[62] This obviously presents a problem for the Green Party, which leans decidedly to the left.

For the minor parties, whether left or right, the high cost of buying time on radio and television makes access to the media quite difficult. Even George Wallace, who was one of the best-financed minor-party candidates in U.S. presidential election history, was able to buy only one-sixth of the radio and television time of the major party candidates in the 1968 election. In comparison to major parties, minor-party contenders generally are able to buy roughly one-twentieth of the media time.[63] The Green Party clearly does not have the ability to purchase much media time. Big donors do not have much political interest in contributing to this party because of its organizational weakness and, hence, its inability to influence politics and society. Furthermore, big donors do not identify with the Green Party's Ten Key Values, which emphasize replacing the current capitalist system with a more egalitarian, community-based economy. The party thus has difficulty raising funds for electoral campaigns. Even in comparison to the Libertarian (yet more corporate friendly) candidate Gary Johnson, 2012 Green contender Jill Stein had a small election fund, in fact, about three times smaller.[64] This probably helps explain why Stein received only slightly more than a third of the popular votes that Johnson got.[65]

Of course, the extreme financial disadvantage of Green and other minor party presidential candidates is the result of the much greater amount of money not only raised and spent by the major party candidates themselves but also by allied outside groups on their behalf. These groups include the candidates' political parties, sympathetic political action committees (PACS, which are organizations specifically devoted to electoral fundraising), and nonprofit political advocacy groups.[66] For example, the total amount spent by all sources in support of Barack Obama and Mitt Romney in the 2012 presidential election was over $2 billion, yet the largest share of this expenditure actually was done by outside groups rather than the campaigns themselves.[67] Growing PAC and advocacy group money in presidential and other federal races is used to circumvent legal limits on campaign contributions. It is expended for purposes that indirectly favor certain candidates, such as ads that "educate" voters about opponents' stands on issues.[68] While outside money is used to help major party presidential campaigns, it overwhelmingly is not spent on behalf of opposing minor party campaigns, including those of Greens.[69] Most of it originally is donated by the wealthy and corporations, who for reasons explained above, clearly tend to favor candidates from the duopoly. Even the much lesser but still substantial of such funds donated or spent directly by unions overwhelmingly are used to support major party candidates.[70] As described in other chapters in this book, the leadership of organized labor remains strongly committed to the Democratic Party and its candidates.

In the end, the election system still depends on the "golden rule" model of the political process: "Those with the Gold Rule in Political Races."[71] Those without the gold are left behind. All of the Green Party candidates, including Nader, remained far behind—whether raising, spending, or having cash on hand in comparison to the major party candidates.[72]

Of course, none of the Green Party presidential candidates that came after Nader were able to raise the amount of money that he collected both as a Green and as an independent candidate. In 2000 Nader raised $8.4 million, and in 2004 and 2008, he raised about $4.6 million and $4.3 million, respectively.[73] David Cobb, Cynthia McKinney, and Jill Stein raised approximately $500,000, $200,000, and $900,000, respectively—an even more meager amount of money in comparison to major party contenders.[74] This greatly disadvantaged these Greens. In addition to suffering from a late campaign start and a lack of name recognition, their shortage of money helps explain why they couldn't secure third place or garner the same percentage of votes as Nader.

Superior access to financial resources certainly helps in securing better election results. Ross Perot's money-driven relative success in the elections of 1992 and 1996 (in which he won 18.87 percent and 8.4 percent of the popular vote, respectively) reveals that it is possible to get many votes without having a strong organization. Yet, it is important to remember that money isn't everything. A well-developed grassroots organization also can be critical, not only for stimulating donations but also for identifying and mobilizing supportive voters and for recruiting well-known candidates in the first place. The major parties have an obvious, enormous edge in generating such organization due to their strong political networks throughout the country. In turn, such networks are sustained in part by these parties' superior funding.

In sum, the major parties have a variety of cumulative, mutually reinforcing electoral advantages over minor parties like the Greens. Consequently, if winning elections were the Greens' only method of transforming society, they might have little hope for future success. Yet, they do have another strategy that inspires them.

Countercultural Politics

One basic difference between the major parties and the Green Party is that whereas gaining success in elections is the chief goal for the major parties, the Greens mainly are struggling to establish what Antonio Gramsci called "a counter hegemony within an established hegemony."[75] Nicola Pratt explains counter-hegemony as "the creation of an alternative hegemony on the terrain of civil society in preparation for a political change."[76] Put simply, this involves the slow development of an oppositional, revolutionary culture within the dominant culture. Gramsci described this strategy as a "war of position," which gradually constructs the social foundations for a new state. He further identified this process as a "passive revolution," the beginning of social transformation that did not require a popular revolt against the state.[77] John Rensenbrink's argument regarding Green electoral strategy supports the idea that the Green Party mainly is active in order to organize a passive revolution. According to Rensenbrink, Green activists have used electoral politics as a strategy to initiate "fundamental transformation," which will bring "profound changes in social institutions, in culture, in economy, as well as in the government."[78] As mentioned earlier, electoral campaigns are seen by many Greens as a direct opportunity to raise public consciousness about Green ideals and policy alternatives. They also are viewed as a chance to indirectly foster this process by recruiting new party members who will get involved in both the electoral and social movement activism of the Green Party. If Green electoral efforts increasingly can build support for and participation in Green politics, it is felt that this eventually will lead to a more widespread, potent, and effectual public demand for sweeping systemic change.

However, a strong political organization is a fundamental prerequisite for initiating a "passive revolution" in any society or state. Only a party with this asset can effectively disseminate its messages to various strata of society. Moreover, in order to build its cultural influence or counter-hegemony among various classes and groups, a party needs to communicate with them in a way that is easily understandable to them. These same strong organizational networks also are essential for building better electoral campaigns and collecting funds for these campaigns.

Yet, after more than 20 years of trying to reconstruct American state and social systems on the basis of their Ten Key Values, the Greens still have not had much success in developing their party organization—an essential component for achieving their goals. Party activists like Rensenbrink say they do not want to measure their success "in terms of winning the presidency but in terms of developing and supporting the power of grassroots; and in terms of the impact a strong showing for an alternative has on the constellation of powers in society and on the policies pursued by society."[79] But, they have not been very effective in this regard. Greens have not built a truly strong grassroots basis for influencing local, state, or national politics. Today most localities in the United States are relatively untouched by Green Party organization, and the electoral projects of Green chapters chronically are hampered by a lack of active party members.

Green Party leaders often portray presidential campaigns as a critical way to expand state and local party organization. The Nader campaign of 2000 was such a strong catalyst; the party grew rapidly in its wake. The Green Party's number of state and local chapters, candidates, local officeholders, registered voters, as well as its national budget, all increased dramatically in the year during the campaign and for the next couple of years.[80] Yet, the subsequent Green presidential campaigns run by poorly known candidates with inferior funding have not been the best agents for member recruitment, chapter development, and other aspects of party growth. When these candidates predictably have gotten less than 1 percent of the vote and failed to achieve third place, the result has not been an inspiring "strong showing for an alternative."

Regardless of the methods employed, Greens also have achieved very limited success in attracting members from the general public, and, unfortunately, few of them have come from diverse backgrounds. In the late 1980s, during the Green Party's formative period, Bharat Patankar identified the pattern of the Green membership as a "monochromatic green gathering" where most of the members were "university based." Most Green activists were from a "white middle-class" background. [81] By the late 1990s, despite their initiatives in overcoming class and racial imbalances, Greens had made only minimal progress in organizing among nonprofessional workers and racial minorities, or in promoting Green activism with the support of people from these groups. [82] There is no indication that such problems have abated much if at all in subsequent decades. [83]

A longstanding impediment to Green Party member recruitment among a wider segment of the public may be the party's failure to articulate a message of systemic change that is easily understandable to the general public and resonant with American political culture. David Gillespie commented that "American third parties, [drawn] much closer to the politics of redemption, have been far more inclined than the major parties to expositions" (that is, extended political discourses and manifestos). [84] The Green Party is no exception to this rule. The Ten Key Values mentioned earlier are the common core of the Green vision. However, the Greens' public documents do not elaborate simply and clearly enough how they would implement these values in the United States. For example, Green Party website lacks a concise, easily digestible explanation regarding how Green activists would transform the present capitalist economy into a community-based economy. [85] Moreover, Green activist Charlene Spretnak expresses doubts about the implied meanings of the terms the Greens are using and Greens' "ability to communicate" with U.S. citizens on the basis of these vocabularies. [86] Capitalist values are foundational cornerstones of the U.S. political culture. Merely challenging these values without plainly articulating how the Green alternatives still are consistent with ordinary Americans' everyday experiences and aspirations can make it hard for the Green Party to succeed in its electoral or counter-hegemonic politics. Without enough attention to their popular resonance, the Green Party's positions and related proposals may have very limited appeal to the public at large. This may constrain the Greens' ability not only to expand their grassroots organization but also, ultimately, to attract well-known candidates, raise money, and do better in various elections, including those for president.

Conclusion

The vision of the Greens is to transform the current political, social, and economic structures on the basis of their Ten Key Values. Engaging in the electoral process is one strategy to advance their politics. Without eventually achieving more electoral success, however, it will be almost impossible for the Green Party to carry out its broad agenda. Such success is necessary in order for the party to be perceived as more efficacious and, therefore, more worthy of broader public attention and support. This attention and support is strategically indispensable, regardless of whether the Greens are trying to pressure the state to implement reforms (as third parties have done in the past) or transform popular consciousness for the sake of a passive revolution. Consistently winning a more significant share of the presidential vote is one way for the Green Party to advance electorally.

The implication of this analysis is that three things need to be accomplished by the Green Party in order to make that possible. First, nominating stronger, especially better known candidates is essential. Second, it is important for the Greens to begin to lessen if not resolve their crisis of inadequate funding. Third and finally, building a stronger and more extensive grassroots organization also is critical. Toward this last end, it is important for the Green Party to present its ideas to the public in a way that is more popularly appealing. Greens even may need to modify some of their agenda, to the extent that is possible without violating core Green philosophies. As suggested throughout this chapter, progress in any one of the above three areas may enhance the possibilities for progress in the other areas.

At the same time, improvement in only one area of deficiency may not necessarily be sufficient. If the candidate or the party does not have enough funds or organization, merely nominating a well-known candidate may not bring electoral success. For example, in 1996 a famous Green Party presidential candidate (Nader) attracted a relatively small percentage of popular votes (0.71 percent), perhaps due to the lack of funds (totaling less than $5,000 spent) or substantial campaign structure.[87] Likewise, just spending money may not bring electoral success if the candidate, the party organization, or both are weak. Last, beefed-up organization may not do much to advance a presidential campaign if the candidate is too unknown or underfunded. Thus, it is important for the Green Party to try to make progress on all three interconnected fronts simultaneously.

This chapter has identified big obstacles to Green Party advancement in all the key areas central to improving its performance in presidential campaigns. Yet, the analysis also suggests that a shift in the party's basic orientation could help it to move forward. If the Greens can build a somewhat more candidate-centered party, they may be better able to recruit more viable candidates, raise more money, and strengthen their grassroots organization. A consistently stronger, more explicit appreciation for the value of winning many votes and making a good showing on election day (and not just further educating and mobilizing the already converted few) could help attract better known candidates, sympathetic donors, skilled activists, and voters. This eventually could inspire another famous, courageous public figure to run for president on behalf of the Green Party.

Having learned lessons from the Nader experience and reoriented the party toward placing a greater priority on electoral achievement, the Green Party might be able to do better than it did in 2000. This of course would require winning over more voters who are not so susceptible to the short-term fear of "spoiling" the election for the Democrat, and who are more interested in building a viable progressive alternative to the duopoly in the long term. In order to do this, the Green candidate and the party would have to concertedly reach out to independents, habitual nonvoters, and younger left-leaning voters (who are not old enough to have been directly affected by the post-2000 anti-Nader backlash). If Greens can do the above, they might even be able to breach the 5 percent presidential vote threshold; this would enable them to collect millions of dollars in federal funds for use in the next presidential election.[88] Such an advance could lead to substantial growth in party organization and more breakthroughs in subsequent elections at different levels.

However, it is unclear whether the Green Party is capable of making the above shift toward more of a focus on narrowly defined electoral success. Much of its leadership and membership may equate this change with "selling out." A debate within the party and an infusion of new and different types of members, spearheaded by its more pragmatic members, would be needed to try to tip the balance. The alternative, of course, would be for such members to join others outside of the party who are similarly inclined to form a new party. This party would be more of a progressive value/candidate-centric hybrid. It would aim to compete for power more seriously, not only in the culture but also in the ballot box.

Notes

1 Stephens, *The Transition from Capitalism to Socialism*.
2 Reynolds, *Democracy Unbound*, 47–48; and Rosenstone, Behr, and Lazarus, *Third Parties in America*.
3 Reynolds, *Democracy Unbound*, 24–25; Berg, "Greens in the USA," 250, 252; Sifry, *Spoiling for a Fight*, 2; and Green Party of the United States, "All Candidates for Office." The presidential campaigns of Eugene Debs and Ralph Nader played a significant role in inspiring such activism within the Socialist Party (in the early twentieth century) and the Green Party (in the early twenty-first century), respectively.
4 Leip, "United States Presidential Election Results."
5 Ibid.
6 Hicks, *Third Party Tradition*, 4.
7 Mazmanian, *Third Parties in Presidential Elections*, 4.
8 Leip, "United States Presidential Election Results." Roosevelt received 27.39 percent of the popular vote.
9 Disch, *The Tyranny of the Two-Party System*, 5.
10 Duverger, *Political Parties*, 217.
11 Patterson, *American Democracy*, 223–24.
12 Leip, "United States Presidential Election Results."
13 Gillespie, *Challengers to Duopoly*; and Rosenstone, Behr, and Lazarus, *Third Parties in America*.
14 Leip, "United States Presidential Election Results."
15 Ibid; Gillespie, *Challengers to Duopoly*; and Rosenstone, Behr, and Lazarus, *Third Parties in America*.
16 King, *The New American Political System*.
17 See Pomper, *Voters' Choice*, 147–52; Burnham, *Critical Elections*, 71–90; Dennis, "Trends in Support"; and Patterson, *American Democracy*, 379–80.

18 Herrnson, "Two-Party Dominance," 32; and Sorauf, "Political Parties and Political Action Committees." For details about FECA, see Federal Election Commission "The FECA and the Federal Campaign Finance Law."

19 Wattenberg, *The Rise of Candidate-Centered Politics*, 163.

20 Nie, Verba, and Petrocik, *The Changing American Voter*, 48.

21 Herrnson, "Two-Party Dominance," 32.

22 Rosenstone, Behr, and Lazarus, *Third Parties in America*, 81–88, 93–107.

23 Herrnson, "Two-Party Dominance," 35.

24 Smallwood, *The Other Candidates*, 19; and Key, *Politics, Parties and Pressure Groups*, 281.

25 Rensenbrink, *Against All Odds*, 4.

26 Green Party of the United States, "Ten Key Values of the Green Party."

27 Gaard, *Ecological Politics*, 129.

28 Rensenbrink, *Against All Odds*, 111.

29 Herrnson, "Two-Party Dominance," 35–36.

30 Herrnson, "Two-Party Dominance," 36.

31 Green Party of the United States, "States."

32 Winger, "March 2014 Registration Totals"; and Green Party of the United States, "Current Green Officeholders."

33 Nash, *Third Parties in American Politics*, 268; Reynolds, *Democracy Unbound*, 24; and Busky, *Democratic Socialism*.

34 Gillespie, *Challengers to Duopoly*, 174–76; Reynolds, *Democracy Unbound*, 18–26; and Leip, "United States Presidential Election Results."

35 Leip, "United States Presidential Election Results." The Socialist Party achieved third place in presidential elections seven times, all between 1904 and 1940. The Libertarian Party is the only other doctrinal party that also secured third place on several occasions, specifically four times between 1976 and 2012.

36 Gillespie, *Challengers to Duopoly*, 178; Reynolds, *Democracy Unbound*, 27; Leip, "United States Presidential Election Results"; and Marxist Internet Archive, "Norman Thomas."

37 Leip, "United States Presidential Election Results"; and Henderson, *Darlington Hoopes*.

38 Gillespie, *Challengers to Duopoly*, 178.

39 Gillespie, *Challengers to Duopoly*, 176–79; Reynolds, *Democracy Unbound*, 26–27; and Rosenstone. Behr, and Lazarus, *Third Parties in America*, 90–91. Specifically, for a discussion of the ideological chasms inside the party and how these conflicts affected the party's organization, see Myers, *The Prophet's Army*, 123–42; and Warren, *An Alternative Vision*, 49–120.

40 Rosenstone, Behr, and Lazarus, *Third Parties in America*, 37.

41 Herrnson, "Two-Party Dominance," 31.

42 Ibid.

43 Green Party of the United States, "States."

44 Graham, *Ralph Nader*, 107.

45 See Nader, *The Ralph Nader Reader*.

46 Leip, "United States Presidential Election Results."

47 Hawkins, *Independent Politics*.

48 Federal Election Commission, "Federal Elections 2004"; and Federal Election Commission, "Federal Elections 2008."

49 Federal Election Commission, "Federal Elections 2008."

50 Leip, "United States Presidential Election Results."

51 Waldman, "How Our Campaign Finance System Compares to Other Countries."
52 Heard, *The Cost of Democracy*, 16.
53 Herrnson, "Two-Party Dominance," 27.
54 Federal Election Commission, "2012, 2008 Presidential Campaign Finance."
55 Rosenstone, Behr, and Lazarus, *Third Parties in America*, 27; and Sewell, *Ballots for Freedom*, 167.
56 Rosenstone, Behr, and Lazarus, *Third Parties in America*, 27.
57 Ginsberg, "Money and Power," 171.
58 Ibid., 164.
59 Ostrogorski, *Democracy and the Organization of Political Parties*, 285.
60 Ginsberg, "Money and Power," 164.
61 Ibid., 174.
62 Ibid., 164.
63 Rosenstone, Behr, and Lazarus, *Third Parties in America*, 30.
64 Federal Election Commission, "2012, 2008 Presidential Campaign Finance."
65 Leip, "United States Presidential Election Results."
66 Center for Responsive Politics, "Outside Spending."
67 Center for Responsive Politics, "2012 Presidential Race." This fact pertains to total spending by the two candidates. The amount of spending effectively on behalf of the candidates that was not spent by their campaigns was 65 percent for Romney and 48 percent for Obama.
68 Center for Responsive Politics, "Outside Spending"; Center for Responsive Politics, "Politicians and Elections"; Parenti, *Democracy for the Few*, 185; and Eitzen, Baca Zinn, and Eitzen Smith, *Social Problems*, 38–44.
69 Center for Responsive Politics, "Active Presidential Candidates."
70 Center for Responsive Politics, "Outside Spending"; and Center for Responsive Politics, "Labor: Top Recipients."
71 Miller, "Those with the Gold Rule."
72 Center for Responsive Politics, "2004 Presidential Race"; "2008 Presidential Election"; and "2012 Presidential Race."
73 Center for Responsive Politics, "Ralph Nader (I)."
74 Center for Responsive Politics, "2004 Presidential Race"; "2008 Presidential Election"; and "2012 Presidential Race."
75 Gill, *Gramsci*, 53.
76 Pratt, 335
77 Gill, *Gramsci*, 54.
78 Rensenbrink, *Against All Odds*, 132.
79 Ibid., 135.
80 Berg, "Greens in the USA," 250, 252; Sifry, *Spoiling for a Fight*, 2; and Green Party of the United States, "All Candidates for Office."
81 Patankar, "Monochromic Green Gathering," 71.
82 Gaard, *Ecological Politics*, 196, 231.
83 Green Pages, "The Color of Green"; and Teal, "More Diverse Candidate Pool Crucial."
84 Gillespie, *Politics at the Periphery*, 284.
85 See Green Party of the United States, "IV. Economic Justice and Sustainability."
86 Gaard, *Ecological Politics*, 106.
87 Sifry, *Spoiling for a Fight*, 176–78.
88 Dao, "The 2000 Campaign."

Bibliography

Berg, John C. "Greens in the USA." In *Green Parties in Transition: The End of Grass-roots Democracy?* Edited by Gene E. Frankland, Paul Lucardie, and Benoit Rihoux, 245–56. Farnham, England: Ashgate, 2008.

Burnham, Walter Dean. *Critical Elections and the Mainsprings of American Politics.* New York: Norton, 1970.

Busky, Donald F. *Democratic Socialism: A Global Survey.* Westport, CT: Praeger, 2000.

Center for Responsive Politics. "Active Presidential Candidates." OpenSecrets.org. Accessed September 14, 2014. www.opensecrets.org/pres12/summary_active.php.

———. "Labor: Top Recipients." OpenSecrets.org. Accessed September 14, 2014. www.opensecrets.org/industries/recips.php?ind=P&cycle=2012&recipdetail=P&mem=N&sortorder=U.

———. "Outside Spending." OpenSecrets.org. Accessed September 15, 2014. www.opensecrets.org/outsidespending/.

———. "Politicians and Elections." OpenSecrets.org. Accessed September 14, 2014. www.opensecrets.org/elections/.

———. "Ralph Nader (I)." OpenSecrets.org. Accessed September 14, 2014. www.opensecrets.org/pres08/summary.php?cid=N00000086.

———. "2008 Presidential Election." OpenSecrets.org. Accessed September 14, 2014. www.opensecrets.org/pres08/index.php?cycle=2008&type=SF.

———. "2004 Presidential Race." OpenSecrets.org. Accessed September 14, 2014. www.opensecrets.org/pres04/.

———. "2012 Presidential Race." OpenSecrets.org. Accessed September 14, 2014. www.opensecrets.org/pres12/#out.

Dao, James. "The 2000 Campaign: The Green Party: History Could Be Green Party's Toughest Opponent." *New York Times*, November 2, 2000. www.nytimes.com/2000/11/02/us/2000-campaign-green-party-history-could-be-green-party-s-toughest-opponent.html.

Dennis, Jack. "Trends in Support for the American Party System," *British Journal of Political Science* 5 (1975): 187–230.

Disch, Lisa Jane. *The Tyranny of the Two-Party System.* New York: Columbia University Press, 2002.

Duverger, Maurice. *Political Parties: Their Organization and Activity in the Modern State*, 2nd ed. Translated by Barbara North and Robert North. New York: Wiley, 1954.

Eitzen, Stanley D., Maxine Baca Zinn, and Kelly Eitzen Smith. *Social Problems*, 13th ed. Boston: Pearson, 2014.

Federal Election Commission. "The FECA and the Federal Campaign Finance Law." Accessed September 19, 2014. www.fec.gov/pages/brochures/fecfeca.shtml.

———. "Federal Elections 2008." Accessed September 19, 2014. www.fec.gov/pubrec/fe2008/federalelections2008.pdf.

———. "Federal Elections 2004." Accessed September 19, 2014. www.fec.gov/pubrec/fe2004/tables.pdf.

———. "2012, 2008 Presidential Campaign Finance." Accessed September 14, 2014. www.fec.gov/disclosurep/PCandList.do.

Gaard, Greta. *Ecological Politics: Ecofeminists and the Greens.* Philadelphia: Temple University Press, 1998.

Gill, Stephen, ed. *Gramsci, Historical Materialism and International Relations.* Cambridge: Cambridge University Press, 1993.

Gillespie, David J. *Challengers to Duopoly: Why Third Parties Matter in American Politics.* Columbia: University of South Carolina Press, 2012.

————. *Politics at the Periphery: Third Parties in Two-Party America.* Columbia: University of South Carolina Press, 1993.

Ginsberg, Benjamin. "Money and Power: The New Political Economy of American Elections." In *The Political Economy: Readings in the Politics and Economics of American Public Policy.* Edited by Thomas Ferguson and Joel Rogers, 163–79. Armonk, NY: M. E. Sharpe, 1984.

Graham, Kevin. *Ralph Nader: Battling for Democracy.* Denver: Windom, 2000.

Green Pages, "The Color of Green: An Interview with Darryl L. C. Moch, DC Statehood Green Party." *Green Pages.* Last modified April 18, 2012. http://gp.org/greenpages-blog/?p=2970.

Green Party of the United States. "All Candidates for Office." Accessed November 1, 2014. http://gp.org/elections/candidates/index.php.

————. "Current Green Officeholders." Accessed September 13, 2014. http://www.gp.org/officeholders.

————. "IV. Economic Justice and Sustainability." Accessed September 18, 2014. http://www.gp.org/economic_justice_and_sustainability.

————. "States." Accessed September 21, 2014. http://www.gp.org/state_parties.

————. "Ten Key Values of the Green Party." Accessed September 13, 2014. http://www.gp.org/four_pillars_10_kv.

Hawkins, Howie. *Independent Politics: The Green Party Strategy Debate.* Chicago: Haymarket Books, 2006.

Heard, Alexander. *The Cost of Democracy.* Chapel Hill: University of North Carolina Press, 1960.

Henderson, J. Paul. *Darlington Hoopes: The Political Biography of an American Socialist.* Glasgow, Scotland: Humming Earth, 2005.

Herrnson, Paul S. "Two-Party Dominance and Minor Party Forays in American Politics." In *Multiparty Politics in America.* Edited by Paul S. Herrnson and John C. Green, 21–42. Lanham. MD: Rowman and Littlefield, 1997.

Hicks, John D. "The Third Party Tradition in American Politics." *Mississippi Valley Historical Review* 20, no. 1 (1933): 3–28.

Key, V.O., Jr. *Politics, Parties and Pressure Groups,* 4th ed. New York: Thomas Y. Crowell, 1958.

King, Anthony, ed. *The New American Political System,* 2nd ed. Washington DC: American Enterprise Institute, 1990.

Leip, David. "United States Presidential Election Results." *Dave Leip's Atlas of U.S. Presidential Elections.* Accessed September 19, 2014. http://uselectionatlas.org/RESULTS/.

Marxist Internet Archive. "Norman Thomas (1884–1968)." *Encyclopedia of Marxism.* Accessed September 21, 2014. www.marxists.org/glossary/people/t/h.htm.

Mazmanian, Daniel A. *Third Parties in Presidential Elections.* Washington, DC: Brookings Institute, 1974.

Miller, Ellen S. "Those with the Gold Rule in Political Races." *Christian Science Monitor,* June 16, 1995. www.csmonitor.com/1995/0616/16192.html.

Myers, Constance A. *The Prophet's Army: Trotskyists in America, 1928–1941.* Westport, CT: Greenwood Press, 1977.

Nader, Ralph. *The Ralph Nader Reader.* New York: Seven Stories Press, 2000.

Nash, Howard P., Jr. *Third Parties in American Politics*. Washington, DC: Public Affairs Press, 1959.

Nie, Norman H., Sidney Verba, and John R. Petrocik. *The Changing American Voter*. Cambridge, MA: Harvard University Press, 1979.

Ostrogorski, Moisei. *Democracy and the Organization of Political Parties*. New York: McMillan, 1902.

Parenti, Michael. *Democracy for the Few*, 9th ed. Boston: Wadsworth Cengage, 2011.

Patankar, Bharat. "Monochromic Green Gathering," *Race and Class* 31, no.2 (1989): 68–73.

Patterson, Thomas E. *The American Democracy*. Boston: McGraw-Hill, 1999.

Pomper, Gerald. *Voters' Choice: Victories of American Behavior*. New York: Dodd, Mead, 1975.

Pratt, Nicola C. "Bringing Politics Back In: Examining the Link between Globalization and Democratization." *Review of International Political Economy* 11, no. 2 (2004): 311–36.

Rensenbrink, John. *Against All Odds: The Green Transformation of American Politics*. Raymond, ME: Leopold Press, 1999.

Reynolds, David. *Democracy Unbound: Progressive Challenges to the Two Party System*. Boston: South End Press, 1997.

Rosenstone, Steven J., Roy L. Behr, and Edward H. Lazarus. *Third Parties in America: Citizen Response to Major Party Failure*. Princeton, NJ: Princeton University Press, 1984.

Sewell, Richard H. *Ballots for Freedom: Anti-Slavery Politics in the United States 1837–1960*. New York: Norton, 1976.

Sifry, Micah, L. *Spoiling for a Fight: Third Party Politics in America*. New York: Routledge, 2003.

Smallwood, Frank. *The Other Candidates: Third Parties in Presidential Elections*. Hanover, NH: University Press of New England, 1983.

Sorauf, Frank J. "Political Parties and Political Action Committees: Two Life Cycles." *Arizona Law Review* 22 (1980): 445–64.

Stephens, John D. *The Transition from Capitalism to Socialism*. Urbana: University of Illinois Press, 1986.

Teal, Penny. "More Diverse Candidate Pool Crucial." *Green Pages*. Last modified March 21, 2009. http://gp.org/greenpages-blog/?p=1118.

Waldman, Paul. "How Our Campaign Finance System Compares to Other Countries." *The American Prospect*. Last modified April 4, 2014. http://prospect.org/article/how-our-campaign-finance-system-compares-other-countries.

Warren, Frank A. *An Alternative Vision: The Socialist Party in the 1930s*. Bloomington: Indiana University Press, 1974.

Wattenberg, Martin P. *The Rise of Candidate-Centered Politics: Presidential Elections of the 1980s*. Cambridge, MA: Harvard University Press, 1991.

Winger, Richard. "March 2014 Registration Totals." *Ballot Access News*. April 1, 2014. www.ballot-access.org/2014/04/april-2014-ballot-access-news-print-edition/.

8

LABOR PARTY TIME? NOT YET*

Mark Dudzic and Katherine Isaac

During the first of the 2012 presidential debates, President Barack Obama opined to Governor Mitt Romney, "I suspect that on Social Security, we've got a somewhat similar position." This should have come as no surprise to those of us paying attention. Since at least July of the previous year, President Obama had been dangling a "grand bargain" in front of congressional Republicans: cuts in Social Security and Medicare in exchange for a temporary agreement to raise the federal debt ceiling. While the two sides never consummated this deal (mainly because the Republicans held out for deeper cuts and more extensive concessions), as of this writing all indications are that the offer remains on the bargaining table.

That a Democratic president would have been willing to trade away the crown jewels of the social safety net that have defined the party's identity in the minds of millions of Americans for generations is astounding. This betrayal came *after* the Obama administration's various first-term betrayals of ordinary Americans—such as the failure to deliver on its campaign promises to labor regarding job creation and labor law reform; the basic embrace of the "Bush Doctrine" in foreign policy and the escalation of war in Afghanistan; and the repeated capitulations in the fight to pass substantive health care legislation. Thus, the proposed gutting of Social Security and Medicare should have marked the date when labor finally disowned the Democratic Party and declared its support for the establishment

* Originally published in a slightly different form on the website of the Labor Party, December 2012, www.thelaborparty.org/d_lp_time.htm. Reprinted by permission of the authors/publishers.

of a political party with a working-class agenda. Instead, one union after another rushed to endorse Obama for a second term, asking for little or nothing in return.

Obama owed his reelection to the labor movement. Its massive ground campaign mobilizations surely made the difference in the key battleground states of Ohio, Pennsylvania, Michigan, Wisconsin, and Virginia. Labor did so mainly because the "greater of two evils" alternative—the inauguration of a national union-busting Republican regime committed to a Greek-style austerity program—was, quite simply, unacceptable. But despite labor's massive contribution to Obama's victory in 2012, no one could credibly claim that labor, as a social movement, would be stronger after four more years, nor that the lives of working people would be better or more secure.

The history of Obama's first term is instructive. Despite winning the presidency and both houses of Congress in 2008 on a platform of hope and change, the Democratic Party abjectly failed to articulate, much less implement, a program enabling ordinary Americans to recover from the worst economic meltdown since the Great Depression. This failure generated a political crisis with two exceptionally different expressions. On the one hand, it fueled a right-wing, populist rage that pitted workers who have lost secure jobs and decent benefits against those workers—many in the public sector—who have managed to maintain them. By scapegoating "underwater" homeowners, immigrants, and other victims of the economic crisis, this "populism" diverted anger away from the Wall Street bankers who caused the crisis. Meanwhile, it pursued a political agenda that threatened to repeal the major social gains of the past 100 years. Although it purported to speak for small business folks and hardworking Americans, this Tea Party movement offered nothing in the way of real relief. Its momentum may have peaked shortly after its stunning successes in the 2010 midterm elections. However, the results of the June 2012 Wisconsin recall election (favorable to the Tea Party) and their repeated use as a Republican trope in the fall elections bore testimony to the continuing appeal of a well-financed and well-publicized right-wing popular base (which used the familiar themes of racism, religious and nationalist bigotry, and intraclass resentment to advance its antigovernment agenda).

On the other hand, the post-2008 political crisis also was the reason that the Occupy Wall Street movement resonated with many Americans. For all its shortcomings, it successfully articulated the impact of the current economic crisis in class terms. Occupiers focused on a critique of the deficiencies of capitalism rather than simply a temporary quick fix to the current crisis. It may have been the first critique of neoliberalism to gain significant traction in the United States. The movement may have helped shift the terms of debate. However, its lack of organizational unity, ideological coherence, and institutional support clearly were factors in its inability to coalesce into a serious alternative to our current two-party political party system (which obviously is dominated by "the 1 percent").

Unlike nearly every other industrialized country in the world, the U.S. working class has not succeeded in developing a class-based political party substantial enough to contend for political power. As a result, the United States does not have even a moderately strong welfare state to serve the public as a whole. Instead, from the Great Depression through the 1970s, a "private welfare state" was negotiated via individual union contracts; it also was adopted by "me-too" non-union corporations that often matched union wages and benefits as part of a sophisticated anti-union strategy. This was supplemented by a relatively meager social safety net. The above changes together provided a rising standard of living and a modicum of security for working Americans.[1] This arrangement, however, has made working people in the United States particularly vulnerable to the ravages of neoliberalism. Indeed, for the past 30 years, we have experienced an unrelenting assault on the standard of living and well-being of the vast majority of Americans who work for a living. As a result, wealth and power increasingly are concentrated in the hands of a globalized elite.[2]

We would be hard-pressed to identify a period of U.S. history where the need for a labor-based political party was greater than it is now. After all the events since the financial meltdown of 2008—the "Wisconsin Winter,"[3] the "Occupy Wall Street Autumn," another "lesser of two evils" election season, the sequestration crises, the food stamp cuts coupled with giveaways to agribusiness in the bipartisan Farm Bill of 2014, and the revival of fast-track trade authority—the next logical step might seem to be the launching (or relaunching) of just such a party. Yet the short-term prospects of an independent, proworker political movement emerging on the American scene are virtually nonexistent.

Below we review the contemporary movement to build a viable labor party in the United States and reflect upon the lessons for future labor party organizing. We describe the rise of the movement and the establishment of the Labor Party in the 1990s. We then explain why the movement and party declined thereafter. We focus on the inability of most national labor unions to overcome their deep attachment to the Democratic Party, as well as an increasingly anti-union economic and political environment. Ultimately, we suggest that a stronger labor movement is essential for successfully building a labor party. We also propose certain steps that may lay a foundation for the future reestablishment and growth of an independent political voice for working people in the United States.

A Party of Our Own

Hard as it may be to believe today, in the mid-1990s, a group of progressive unions and individual activists initiated a substantial organizing project to create just such a party. In 1996, after five years of intensive organizing, 1,400 delegates from unions representing more than 2 million workers met in an overflowing convention hall in Cleveland, Ohio, to launch the Labor Party.[4] After contentious debate about issues from abortion to running candidates, we adopted a comprehensive program—"A Call for Economic Justice"—and began the difficult yet exhilarating task of developing an organizing strategy to wean the labor movement from the corporate-dominated two-party political system.[5]

This Labor Party moment reflected the confluence of a number of significant developments in the 1990s:

1. A belated understanding on the part of broad sections of the labor movement that the PATCO debacle of the previous decade (when newly elected President Ronald Reagan busted the air traffic controllers' strike and fired all the strikers without any significant response from the labor movement) signaled the end of the postwar collective bargaining regime.
2. A growing fury among union members against the Democratic Party's support—via Bill Clinton's version of neoliberalism—for the North American Free Trade Agreement (NAFTA). NAFTA was the first of many trade agreements that implemented a globalization program that enriched a global elite at the expense of workers everywhere.
3. Resurgence, after decades of marginalization, of the longstanding labor/left tradition that had focused on class-struggle unionism and independent political action. This tradition helped to inform and inspire a new generation of union leadership.

After 15 years of retreat, disorganization, and defeat, we witnessed in the mid-1990s an upsurge of trade union militancy, focused on taking the offensive against corporate greed. This upsurge was forged in the crucible of the Pittston coal strike of 1989–90 (where the United Mine Workers of America put their union on the line and won), and in militant corporate campaigns against BASF, Ravenswood Aluminum, and other multinational corporations (where unions embraced new tactics and a mobilization model that was able to beat back the worst of the corporate offensive against labor). In 1991, Ron Carey won the presidency of the Teamsters, the largest union in America. This set in motion a member-driven upsurge of militancy and activism, and it helped solidify the union's recent reunification with the AFL-CIO. In 1993, the revitalized labor movement turned Decatur, Illinois, into a "war zone" to confront megacorporations Staley, Bridgestone/Firestone, and Caterpillar. In 1995, workers at the *Detroit News* and *Detroit Free Press*—in the very city that gave rise to the modern labor movement—were forced to strike and subsequently were locked out. Unionists everywhere vowed that these battles would not end in another defeat for workers.

In response to growing demands for change, the New Voice slate of John Sweeney and Richard Trumka swept into office in 1995 in the only contested election in the history of the AFL-CIO. They promised a revitalized labor movement with the goal of organizing one million new members per year. A "labor spring" emerged in which the Cold War–inspired anti-intellectualism of the labor movement gave way to new leadership, welcoming academics and activists from other social movements to bring their experience and energy to help revitalize the movement.

It was no accident that many of the unions and activists involved in these struggles also led the effort to launch a labor party. A small number of unions associated with the labor left, including the United Electrical, Radio and Machine Workers of America (UE), had long agitated for independent political action. However, the effort took a leap forward when the Oil, Chemical, and Atomic Workers Union (OCAW) allocated the necessary resources to implement an organizing effort both internally and within the labor movement as a whole. As experienced by many industrial unions, deindustrialization, offshoring, and automation had begun to decimate the industries where OCAW unionization had thrived. OCAW's long history of anticorporate activism and rank-and-file mobilization includes its 1973 strike against Shell Oil, during which one of the first labor-environmental coalitions was forged. Its advocacy on health and safety legislation for workers, which received national attention when union activist Karen Silkwood was killed in the midst of her attempts to blow the whistle on the nuclear industry, was embraced by both the feminist and antinuclear movements. In 1988, a progressive caucus led by Bob Wages and Tony Mazzocchi won election to national office in the OCAW.

Mazzocchi was widely regarded as a visionary at the forefront of the labor movement's involvement in the major struggles for social justice in the postwar period. He was active in the movements for civil rights, against nuclear proliferation and the Vietnam War, and for environmental justice. Mazzocchi (and the OCAW) played a crucial role in the movement for occupational health and safety. He conceptualized health and safety issues as a fight against corporate power and for worker empowerment. Wages and Mazzocchi campaigned on the promise of breaking away from labor's lockstep allegiances to the Democratic Party.[6]

To counter skeptics who claimed that the union's members would not support such a radical move, Wages and Mazzocchi commissioned a survey of international staff, local union officers, and rank-and-file members. The survey found that 65 percent of members agreed that, "Both the Democratic and Republican Parties care more about the interests of big business than they do about working people." In addition, 53 percent of respondents agreed that, "It's time for labor to build a new political party of working people independent of the two major parties."[7] These survey results facilitated top-to-bottom discussion of political alternatives within the OCAW and led the executive board (made up of both nonvoting union officers and voting rank-and-file union members) to pass a resolution calling for a "new crusade for social and economic justice."[8]

The survey became an organizing tool in its own right, prompting open discussions about politics and labor within the OCAW. Mazzocchi spread the idea to other unions. No matter what union administered it, regardless of geography, occupation, race, or gender, the results were strikingly similar. More than 50 percent of survey respondents agreed that neither political party represented the interests of working people and that the time had come to build a new party of labor.[9]

Building on its successful worker-led small group trainings on occupational health and safety issues, the OCAW commissioned the Labor Institute to develop training materials (which later evolved into the Labor Party's Corporate Power and the American Dream training curriculum) to engage thousands of union members in discussion and debate. It was during one of these sessions that a union member coined what would become the Labor Party's slogan: "The bosses have two parties. We should have one of our own!" Local unions established labor party committees and began to reach out to potential allies in their communities and in the broader labor movement. One popular organizing tool was the video *Mouseland*, narrated by Tommy Douglas, leader of Canada's New Democratic Party. The video is an animated story of a mouse that faces the false dilemma of voting for either a black cat or a white cat, parties that clearly do not represent the interests of the mouse.[10]

By the early 1990s, the Labor Party movement was in full swing. The OCAW assigned Mazzocchi (who had stepped down from his position as international secretary-treasurer) to work full time on building Labor Party Advocates (LPA) within the broader labor movement. The LPA organizing committee was established solely to organize debate within the labor movement—not unlike an organizing committee in a union representation campaign. OCAW president Bob Wages used his national office and position on the AFL-CIO executive council to reach out to other national union leaders. OCAW funded the organizing work of veteran activist Bob Kasen, who produced the newsletter, *Labor Party Advocates*. On the West Coast, organizer Leo Seidlitz worked out of the offices of the San Francisco Labor Council. Other unions contributed significant in-kind resources.

On April 7, 1991, the loosely formed, multi-union LPA organizing committee issued "An Invitation from Tony Mazzocchi to Join Labor Party Advocates" to 5,000 union leaders and activists to better gauge support within the labor movement. In August of that year, conventions of the OCAW, the UE, and the Pennsylvania Federation of the Brotherhood of Maintenance of Way Employees (BMWE), one of the old railroad brotherhoods and now a division of the Teamsters, became the first three union bodies to endorse LPA officially. The following year the California State Federation became the first state AFL-CIO body to endorse. By the end of 1992, more than 300 trade unionists attended an LPA educational conference sponsored by LPA chapters in Detroit and Cleveland.

Momentum grew for the Labor Party as passage of the NAFTA trade agreement at the end of 1993 made the newly elected Clinton administration's neoliberal loyalties painfully clear. The first LPA interim steering committee convened in Chicago in October of that year, and it was attended by 80 labor leaders representing unions with more than half a million workers. The committee called for a founding convention within two years and urged local groups to begin holding hearings about what a real Labor Party would look like.

The national convention of the BMWE, instigated by Pennsylvania Federation (Penn Fed) chairman Jed Dodd, endorsed LPA in 1994 as did the International Longshore and Warehouse Union (ILWU), a union with a long militant history, in 1995. The California Nurses Association, which had just emerged from a period of internal turmoil to embrace a militant and organizing-oriented union model, soon followed. Organizations that sought to organize marginalized and excluded workers such as the Farm Labor Organizing Committee (FLOC) and the Kensington Welfare Rights Union (KWRU) also joined. Respected and innovative leaders like the Nurses' Rose Ann DeMoro and American Federation of Government Employees (AFGE) vice president Ken Blaylock joined the national council—which, in January 1995, issued a call for a spring 1996 founding convention of the Labor Party and appointed convention committees. By January 1996, affiliations included the 50,000-member California Council of Carpenters, the 20,000-member regional health care union 1199 New England, the 12,000-member Chicago Teamsters Local 705, and Machinists Local 1781 in San Mateo, California, with more than 13,000 members.

The year leading up to the founding convention was a period of intense public discussion and debate almost unprecedented in the history of the labor movement. Thousands of members began to pay membership dues and worker-activists (as well as a number of groups with various ideological axes to grind) formed dozens of LPA chapters around the country. LPA moved out of the cubicle donated by Ralph Nader to open our own office and begin planning for the convention. LPA sent a convention call to every local union in the country and set up convention committees for rules, program, and a constitution. Resolutions and affiliations from hundreds of unions and LPA members began pouring into the new office.

Unlike previous party-building efforts led by the labor left, Labor Party Advocates had established enough legitimacy and breadth of support that mainstream union leaders did not publicly denounce it. Instead, our efforts blended with the broader flowering of "new activism" and debate surrounding the election of new AFL-CIO leadership. Newly elected AFL-CIO president John Sweeney, while skeptical about the Labor Party's chances for success, commented: "I would be the last person, however, to discourage the dedicated brothers and sisters who are organizing the Labor Party movement from taking their best shot, and I hope the progress they are making sends a clear signal to a Democratic Party that has moved away from working families, just as surely as it has moved away from the old, the young, the disabled, and the poor."[11]

In preparation for the founding convention, LPA held hearings around the country to draft a constitution, program, and structure for the new party. LPA members also debated what the party would do, once founded. The majority understood that, despite the movement's rapid growth, it would not be possible to intervene immediately in a serious way in electoral politics. Thus, most members advocated a longer-term organizing approach that focused on building power and density and on conducting broad issue-oriented campaigns. Three key factors influenced the debate about whether or not to run or endorse candidates at the outset. First, because of legal restrictions on the use of union membership dues (treasury funds) for direct political purposes, Labor Party engagement in electoral politics would have cut off its access to union treasury funds then financing the party.[12] Second, the newborn party would have immediately lost the support of key unions that were not yet ready to divorce the Democratic Party; and, third, it would have exposed the fact that the burgeoning party was not yet strong enough to win campaigns, much less keep elected officials in line.

The founding convention ratified this perspective. As Labor Party activist and political scientist Adolph Reed Jr. described this organizing model of politics in his *Progressive* column in 1996, "The idea is to build a coalition on the model of union solidarity: developing a base, consolidating it, expanding it, consolidating again, and so on." This "organizing approach to politics is based on intensive, issue-based organizing of the old-fashioned shop-to-shop, door-to-door technique. The paramount objective is to reach out to people who aren't already mobilized in left politics, to begin a conversation that builds a movement."[13]

The founding convention in 1996 was a boisterous four-day event attended by 1,400 delegates and endorsed by 9 international unions and 117 state or local union bodies. Invited speakers Jim Hightower and Jerry Brown brought delegates to their feet with anticorporate messages. Brown, then out of elected office, declared himself a "recovering" politician who had to tell the truth. Ralph Nader, running for president on the Green Party ticket, spoke from the floor as an at-large delegate. Nader said, "This convention will be looked upon as the rebirth of the labor movement after so many years of being subordinated to corporate power."[14]

Inspiring as the speakers were, it was the delegates who set the tone and energy of the convention. Committees met into the wee hours of the night to craft resolutions and work out compromises on the program and constitution. Threats were made to walk out over yet-to-be resolved disagreements. An impromptu march to city hall was organized to denounce the anticollective bargaining initiatives of Cleveland's mayor, and funds were raised for various unions on strike, including the Detroit newspaper workers.

The new party's program, "A Call for Economic Justice," included support for an amendment to the U.S. Constitution to guarantee a job at a living wage; restoration of the rights to organize, bargain, and strike; universal access to quality health care; access to quality public education; an end to the corporate abuse of trade; an end to corporate welfare; and revitalization of the public sector.[15] The program was visionary and yet could pass Mazzocchi's often-repeated litmus test: "Can you get this passed in your local?"

Delegates to the founding convention set up a governing structure that assured that unions and worker organizations would play the predominant role in the party, and provisions were made for a committee to define conditions under which the Labor Party would embark on an electoral strategy. The list of new affiliate unions continued to grow, including the American Federation of Government Employees (AFGE) and the United Mineworkers of America (UMWA).

Between 1996 and 2002, much of the Labor Party's organizing focused on campaigns to organize labor support for issues including single-payer health care and worker rights. The Labor Party launched its Just Health Care campaign with a nationwide radio show hosted by Pacifica's Amy Goodman, and our financing plan was adopted by single-payer advocates in the U.S. Congress, including Paul Wellstone and John Conyers.[16] We also launched the Free Higher Education campaign, which called for free, publicly funded higher education.[17] The Campaign for Worker Rights based an expansive view of worker rights on constitutional principles that went far beyond calls for expedited union election procedures.[18] We published a monthly newspaper, *Labor Party Press*, edited by labor journalist Laura McClure and designed by the Labor Institute's Michael Kaufman.[19] Veteran UE organizers Ed Bruno and Bob Brown joined the national organizing staff. We developed an electoral strategy that committed the party to electoral politics as an important tactic, but not the only tool needed to achieve working-class power.[20]

Labor Party chapters hosted public events in dozens of cities, launched a number of issue campaigns, and, in Massachusetts, Maine, and Florida, initiated and won nonbinding referenda in support of single-payer national health care. The Labor Party also encouraged a vigorous cultural celebration of workers in theater, film, music, and art, including the establishment (in conjunction with the American Film Institute and the Washington Metropolitan Council of the AFL-CIO) of the annual DC Labor FilmFest.[21]

In the first few years of the new century, however, a number of events contributed to a significant loss of momentum in the movement to establish a labor party. The effects of globalization and deindustrialization had ravaged the membership of many of the sponsoring unions. Several ceased to exist, including the OCAW, which merged with the Paperworkers Union in 1999. Soon thereafter, the leadership of the newly merged union, PACE, ceased its active support for the Labor Party. (PACE later merged into the United Steel Workers of America.) The debacle of the stolen 2000 presidential election—and the subsequent scapegoating of Green Party candidate Ralph Nader as a spoiler—created an environment hostile to any attempt to build an independent political movement. The attacks on September 11, 2001, and the subsequent rush to war also had a chilling effect on efforts to promote a radical break with the two-party system. The Bush administration's attacks on unions and the entire social insurance model gave rise to an "anybody but Bush" mindset within much of the labor movement. This squelched any political vision beyond the urgency of defeating Bush and his political allies and defending the remnants of the New Deal and Great Society programs.

In 2002, Tony Mazzocchi, the founding brother of the Labor Party movement, died after a yearlong illness. While Mazzocchi had been careful to avoid the "cult of personality" that has plagued many political movements and had cultivated a diverse group of committed leaders and organizers, his death was nonetheless an organizational setback. The Labor Party lost his years of experience, his strategic vision, and the vast respect that unionists at all levels had for him.

The 2002 Labor Party convention reflected these diminished prospects. Delegates opted to focus efforts on our issue-oriented organizing campaigns. While a step back from the dream of a fully developed party with the capacity to contend for power in the political sphere, these campaigns were far-reaching in their analysis; they continue to inform the political discourse in the labor movement today. And many of the activists who founded U.S. Labor Against the War (USLAW) worked together in the Labor Party and participated in its 2002 discussion about how labor should respond to President Bush's growing threat to invade Iraq. Labor Party National Council members Noel Beasley and Jerry Zero hosted the first meeting of USLAW in Chicago early the next year.

In 2004, the Labor Party's analysis of labor's role in that year's disastrous election campaign received wide attention in progressive circles. The party also weighed in on the contentious debates about the future of the AFL-CIO.[22] Despite these efforts to find some strategic traction, the momentum was no longer there. The labor movement itself was in broad retreat. Huge sections were aligning themselves with a new global company union perspective that had no room for an expansive, anticorporate political movement like the Labor Party. Much of the rest of labor was embroiled in losing defensive battles, and it could no longer conceive of the possibility of a broad political advance for working people.

The last formal initiative of the Labor Party was a petition campaign to gain ballot access for the South Carolina Labor Party in 2006. With almost unanimous support from South Carolina's small but feisty labor movement, led by state AFL-CIO president Donna Dewitt, organizers fanned out across the state. (Flea markets in addition to union halls were the ideal venue to address working people.) We spoke one-on-one with thousands of South Carolinians who agreed that working people needed—what became the slogan of the South Carolina Labor Party—"Another Choice for South Carolina." With minimal resources, Labor Party activists gathered more than 16,000 signatures from registered voters, securing, in the fall of 2006, a ballot line and proving that we could build a party of labor in the heart of the right-to-work South. Even this inspiring effort, however, fell victim to the growing marginalization of the labor movement and the rising tide of Obamamania.[23] By the end of 2007, the Labor Party ceased accepting individual memberships and union affiliations and suspended its active operations.

Lessons Learned

Mistakes were certainly made in the short history of the Labor Party, and some obstacles proved too difficult to overcome. Perhaps the most difficult was the development of a strategy to extract the labor movement from the tentacles of the two-party electoral process. An organizing dynamic took hold in which enthusiasm for developing an alternative to the Democrats peaked in the off-cycle election years and diminished as unions mobilized for yet another round of elections. This dynamic cannot solely be attributed to muddled, compromised, or timid union leadership. Unions, and working people in general, have real, concrete interests and concerns that must be defended in the electoral arena, even as we work to transcend the boundaries set by the two parties of the bosses. The prospect of breaking completely with the Democratic Party without an established alternative was too risky for even the most militant unions, and it remains the biggest challenge to any effort to build an independent labor politics.

The somewhat disjointed internal structure of the Labor Party also gave rise to conflict between union-based organizing and chapter-based organizing. Although a number of local chapters developed with a strong union base, many others were organized with no base to which they could be held accountable. Many chapters contributed significantly to the advancement of the Labor Party's goals, but others devolved into sectarian debating societies, drove out serious worker activists, and sucked resources from the organization. Another constant topic of debate was how high to raise expectations of this newly created party. Many unions and activists pressured Mazzocchi and other early LPA leaders to hold the founding convention in 1996 to capitalize on that year's momentum. In retrospect, it may well have been wiser to secure more significant support from the labor movement, to retain a looser Labor Party Advocates structure rather than create the raised expectations of a formal party.

None of the internal mistakes and weaknesses would have proved fatal if the labor movement had continued to gain strength from its revival in the mid-1990s. Instead, the pressures of neoliberalism, deindustrialization, and globalization led many unions to cut their losses and focus on holding the line. Even the most dynamic unions put their efforts into organizing union density (increasing the percentage of unionized workers in an industry or geographic area) rather than political power. Ultimately, it was this structural decline of the labor movement that made the Labor Party untenable.

Those of us who worked to build the Labor Party have little to regret. The fact remains that this was the most successful effort to construct an independent working-class party since the La Follette campaigns 75 years earlier. The Labor Party did many things right, including the following:

- It adopted a party-building model that was patient and inclusive. We resisted attempts to convene a body of self-appointed leaders with a shopping list of demands for the working class to follow. Rather, we focused on building a broad movement of working-class institutions, leaders, and activists to speak on our own behalf.

- The Labor Party understood that unions had to be at the core. As the only institutions with the resources and the capacity to implement a broad political strategy, no viable progressive party can exist without the support and participation of a significant percentage of the national labor movement. At the same time, success also depends on being inclusive enough to resonate with the interests and concerns of unorganized workers as well.

- The Labor Party avoided the expediency of identity politics and liberal talking points and instead organized around broad class-based interests and concerns. When faced with controversial or socially divisive issues, we built consensus by developing a program and a vision that can appeal to and educate the broadest possible constituency without sacrificing a working-class agenda. For example, Clinton's 1996 "reform" of welfare demonized welfare recipients in ways that could have divided workers. The Labor Party framed it as a class issue and as a mechanism to undermine union rights, and members rallied in opposition. *blah*

- The Labor Party understood that elections were not about playing the spoiler or about bearing witness. Rather, the electoral process should be about building power for working people. The Labor Party's "Call for Economic Justice" is an eloquent statement of what politics would look like if workers had a party of our own.[24] Our electoral strategy, crafted after two years of internal debate, stands as a concise statement of what is required for an independent working-class party to intervene seriously in electoral politics. The strategy includes independence from corporations, accountability to party membership and program, and sustained activity before, during, and between elections to politically educate and mobilize the working class.[25]

There Is No Alternative

Many consider the perennial efforts to build a party of labor to be a fool's errand. Indeed, the challenges do appear insurmountable. Those who would build a labor party must find a way to extract a labor movement that is enmeshed in all types of instrumental political relationships from an entrenched two-party system where the winner takes all. In addition, a labor movement that now represents only 7 percent of the private sector has difficulty setting terms and conditions of debate, much less building and sustaining political power. Is there an alternative to the labor party strategy in which working people can build such power? Activists within and outside of the labor movement have engaged in a number of significant yet flawed attempts during the past two decades, including the following.

Reform the Democratic Party. Although individual progressive or prolabor candidates have won office on the Democratic ticket and have impacted the party's platform, their efforts have not transformed the party into a vehicle for a working-class political agenda. One reason is that the Democratic Party defines itself as a multiclass party, claiming to represent both working-class interests and the economic program of "progressive" capital, thus blurring working-class concerns with and subordinating them to a neoliberal agenda. But more significantly, neither of the two major parties has a structure that would hold them accountable to a living, breathing constituency. Rather, the parties exist in the political ether as a series of unaccountable relationships between funders, candidates, and interest groups. Instead of accountability to masses of voters, the overriding party allegiance (especially since the rise of neoliberalism) is to a globalized capitalism whose interests trump all other concerns. In this context, the periodic emergence of "insurgent" candidates may pull those who would stray from the Democratic Party back into the fold. But when the dust settles, we are left with the same unaccountable and unresponsive national party, a political graveyard for progressives.

Organize first, build political power later. This position has both a "left/syndicalist" (all power springs from the active organization of workers at the point of production) and a "right/opportunist" (organization of workers can only be achieved by building a broad partnership with the bosses) variation. Both ignore the reality that the ability to organize and defend the broad social insurance programs that make it possible for workers to live a decent life is determined politically.[26] After almost seven years of trying such an "organize first" approach, those unions that formed the Change to Win alliance to pursue that strategy (based on the belief that the AFL-CIO was spending too much of its resources on political activities rather than on organizing) have not met with any breakthrough successes.[27] In fact, many of them now are expending a higher percentage of their resources on political activities than many of the old AFL-CIO unions.

Green Party/Nader electoralism. The Greens have maintained that the way to build a new political movement is to first engage in electoral politics. They have been at it for more than 20 years and have won hundreds of local offices, though many are in nonpartisan elections. In 2000, presidential candidate Ralph Nader garnered 2.7 percent of votes cast. The party's economic program is inclusive enough to be considered a labor program. However, the party is unable to mobilize the institutional resources necessary for a credible electoral effort that even a weakened labor movement can still marshal. In fact, the party continues to promote many candidacies that mainly serve to protest the status quo. While that may assuage the consciences of the politically pure, it has not produced transformative political results.

Fusion. Several states allow candidates to be endorsed by multiple political parties. New York State, in particular, has a venerable tradition of "fusion," wherein minor parties endorse major party candidates in an attempt to gain some leverage and influence in the major party's administration. It has proven to be an effective tool to build some power within the current political system. In New York, the Working Families Party has for nearly 15 years used cross endorsements to win increases in the minimum wage and other benefits for working people (though activists in other states have also succeeded in raising the minimum wage and other similar initiatives through old-fashioned lobbying and pressure campaigns). However, fusion advocates have not been able to transform this power into a tool for advancing a broad working-class agenda. Rather, fusion parties have become creatures of the major parties that they were hoping to transform. For example, in 2010 New York witnessed the disgraceful spectacle of the Working Families Party begging to endorse Andrew Cuomo, the Democratic candidate for governor, who *even before the election* promised to attack public worker unions and undermine public worker benefits. It is possible that proworker fusion parties where they exist could become allies in a revived Labor Party movement, but efforts to build new fusion parties in states that have no history of such politics and no legal framework of cross-endorsement appear to be a colossal waste of energy and resources.

In the end, the creation of a party of our own remains is the great unfinished task of the U.S. working class and the only real way out of the two-party political wilderness. There are no political shortcuts. Nor is it conceivable that such a party could emerge without having, at its core, a revived and revitalized labor movement. While these tasks may be even more daunting today than they were in the 1990s, it doesn't make them any less urgent or necessary.

Next Steps

This is a time of tremendous opportunity. After years of economic crisis and political impotency, working people are questioning the legitimacy of the entire political system and exposing its corrupt domination by a rich oligarchy. The Occupy movement struck a chord with so many because its organizers understood that the system is rigged to generate inequality. Unfortunately, because of the reasons enumerated above, this is not yet a time when the revival or relaunching of a working-class political party is in order. No matter what individual activists may desire, the simple fact remains that you cannot build a party of labor when the labor movement itself is in disarray and retreat.

While this is not the time to dust off the Labor Party, it certainly is the time for working-class activists to begin the discussion of what it would take to build an independent, class-based political party. That discussion can be greatly informed by the history of the Labor Party movement, and we need to encourage a broad discussion of this history and its lessons for today. Many current leaders and activists in the labor movement were not around when the Labor Party was at its heyday more than a decade ago. Many of the key participants in the Labor Party are nearing retirement, and they have valuable lessons to share with a new generation. We believe that the current political moment is a time when people will be very responsive to such a discussion.

We should also work to support initiatives that could promote class politics. Groups such as the Labor Campaign for Single Payer and U.S. Labor Against the War (USLAW) fight for issues of broad concern to working people, and they require the construction of a powerful anticorporate movement to achieve their goals.[28] They help to educate working people about the nature of the political system and bring together the best and the brightest activists across geographic lines and union jurisdictions. They challenge labor to fulfill its historic role to lead a social movement of working people. In addition, unions should embrace internal mobilization projects that educate members about a real working-class agenda, identify and develop new leadership, and build relationships with potential allies. National Nurses United's Robin Hood Campaign to impose a financial transaction tax on Wall Street speculators is one concrete example of how thousands of union members can be moved to action around issues not directly tied to the next election cycle.[29]

It might also be time to revive the Labor Party Advocates political survey. The history of the Labor Party shows how political action questionnaires can be a valuable organizing tool. In the current period, it would provide an immediate task to engage advocates, a low-commitment "ask" for union leaders at all levels, and an opportunity to gather valuable information about the state of mind and political attitudes of union members, activists, and leaders.

The 10 Percent Solution

It is not realistic to demand that today's labor movement completely disengage itself from its current ties with the Democratic Party. However, the ongoing economic crisis and the failures of the Obama administration seem to provide an opening to begin to challenge labor to move some of its resources toward a long-term project. Such an effort would advance a broad working-class program that goes beyond the next election and that is geared to building independent political power for working people. We could launch such a venture if labor contributed just 10 percent of the resources and finances that it spent in the 2012 election cycle.

What could we do with those resources and commitments? We could connect with the tens of millions Americans who either are unemployed or underemployed, underwater on their mortgages, reliant on food stamps to feed their families, still lacking sufficient health care coverage, condemned to a lifetime of student debt peonage, deprived of a more secure life via citizenship rights, or trapped in a series of Walmart-style jobs (and facing the possible loss of even the minimal social insurance benefits that used to be the birthright of everyone in the United States). In short, we could begin to mobilize and speak on behalf of a working class that has become fragmented and disenfranchised because of a political system that inexorably distributes wealth and power upward to "the 1 percent."

There is much to learn from the Labor Party movement. Until we (working people) have a party of our own, we are doomed to fight with one hand tied behind our back. "This is the struggle of our generation," said the Labor Party founders in 1996. "The future of our children and their children hangs in the balance. It is a struggle we cannot afford to lose."[30]

Notes

1 See Klein, *For All These Rights*; and Gottschalk, *The Shadow Welfare State*.
2 See Harvey, *A Brief History of Neoliberalism*.
3 This was a series of mass protests in Wisconsin in the winter of 2011 that unsuccessfully attempted to prevent the state legislature from enacting a series of anti-union measures proposed by Governor Scott Walker.
4 Labor Party, "About the Labor Party." This source and all subsequent citations of sources authored by the Labor Party are from the Labor Party website.
5 Labor Party, "A Call for Economic Justice."
6 Labor Party, "Labor Party National Organizer: Tony Mazzocchi." See also Leopold, *The Man Who Hated Work and Loved Labor*.
7 Leopold, 443–45.
8 Oil, Chemical, and Atomic Workers International Union, AFL-CIO, *Proceedings* (1991), 59.
9 Leopold, 443–45.
10 Douglas-Coldwell Foundation, "The Story of Mouseland."
11 Sweeney, "John Sweeney Responds," 28.
12 Federal election laws prohibit the use of union membership dues (treasury funds) for contributions to political candidates. Most unions collect separate, voluntary contributions via a committee on political education (COPE) or political action committee (PAC). As a nonelectoral social advocacy organization, the Labor Party was not subject to federal election law restrictions. Consequently, unions were able to support it with treasury funds. Engaging in electoral politics would have cut off access to treasury (dues-based) funds and forced the new party to compete for the much more limited COPE or PAC funds, thus effectively defunding the party. Recent Supreme Court decisions have made it easier for unions (and corporations) to make political contributions through Super PACS (though direct contributions to candidates are still restricted). These rules were not in effect at the time the Labor Party was launched.
13 Reed, "Building Solidarity," 21.
14 La Botz, "Founding the Labor Party."

15 Labor Party, "A Call for Economic Justice."
16 Labor Party, "Just Health Care."
17 Labor Party, "Free Higher Education."
18 Labor Party, "Campaign for Worker Rights."
19 Labor Party, "Labor Party Press Archives."
20 Labor Party, "Electoral Strategy of the Labor Party."
21 Washington, DC, Metro Council, AFL-CIO, "DC Labor FilmFest."
22 Dudzic, "The Debate Continues."
23 Labor and progressive activists in South Carolina turned their attention to mobilizing for the 2008 election cycle with the recurring hope that the next Democratic presidential candidate (in this case, Obama) would be better than the last (or at least would be the lesser of two evils). See the next section, "Lessons Learned," for further explanation.
24 Labor Party, "A Call for Economic Justice."
25 Labor Party, "Electoral Strategy of the Labor Party."
26 Union rights and representation procedures in the private sector are defined by a series of federal laws (Wagner Act, Taft-Hartley Act, Landrum-Griffen Act, Railway Labor Act, etc.), and these rights and procedures tend to be modified based on the relative political strength of labor and capital. Likewise, public employee rights are determined by state legislation and policies that can be easily and quickly overturned or expanded by a new administration. All other components of social insurance benefits have the same characteristics.
27 In its six years of existence, Change to Win organized only a fraction of the new members it promised at its inception. See Early, 230–35.
28 See the websites of the Labor Campaign for Single Payer Healthcare and U.S. Labor Against the War.
29 The Robin Hood Tax, "ROBINHOODTAX."
30 Labor Party, "A Call for Economic Justice."

Bibliography

Douglas-Coldwell Foundation. "The Story of Mouseland: As Told by Tommy Douglas in 1944." Accessed June 30, 2014. www.dcf.ca/en/mouseland.htm.

Dudzic, Mark. "The Debate Continues: A Revitalized Labor Movement Needs a New Vision of Politics." Last modified March 5, 2005. www.thelaborparty.org/d_debate.htm.

Early, Steve. *Save Our Unions: Dispatches From A Movement in Distress.* New York: Monthly Review Press, 2013.

Gottschalk, Marie. *The Shadow Welfare State: Labor, Business, and the Politics of Health Care in the United States.* Ithaca, NY: ILR Press, 2000.

Harvey, David. *A Brief History of Neoliberalism.* Oxford: Oxford University Press, 2005.

Klein, Jennifer. *For All These Rights: Business, Labor, and the Shaping of America's Public-Private Welfare State.* Princeton, NJ: Princeton University Press, 2006.

Labor Campaign for Single Payer Health Care. "The Labor Campaign for Single Payer Healthcare." Accessed March 20, 2014. www.laborforsinglepayer.org/.

Labor Party. "A Call for Economic Justice: The Labor Party's Program." Accessed March 20, 2014. www.thelaborparty.org/d_program.htm.

———. "About the Labor Party." Accessed March 20, 2014. www.thelaborparty. org/a_tm.htm.

———. "Campaign for Worker Rights." Accessed March 20, 2014. www.thelaborparty. org/c_workerrights.html.

———. "Electoral Strategy of the Labor Party." Accessed March 20, 2014. www.thelabor party.org/d_electoral.htm.

———. "Free Higher Education." Accessed March 20, 2014. www.thelaborparty.org/a_ fhe.html.

———. "Just Health Care." Accessed March 20, 2014. www.thelaborparty.org/c_jhc.html.

———. "Labor Party National Organizer: Tony Mazzocchi." Accessed March 20, 2014. www.thelaborparty.org/a_tm.htm.

———. "Labor Party Press Archives." Accessed March 20, 2014. www.thelaborparty. org/d_lpp_news.htm.

La Botz, Dan. "Founding the Labor Party." *Against the Current* 63 (1996). Accessed March 19, 2014. www.solidarity-us.org/site/node/765.

Leopold, Les. *The Man Who Hated Work and Loved Labor: The Life and Times of Tony Mazzocchi.* New York: Chelsea Green, 2007.

Oil, Chemical, and Atomic Workers International Union, AFL-CIO. 1991. *Proceedings of the 20th Constitutional Convention,* Denver, Co., August 12–16, 1991. St. Louis, Mo.: The Union.

Reed, Adolph, Jr. "Building Solidarity." *The Progressive,* August 1996, 20–21.

Sweeney, John. "John Sweeney Responds." *Labor Research Review* 1, no. 24 (1996): 26–29. Accessed December 9, 2014. http://digitalcommons.ilr.cornell.edu/cgi/viewcontent. cgi?article=1264&context=lrr.

The Robin Hood Tax. "ROBINHOODTAX." Accessed March 20, 2014. http://robin hoodtax.org/.

U.S. Labor Against the War. "U.S. Labor Against the War." Accessed March 20, 2014. www. laborforsinglepayer.org/.

Washington, DC, Metro Council, AFL-CIO. "DC Labor FilmFest." Accessed March 20, 2014. www.dclabor.org/ht/d/ProgramDetails/i/23256.

9

DON'T WAIT FOR LABOR

The Necessity of Building a Left Third Party at the Grassroots

John Halle

In late 2013, AFL-CIO head Richard Trumka made an unusually politically provocative pledge. Taking stock of the Obama administration's long record of broken promises to labor, which culminated in its proposal to reduce Social Security benefits by changing how they are inflation-adjusted, Trumka issued the following declaration: "No politician . . . I don't care the political party . . . will get away with cutting Social Security, Medicare, or Medicaid benefits. Don't try it."[1] "This warning goes double for Democrats," he continued. "We will never forget. We will never forgive. And we will never stop working to end your career."[2] Trumka's chief deputy, Damon Silver, chimed in on the same theme a few days later: "We're being really clear. We're not going to give cover to Democrats who think it's a good idea to take away economic security from our most vulnerable citizens."[3]

How the AFL would carry out these threats was left unspecified, though elementary logic dictated that if Trumka were serious about "ending the careers of Democrats," two options were available. One option, issuing Democratic primary challenges, unions had occasionally attempted, although with mixed results, as doing so carried the danger of weakening the eventual nominee and resulting in a "greater evil" Republican victory. The other option, higher risk but also offering potentially greater rewards, would be that which labor has consistently avoided for virtually its entire history. This would involve pledging support to an existing third party or its candidates, or else forming a labor party and targeting those Democrats who fail to reciprocate for labor's routine and costly investments in their campaigns.

However, unprecedented conditions require unprecedented responses, and there was reason to believe the time might be right to break with the Democrats should national labor leadership decide to make an uncharacteristically bold move. Most conspicuously favorable was the evident public distrust for all elected officials, with the president, Congress, and the two major parties laboring under historically low approval ratings.[4] Mirroring this sentiment was support for third parties edging upward and a majority of younger people registering a positive view of socialism, according to recent polls.[5]

This chapter will address the main question raised by Trumka's announcement: whether it makes sense for those committed to advancing a left agenda to push for the formation of a labor party under the auspices of existing unions. But before considering this, it is worth noting that Trumka's remarks fell on deaf ears. They only found their way into a couple of stories filed by reporters on the ever-dwindling labor beat, before quickly disappearing from the news cycle. More significant was the nonresponse emanating from both administration officials and Democratic Party leadership. This initially might seem surprising. The Democrats, after all, rely on the unions for financial support and, more importantly, for on-the-ground political muscle during campaigns. Union locals assume a major role in Democrats' grassroots electoral work, such as phone banking, lawn sign distribution, and election day get-out-the-vote operations.

Yet, it seems likely that the silence was itself a statement—a tacit demonstration that both the unions and the Democrats knew perfectly well that Trumka's threat would not materialize. Having only rarely supported primary challenges and virtually never endorsed third party candidacies, the unions had nowhere to go, that is, no electoral means to discipline wayward Democrats. Most notable among errant Democrats were those who signed off on right-wing efforts to impose austerity, rewarded by the huge pool of financial support routinely available to those who side with capital against the interests of workers. For so long having outsourced the selection and development of candidates to the Democrats, unions lack any internal mechanism for recruiting and advancing independent candidates for national office. Nor is there any indication that labor has any intention to develop such a mechanism, much less a broader long-term strategy for declaring electoral independence from the Democrats.

Below I argue that a strategy does exist for the development of a labor-based party and that the benefits of pursuing it are likely to significantly outweigh the costs. Of course, that does not imply that any such strategy will be pursued by the unions, or that it will have any significant influence on their direction in the years to come. Indeed, there is good reason to believe, based on their history and institutional structure, that unions not only will resist developing an independent electoral strategy; they also will function as a significant obstacle to any internal or external elements that would attempt to pursue such an approach. Given this reality, leftists should be aware that a main obstacle preventing the development of a third party (arguably the most important goal of left political organizing) will be union leadership. For reasons that will be discussed, it is clear that if the Left requires that an insurgent party take its initiative from this source, it is sure to be disappointed.

I begin with a brief discussion of the potential advantages for labor in having local officials who willingly pursue aspects of its agenda. I note several places where sympathetic local government has achieved concrete results. Included among these is New Haven, Connecticut. There I briefly served as a Green Party official working to achieve gains for the local unions then involved in a strike against the city's largest employer, Yale University. Next, I discuss some of the general lessons this experience offers while highlighting certain potential that remains untapped in New Haven and elsewhere. Other cities, I argue, offer considerable opportunities for insurgent third parties to go beyond what was accomplished in New Haven, particularly if the party is explicitly identified with local labor unions. The case of Lorain, Ohio, is briefly considered in this light, as is the case of the now defunct Labor Party. The latter, I maintain, failed to take advantage of available electoral opportunities at the local level. Finally, I provide a brief survey of the fraught relationships between organizers of radical third parties and national labor unions, showing how and why these unions usually have been serious obstacles to the establishment of an independent working-class party. In view of the above analysis, I conclude that a viable labor-oriented third party only can be built if it adopts a locally based, bottom-up approach that operates independently of the leadership of the major national unions.

Union Power, Local Government, and Electoral Discipline

As suggested above, organized labor's inability to impose electoral discipline on Democrats siding with labor's enemies insures that their national agenda will continue to be routinely ignored. At the same time, it is important to recognize, as has been sporadically demonstrated, that unions have the capacity to respond much more effectively at other levels of government. In particular, unions can wield significant electoral power at local and occasionally regional levels, in many cases serving as the dominant influence.

The lower level focus by unions frequently has paid dividends, as writer Kristian Williams has documented.[6] At the peak period of radical labor activism a century ago or more, broad cooperation between city government and organized labor was taken for granted, and union organizing drives substantially benefited from these relationships. Instances of cooperation cited by Williams extend back to 1874, when "the mayor and sheriff of Braidwood, Ill., refused to deputize Pinkerton guards. Instead they deputized striking miners, disarmed the Pinkertons, and arrested strikebreakers."[7] During a 1902 streetcar strike in Pawtucket, Rhode Island, "the mayor . . . openly sided with the striking workers and the police did almost nothing to impede their activities,"[8] while during another 1902 strike in New Orleans "the police didn't just stand aside, but actually attacked the scabs, arresting them on weapons charges and (as one newspaper put it) 'slamming them about unmercifully.'"[9] Other examples include the 1919 Cleveland steel strike, where "Mayor Harry Davis ordered police to treat scabs as suspicious persons."[10] Also, "during the 1934 Milwaukee Electric Railway and Light Company strike, Mayor Daniel Hoan ordered the arrest of 150 strikebreakers."[11]

Williams notes that local police departments' behavior is circumscribed by local government, citing the conclusions of historian James Richardson that "police tended to follow the lines of power. . . . If the authorities favored the workers or were at least neutral, the police remained neutral. If on the other hand, political leaders . . . viewed the strikers as un-American radicals . . . then the police acted as agents of employers in their strikebreaking activities."[12]

Given the crucial role of local government and law enforcement during strike actions, it would seem that the labor unions should make achieving close working relationships with, or at best, actual representation in city councils a top priority. For a variety of reasons, collaboration between unions and local government has become the exception rather than the norm. Of the relatively few such examples from the postwar period, the last Williams mentions was in 1997 in Houston, where the police chief gave orders to ticket scab truckers.

New Haven: Scope and Limits of Local Reform

While it is rarely actualized, the potential remains for municipal authorities to intercede with local government to ensure favorable treatment for unions during strikes and organizing drives. An example of this in which I myself played a role as a New Haven alderman occurred during the 2003 strike of Yale unions. Part of this strike involved the attempted organizing of health care workers at Yale-New Haven hospital. In an attempt to undermine the organizing drive, the Yale administration ordered the Yale University police force to arrest union leafleteers on hospital property. Following the activists' arrest, a union organizer suggested to me the possibility of submitting a resolution to remove the Yale police's deputizing authority. It was quickly drafted and then passed by the full board, enabling the organizing drive at Yale hospital to proceed unhindered by police disruption.[13]

Although I did not run on a labor party line (since the Labor Party, as will be discussed subsequently, was not available as a ballot line), I was a third party member, specifically of the Green Party. Elected in 2001, I was committed to locally advancing the party's key value of economic justice.[14] The goal, for which union support was central, was understood by the local party chapter to be the creation of a comprehensive program to address New Haven's high levels of wage and income inequality. The chapter's platform also included raising city revenue by targeting wealthy nonprofit corporations (most notably Yale), passing a local living wage ordinance, strengthening largely toothless protections for renters, and creating a municipal utility to provide low cost cable television and Internet service. Many of these ideas came from the unions through their locally based think tank, the Connecticut Center for a New Economy. Others came from union members who, as participants in chapter deliberations in an unofficial capacity, helped to formulate the platform and actively supported local Green Party campaigns.

On the strength of these proposals, we elected 2 candidates to the office of alderman and narrowly missed electing 2 others to the 30-member board in 2001. A few years after my departure in 2003, a Green would be elected in another ward, though he would be defeated in his reelection bid in 2009. This resulted in the return of Democratic control for all 30 board seats. Unfortunately, the New Haven unions chose not to advance the third party precedent that the Green Party had established during this period. The unions would maintain a strong electoral presence. However, rather than developing an independent electoral alternative, they focused on expanding their influence on what had already been a mostly sympathetic though, at crucial moments, an insufficiently supportive board of aldermen. They did so by electing a majority of current union members to serve on the board.[15] The unions also moved to take control of the Democratic town committee, thus ensuring that endorsed candidates would be reliable supporters of the union agenda. In so doing, they chose to work within the system that had served them well, at least within circumscribed limits.

Yet there is a serious drawback for the unions in pursuing the above pro-Democratic strategy. At higher levels of government, which have played a key role in the rollback of labor as a social and political force in the past several decades, the Democrats have been dubious allies at best. New Haven politics provides a revealing case study. Various labor-friendly Democratic Yale campus activists have later served in higher political office. But when they have done so, they have often neglected their roots, advancing and implementing legislation undermining unions and the communities in which they are based. Of these politicians, the most notorious is former alderman and U.S. senator Joseph Lieberman. As a senator, he would become an iconic neoliberal Democrat, or, in other words, an archetypical Democratic proponent of policies that benefit corporations and the wealthy at the expense of subordinate classes. He actively promoted antilabor deregulation policies and free trade agreements, while doing little to roll back antiworker legislation passed during Republican administrations. (Notably, the New Haven unions would continue to support him, including during his third party campaign against the successful primary challenge from a more progressive Democrat, Ned Lamont.) Another Yale Democrat is former alderman Anthony Williams. Later, in his executive capacity as mayor of Washington, DC, he would impose a harsh austerity budget accompanied by strikingly right-wing initiatives, including a flat tax and school vouchers. A third figure who got his start in New Haven politics was Bill Clinton. His memoirs, which draw a highly sympathetic portrait of local machine boss Arthur Barbieri, illustrate how close he was to the local Democratic establishment.[16] As president, Clinton would end up pushing and signing off on free trade agreements that would devastate what remained of New Haven's unionized industrial base. Additionally, Clinton's conservative welfare reform and drug war initiatives took a heavy toll on New Haven's largely nonwhite population, a major part of the local Democratic electoral base.

New Haven has frequently functioned as a training ground for ambitious Yale College Democrats, imparting to them instruction in retail political skills through connections with local activist, community, and labor groups. At the same time at Yale, most often through its law and business schools and network of corporate alumni, these Democrats have been able to forge and cement connections with elite elements of corporate capital. The unions deciding to declare their independence would have challenged these longstanding arrangements—by which budding corporate Democrats posture as supporters of urban working-class initiatives while preparing to jettison these sympathies when elites require they do so. Unfortunately, the unions did not choose to disrupt the role the New Haven Democratic Party plays within this plutocratic system. Possibly this was the case because the partisan status quo serves immediate union interests (through such actions as minimally favorable appointments to the National Labor Relations Board and the courts, as well as the passage of occasional, albeit increasingly rare, proworker legislation).

Of course, it is possible that the precedent set by the Green Party eventually may result in the unions taking a more adversarial path. If they do so, this would mark a fundamental shift in their orientation with potential national as well as local ramifications. It would be indicative of a left beginning to develop the capacity to seriously challenge elite control through the electoral system. Such an action, if it ever occurs, would be worthy of the Left's close attention.

Lorain County, Ohio, and the Independent Labor Challenge

What did capture the attention of sectors of the national Left during the 2013 electoral cycle was a much more radical, albeit small-scale, break with existing arrangements, emerging in the November municipal elections in Ohio. There, in the County of Lorain, unions supported 14 prolabor candidates, some of whom were not backed by the local Democratic Party, including three independents, all of whom were elected. One ran unopposed in the city of Elyria and the other two ran in the city of Lorain against candidates endorsed by the Democrats.[17] Rather than work exclusively within the Democratic Party by automatically supporting its favored candidates, county union leaders had decided to act more autonomously for a change.[18] They even unofficially dubbed efforts to promote their renegade slate "the Lorain Independent Labor Party."[19] The *Lorain Chronicle*'s election roundup reported the specific explanation for the decision to break with the Democrats; it was articulated by one of the rebel labor leaders, Joe Thayer (a Sheet

Metal Workers Union organizer, former county AFL-CIO head, and Democratic Party precinct committeeman[20]):

> The Democratic Party, Thayer said, hasn't been meeting its obligations to organized labor recently. He said [the Lorain City] Council's March vote to water down unionization and local-hire requirements on contractors bidding for city projects [the Project Labor Agreement, or PLA] was one example. . . . Another problem, Thayer said, is that city officials, including Mayor Chase Ritenauer, essentially acted as "strikebreakers" when they collected trash in the city during a weeklong strike by Republic Waste workers in April. "If we can't get a party that we've always supported hands down to support us, we're going to look elsewhere," Thayer said.[21]

Democratic Party leaders in the city of Lorain quickly sanctioned the orchestrators of the breakaway, likely recognizing the dangers that independent labor party activism posed to the electoral foundation of the Democrats.[22]

It is important to appreciate the larger electoral context of this unusual falling out between the labor and the Democratic Party. Like many other heavily postindustrial areas in the East and Midwest in recent decades, Lorain County largely has been under Democratic control, with the Republican minority having almost been reduced to rump party (noncompetitive) status.[23] Under these circumstances, with the spoiler factor removed, a labor (or Green) party functions as a de facto second party in the races in which it chooses to compete. Here, Democrats' failure to support organized labor becomes a chief campaign issue, rather than being swept under the rug, as would be the case if there commonly were viable right-wing Republican challengers.

The Lorain County, Ohio, case offers a direct contrast to the model pursued by the unions in New Haven in two respects. On the one hand, as already mentioned, the creation and use of an independent ballot designation constitutes a sharp break with the position of national unions, a strategy that the New Haven unions have not pursued. On the other hand, unlike the New Haven unions, the Lorain Independent Labor Party (ILP) officeholders at present are committed to advancing a limited economic program that protects longstanding arrangements between the unions and local government, including, most notably, the reinstatement of the PLA. As of this writing, they have not pursued broad redistributionist programs of the sort sought by the New Haven unions. However, various statements by ILP coalition members suggest that the party will attempt to move forward with similar sorts of initiatives and function as an alternative to a Democratic Party that, in their view, has severed its roots in the working class.[24]

How far the Lorain Independent Labor Party will continue in the above direction is unclear. In contemplating that possibility, it is worth noting that the city of Lorain elected a socialist mayor and city council in the municipal elections of

1912.[25] The current ILP occupants of the Lorain City Council have made no reference to this history in their public statements. However, it seems at least possible that awareness of their role in a political party that opposes what they call the two parties of "the bosses" has some connection with a radical past.[26] If so, such awareness could foster a willingness to persist in expanding the party and putting forth new progressive economic initiatives. Additionally, a possible indicator of the ILP's ability to continue to challenge the status quo is the fact that Lorain is a stronghold of support for Representative Marcy Kaptur, one of the few reliable liberals remaining in the Democratic Congressional Caucus and a staunch advocate for homeowners victimized in recent years by banks' marketing of subprime loans in low income communities. Yet, regardless of what ILP does in the future, the fact that it has been able to establish a foothold in municipal government shows that it is possible for today's local unions to begin to engage in viable third party efforts. This approach contrasts with unsuccessful top-down strategies favored by certain other progressive third party activists, including those who founded the ill-fated Labor Party in the late 1990s.

The Labor Party

The electoral activism of Lorain unionists was a local reflection of a broad-based disenchantment with the Democratic Party and its failure to deliver on core components of the labor agenda, as echoed in the remarks of Richard Trumka cited at the opening of this chapter. These were by no means the only expressions of disillusionment directed toward Democratic leadership from the labor movement in recent years. In 2012 a more pointed criticism was issued by organizers of the now dormant Labor Party, Mark Dudzic and Katherine Isaac, a revised and expanded version of which appears in Chapter 8 of this book. In this piece, the authors initially present a list of labor grievances against President Obama and the Democrats that seem to prepare the reader for a renewed call to build the party.[27]

But rather than taking up arms, Dudzic and Isaac announced that now is not the time to reestablish the Labor Party, which was initially formed in 1996 and disbanded in 2006. Their verdict, expanded on by Dudzic in a subsequent interview, was "not yet."[28] That meant, in their opinion, that the conditions and forces were not properly aligned for launching a labor party now or at any time in the foreseeable future.[29] The main reason they gave for their efforts' lack of success was that the national unions had since the time of the George W. Bush presidency (and its increasingly anti-union politico-economic context), "reverted to a survival mode that precluded the embrace of transformative efforts like the Labor Party."[30] Dudzic counterposed this to the period of the Labor Party's founding, when an emboldened labor movement seemed to offer the prospect of a transformation in the relationship of labor unions to the existing bipartisan arrangements—specifically organized labor's longstanding commitment to support Democratic candidates.[31]

While the Labor Party did indeed grow somewhat quickly in this initial phase, Dudzic and Isaac note that there were indications that optimism about union leadership being ready to rethink its longstanding support for Democratic Party candidates should have been muted at best.[32] They likely were correct in their skepticism. As will be discussed in the next section, that which occurred during the second Bush and Obama administrations should be seen not as an aberration but as a return to normal pattern of union subservience to the Democrats.

Furthermore, contrary to what Dudzic and Isaac suggest, union intransigence does not have a pragmatic basis. It does not follow either logically or empirically that crisis conditions should necessarily mandate the closing down or scaling back of strategic visions. In many instances, crises demand that new ideas, including radical ones, be seriously considered, requiring attendant risks that would not be necessary under normal circumstances. In particular, the Lorain case is an example of local unions having recognized that in the face of crisis their survival required that they embrace "transformative efforts" rather than preclude them. Attacks on municipal employees in Lorain were proceeding apace under supposedly labor friendly Democratic mayoral administrations. This mirrored a national politics in which the undermining of unions was a bipartisan project promoted by the political class at all levels (albeit generally pursued with less enthusiasm by Democrats). Lorain mayor Ritenauer, in serving as a de facto strikebreaker and promoting outsourcing, mirrored numerous other prominent centrist Democrats (most notably Chicago mayor Rahm Emanuel, who has made no secret of his active hostility to unions in general and the Chicago Teachers Union in particular).

As the pressures increase for such ambitious politicians to establish a fundraising base for their campaigns for higher office, their service to capital at the expense of labor becomes increasingly inevitable. While intraparty primary challenges have the potential to register occasional victories, the business model of the Democratic Party dictates that only a few of these will succeed and that the institutional center of gravity will remain where it has been for the past four decades, with economic elites.

Labor unions will need to be able to combat these Democratic attacks with an electoral alternative. Fortunately, as the Lorain example shows, they can do so at reduced risk in single party localities where the danger of electing a Republican is minimal. In retrospect, it's a bit hard to see why the Labor Party did not attempt to adopt this organizing model for itself. That local positions were eminently achievable should have been apparent, if not at the founding Labor Party convention in 1996, at least soon thereafter. For in the wake of the failed Nader Green Party candidacies, many activists recognized the logic of building a party up from local roots. The New Haven victories mentioned above were part of the activist wave that also resulted in Greens being elected to city councils in Portland,

Maine; Minneapolis; Madison, Wisconsin; Santa Monica; and other locales. Also notable at that time were the electoral results in San Francisco, where the Greens secured three seats on the board of supervisors, two on the school board, and, most dramatically, achieved the near victory of Matt Gonzalez in his run for mayor in 2003.

The Labor Party could have chosen to work with the Greens in these areas, with an eye toward an eventual merger of the two parties, or to run their own local campaigns in areas where they had a strong local presence. In this connection, it should be understood that the nascent Labor Party did not, in principle, foreswear running candidates. Rather, it committed to doing so only in those instances, according to their electoral strategy statement, "where a credible campaign can be run."[33] As just mentioned, this mandated that initial electoral outings be staged at local levels, since higher level offices were seen as inaccessible to a newly established third party. An exception to this rule would have applied had the Labor Party managed to acquire the institutional resources and sanction of the national unions. If so, the party could have immediately mounted credible campaigns for selected national offices. Yet this was an unrealistic expectation, as Dudzic later realized. The failure to achieve national union support required that the party limit itself to local campaigns. They can be run successfully with minimal financing on a door-to-door, volunteer basis, particularly if the resources of union locals are available.

As Dudzic and Isaac note, instead of running candidates, the Labor Party committed itself to single issue initiatives that complemented rather than competed with the agenda of the left wing of the Democratic Party. Included among these were "campaigns to organize labor support for issues including single-payer health care and worker rights."[34] Later, it would devote itself to the Free Education Now campaign.[35] While entirely worthy objectives, these initiatives pose a conundrum for an aspiring third party. For insofar as they can be achieved by social movement activists working with and even through the existing two major parties, they argue against the need for a left third party. Moreover, if these activist efforts by such a party don't succeed, the failure raises questions about the party's organizational competence and its ultimate ability to function effectively in an electoral setting. As it was, the latter materialized. None of the specific policies advocated by the Labor Party would come close to being enacted, even with the election of an ostensibly liberal Democratic administration in 2008. The result was a double defeat; the possibility of achieving minimal progressive economic change within the two-party system became more remote, as did the prospect of developing a third party politics truly able to advance an agenda of downward redistribution. Taking the above in totality, the Labor Party experience should be seen not so much as offering a negative prognosis regarding the prospects for a future insurgent third party, but as an indication of the strategic limitations of even the most forward thinking elements of the labor movement.

Labor Parties: The Case for Reduced Expectations

As suggested above, the expectation that the major unions would function as anything other than an obstacle to the development of any independent party, including a labor party, was probably naïve. As many on the left are aware, there are various characteristics of union leadership that discourage bold progressive action on most political fronts. One of the less visible yet more potent restraining qualities may be labor leaders' numerous administrative connections with the Democrats. Examples include the assurance of sufficient, stable salaries for union staff by Democratic supported laws mandating payment of union dues; the management by former Democratic officials of union-sponsored think tanks that assist union directors with relevant policy research and advocacy; and possible opportunities for union officers to serve as staff for Democratic legislators or for relevant government agencies during Democratic administrations.[36] These and other ties between labor leadership and the Democratic Party may contribute significantly to unions' ingrained organizational conservatism—particularly their entrenched unwillingness to do anything that might strongly challenge the Democrats from the left or from below. This tendency is typified by one contemporary labor leader who admitted that unions have largely refrained from this type of political militancy because "it was better to be at the table and not listened to than it would be to be outside."[37] Such striking compliance also explains union heads' willingness to function as political insiders brokering backroom deals, including those with their supposed capitalist class antagonists.[38] What relatively few on the left may know is that these regressive labor tendencies are historically deeply rooted and seemingly highly resistant to change. Reversing the tide of neoliberalism (the modern surge of procorporate polices) in the political and economic spheres will, therefore, require a much more radical transformation of unions than many on the left are willing to recognize. This is an important implication of the analysis in Eric Chester's 2004 book *True Mission*, which reviews attempts to build left third parties since the Reconstruction era.[39]

As Chester demonstrates, labor parties, defined as those developed at the behest of or with the support of unions have taken various forms. Given their foundation in organized labor, it has often been assumed that these would necessarily be sympathetic to a progressive economic platform, one that is socialist in orientation, at or at least somewhat downwardly redistributionist. As Chester shows, this is a misconception. Rather, the defining priority of labor parties has not been to advance the interests of the majority of the population generally or the working class specifically, but rather, to advance the interests of the union leadership or possibly, at most, union membership. In periods of strong union representation, there is, of course, a significant overlap between the agendas of organized labor and that of the Left, so that what's good for the AFL–CIO has tended to be what's good for the working class. However, when relatively few workers benefit from union contracts, union interests are not those of the many; instead, they mostly are the parochial concern of a few.

While the relevance of the above point to the present period (in which very few workers belong to a union) may seem obvious, Chester's real goal is to show how the argument clearly applies to labor and political history going back to the turn of the previous century. One of his illustrations is the case of the Union Labor Party (ULP), which ran union officials for municipal offices in San Francisco in 1901 and later in Los Angeles. According to Chester, once assuming office, the ULP "would accomplish virtually nothing in the way of progressive legislation" while "lining their pockets with bribes from corporations seeking municipal franchises and waivers from the city's regulatory agencies."[40] Chester observes that rather than being repudiated, the blatant corruption of the San Francisco branch of the ULP would be a model for Los Angeles trade union officials who, running their own slate of candidates the next year, "eagerly sought to emulate its success" in shaking down local businesses.[41] Chester finds it "difficult to understand" why unionists would regard implementing a criminal venture as worthy of emulation.[42] A possible explanation for this pattern is advanced by Robert Fitch in his 2006 study *Solidarity for Sale*. Fitch identifies a key strain of union culture as routinely prioritizing individual self-advancement above collective solidarity. As he notes, these tendencies have, with alarming frequency and predictability, crossed the line into outright criminality.[43] In any case, the ULP would serve as a cautionary indication that labor parties could not necessarily be relied upon to serve the interests of the trade union base, much less the working class as a whole, and that pressures to cooperate with and capitulate to capital would be a recurrent pitfall.

Another representative instance cited by Chester with indirect links to labor party politics in the United States involves the founding of the Independent Labor Party in Britain. Labor's initial electoral success was tied to a secret agreement in which the Labor Party pledged not to contest the Liberal Party in 30 parliamentary districts, thus allowing the Liberals to return to power in 1906 following their defeat in 1900. For Chester, this episode would be revealing in two respects. First, the evident willingness of Labor to negotiate with the representatives of capital in order to achieve a "lesser evil" victory for the Liberals against the ruling right-wing Conservative Party would be continually repeated in much of subsequent labor history. Another reoccurring problem illuminated by this episode would be the willingness to undertake such negotiations in secret, presenting the outcome to the rank and file as a done deal, along with the expectation that the leadership's decision would not be challenged or questioned.

Following the agreement with the Liberals, Labor Party founder Keir Hardie would be quickly legitimated in establishment circles. His prior role in fomenting miners' strikes in the North would be forgotten or at least forgiven. Hardie would parlay his reputation for pragmatism into worldwide celebrity status. He would receive respectful coverage in the establishment media of the day for seeking, in his words, to "eliminate the impossibilist element which for the moment dominates the movement, and which has to be downed everywhere—as a preliminary—for Socialism to become a living, vitalizing power."[44]

In 1908 and 1909 Hardie would spread his pragmatic message while in the United States. Here he argued for the necessity not only to create a reformist labor party comprised of Socialist Party (SP) members and unionists, but also to simultaneously isolate the radical wing of the burgeoning SP. The latter could be accomplished by, in his words, "mak(ing) it too hot for the IWW type."[45] Here he was referring to the need to ostracize SP members who also were supporters of the International Workers of the World—a radical mass party of the working class led by Bill Haywood, Emma Goldman, and others whom he regarded as dangerous extremists. Revealingly, Hardie's main supporters were in the Socialist Party's moderate wing, many of whom were drawn from the ranks of upper-class New York families. In this capacity they in fact would serve as active promoters of a "pragmatic" strategic alliance between SP members and the union activists.[46] Even though most union leaders involved in this effort made no secret of their active hostility to the Socialist Party,[47] cooperation between the two groups eventually resulted in the founding during 1919 and 1920 of the short-lived national Farmer-Labor Party.[48] SP moderates would also follow Hardie's call for the repudiation of the IWW. They thereby would become instrumental in the undermining and eventual expulsion from the Socialist Party of its radical wing, and thus, the party's elimination as a significant challenger to U.S. capitalism.[49]

In the case above, Chester portrays some Socialist Party moderates who supported a labor party, including the wealthy among them, as at least potentially well intentioned though strategically misguided.[50] But a parallel, more cynical reading of this and other similar examples by Chester is that enlightened sectors of capital may have been willing to accept the rise of labor parties on the left as the price of heading off the much more serious danger posed to elite dominance by radical labor movements. Such movements in the early twentieth-century United States were represented politically by the IWW and the left wing of the Socialist Party, as it began to gain an electoral footing.

Probably the most transparent example cited by Chester of a co-optation strategy undertaken by elite elements of capital, also involving a labor party backed by Socialist Party moderates in the United States, occurred during the New York mayoral elections of 1936. According to Chester, the SP had reestablished a strong presence and was preparing to nominate a candidate to compete against the incumbent New Deal Republican, Fiorello La Guardia, as well as a Democrat backed by the corrupt local political machine, Tammany Hall. Moderate elements led by the SP's standard bearer, Norman Thomas, were concerned with the potential for splitting the left vote, resulting in a defeat for La Guardia (an ally of then-president Franklin Delano Roosevelt). Thomas and his allies pushed for a referendum calling on the party to withdraw its candidacy, while urging a vote for La Guardia to be the fusion nominee of the American Labor Party. The ALP, formed at the instigation of some of the city's major unions, most notably, the International Ladies' Garment Workers' Union, was an ad hoc party ballot line that would enable working-class voters to support FDR's preferred candidate without casting a vote for the "party of business."[51]

It soon became apparent to the SP moderates that a referendum victory necessary to secure a La Guardia endorsement could only be achieved if underwritten with substantial financial backing. The unions behind the ALP were themselves cash-strapped and unable to come up with the requisite funds. Stepping into the breach would be New York governor and Wall Street millionaire Herbert Lehman, who would loan the party $50,000. This was a sufficient sum to manipulate the internal workings of the Socialist Party organization in favor of withdrawal.[52]

The salient aspect of this transaction was that the loan was anonymous; for obvious reasons, Lehman was not eager to make public his support for a Republican running against a Democrat. The same was true to an even greater degree for Thomas and the Socialist Party moderates. Had it become widely known that they had collaborated with a widely detested representative of the Wall Street plutocratic class, the result would have been widespread outrage. As it was, the ALP would later repay the favor by providing Lehman with its endorsement in the gubernatorial election of 1938. Thereafter, the Socialist Party would disintegrate gradually, abandoned by a Left apparently willing to accept the New Deal variant of capitalism. This was the same form of capitalism that the SP itself unofficially had endorsed through its aforementioned electoral pragmatism, thereby refusing to stand up for the core anticapitalist principles espoused by its radical wing.[53]

Chester's characterization of the ALP as "descending into the murky and secretive world of covert operations" would be a defining feature of the history of labor parties in advanced capitalist countries through much of the second half of the twentieth century (and beyond).[54] In particular, backroom deals with official labor parties would be the locus by which elites would project their influence into, and succeed in their counterattack against, populist mass movements.[55] The imposition by contemporary European labor and similar so-called "socialist" parties of neoliberal austerity (fiscal cutbacks favored by big business and its allies) can be seen, in retrospect, as the purest realization of this strategy thus far.[56] It shows capital as having finally succeeded to such an extent that the ostensible party of the working class willingly signs off on policies that have at their very basis an attack on the working class and its standard of living.

Chester's history shows that elements within the U.S. Socialist Party were aware of this potential from the very beginning. In particular, Socialist Party presidential candidate Eugene Debs recognized the danger of accommodating labor bosses (such as Samuel Gompers) who were neither temperamentally sympathetic nor philosophically committed to socialism in any way. Debs insisted that "only a socialist party could represent the interests of the working class."[57] He repeatedly would struggle against moderate attempts to engineer an alliance leading to the formation of a Labor Party or the endorsement of candidates running on Labor Party lines. The party's sole objective should be, in Debs words, "the overthrow of capitalism," and Debs repeatedly professed his intolerance for those who set their sights any lower.[58] After more than a century of organized labor's efforts to convince the establishment of unions' moderation and pragmatism through their willingness to compromise, Debs's uncompromising line in the sand may come across as shrill and overly idealistic today. However, with capital's nearly unbroken, decades-long string of successful assaults against labor now reaching its endgame in the United States (with the last remaining union stronghold in the public sector coming under direct, sustained attack), the Left should see Debs' claim as prophetic. It is the minimum of what is required for workers to mount a viable political defense against capital.

Conclusion

Chester's observations above may strike many as dispiriting. But that is not how they were intended, nor is it how they should be received. Rather, they may be seen as arguing for what has been stressed in the previous sections of this chapter—the importance of building political capacity at the local level that is based on existing local concerns and activist initiatives, as was done in New Haven and in Lorain, Ohio. As was shown, local left third-party candidates can be recruited, and a party infrastructure from those involved at the grassroots can be developed.

What then should be the function of a national party? This is the role that the Labor Party attempted to fill at the turn of the twenty-first century in the United States, as discussed earlier. As already suggested in reference to that party, a national organization, at least at first, should serve to coordinate local efforts rather than operate in a top-down fashion. It should connect such efforts to one another through articulation of a common ideological and programmatic orientation, and thereby define a national party identity. It also may assume a role in pinpointing locations where conditions for third-party challenges appear favorable; identifying viable candidates from sympathetic activist organizations; and pooling national resources to direct funds to promising local campaigns. But in assuming these functions, it does not follow that such a national organization should attempt to engage with national politics and politicians beyond what is necessary to facilitate the growth of local, potentially winning campaigns. The established path from insurgent municipal to state to national office, the trajectory by which Bernie Sanders rose from a local politician in Burlington, Vermont, to U.S. senator, needs to be kept in mind as a guide. The Labor Party's election guidelines were correct in noting the importance of serious campaigns and the demoralizing effects of perpetual symbolic, losing races.[59]

The failure of the Labor Party reflected shortsightedness in two respects. First, as mentioned previously, it placed inordinate faith in the Left's ability to, in Mark Dudzic's words, "craft a strategy to really extract the labor movement from its instrumental relationships with the Democratic Party."[60] While such hopes are perennial among the Left, they are based on persistent, overly optimistic assumptions about labor leadership—assumptions that Chester's book provides a solid basis for rejecting. Rather than taking remarks such as Trumka's as a sign that labor leadership has finally recognized the necessity of electoral independence, they should be seen as one more entry in a long history of idle threats that will elicit no more than guffaws from Democratic Party insiders.

Second, and just as important, the Labor Party's perspective reflected an overly pessimistic assessment of the potential of locally based activism and the capacity of municipal politics to provide a foundation for a broader political insurgency. It is inevitable that national organizations, and national unions in particular, will look askance at unauthorized independent campaigns undertaken by locals and may attempt to rein them in. Nevertheless, local union members should follow the Lorain, Ohio, example in taking the initiative to act independently. In doing so, they will incur the displeasure of Democratic Party loyalists both within the union and outside. Yet these local mavericks should be aware that going it alone need not end in defeat and ostracism. Electoral success (which clearly is obtainable at lower levels) and the statutory power wielded by those who achieve it immediately command respect and deference from former critics. Those who have served in local office can attest to this.[61]

The same strategic imperative applies even more so to those of us without formal affiliations to the unions. Our interest in economic justice derives from being among the overwhelming majority victimized by a political system now under almost complete control of economic elites. Many of us have long since recognized the crippling results of unions' unhealthy relationship to electoral politics on the broader left. It is now more necessary than ever that the Left seriously consider carefully argued, well supported critiques of labor and the operative assumptions behind its electoral strategy, as well as broad visions for achieving and exercising power on whatever level power can be obtained.

Notes

1 Schroeder, "Labor Warns Democrats."
2 Ibid.
3 Foote, "Watch This Labor Leader Crush Lies."
4 McCarthy, "Americans Losing Confidence in Gov't"; and Dugan, "Democratic Party Seen More Favorably."
5 Jones, "In U.S., Perceived Need for Third Party Reaches New High"; and Pew Research, "Public's Response to 'Capitalism,' 'Socialism.'" According to the latter poll, 45 percent of those between the ages of 18 and 29 view socialism positively.

6 Williams, "Cops for Labor?"

7 Ibid.

8 Ibid.

9 Ibid.

10 Ibid.

11 Ibid.

12 Ibid.

13 Kearney and Leibenluft, "Hospital Police to Lose Power of Arrest."

14 Green Party of the United States, "Ten Key Values of the Green Party."

15 Resnikoff, "How Community Organizing Transformed New Haven."

16 Clinton, *My Life*, 188.

17 Harry Williamson (president, Lorain County AFL-CIO), e-mail message to editor's research collaborator, Russell Weiss-Irwin, August 8, 2014; LorainCounty.com, "Lorain County 2013 General Election Results"; Saltamontes, "A Union County"; and Essif, "After Defeating Democrats."

18 Essif, "After Defeating Democrats"; Saltamontes, "A Union County;" and Dicken, "Lorain Democrats Warn 3 Men to Stick to Party Line."

19 Essif, "After Defeating Democrats."

20 Goodenow, "2 Independents Get Union Help."

21 Dicken, "Lorain Democrats Warn 3 Men to Stick to Party Line."

22 Ibid.; and Essif, "After Defeating Democrats."

23 Dicken, "County Dominated by Dems"; and Lorain.com, "City Guides for Lorain."

24 For example, see Johnson and Paleczny, "Joshua Thornsberry," for a relevant statement by ILP Councilman Joshua Thornsberry on WEFT radio.

25 Judd, "Out of the Hands of Victory."

26 Johnson and Paleczny, "Joshua Thornsberry."

27 Dudzic and Isaac, "Labor Party Time? Not Yet."

28 Ibid.; and Seidman, "Looking Back at the Labor Party."

29 Dudzic and Isaac, "Labor Party Time? Not Yet."

30 Seidman, "Looking Back at the Labor Party."

31 Ibid.

32 Dudzic and Isaac, "Labor Party Time? Not Yet."

33 Labor Party, "Electoral Strategy of the Labor Party."

34 Dudzic and Isaac, "Labor Party Time? Not Yet."

35 Labor Party, "Statement in Support of Free Higher Education."

36 A recent instance of a "revolving door" between unions and Democratic administrations is President Obama's appointment to the National Labor Relations Board of former SEIU general counsel Craig Becker. Two leading Democratic managed, union sponsored advocacy organizations are American Rights at Work (founded by former Democratic House majority whip David Bonior and funded by the AFL-CIO, the Teamsters, the SEIU, and the United Farm Workers) and Working America (directed by former Clinton administration Labor Department official Karen Nussbaum and funded by the AFL-CIO).

37 Henwood, "Labor's Many Dead Ends." According to left economic analyst Doug Henwood, this remark was attributed by former AFL-CIO official, labor activist, and writer Bill Fletcher Jr. to an unnamed labor leader.

38 Fletcher and Gapasin, *Solidarity Divided*.

39 Chester, *True Mission*.
40 Ibid., 53.
41 Ibid., 54.
42 Ibid.
43 Fitch, *Solidarity for Sale*.
44 Chester, *True Mission*, 52.
45 Ibid., 51.
46 Ibid., 44–53.
47 Ibid., 59.
48 Ibid., 84–91.
49 Ibid., 82.
50 Ibid., 44–91.
51 Ibid., 146–49, 171.
52 Ibid., 171–72.
53 Ibid., 172–73.
54 Ibid., 170; and Moschonas, *In the Name of Social Democracy*.
55 Moschonas, *In the Name of Social Democracy*.
56 Ibid. For a recent illustration of this dynamic, see Bickerton, "What's the Matter with France?" The most conspicuous example of how supposedly left-wing parties have pursued fiscally conservatism in recent years is in heavily indebted countries such as Greece, Ireland, and Spain. For instance, see Mavroudeas, "The Greek External Debt."
57 Chester, *True Mission*, 77.
58 Ibid., 41.
59 Seidman, "Looking Back at the Labor Party: Mark Dudzic."
60 Dudzic and Isaac, "Labor Party Time? Not Yet."
61 Halle, "Why I Ran."

Bibliography

Bickerton, Chris. "What's the Matter with France?" *Jacobin*, July 9, 2014. www.jacobinmag.com/2014/07/whats-the-matter-with-france/.

Chester, Eric Thomas. *True Mission: Socialists and the Labor Party Question in the U.S.* London: Pluto Press, 2004.

Clinton, Bill. *My Life*. New York: Alfred A. Knopf, 2004.

Dicken, Brad. "County Dominated by Dems, But GOP Base Growing." *Chronicle Online*, October 28, 2012. http://chronicle.northcoastnow.com/2012/10/28/county-dominated-by-dems-but-gop-base-growing/.

———. "Lorain Democrats Warn 3 Men to Stick to Party Line." *Chronicle Online*, September 24, 2013. http://chronicle.northcoastnow.com/2013/09/24/lorain-democrats-warn-3-men-to-stick-to-party-line.

Dudzic, Mark, and Katherine Isaac. "Labor Party Time? Not Yet." Labor Party. Last modified December, 2012. www.thelaborparty.org/d_lp_time.htm.

Dugan, Andrew. "Democratic Party Still Seen More Favorably than GOP: Both Parties Face 'Up-side Down' Favorability Ratings." Gallup Politics. Last modified May 16, 2014. www.gallup.com/poll/169091/democratic-party-seen-favorably-gop.aspx.

Essif, Amien. "After Defeating Democrats, Will Ohio Union Form a New Party?" *In These Times*, October 8, 2014. http://inthesetimes.com/working/entry/17227/defeat_democrats_independent_labor_party_ohio_lorain_county_unionists.

Fitch, Robert. *Solidarity for Sale: How Corruption Destroyed the Labor Movement and Undermined America's Promise*. New York: Public Affairs, 2006.

Fletcher, Bill, Jr., and Fernando Gapasin. *Solidarity Divided: The Crisis in Organized Labor and a New Path Toward Social Justice*. Berkeley: University of California Press, 2008.

Foote, Doug. "Watch This Labor Leader Crush Lies About Social Security on CNBC." *Main Street, A Project of Working America: Community Affiliate of the AFL-CIO* (blog), October 18, 2013. http://blog.workingamerica.org/2013/10/18/watch-this-labor-leader-crush-lies-about-social-security-on-cnbc/.

Goodenow, Evan. "2 Independents Get Union Help in Lorain Races." *Chronicle Online*, November 7, 2013. http://chronicle.northcoastnow.com/2013/11/07/2-independents-get-union-help-in-lorain-races/.

Green Party of the United States. "Ten Key Values of the Green Party of the United States." Accessed July 5, 2014. www.gp.org/tenkey.php.

Halle, John. "Why I Ran." *Progressive Review*. Accessed July 10, 2014. http://prorev.com/whyiran.htm.

Henwood, Doug. "Labor's Many Dead Ends." Opinion Nation: Labor's Bad Recall? (blog), *The Nation*, July 19, 2012. www.thenation.com/blog/168435/opinionnation-labors-bad-recall#.

Johnson, David, and Paleczny, Bob. "Joshua Thornsberry." Illinois World Labor Hour. The A-Infos Radio Project. Podcast audio. March 1, 2014. www.radio4all.net/index.php/program/74736.

Jones, Jeffrey M. "In U.S., Perceived Need for Third Party Reaches New High." Gallup Politics. Last modified Oct. 11, 2013. www.gallup.com/poll/165392/perceivedneed-third-party-reaches-new-high.aspx.

Judd, Richard W. "Out of the Hands of Victory: Lima and Lorain, Ohio." Chapter 6 in *Socialist Cities*. Albany: State University of New York Press, 1989.

Kearney, Brendan, and Jacob Leibenluft. "Hospital Police to Lose Power of Arrest." *Yale Daily News*, March 3, 2003. http://yaledailynews.com/blog/2003/03/03/hospital-police-to-lose-power-of-arrest/.

Labor Party. "Electoral Strategy of the Labor Party." Accessed January 18, 2014. www.thelaborparty.org/d_electoral.htm.

———. "Statement of Academics in Support of Free Higher Education." Accessed March 29, 2014. www.thelaborparty.org/c_fhe_statement.htm.

Lorain.com. "City Guides for Lorain." Accessed October 10, 2014. www.lorain.com/places/cityguides.html?cgid=3.

LorainCounty.com. "Lorain County 2013 General Election Results." Last modified January 22, 2014. www.loraincounty.com/government/2013-general/.

Mavroudeas, Stavros, "The Greek External Debt and Imperialist Rivalries: One Thief Stealing from Another." *MRZine*, February 20, 2010. http://mrzine.monthlyreview.org/2010/mavroudeas200210p.html.

McCarthy, Justin. "Americans Losing Confidence in All Branches of U.S. Gov't: Confidence Hits Six-Year Low for Presidency; Record Lows for Supreme Court, Congress." Gallup Politics. Last modified June 30, 2014. www.gallup.com/poll/171992/americans-losing-confidence-branches-gov.aspx.

Moschonas, Gerassimos. *In the Name of Social Democracy: The Great Transformation 1945 to the Present*. London: Verso, 2002.

Pew Research Center for the People and the Press. "Little Change in Public's Response to 'Capitalism,' 'Socialism.'" Last modified December 28, 2011. www.people-press. org/2011/12/28/little-change-in-publics-response-to-capitalism-socialism/.

Resnikoff, Ned. "How Community Organizing Transformed New Haven." MSNBC. Last modified September 9, 2013. www.msnbc.com/the-ed-show/how-community-organizing-transformed-new-have.

Saltamontes, Russell. "A Union County." *Jacobin*, October 6, 2014. www.jacobinmag. com/2014/10/a-union-county/.

Schroeder, Robert. "Labor Warns Democrats on Social Security, Medicare Ahead of Budget Talks." *Wall Street Journal Capital Report* (blog), October 21, 2013. http:// blogs.marketwatch.com/capitolreport/2013/10/21/labor-warns-democrats-on-social-security-medicare-ahead-of-budget-talks/.

Seidman, Derek. "Looking Back at the Labor Party: An Interview with Mark Dudzic." *New Politics*, March 23, 2014. http://newpol.org/content/looking-back-labor-party-interview-mark-dudzic.

Williams, Kristian. "Cops for Labor? Police Support for Protesters in Wisconsin Was an Exception to the Historical Rule." *Dollars and Sense*, September/October 2011. http:// dollarsandsense.org/archives/2011/0911williams.html.

Wolff, Richard, *Democracy at Work: A Cure for Capitalism*. Chicago: Haymarket Press, 2012.

10

A NEW PROGRESSIVE PARTY

How the Working Families Party Can Change Electoral Politics*

Daniel Cantor

> I am not a Christie-crat. I am not a Corporate-crat. And I am not a Chicken-crat. I'm a Working Families Demo-crat!
>
> Hetty Rosenstein, Communication Workers of America and New Jersey Working Families leader at the 2014 New Jersey Democratic Party Convention

Consider the example of the Tea Party Republicans. A minority force in a minority party, they now dominate politics in Washington, DC, and in many statehouses. They have exploited racial, cultural, and economic anxieties among a subset of white voters and created a political vehicle capable of winning primary and then general elections. In power, they promote an agenda focused less on the dwindling prospects of their constituents and more on enhancing the life chances of the 1 percent. It's a scam that economist Paul Krugman, writer Thomas Frank, and others have been on to for a long time, but it continues to work all too well in the absence of a convincing alternative from Democrats.

What progressives should do in response is not hard to fathom, and it informs the strategy of the Working Families Party (WFP) and its allies. Since its founding in 1998, working both inside and outside the Democratic Party, the WFP has tried to yank and pull and prod the Democrats to the left. It's the job of the Democrats to defeat Republicans, and it's our job to make sure that they defeat them for

---

* Originally published in a slightly different form as "A New Progressive Party" in *The Nation*, July 7–14, 2014, 19–20. Reprinted by permission of the author and *The Nation*.

the right reasons, and with the right people (that is, progressive Democrats like Massachusetts senator Elizabeth Warren, Oregon senator Jeff Merkley, Minnesota congressman Keith Ellison, and New York City mayor Bill de Blasio).

This means building independent political power and independent organizations. It means thinking more about top versus bottom than left versus right, and tapping the anger at the 1 percent that the Tea Party discusses more than the Democrats do. It means growing a base of engaged citizens to change the ideological atmosphere in which all citizens breathe. This is easy to say but not so easy to accomplish. Yet it is not impossible, as the record in a growing number of states suggests.

For the WFP, in New York and nationwide, the fundamental challenge is how to navigate the tension between the ideal and the possible. We are constantly trying to walk that tightrope between independence and relevance, finding our way to the left wing of the possible. This requires a nimble approach, not a single tactic. Sometimes we've endorsed prominent Democrats and worked hand in glove with them to achieve progressive outcomes—like winning the nation's first statewide paid-sick-days law in Connecticut with the support of Governor Daniel Malloy.

Quite often, we've challenged incumbent or machine Democrats—in Clackamas County, Oregon, in Newark, New Jersey, in Bridgeport, Connecticut—who were either indistinguishable from Republicans or firmly in the pocket of the Democrats' own big-money crowd. And sometimes we just aim to help Democrats beat truly awful Republicans, like the race in Pennsylvania in 2014 against Governor Tom Corbett.

In late May 2014, the New York WFP debated at its quadrennial convention in Albany how best to pull Democrats in a progressive direction. Some 800 attendees, most traveling on their own dime, gathered to choose the person we would endorse for governor for the upcoming election. Incumbent governor Andrew Cuomo was actively seeking WFP support, even as he was aware of unhappiness among some party leaders and rank-and-file over aspects of his fiscal and education policies. He was being challenged by Fordham University law professor Zephyr Teachout, one of the nation's leading experts on corruption and political money.

For four hours, people were on the edge of their seats, as activists well known and obscure rose to speak in an unscripted debate. Hector Figueroa and George Gresham, the top two Service Employees International Union leaders in the state, made impassioned pleas for the party to support Cuomo in order to ensure a united front against the Republicans, who control the state senate. Bertha Lewis of the Black Institute, a founder of the WFP, countered that the governor's record did not warrant our support and that we should back Teachout. Hundreds of community activists and unionists, environmentalists and fast-food workers, students, and retirees were paying close attention as the voting came to an end, as were thousands of Twitter users following scores of journalists. This was authentic political debate, the kind that barely exists in the meticulously controlled world of two-party politics.

In the end, Cuomo won by 58 to 42 percent. He announced a set of electoral and policy commitments that carried the day—which, when you think about it, is how politics is supposed to work.

The electoral commitment came first. After nearly four years of Republican dominance in the state senate—with right-wing views on inequality and the economy thus determining the limits of state policymaking—the governor announced a public and forceful commitment to end Republican control of the state's upper chamber. For readers outside New York, this may not seem earth-shaking. But when Mayor de Blasio took the stage and called it "a transcendent moment," members were on their feet. The Republicans have controlled the state senate for all but 2 of the last 70 years, and it is the main reason progressive policy reforms fail. It took us 5 *years* to overcome Republican opposition and get a minimum wage increase passed in 2004. If we were to retake the senate with a Democratic–Working Families majority, it shouldn't take 5 *weeks*. That was the core argument made by the pro-Cuomo forces, and it was a good one.

Cuomo also made policy promises, pledging vigorous support for New York's version of Seattle's $15 minimum wage. That promise, in turn, won the critical support of the low-wage worker organizing groups inside the WFP. Cuomo also announced via video that in the next legislative session (based on the assumption that he would lead the "Take Back the Senate" coalition to victory), we would see several progressive breakthroughs. These advances would include passage of public funding for elections to reduce the power of big money in Albany; enactment of the DREAM Act to provide college access to the children of immigrants; decriminalization of possession of small amounts of marijuana in public; approval of the remarkable Women's Equality Act (which would strengthen laws against salary discrimination, domestic violence, and sexual harassment); and funding for a hundred new community schools.

A perfect solution? That doesn't exist in politics. An advance for progressive values, power, and organization? Absolutely. The WFP was able to construct a powerful compromise—one that keeps us building something together in which our principles and vision remain paramount. The winners on that Saturday night didn't gloat, and the losers didn't stalk away in anger. They were all aware that an organization that makes it possible to have such a debate in the first place is a precious thing indeed.

The WFP doesn't just want to speak truth to power: We want the middle class, the working class, and the poor to share in that power. As political scientist Joel Rogers often says, the task of progressives is to move from "grievances to governance, from protest to policy."[1]

So what's next? We need to recruit and support hundreds—and then thousands—of leaders and activists across the country to run for local, state, and federal office, challenging corporate Democrats and articulating a bold and sustainable vision for our economy and society. We need to help them become the kind of leaders that we need in office. And we'll know we've succeeded when the phrase "I'm a Working Families Democrat" means a pathway to victory for the values of decency and equality that are at the heart of modern progressivism.

Note

1 Confirmed by Joel Rogers, e-mail message to editor, November 9, 2014.

11

BREAKING THROUGH BY BREAKING FREE

Why the Left Needs to Declare Its Political Independence*

Thomas Harrison

Third party sentiment among liberal and left voters surged in 2000 with the Ralph Nader campaign, only to recede sharply as most of these same voters, terrified by the prospect of Republican rule, retreated back to the dead-end politics of lesser evilism. Now that President Barack Obama is well into his second term in office, however, there are distinct signs of a revival.

In contrast to the "Yes We Can" euphoria that seized Obama voters in 2008, it seemed that the dominant emotion in the run-up to the 2012 election was fear, a well-founded fear of the Republicans' brutal agenda. This agenda, driven by the GOP's antipathy for the "losers" of American society, has been on display in Congress and state governments ever since (for example, through efforts to block the extension of unemployment benefits for millions and cut food assistance for the poor). Frightened Democratic voters had exceedingly low expectations; once the election results were in, the prevailing mood seemed to be one of relief, rather than hope for a brighter future.

* Originally published in a somewhat different form as "The Left Should Declare Its Independence from the Democrats," on the website of the journal *New Politics*, May 4, 2012, http://newpol.org/content/left-should-declare-its-independence-democrats; and "After the Elections: Which Way for the Left?," *New Politics* 14, no. 2 (winter 2013), http://newpol.org/content/after-elections-which-way-left. Reprinted by permission of the author and publisher. The author thanks Jonathan H. Martin for his meticulous editing and for many valuable suggestions. He also thanks Joanne Landy and Lois Weiner for constructive criticisms.

Jill Stein's Green Party campaign garnered few votes in 2012 (only 456,000, or 0.36 percent), but since then, evidence has increased that voters are more open to supporting challenges to the Democrats from the left. Perhaps the most significant was the victory in 2013 of Kshama Sawant, who ran a citywide race for a seat on the Seattle City Council. A member of a small revolutionary socialist group, Socialist Alternative, Sawant obtained 90,000 votes. Another Socialist Alternative candidate, Ty Moore, came very close to winning a city council race in Minneapolis. Both Sawant and Moore built a base of progressive union leaders, Greens, and civil rights groups in support of their candidacies. Even before she won, Sawant's campaign moved the whole political discourse in Seattle sharply to the left on the issues of a $15 minimum wage and taxing the wealthy.[1]

There are a few more developments that may signal a political thaw. In heavily unionized Lorain County, Ohio, the central labor council, disgusted with the local Democratic Party organization, backed—albeit with reluctance—its own slate of 14 prolabor candidates for local offices. Some of these candidates were not endorsed by the Democratic Party, and three of them were independents. All these independents were elected.[2] Such steps toward political autonomy by labor, however tentative at first, are especially significant. In Seattle, Sawant was supported by locals of the American Federation of State, County, and Municipal Employees (AFSCME), the Communication Workers of America, the Postal Workers, the American Federation of Teachers, and the Brotherhood of Electrical Workers.[3]

But the election that got the most attention in 2013 was Bill de Blasio's as mayor of New York. Despite his youthful flirtation with left-wing radicalism, de Blasio has spent his entire political career in the neoliberal mainstream of the Democratic Party. Neoliberalism is a particular set of economic policies that, by favoring economic elites, result in the redistribution of wealth and power to the rich and corporations.[4] As a friend of Bill Clinton, who presided over the final triumph of neoliberalism in the Democratic Party, de Blasio is most unlikely to seriously challenge the party's probusiness orthodoxy. Nor is he at all likely to threaten the financial and real estate interests that rule New York City.[5] However, it is significant that he won by positioning himself as an outspoken political liberal—or "populist," as the procorporate media condescendingly dubs him. During his campaign, de Blasio denounced the existence of "two cities" (one for the rich and one for the rest); called for higher taxes on the wealthy; deplored the shortage of housing and decent jobs; and promised to end the racist police tactic of "stop and frisk."[6] This speaks to the existence of a new mood that may be difficult for the Democrats to co-opt and offers opportunities for independent political action by the Left.

But while there appears to be a more restive, left-leaning mood in the country, this chapter argues that its impact will be limited unless it finds organizational expression in the shape of an electoral vehicle, a new political party. Absent that, considering the Obama administration's and Congress's deep commitment to the needs of the corporate world, it would take the pressure of a mass upheaval from below to wring from the government any even moderately significant concessions to popular needs.

In what follows, the case for a new party of the left will be made, in several ways. First, it will be argued that the Democratic Party is not and never can be a progressive "party of the people." Second, left electoral strategies that refrain from consistently challenging the Democrats as well as the Republicans will be critiqued for being ineffective and politically counterproductive. Third, the limitations of recent progressive third-party efforts will be analyzed. Fourth and last, it will be shown that opportunities and promising strategies for building a viable, new third party of the left do exist. It will be proposed that now is the time to launch a broadly based and genuinely independent progressive party that this country has lacked for so long and so desperately needs. The argument begins with an evaluation of Obama and his Democratic allies in Congress from a progressive standpoint.

The Obama Administration's Record

In 2012, Barack Obama was swept back into office chiefly by a de facto coalition of blacks, Latinos, unionized workers, young people, and low-income Americans.[7] It was encouraging that African Americans and Latinos responded to Republican voter suppression efforts by turning out in impressive numbers. Nevertheless, it remains a striking fact that the core of the Obama coalition is made up of the very people who have suffered most from the policies of his administration.[8]

Under Obama, the domination of financial elites over American society has become more absolute than ever. Millions of victims of the Great Recession who have lost their jobs and homes have been left by the government essentially to fend for themselves. A vicious assault on public employees, especially teachers, enabled and often spearheaded by Democratic officeholders, continues.[9] Writing in Salon, Matt Stoller charts the widening gulf since 2008 between corporate profits and home equity, the "main store of savings for Americans who have savings."[10] Under Obama, profits have recovered since 2008, but home equity levels have not—an unprecedented divergence. Stoller explains how administration policy clearly has favored the property rights of rich creditors responsible for the economic crash at the expense of ordinary debtors:

> The bailouts and the associated Federal Reserve actions were not primarily shifts of funds to bankers. They were a guarantee that property rights for a certain class of creditors were immune from challenge or market forces. The foreclosure crisis, with its rampant criminality, predatory lending, and document forgeries, represents the flip side. Property rights for debtors simply increasingly exist solely at the pleasure of the powerful. The lack

of prosecution of Wall Street executives, the ability of banks to borrow at 0 percent from the Federal Reserve while most of us face credit card rates of 15–30 percent, and the bailouts are all part of the re-creation of the American system of law around Obama's oligarchy.[11]

Noting how these policies accelerated upward redistribution, Stoller shows that whereas under Bush 65 cents of every dollar of income growth went to the top 1 percent, under Obama it was 93 cents.[12] Such an accomplishment by a Democratic administration brings to mind a statement by David Bromwich, a Yale English professor and political essayist, who observes, "redistribution of wealth and power more than three decades in the making has now been carved into the system and given the stamp of permanence. Only a Democratic president, and one associated in the public mind (however wrongly) with the fortunes of the poor, could have accomplished such a reversal with such sickening completeness."[13]

The Affordable Care Act (ACA)—Obamacare—has been the president's most important domestic achievement so far, and it illustrates the limits of reform in the era of neoliberal hegemony. ACA does reduce the number of uninsured Americans and contains some badly needed restrictions on the private health care industry, such as banning the use of preexisting conditions as an excuse to deny coverage. Of much greater significance though is the way in which the law actually strengthens the industry and stands in the way of a single-payer universal free health care system. ACA delivers more than $1 trillion in subsidies over 10 years to private insurers, as well as millions of new customers by compelling the uninsured to purchase coverage or face a penalty.[14] The "Cadillac tax" on more expensive insurance plans that are offered through employers and that often are the result of union bargaining, will encourage employers to shift more and more of the costs of medical insurance onto their employees. Skepticism that government can play any useful role in this area likely will deepen among the general public.[15]

Arguably, U.S. foreign policy under Obama is even more militarized, more arrogantly imperial than it was under Bush, despite Obama's more muted rhetoric. The president has learned that traditional ground wars like those in Iraq and Afghanistan are difficult to sustain, much less to win. Instead, he substitutes different but still deadly interventions consisting of drones, special operations, and the like. Bromwich argues that Obama, together with Bush, has presided over a new historical stage in U.S. governance characterized by vastly increased "force projection" abroad and a powerfully enhanced national security state of secrecy, surveillance, "kill (assassination) lists," and indefinite detention. The monstrous war machine constructed by Bush to fight "terror" has been greatly expanded under Obama, gravely undermining civil liberties at home and promoting Islamist extremism throughout the world.[16]

Environmentalists know that the Obama administration has been aggressively indifferent to global warming and the need for a more environmentally sound energy policy. Obama endorses such ecologically destructive energy practices as hydrofracking, using natural gas in place of coal, building the tar sands pipeline, expanding use of nuclear power, and oil drilling in both the Arctic and the Gulf of Mexico.[17] As Naomi Klein points out, real solutions to the climate crisis—not merely recycling and buying green products—are antithetical to "free market" dogmas, to which the Democrats cling as much as the Republicans. Klein explains that only collectivist measures might make a difference: heavy investment in rail transportation, large-scale development of renewable energy, and, above all, planning based on the common good, not profitability. That would mean a major assault on corporate "rights" and priorities, an offensive that obviously would be fiercely resisted and probably could succeed only by nationalization of industries.[18] The Obama administration's permissive and even accommodating treatment of culpable bankers and hedge fund managers in the wake of the financial crisis should make it very clear that a serious challenge to corporate prerogatives—let alone nationalization—is simply not on the table for the Democrats.[19]

Regarding fiscal policy, even before the 2012 election, Obama started negotiating a "grand bargain" with the GOP to cut the deficit at the expense of entitlement programs such as Social Security, Medicare, and Medicaid, in return for very modest tax increases on the rich. The budget deal that eventually emerged, however, included no new taxes on the wealthy, but did include increases in military spending and an end to supplemental benefits for the long-term unemployed. This should not have come as a surprise. A year earlier, when the Democrats controlled both houses of Congress, a news analysis in the *New York Times* observed: "Just a few years ago, the tax deal pushed through Congress . . . would have been a Republican fiscal fantasy, a sweeping bill that locks in virtually all the Bush-era tax cuts, exempts almost all estates from taxation, and enshrines the former president's credo that dividends and capital gains should be taxed equally and gently."[20]

But even if there had been a real trade-off, the idea of reciprocity in a society driven by extreme inequality is both ludicrous and obscene. Its only function is to apply a patina of "fairness" to a brutally one-sided austerity regime, and austerity is Obama's number one domestic priority. Obama and the vast majority of Democratic politicians operate entirely within a bipartisan consensus among ruling elites that the U.S. economy can revive only by reducing social spending, crippling public sector unions, generating more cheap energy from fracking and heavy oil, further reducing workers' standard of living, and continuing the upward redistribution of wealth.

Congress, with whom the president must work, itself is more completely in thrall to corporate lobbyists than ever before. The presence of Senators Tammy Baldwin (D-WI), Elizabeth Warren (D-MA), and a few others with progressive reputations will not change the Democratic Party. The White House and the Democrats' congressional leadership—not to mention Democratic funders—understand that Wall Street and the corporations come first. Meanwhile, they treat the party's left wing as a marginal and easily containable nuisance, useful only for getting out the vote. Ralph Nader says of House minority leader and major fundraiser Nancy Pelosi:

> Over ninety percent of the Democrats in the House defer to her and do not press her on such matters as upping the federal minimum wage, controlling corporate crime, reducing corporate welfare giveaways, reasserting full Medicare for all, diminishing a militaristic foreign policy and other policies reputed to be favored by the Party's Progressive Caucus. . . . Instead the Progressive Caucus remains moribund, declining to press their policy demands on leader Pelosi, as the hard core of the Tea Partiers do with their leaders. . . . Today's Democrats, with very few exceptions, are dull, tired and defeatist.[21]

Recently, Obama and the Democratic leadership in Congress have made some gestures to the Left—the president's support for an increase in the long-stagnant minimum wage, for example, and the rejection by Harry Reid and Nancy Pelosi of fast-track approval for the Trans-Pacific Partnership free trade agreement. Some liberals have pointed to these moves as proof that the Democrats are retreating from neoliberalism. One of these is Harold Meyerson, who responded to a much-discussed article in *Harper's* by political scientist Adolph Reed, in which Reed argued that the Left has come to almost completely identify itself with the success of the Democrats, and in so doing has accommodated itself to neoliberalism. Meyerson claimed that "Reed's characterization of the Democrats as neoliberal NAFTA-ites seems frozen in time, that time being the 1990s."[22] He went on to cite the instances just mentioned, as well as the election of Warren and de Blasio. However, if mainstream Democrats have opposed the latest corporate–free trade scheme, it is not because they are less committed to neoliberalism, but because of focused public resistance.[23] Likewise, if they have supported a hike in the minimum wage more actively, it is due to militant social movements like that of the fast-food workers.[24]

Raising the hourly minimum wage to a still-paltry $10.10 (as proposed by Obama and Democratic allies in Congress) will help those workers at the very bottom, of course. However, it does not address the fundamental problem: As more and more jobs are concentrated at or near the minimum wage level, the United States will continue to devolve toward the low-wage economy that proponents of austerity see as essential for raising profitability and competitiveness. In other words, such a minimum wage increase alone does not challenge the neoliberal agenda. A reinvigorated labor movement that devoted itself to the task of organizing the unorganized would do more than anything else to reverse the decline in the living standards of workers as a whole. Strong unions, however, are antithetical to neoliberalism, which is why they have not been fostered by administration policy.[25]

Missed Opportunities

In recent decades, the conservatism of the Democratic establishment induced some elements among labor and the Left to flirt with the idea of a third party. Nothing permanent resulted from these dalliances, but in examining the reasons for their failure, we may find some valuable lessons for the future.

During the 1990s, labor's disappointment with the Clinton administration's aggressive neoliberalism—such as his support for the North American Free Trade Agreement (NAFTA)—provoked a number of progressive union leaders and rank-and-filers to take some hesitant steps toward political independence. The Labor Party was inaugurated in 1996. Until it suspended operation in 2007, the organization focused on nonelectoral campaigns around the right to a job, health care, free higher education, and the right of all workers to organize and bargain—while it kept postponing running candidates.[26] Around the same time, the New Party was founded, also with support from some unions, as well as from the low-income community organizing group ACORN. The New Party pursued a "fusion" strategy of supporting major party candidates (almost always Democrats) through endorsement or, where legally permitted, by putting their names on the party's own ballot line.

The leaders of both organizations believed that progressive third parties could be built without running candidates. The Labor Party's reluctance to break with more conservative elements in the union bureaucracy was the main reason for its refusal to enter the electoral arena.[27] The New Party, on the other hand, always explicitly viewed itself as no more than a pressure group. In the aftermath of the Supreme Court's 1997 decision to uphold state laws banning party cross-endorsements (which exist in most states), supporters of the New Party's strategy shifted their hopes to the Working Families Party (WFP). The WFP is little more than another ballot line for the Democrats in several states, such as New York, that allow cross-endorsement.[28]

A few notable WFP endorsements in recent years illustrate the extent of the WFP's commitment to the Democratic Party. In 2010 the WFP offered its support to a centrist Democrat, Andrew Cuomo, in his run for governor of New York. Cuomo actually refused to accept the offer—thereby supposedly jeopardizing the party's ballot line—until WFP officials agreed to his budget-cutting proposals, including pay freezes for state employees.[29] In fact, gaining the ballot line was only an excuse for WFP's pursuit of Cuomo. New York requires a minimum of 50,000 votes for a party to keep a place on the ballot. However, a genuine progressive, Howie Hawkins, got 59,906 as a Green candidate in the same election. The WFP did not offer him its support, thereby demonstrating its automatic commitment to the Democrats. This commitment was again shamefully apparent in 2013 when the WFP sent in operatives to help defeat Hawkins, this time running a strong Green campaign for the Syracuse city council against a prodeveloper Democratic incumbent.[30] In 2014 the WFP endorsed Cuomo for governor once more. The alleged basis for this decision was a dubious, eleventh-hour pledge from Cuomo to support various WFP legislative initiatives and work for a Democratic takeover of the state senate.[31] Clearly, the WFP's ties to the Democratic Party will always trump its purported progressive agenda.

Unlike the Labor Party, New Party, and WFP, Ralph Nader's presidential campaigns, and particularly the one in 2000, offered a real opportunity for a mass third party of the left to emerge. An NBC/*Wall Street Journal* poll completed several months before the 2000 election showed Nader's support at 7 percent.[32] When the election took place, Nader received 2.8 million votes, or 2.7 percent. However, according to him, the *Washington Post* estimated that there were more than 5 million would-be Nader voters who "got cold feet" at the last minute.[33] In fact, Nader's potential political appeal was far more extensive than that. Polls show that millions more Americans supported his radical-democratic and anticorporate program and agreed with his attacks on the two-party system.[34] In other words, a mass base for a new progressive third-party movement actually existed in 2000.

During the 2000 campaign, Nader was barred from the televised debates. Had he participated, viewers would have been presented with a subject that is the central problem of American society but always is taboo in national political discourse: plutocracy versus democracy, rule by the rich versus rule by the people. Had that happened, Nader might have doubled or tripled his vote in November. Yet far more important would have been the educational impact of such a visible and dramatic confrontation. Even without significant media exposure, the Nader campaign may have changed many people's *consciousness*, including people who didn't vote for him in the end. He exposed them to a well-articulated claim that rarely is heard from a respected public figure—not only that the system is thoroughly corrupt but that something should and actually could be done about it. Had he been able to directly challenge Bush and Gore in a debate format—so different from the few interviews he was allowed on national TV—the political effect might have been enormous and long range.

The Nader campaign was an opportunity to make a breakthrough, to *begin* to create a force that could pull American politics to the left. For most of the organized forces of the Left, however, it was a missed opportunity. Worse than that, it was a deliberately *spoiled* opportunity. The Labor Party and New Party refused to endorse him. In the months leading up to the elections, major progressive groups and leaders (including feminists, environmentalists, civil rights organizations, key unions, and left-leaning journalists) went all out to persuade progressives that "a vote for Nader is a vote for Bush." Not only did they cling to their lesser evil commitment to the Democrats, but they also made every effort to destroy the Nader campaign itself. Led by feminist Gloria Steinem, longtime civil rights leader Jesse Jackson, Massachusetts representative Barney Frank, Michigan representative John Conyers, columnists Anthony Lewis and Bob Herbert, and many others, they relentlessly vilified Nader personally (with "arrogant" and "egomaniacal" being two of the favorite epithets). Nader voters were told that they would be responsible for an antichoice Supreme Court, endless war, and other horrors.[35]

After it appeared that Nader's Florida votes may have enabled Bush to carry that state (with considerable illicit assistance from Republican officialdom), the liberals' rage and venom knew no bounds.[36] AFL-CIO head John Sweeney called the Nader campaign "reprehensible."[37] This remark vividly illustrates the labor movement's political spinelessness and moral decay. Not "noble but misguided" but "reprehensible"—a campaign that called for doubling the minimum wage, paid family leave, a national day care system, single-payer health insurance, a real war on poverty, repealing the anti-union Taft-Hartley law, giving triple back pay to workers fired illegally in organizing drives, and opposing antiworker free trade agreements like NAFTA and the WTO (World Trade Organization) accord? Yet Sweeney had scarcely a word of criticism for Gore, who had offered very little to labor and had served a Democratic administration that arguably was more indifferent (when it was not downright hostile) to labor's agenda than any since Grover Cleveland's.[38]

Of course, Nader had serious political flaws. Key among them was his avoidance of race, gender, and sexual orientation, or his tendency to treat them as "special issues." This made it easier for those like Steinem, Jackson, Conyers, and Frank, who are dogmatically committed to the Democratic Party—and would have opposed Nader even if he were perfect on these questions—to discredit the Nader campaign. Jesse Jackson insisted that minorities and the poor had to stick to the Democrats because these groups had so much at stake.[39] The absurdity of this argument is easy to demonstrate. How realistic is it for the most oppressed to vote for a party that comes close to abolishing welfare (via the 1996 law championed by Clinton), supports mass incarceration, and pushes job-destroying globalization? Minorities and the poor are more victimized than anybody else by the Democrats' collusion in a grossly unjust system. But Nader's failure to explicitly champion the specific needs of communities of color made it almost impossible for him and his supporters to counter this bogus line of reasoning.

Nevertheless, some on the left apparently did realize that the Nader campaign still was an extraordinary opportunity for progressives to tap into popular disillusionment with the two-party system and to take advantage of a well-known and highly respected candidate. Within the labor movement, for example, a handful of small unions like the California Nurses Association and various individual labor leaders and activists did endorse Nader. So did an assortment of prominent leftists in academia and elsewhere. Yet, as noted above, many of the most eminent left-of-center organizations and individuals not only let the opportunity pass; they also worked furiously to crush the campaign, demonize Nader personally, and discredit the very idea of an electoral alternative to the Democrats.[40] They, not Nader or his supporters, were the real "spoilers" of the election.

The Democrats: From Bad to Worse

Instead of creating an electoral alternative, most of the influential left-leaning leaders and organizations in the United States persist in a futile attempt to push Democrats to live up to their allegedly progressive ideals. Liberal critics of Obama and his party often bewail their "cowardice" in the face of Republican militancy and their "capitulation" to corporations and the military, or explain their policies as opportunistic bids for the votes of conservatives and centrists. But this is a fundamental misunderstanding of what drives Democratic policy. Mainstream Democrats have been abandoning the politics of welfare state liberalism, of regulated capitalism, since the 1970s.[41] Except for a small and thoroughly powerless left wing, they have long embraced the neoliberal dogmas of free markets, privatization, reduced government spending, and low taxes on the rich. Democrats may eschew the explicit racism, sexism, and homophobia so rampant among Republicans. They may "feel our pain," in the unctuous words of Bill Clinton. However, they are as committed as their GOP rivals to the health and profitability of a heartless and massively destructive economic system. They also are as certain as the conservative heroine (and late British Prime Minister) Margaret Thatcher that "There Is No Alternative"—a slogan she used to justify her neoliberal policies.

Some progressive magazines such as *The Nation* believe it is possible for the Democrats to "choose" between their financial patrons and their working-class supporters. In fact, since the Democratic Party is little more than a fund-raising machine these days, and has always been led by politicians who see their first duty as shoring up the capitalist system, the "choice" is a foregone conclusion.[42] This doesn't mean that the Democrats cannot be forced to make concessions to their popular constituencies, but only under certain conditions. Such conditions include the pressure of mass upheaval (as with the labor upsurge of the 1930s and the civil rights, antiwar, and women's movements of the 1960s and 1970s) or the palpable threat of a working-class breakaway represented by a third party (such as the Populists in the 1890s and the Socialists in the 1900–1919 period). Only then can the Democrats be forced to move a little to the left.[43]

Labor, minorities, and social movements have never had their own party, controlled by and accountable to them. Instead, the Democrats so far always have succeeded in taming and co-opting labor and popular movements when they have threatened the system from the left. Among progressives, even the harshest critics of Clinton and Obama often have clung to the idea that the Democrats were once a kind of people's party and have tended to see their decline as a recent phenomenon. Even in its most "progressive" phases, however, even during the New Deal, the Democratic Party has always been as thoroughly controlled by business interests as the Republicans.[44] Until the 1960s, the party essentially was an alliance of corrupt northern big city machines and racist southern rural machines, both at the service of capital.[45] Labor and the party's liberal activists were seldom more than an inferior element.[46]

Even at its height during the 1940s, labor's national political influence was exerted by supporting the more liberal wing of the party, which favored substantially expanding the New Deal into the Fair Deal proposed by President Harry Truman.[47] Labor helped Truman, the Democratic incumbent, win his surprise victory in 1948 by providing money, troops to get out the vote, and political cheerleading. However, its power within the party's top decision-making circles was close to nil, as reflected by the subsequent failure to enact most of the Fair Deal and by Truman's repeated use of the anti-union Taft Hartley law to break strikes.[48] How much more might have been won had the unions launched a labor party, as some labor leaders briefly threatened to do at the time. The United States might have acquired a real welfare state similar to those established in Western Europe in the same era—with free medical care, decent government-provided retirement pensions, lengthy vacations, family leave at full pay, redistributionist taxation, and so on.

The civil rights movement and Vietnam War, it is true, shook the Democrats and brought about a brief lurch to the left under 1972 presidential candidate George McGovern. But afterward, from a progressive standpoint, it was all downhill. With successive Democratic presidential candidates (Carter, Mondale, Dukakis, Clinton, Gore, and Obama) the general tendency has been toward closer and closer alignment with the Republicans on the issues most crucial to the well-being of U.S. capitalism—taxation, trade, labor, military spending, and foreign policy.[49] On foreign policy today, there is bipartisan concurrence on the need to aggressively promote capitalism ("free markets") and keep the United States on top as the unassailable number one global superpower. There are still some important differences between the two parties, of course, but consider the vast areas on which there is now fundamental agreement, except for weak dissent by a mere handful of Democratic officials. Massive military spending is chief among them. This monumental waste of resources by itself excludes the possibility of any significant social spending and therefore guarantees the perpetuation of poverty, racial inequality, grossly inadequate schooling and resulting mass ignorance, environmental decline, and infrastructural decay.

The Democrats Can Never Be a Party of the People

Could the Left ever take over the Democratic Party? One often hears progressives say that we should imitate the right-wing Christian Coalition and the Tea Party. These groups started at the grassroots, settled into a long-range boring-from-within strategy, and succeeded over the years in permeating and eventually winning considerable power within the Republican Party. The problem, however, is that while the corporate-dominated Republican Party is accessible to the Far Right, the Democratic Party is not, by its own equally probusiness nature, accessible to those on the left and in the labor movement who reject the priorities of corporate America. Outlawing abortions, imposing school prayer, persecuting homosexuals, and other similar or worse actions favored by extreme rightists, are quite compatible with a corporate agenda (maximal profit-making). An anti-imperialist foreign policy, massive cuts in military spending, a real war on poverty and racial inequality, full employment, national health insurance, a shorter work week, and a strong labor movement, are not. These things only can be won by mobilizing, in open political struggle outside and against the two parties, those who do not have a vested interest in the status quo—the vast majority of Americans.

Because the Democrats are a *structurally* capitalist party, not an organization of voters and supporters whose preferences determine its policies, the Left can never compete with corporate power and financing for influence *inside* the party. There, it is "money power" that counts, whereas the Left and labor have only the potential power of organized numbers—a power that, if wielded openly in the electoral arena, could be decisive. If by some incredible turn of events the Left were to win control of the Democratic Party, it would inherit an empty shell, deserted and opposed by big business and its operatives, a mere name. The Left would have seized control only of itself. It still would have to create a new political vehicle, even if it were called the "Democratic Party." Better to start building a new party, rather than to continue pursuing the utterly futile and disastrously time-wasting strategy of trying to transform the Democrats. The U.S. Left for the most part has rarely attempted to create a third party, but it has worked with and within the Democratic Party for decades, with very little to show for it.

Polls show that many Americans today actually are open to socialist ideas,[50] many more perhaps than at any time since the 1930s. Yet our country's uniquely blind faith in the profit system remains dominant. A central component of this ideology is the belief that the demands of capital must always be conceded in the end for fear of jeopardizing investment and jobs. This view is never challenged by the Democrats because they have accepted it, with varying degrees of reluctance or enthusiasm. As long as a probusiness ideology thrives in the current political climate, the Right will always be on the offensive—bringing with it all the other things for which it stands, such as outlawing abortions, driving LGBT people back into the closet, and abolishing affirmative action (just to name the few issues on which the Republicans and Democrats still do differ more substantially). To begin to reverse this trend, to persuade millions of Americans that they do not have to bow to corporate power, we need a politically *independent* left, one without the ties to corporate interests that bind the Democratic Party.

On the other hand, as long as the bulk of the U.S. Left continues to believe that there is no alternative to its perpetual subordination to the Democrats, to the politics of lesser evilism, we may as well give up any hope of the following: substantially cutting bloated military budgets; ending chronic imperial interventions;

reviving a strong labor movement; really addressing climate change; ending poverty; offering quality education to all children; establishing a national system of free medical care; or even saving the remnants of the New Deal and the Great Society.

We Need to Get Started: The CTU Example

Municipal and state elections are a good place to start building a new party and thereby creating an independent left. In fact, in localities where dynamic social movements have arisen, independent political action is an essential means of strengthening these movements and preventing them from being weakened or even neutralized by entanglement with Democratic Party machines. Chicago provides a current example of how steps can be taken in this direction. The Chicago Teachers Union (CTU) recently launched an Independent Political Organization (IPO), bringing together unions, progressives, and community groups to establish a "pipeline for candidate development to identify and train people who are part of our movement to become elected officials."[51] The IPO's plan is for these candidates "to be held accountable to the people who helped put them in office."[52] This is just the sort of thing that progressive elements in the labor movement, along with their allies in the community, need to be doing. But a question of no small importance is the following: Will the IPO run its own candidates as Democrats and endorse other Democrats, or will it run them as independents, maybe even as part of a nascent third party?

Micah Uetricht, a Chicago-based former organizer and editor at *In These Times*, writes in *Jacobin* that the "CTU has entered into open opposition with the neoliberal wing of the [Democratic] party" by demanding smaller class sizes; enriched curricula; and funding for basic services such as libraries, arts programs, nurses, and social workers—all paid for by progressive taxes. The Democrats, including Obama, he notes, have embraced an agenda of "high stakes standardized testing, merit pay for teachers, school closures, privatization, and union busting through charter school expansion" and "an unshakeable faith in the free market as the Great Liberator of the wretched, over-regulated student masses."[53]

Uetricht, however, after listing the Democrats' crimes against teachers, students, and their families, and deploring the $30 million given to Democratic candidates by the National Education Association and the American Federation of Teachers in 2012, dismisses the possibility of the CTU or labor in general breaking with the Democrats "today, or at least in the near future." He explains, "The relationship between the two is too well-cemented. . . . The political formations to the left of the Democrats are in too great a disarray. And the stakes at the national and local legislative levels are far too high for unions to bow out. . . . Radicals often fetishize a clean break with the party, as if the ideological purity of such a stance could somehow make up for the loss of power it would entail."[54] Loss of power? What power? Surely Uetricht realizes that labor's "power" to influence Democratic policy on education or anything else is at a historic low—so low as to be nearly nonexistent.

Political independence on the other hand would actually increase the power of labor and progressives in Chicago and elsewhere. It would put the Democrats on notice that they can no longer take the votes of working people for granted. It also would force ruling elites to pay attention to popular demands, which without political power behind them, these elites safely can ignore. Militant independence by labor and the Left is the most effective way to squeeze concessions out of the powers-that-be today and start to build a real alternative political pole of attraction for the future.

The Democratic Party does not have a neoliberal "wing" that can somehow be pushed out of power; it has become a neoliberal party, with an inconsequential fringe of dissenters. The slick corporate politics and macho militarism of the "New Democrats" (originally a neoliberal faction that arose within the party in the late 1980s) have become the party's very essence. This essence is exemplified perfectly by Obama himself. This is so despite the fact that he, unlike both Clintons and Al Gore, never was part of the conservative Democratic Leadership Council (a group that overtly tried to push the Democrats rightward) and once was considered to be one of the more liberal senators. This is what decades of blind, dogmatic subordination by labor and the Left to one of the country's two capitalist parties—an irrational *fetish* if ever there was one—has come to. It is precisely the "cement" to which Uetricht refers that must be cracked and eventually smashed if there is any hope for progressive reforms, including his goal of high-quality public education.

Uetricht has written a superb book about the Chicago teacher's strike (which the CTU organized in 2012), *Strike for America: Chicago Teachers against Austerity*. It shows how the CTU was transformed by a determined internal opposition into a militant democratic union, which built an almost unique coalition with parents and community organizations and won massive concessions from Chicago's Democratic city government. Yet elsewhere Uetricht states that CTU members, for the sake of defending their jobs and benefits, "want to see lobbying, horse-trading, backroom deal-making, traditional bourgeois politicking, and would likely revolt against any leadership that refused to do so."[55] Every union must politick and make deals, obviously, but the story of the CTU proves that these things should not and need not define the limits of labor and political activism. People's political consciousness—their understanding of power relations and their ability to imagine alternatives—can be profoundly changed by movement campaigns. Yes, the Left is in "disarray," but its fragmentation into multiple separate movements and its inability to contend for real political power—something that a new party would provide—largely are to blame. Uetricht's prophecy of permanent bondage to the Democrats is self-fulfilling.

Obviously the decision to break with the Democrats will not be easy. Major obstacles include, at least until the 2016 election, the enormous credibility that Obama enjoys among African Americans and, more chronically, the deep ties that bind many community groups in Chicago and elsewhere to Democratic machines. Yet if the CTU understands that defending teachers and public education means uncompromising opposition to the conservative policies of Democratic mayor Rahm Emanuel,[56] it needs to extend that understanding to the Democratic Party as a whole. Emanuel may be a particularly aggressive and personally nasty "New Democrat" specimen, but he is no political aberration as far as the Democratic mainstream is concerned.[57] The CTU has created strong networks of allies on issues such as school closings, and these networks can be the basis of independent electoral campaigns.

For Chicago teachers and their allies, political independence is the logical continuation of the struggle they have waged on the picket lines against the city's Democratic administration and its allies in Washington. They have been the spearhead of a militant oppositional trend in Chicago and throughout the country in recent years.[58] For them to become involved in Democratic Party politics would be a step backward. Instead of digging in, the CTU should be breaking out.

"Acting Locally" Is Not Enough

At the same time, while the case of the CTU points to the pressing need—and the real possibilities—for independent political action at the local level, it is vitally important to start building a national party of the left as soon as possible. Many who recognize the need for a new party insist that it must *first* build up a base at the local level before it can consider contending for power on the national level. However, the idea that a third party can be built by focusing exclusively on the grassroots and deferring independent campaigns for national office until a later date is seriously misguided. In less than a year of combined active presidential campaigning in 1996 and 2000, Nader and the Greens appear to have done more to raise people's consciousness and build a third party movement than the prior 10 years of efforts to pass ballot initiatives and elect people to school boards and city councils—as suggested by the relatively rapid growth of the Green Party nationwide after the two Nader campaigns.[59] The point is not that local elections and ballot initiatives are unimportant, but that they cannot be a substitute for electoral initiatives that reach far more people and inspire them to feel part of a growing *national* alternative. Moreover, campaigning for high-profile offices actually can be a very effective way of recruiting and training people at the grassroots.

Whatever the motives, the effect of counterposing local community action to national politics is to forego any real challenge to the centers of power, which are, of course, national and indeed increasingly international. Fighting to keep fundamentalists off school boards, for example, is undeniably important. But is there any hope for our schools without a national fight to shift resources from the military to education?

It is especially during presidential elections that interest in political issues is at its height, even among those who are normally apathetic. At the same time, feelings of hopelessness and submissiveness are at their most intense, particularly now among progressives, because of the rightward degeneration of the Democratic Party. For the Left, there is no better "teachable moment" than presidential elections.

Strategic Voting

In addition to striking a good balance between local and national electoral efforts, building an independent party of the left requires clarity about what real independence means. Even among those progressives who support the idea of a third party, there is a strong reluctance to "do harm" to the Democrats in an election. This inhibition is understandable, but illogical and self-defeating; it will stymie third party efforts endlessly until it is overcome.

In the weeks before the 2000 election, as panic mounted at the prospect of a Republican victory, many Nader supporters proposed "strategic voting." This entailed voting for Nader only in states considered "safe" for either Gore or Bush, in other words states where it was thought that votes for Nader couldn't swing the outcome decisively in favor of Bush. Four years later, the proponents of a safe-state strategy managed to get control of the Green Party and put up David Cobb for president. Cobb's name appeared only on the ballots of those states deemed safe for Kerry. Nader, running as an independent, rightly dismissed this strategy as a capitulation to lesser evilism that contradicted the whole point of independent political action; no independent party of the left can succeed unless it is willing to compete across the board with Democrats as well as Republicans. This is because Democratic voters—as well as nonvoters—constitute much of the potential base for such a party.

Efforts by the Democrats and their supporters in the labor movement and liberal punditry to destroy Nader in 2004 were even more hysterical than in 2000 and included efforts to keep him off the ballot in every state possible. However, as it turned out, the Cobb campaign was effectively invisible, in part because of its exclusive focus on safe states. It won 130,000 votes, as compared to Nader's 550,000, even after Nader had been kept off the ballots of 6 of the 10 states where he had gotten his biggest support four years earlier. Moreover, the Greens lost ballot lines in more than one-third of the states, including Massachusetts, New Mexico, and Connecticut.

The logic of strategic voting is fatal to third party politics because it clings to the premise that we can build a party only when and where it will not threaten the Democrats. This is impossible. A viable progressive third party must win mass support from nonvoters, who make up close to half of the voting age population and tend to be more supportive of progressive policies. These nonvoters overwhelmingly include the poor and working class, and they disproportionately consist of minorities.[60] These are groups who would benefit most from a progressive agenda. Yet, a competitive left third party eventually also must win over the bulk of the Democratic Party's voting base, which is predominately less affluent, heavily nonwhite, and potentially more receptive to left politics as well.[61] Obviously, insofar as former Democratic voters vote for a new party, and that party is not yet strong enough to get its own candidates elected, Democratic candidates may lose and Republicans may win. So, yes, a serious effort to build a progressive third party means accepting the short-term possibility of electing Republicans in some places. How else can a third party eventually grow large enough to defeat *both* Democrats and Republicans? In other words, a left third party *must* "do harm" to the Democrats (and Republicans), and it must frankly declare that it intends to do so.

The Greens

If strategic voting and a policy of competing only for local offices are political dead ends, what then is the role of the Green Party in building a progressive third party movement in the contemporary United States? As suggested earlier, the Greens, despite the Cobb episode, have contributed much to the development of left third party politics. In addition to having established state and local chapters and routinely running candidates throughout the country, in recent years they have had mayors in a number of municipalities—including Richmond, Fairfax, Marina, and Sebastopol, California; Antelope and Westfir, Oregon; Ward, Colorado; Boswell, Pennsylvania; and Cobleskill, New Paltz, Victory, and the Village of Greenwich, New York.[62] They also have been the second largest party in a big city—Washington, DC.[63] Some of the most striking Green successes have been in California. There in the past couple of decades, over 20 Green mayors have been elected or appointed; a Green (Matt Gonzales) came close to being elected mayor of San Francisco; Greens have held majorities at times on several city councils; a Green state representative was elected in Oakland; and two-time Green gubernatorial candidate Peter Camejo made a favorable impression on a significant segment of the public.[64] It seems that California Greens were able to accomplish this by astute campaigning, working with liberal Democrats without sacrificing independence, and tapping into voters' real concerns.

Nevertheless, it appears unlikely that the Green Party can simply grow, through slow accretion and without significant institutional support, into the mass party that we need, one that can really contend for power on a national scale. To bring that into being, there must be a political fight within the labor movement and within the big environmentalist, women's, civil rights, antiwar, and LGBT movements to liberate them, or at least large parts of them, from enslavement to the Democrats. Out of these movements can come the needed critical mass. Labor in particular can contribute serious numbers and resources. It is crucial to win sectors of the unions to the idea of a real third party—not the ineffectual initiatives represented by the Labor Party, New Party, and WFP, which are doomed to fail because of their de facto strategy of nonindependence.

A Latent Third Party

A viable new progressive third party can be built because its mass base already exists. There has been no shortage of evidence in recent years that vast numbers of people are fed up and willing to fight back—the 2011 Wisconsin uprising (against an attack on state workers' collective bargaining rights), the Occupy movement, and the Chicago teachers' strike being the most dramatic examples.

For a while, Occupy looked like an unofficial nascent third party; it managed to electrify the nation and the world, winning the sympathy of many millions. It eclipsed the Tea Party and almost overnight forced national political discourse to address the problem of inequality, jobs, and housing rather than just taxes and "big government." Occupy gave us a glimpse of the potential for bringing a radical critique of the status quo into the living rooms of millions of Americans and inspiring hope.

However, Occupiers showed virtually no interest in helping to create that third party. Driven out of public spaces by massive police actions (apparently in coordination with the Justice Department) and undoubtedly undermined by the perceived imperative to reelect Obama, Occupy faded from the scene. It survived in the form of "flash movements," such as its dramatic humanitarian intervention in the Hurricane Sandy crisis, that flare up but then quickly evaporate.[65]

Nevertheless, public support for a third party remained high and even seemed to increase. In early 2013, during the government shutdown, a Gallup poll asked: "In your view, do the Republican and Democratic parties do an adequate job of representing the American people, or do they do such a poor job that a third party is needed?" Sixty percent responded in favor of a third party, which is the largest amount since Gallup began asking this question in 2003. About half of Democrats were pro-third party, as were half of Republicans and 71 percent of independents.[66] Obviously, the government shutdown at the time contributed to this low point in people's satisfaction with the two-party system. But this was no ephemeral plunge in public opinion; Gallup's polling had shown since 2006 that at least half of respondents believed a third party was needed.[67] Moreover, the shutdown was just the sort of crisis that an *existing* third party could have exploited.

There is, right now, a mass base, as yet unorganized, for progressive independent political action. For decades, polls have shown that on such issues as health care, economic inequality, taxes, war and foreign policy, and other matters, most Americans, not just a radical fringe, are to the left of the Democrats.[68] Today, a large majority is disgusted with corporate crime, the control of politics by money, and the gross celebration of greed and excess—all of which have flourished under both parties' administrations for decades.[69]

Envisioning a New Party

The kind of progressive party that the United States needs must not be a candidate-centered operation that concentrates exclusively on getting votes, like the two old parties. Rather, it should be a movement-type party filled with activists and democratically controlled by its membership. It should campaign systematically for its views through demonstrations, literature, speakers' bureaus, and forums of all kinds—not just campaigns for elective office. It should provide a continuous, national political voice that would speak for nonelectoral movements, sustain them through the inevitable ups and downs, connect them to each other, and enable them to be more than pressure groups.

It often is argued that the U.S. electoral system, with its ancient two-party system and its one-round, winner-take-all voting makes third parties impossible. Yet Britain and Canada both have the same system in the election of their national legislatures, and both have had successful third parties. Conversion to a system with proportional representation and instant runoff voting (IRV) would be a vital democratic reform in its own right because it would permit a much wider spectrum of political opinions to be represented in government and would increase the odds in favor of third parties immensely.[70] However, the current absence of these alternatives is no reason to postpone creating a third party. Actually, the pressure of an effective third party, able to mount protests and exercise political clout, is probably the only thing that can force the two-party duopoly to loosen its grip on the U.S. electoral system.

If a new party ran candidates now for congressional, gubernatorial, and mayoral offices—not to mention for president—it is likely of course, that it would win only a few contests or maybe even none the first time around, and perhaps likewise for several rounds thereafter. Initially, its candidates might not get more than 5 or 10 percent of the vote. While this may not seem like much, 5 percent for a third party candidate represents a very significant number of voters. These voters would have made the extremely difficult decision to break old political habits, to "just say no" to the crippling addiction of lesser evilism and opt for a real alternative. That 5 percent would be more important than the much larger percentage that might vote for the same old unaccountable politicians, including so-called "liberal" politicians (who remain committed to the Democratic Party, even as it moves steadily to the right on issues ranging from welfare to civil liberties, foreign policy, and military spending). That 5 percent would mean hundreds of thousands or even millions of people who have taken a stand in opposition to the establishment, as compared with the far smaller number who ordinarily take part in movement activities.

Again, a progressive third party would treat elections not just as opportunities to win office, but also as occasions to get people to think about alternatives of which they may not have been aware, and thereby to change public opinion and raise consciousness. Indeed, while those with consistently radical politics still are in a minority, it is the educational value of elections that counts most. Elections are, in fact, just about the only time when most Americans are paying attention to political issues at all.

It has been an unfortunately commonplace view among American left activists that elections are a diversion from the work of building movements. On the contrary, electoral activity can be an invaluable opportunity precisely for the kind of political education that also builds social movements and fosters militant struggle. Unlike the Right, the Left needs to promote among its supporters a sophisticated critical understanding of history, social problems, and the structures of power. It cannot, like the Right, simply declare its loyalty to existing conventions and traditions, or appeal to prejudices and religious dogma. It must, to a great extent, swim against the stream, push against the enormous weight of deference to authority, passivity, and fatalism with which we are indoctrinated from birth. Electoral campaigns would enable the Left to get its message out, to make its case to far more people than are reached by nonelectoral movements, and to inspire them to feel part of a growing national alternative.

By contrast, the dominant progressive habit of relegating electoral activity to simply going to the polls in order to stop the Republicans—after which the same conservative trends continue whether or not the Democrats are in office—is profoundly demoralizing politically. It makes it harder to build strong social movements, to organize the unorganized into unions and so on. This, in turn, makes it less likely that labor and social movements will be able to hold the Democrats' "feet to the fire."

Lesser evil thinking also is conservatizing. Being paralyzed by fear of electing Republicans means that millions of Americans do not feel free to vote for candidates who stand for what they actually believe in, like Nader, and instead vote for politicians whom they often despise. Then, having made that commitment, and desperate to convince themselves that they've done the right thing, they begin to discover hitherto unsuspected virtues in their chosen candidate. They also turn against militant activity of a kind they would support at any time other than during elections, because they fear it will play into the hands of the Republicans. In 2004, for example, a great many progressive Kerry supporters were upset about mass same-sex weddings in San Francisco and New Paltz, New York, thinking they would only help reelect Bush.[71] Likewise, in 1964 the civil rights movement was urged to suspend its demonstrations to ensure Johnson's election.[72]

During the 2000 election, those progressives who admired and agreed with Nader but opted for Gore, liked to describe their choice as a vote of consequence rather than a vote of conscience (or voting with their head rather than voting with their heart). But there is nothing hard-headed or realistic about voting for Gore or Obama. Its consequence is the continuation of a brutal, unjust, and ever-worsening status quo. Voting for Nader was the most tough-minded realism; it was a recognition that bringing about constructive change requires clarity, consistency, and radicalism. That is the case a progressive third party must make.

The First Step: A Declaration of Independence

A declaration of independence from the Democrats by significant segments of the progressive community would be a major breakthrough, one that points the way forward toward a new, broadly based political party of the left. With as much support as it is possible to garner from progressive leaders and publications, trade unionists, and social movement activists, such a declaration would announce to the public that at least a portion of the Left has decisively rejected the idea that progressive change can come from the Democrats. It should forthrightly state the need for political *opposition* to the Democrats, as well as Republicans, not just technical organizational independence in the manner of the Working Families Party and other "fusionist" initiatives (which almost always end up urging their followers to vote for Democratic candidates, either directly or on an independent ballot line). Once a reasonable amount of popular support has been mobilized, political opposition means running candidates against Democrats (and Republicans, of course).

As a preparatory step toward the creation of a new political party, it might be possible to convince a prominent progressive figure—someone similar to Ralph Nader—to run for president as an independent. This would be a third ticket, not yet a third party. As I finished this chapter, there was talk of the possibility of such a campaign by Vermont senator Bernie Sanders in 2016.[73] Though nominally an independent, Sanders has been a de facto Democrat throughout his career and never has shown any interest in building a third party nationally. However, he has emerged as an outspoken critic from the left of the Obama administration's domestic and foreign policies, and he has become something of a national figure. Sanders's ultimate preference was to run in the Democratic primaries. The likely effect of his campaign will mainly be to corral independent-minded voters back into the Democratic Party (as progressive Democrat Dennis Kucinich did in 2000), since many of them will feel that they will have nowhere else to turn in the general election. Sanders, if he loses, will not be able to affect the politics of the Democratic winner in 2016, as he might intend. The Democratic nominee, whether it be Hillary Clinton or someone else, will know as usual that she or he need not let any concern about the loyalty of labor and progressives inhibit the pursuit of neoliberal policies. On the other hand, a centrist Democratic presidential candidate would have serious reason to worry, and therefore an incentive to run on a more progressive platform, if an independent ticket challenged that candidate from the left.

A postprimary movement to draft Sanders to run as an independent in the 2016 general election, even without previously organizing a third party, could be a third party catalyst. It would give substance to the idea of such a party and lay the perceptual basis for one. This would be true even if Sanders declined in the end to run as independent; many of his supporters would have learned something about the necessity of independent political action. Out of the uncertain, inconsistent consciousness of third ticket Sanders supporters—who initially would view the campaign as a one-time protest and no more than that—might come a realization that an ongoing third party is needed. They could be assisted in coming to that conclusion by independent-minded leftists working within the third ticket campaign and pushing for a complete break with the Democrats, no matter what Sanders thinks or does.

The advantage of Sanders or someone like him is precisely that he symbolizes those who are in transition—disgusted with the current politics of the Democrats yet still hesitant to break away from them. Whatever Sanders's current views on the Democratic Party might be, those who admire his semi-independence are the very forces that must be won over to the idea of a progressive third party.

Predictably, Sanders's flirtation with an independent candidacy soon elicited urgent appeals to him from liberal opinion-makers to abandon the idea and stick to the Democratic primaries. A statement for Progressive Democrats of America by Tom Hayden made this point categorically and in a way that said much about the bankruptcy of the insider strategy today.[74] Leftists who advocated working within the Democratic Party used to envision a "realignment" of the two-party system, in which progressives drove conservatives out of the party and into the Republican Party. Hayden, however, quoted Jesse Jackson's formula that the Democrats "need two wings to fly"—one of them being the neoliberal establishment represented by Hillary Clinton. Sanders's job, according to Hayden, is to mobilize progressives to support Clinton's "assumed" candidacy in 2016—also to "challenge neoliberal orthodoxy" and "build a more powerful progressive base," but in a way that avoids "an intraparty civil war" and instead "forges consensus against the Republicans."[75] The notion that neoliberal orthodoxy can be challenged while forging consensus with neoliberals like Hillary Clinton is so wildly illogical that further commentary would seem to be superfluous. But such are the mental contortions that liberals like Hayden are forced to undertake.

Of course, even many of those who have no illusions about the Democrats still will say that whomever the Republicans nominate (in 2016 or a subsequent election year) is so dangerous that this is "not the time" to consider political independence. The same thing was said in 2012, 2008, 2004, 2000, and for a very long time before that, and it is nothing but a counsel of despair for the Left. Because the Republicans will get worse, with the Democrats following in their wake, continuing adherence to lesser-evil politics will mean perpetual political enslavement to a rightward-moving Democratic Party. The consequences are dire. As Adolph Reed puts it, writing in *Harper's*:

> If the left is tied to a Democratic strategy . . . before long the notion of a political left will have no meaning. . . . If the right sets the terms of debate for the Democrats, and the Democrats set the terms of debate for the left, then what can it mean to be on the political left? The terms "left" and "progressive" . . . now signify a cultural sensibility rather than reasoned critique of the established order. Because only the right proceeds from a clear, practical utopian vision, "left" has come to mean little more than "not right."[76]

The real differences between Republicans and Democrats will continue to be used to justify supporting the Democrats as a lesser evil, and consequently for deferring the creation of a new party. The point that independent leftists need to emphasize is that while these differences are important to Democratic voters, they are marginal to what the Democratic Party is *about*. The party does not exist *in order* to defend the labor movement, abortion rights, and LGBT rights. Those are not the issues that drive the party, which is why it defends them so feebly and ineffectually, when it defends them at all. When it comes to protecting Wall Street and the corporations, on the other hand, the Democrats are tireless and focused like a laser.

We urgently need a political party that exists solely to fight for the interests of working people (including women, minorities, and LGBT people), a party that would relentlessly pursue this core objective because it is controlled by working people. Such a party would embody the future possibility of creating a truly democratic government and society by overthrowing elite rule.

Notes

1 Johnson, "A Rare Elected Voice for Socialism"; and Moore, "City Council Socialism."
2 For clear evidence of the hesitancy by organized labor in Lorain County to take this step, see Bostick, "Ohioans Elect Two Dozen City Councilors on Independent Labor Ticket." However, the number and affiliation of the labor-endorsed candidates reported in this article were inaccurate. For sources of the correct facts provided here, see Chapter 9, note 17. Other information on the Lorain County case can be found in this chapter.
3 Vote Sawant, "Endorsements for Seattle City Council."
4 Neoliberalism promotes reducing government regulations on business activity, privatizing public goods and services, lowering taxation rates on high incomes, eliminating deficits, and weakening the power of labor unions. Beginning in the 1970s, it was

embraced by both parties on the grounds that any downward redistribution of wealth is counterproductive if not utopian in the context of diminished economic growth and increasing international economic competition. Neoliberals claimed that there is no desirable alternative to an essentially unfettered capitalist system. Neoliberalism's pro-corporate policies also were justified by their Republican and Democratic proponents as the route to greater economic prosperity for all (a claim that was contradicted by subsequent decades of stagnating and declining incomes for most ordinary Americans, paired with dramatic financial gains for the already wealthy few).

5 For a review of various ways in which Mayor de Blasio had failed to meet progressive expectations after six months in office, see Katch, "How's He Doin'?"

6 Greenberg Quinlan Rosner Research, "The Underdog Race for New York Mayor"; and Packer, "Bill de Blasio's Vision."

7 Among many other post-election analyses, see Silverleib, "Analysis: Obama's New Democratic Majority."

8 The overall turnout was relatively high by U.S. standards—60 percent. Nevertheless, the "party of nonvoters" remains the largest; some did not go to polls because they live in solidly blue states, but most are habitual nonvoters, disproportionately young and lower income, with a large proportion of Hispanics. Polls show that nonvoters lean left politically by around two to one. See Pew Research Center, "Nonvoters: Who They Are, What They Think." As discussed later in this chapter, it is among these nonvoters, as well as a substantial part of the Democratic Party's current constituency, that there is much of the potential base for a left third party.

9 Democratic officials who have wielded the budget ax against public employees in recent years include Iowa governor Chet Culver, Massachusetts governor Deval Patrick, and Pennsylvania governor Ed Rendell.

10 Stoller, "The Progressive Case against Obama."

11 Ibid.

12 Ibid.

13 Bromwich, "Symptoms of the Bush-Obama Presidency."

14 Ralston Reports, "Making Inequality Worse."

15 Thus, support for single-payer health insurance was overwhelming in the 1990s but has declined precipitously, almost certainly in response to the introduction of the ACA. See Coates, "Two-thirds of Americans Support Medicare-for-all," which cites a 2009 Harvard/Harris poll; and more recently, Rasmussen Reports, "40% Favor Single-Payer Health Care, 44% Oppose."

16 Bromwich, "Symptoms of the Bush-Obama Presidency."

17 Brookes, "Must Read: Obama's Lousy Environmental Record."

18 Klein, "Capitalism vs. the Climate."

19 See especially Frontline, "The Untouchables."

20 Weisman, "Lines of Resistance on Fiscal Deal."

21 Nader, "The Democrats Can't Defend the Country from GOP."

22 Meyerson, "The Left, Viewed From Space"; and Reed, "Nothing Left: The Surrender of American Liberals." NAFTA refers to the North American Free Trade Agreement, an international accord that reduced barriers to corporate globalization, to the benefit of big business and the detriment of U.S. workers. It was championed by President Clinton and approved by a Democratic-controlled Congress in 1993.

23 See Zeese and Flowers, "Trans-Pacific Partnership."

24 Among many reports on this movement, see Greenhouse, "Wage Strikes Planned at Fast Food Outlets."

25 Shamus Cooke, a left writer who often focuses on labor issues, notes that Obama "fulfilled none of his promises to labor in 2008, and essentially ignored all labor issues in his 2012 campaign." Cooke also observes that Obama and his secretary of education, Arne Duncan, have aggressively targeted teachers' unions through promotion of charter schools and support for the closing of "failed" public schools. See Cooke, "Bad Romance: Labor, Obama and the Democrats."

26 Dudzic and Isaac, "Labor Party Time? Not Yet."

27 Ibid.

28 Sifry, *Spoiling for a Fight*, 258–61.

29 Jaffe, "Will Cuomo Keep His Promises?"

30 Paul, "The Rise and Fall of the Working Families Party."

31 Jaffe, "Will Cuomo Keep His Promises?"

32 Janofsky, "The 2000 Campaign: Nader Attacks Politics as Usual."

33 Nieves, "A Party Crasher's Lone Regret."

34 For examples of polls in 2000 (and beyond) that show majority support for a progressive agenda and a third party alternative, respectively, see Lotke, et al., *The Progressive Majority*; and Pew Research Center, "Obama Better Liked, Romney Ahead," 13.

35 For a survey of anti-Nader efforts by progressives in the 2000 campaign, see Dao, "Democrats Hear Thunder on Left"; and Nader, *Crashing the Party*, 240–71. As for the belief that we can count on Democrats to help keep conservatives off the Supreme Court, it should be remembered that archconservative Supreme Court Justice Antonin Scalia was confirmed in 1986 in the Democratic-controlled U.S. Senate by a vote of 98–0. Those who voted for him included prominent Democrats Joe Biden and Al Gore. Another ultraconservative, Clarence Thomas, was confirmed in 1991 by a Democratic-controlled Senate even in the face of the Anita Hill scandal (in which Thomas was accused of chronically engaging in sexual harassment). As for endless war, we've had something close to it under Obama. U.S. intervention in Iraq has wound down, but Libya was attacked and, at the time of writing, U.S. troops still were in Afghanistan. Also, American drones continued to rain down missiles on Pakistan, Yemen, and Somalia.

36 For a particularly vivid example of Nader's demonization after the election, see Newfield, "Let This Election Be a Lesson to You" (in which a respected liberal journalist and columnist asserted that Nader should be "shunned and shamed").

37 Corn, "Nader: Is There Life after Crucifixion?"

38 Concerning Sweeny's support of Gore, see Selfa, *The Democrats: A Critical History*, 79–81. Sweeney saw to it that the AFL-CIO endorsed Gore a full year before the election. Regarding Gore's minimal support for labor, see Townsend, "Capitol Hill Shop Steward: Let's Ask Gore"; and On the Issues, "Al Gore on Labor."

39 See Lockman, "Jesse Jackson Urges Yalies to Support Gore-Lieberman."

40 See Dao, "Democrats Hear Thunder on Left"; Nader, *Crashing the Party*, 240–71; and Salon Staff, "The Nader Letters."

41 See Ferguson and Rogers, *Right Turn*; Selfa, *The Democrats*, 65–86; and Hacker and Pierson, *Winner-Take-All Politics*.

42 Selfa, *The Democrats*.

43 For illustrations of this dynamic, see Selfa, *The Democrats*, 87–125.

44 Because of the fierce hostility of the great majority of capitalists to the Roosevelt administration, it is widely believed that business did not directly control the Democratic Party during the New Deal. In fact, key members of the business class were farsighted enough to understand that drastic departures from laissez-faire policies and significant concessions to the working class were essential to the very survival of American capitalism. The First New Deal (1933–1934) was not only supported but to a large extent devised by a group of "welfare capitalists." This group was led by Gerard Swope of General Electric, Thomas Watson of IBM, Julius Rosenwald of Sears and Roebuck, Edward Filene of Filene's department stores, the Du Ponts, and most of the investment banks, except for the House of Morgan. The Du Ponts and many of the bankers turned against FDR in reaction to the working-class upheaval of the mid-1930s. Yet the welfare capitalists went on to decisively shape the Second New Deal (1935–1938), and the administration won even more business support with its aggressive pursuit of free trade policies that forced open foreign markets to U.S. exports. See Ferguson, *Golden Rule*; and Rogers, "Industrial Conflict and the Coming of the New Deal."

45 Selfa, *The Democrats*, 40–64.

46 Historian Nelson Lichtenstein observes that in the post–World War II period, a high point of labor's influence on the Democrats, "Even in the urban North the Democratic party rarely offered the representatives of organized labor more than a subordinate role in the development of its political program. The CIO [Congress of Industrial Organizations] bargained with the Democratic party 'much as it would with an employer,' admitted CIO PAC [Political Action Committee] head Jack Kroll in the early 1950s." Lichtenstein, "From Corporatism to Collective Bargaining," 139–40.

47 The Fair Deal was a largely unsuccessful proposal for federal aid to education, universal health insurance, large increases in the minimum wage, full employment, repeal of the anti-union Taft-Hartley law, and other reform proposals.

48 Selfa, *The Democrats*, 100–2.

49 See Selfa, *The Democrats*; and Hacker and Pierson, *Winner-Take-All Politics*.

50 For example, see relevant Pew polls discussed in Eichler, "Young People More Likely to Favor Socialism than Capitalism."

51 Chicago Teachers Union, "Resolution for the Chicago Teachers Union to Launch an Independent Political Organization (IPO)."

52 Ibid.

53 Uetricht, "Strike for America: CTU and Democrats."

54 Ibid.

55 Ibid.

56 Bacon, "Chicago Mayor Rahm Emanuel's War on Teachers and Children."

57 Emanuel is a longtime Obama ally and was Obama's White House chief of staff before he ran for mayor.

58 This tendency is illustrated by the Occupy movement, the 2011 Wisconsin uprising (against a move to abolish public sector collective bargaining rights in the state), the continuing struggle of undocumented immigrants and fast-food workers, the revolt against standardized testing among Seattle schoolteachers since 2013, and repeated victories of oppositional and reformist slates in the Los Angeles teachers' union since 2005. It also includes the so far small-scale incidences of progressive political independence mentioned earlier in this chapter.

59 See Berg, "Greens in the USA," 246–53.

60 See Pew Research Center, "Nonvoters: Who They Are, What They Think."

61 See Pew Research Center, "A Closer Look at the Parties"; and Pew Research Center, "Public's Response to 'Capitalism,' 'Socialism.'"

62 Green Party of the United States, "Green Party Officeholders, U.S."

63 Orvetti, "D.C.'s 'Second Party'?"

64 Green Party of the United States, "Green Party Officeholders, U.S."; and Green Party of the United States, "All Candidates for Office." Right before the election of 2003 to recall Democratic governor Gray Davis, polls taken after televised debates among the candidates gave Camejo the highest rating of all—as reported in Green Party of California, "California Green Party Protests Exclusion of Green Candidates from Debates."

65 Feuer, "Occupy Sandy." After Hurricane Sandy hit the greater New York area in November 2012, veterans of the Occupy Wall Street movement mobilized to provide relief to storm victims. They were widely seen as more effective than established relief agencies such as the Red Cross.

66 Jones, "Perceived Need for Third Party Reaches New High." Gallup's polling results did not indicate the ideological or policy leanings of the pro-third party respondents. Perhaps many of them might have preferred a third party of the right or center. However, polls cited elsewhere in this chapter suggest that a substantial portion, even a majority, probably were discontented on broadly democratic, anticorporate grounds consistent with a preference for a third party of the left.

67 Ibid.

68 For documentation of this tendency in recent years, see Teixiera, "Public Opinion Snapshot: Public Still Backs Government Health Care"; Newport, "Majority Want Wealth Distributed"; Teixiera, "Public Opinion Snapshot: Cut Military, Tax the Rich"; and Drusch, "Poll: Afghan War Opposition Peaks." For extensive documentation of majority support for progressive policies in past decades, see Lotke et al., *The Progressive Majority*.

69 Relevant poll results are cited in Kennedy, "Citizens Actually United: Bi-Partisan Opposition to Corporate Spending"; and Teixiera, "Public Opinion Snapshot: Yes the Rich Are Different." Also, see Porter, "The Spreading Surge of Corporate Crime."

70 IRV allows voters to rank candidates from a field of more than two in order of preference, rather than vote for a single candidate. If no candidate secures more than half the votes, ballots cast for the candidate with the fewest votes are reassigned to those of the remaining candidates who rank next in order of preference on each ballot. This process continues until one candidate wins by obtaining more than half of the votes. IRV already exists for municipal elections in San Francisco, Oakland, Berkeley, Portland (Maine), and Minneapolis.

71 For an illustration of this sentiment, see Lochhead, "Gay Marriage."

72 Lewis, *Walking With the Wind*, 276.

73 See Nichols, "Democrat? Green? Independent? The 'Run Bernie Run' Jockeying." Nichols quotes Kshama Sawant: "We are not, of course, pretending that a mass party of the 99 percent could be built overnight, but if Sanders decided to run as an independent left candidate for president on the basis of using his campaign to help galvanize the forces to launch such a party, it would be an enormous step forward. Concretely, his presidential run could be linked to a national effort to stand a slate of credible left candidates in local and national races in 2016 on an independent basis" (ibid.). However, as this chapter was being finished, the Progressive Democrats of America collected thousands of signatures on a petition urging Sanders to run as a Democrat—as shown

in Progressive Democrats of America, "Encourage Senator Bernie Sanders to Run for President as a Democrat in 2016." Sanders's own comments, recounted by Nichols in the prior source, suggested that he was inclined to do so. In the end he did.

74 Hayden, "You Can Make Democrats the Party of the People Again."

75 Ibid.

76 Reed, "Nothing Left."

Bibliography

Bacon, David. "Chicago Mayor Rahm Emanuel's War on Teachers and Children," *Truthout*. Last modified June 20, 2013. http://truth-out.org/news/item/17091-chicago-mayor-rahm-emanuels-war-on-teachers-and-children.

Berg, John C. "Greens in the USA." In *Green Parties in Transition: The End of Grass-roots Democracy?*, edited by Gene E. Frankland, Paul Lucardie, and Benoit Rihoux, 245–56. Farnham, England: Ashgate, 2008.

Bostick, Bruce. "Ohioans Elect Two Dozen City Councilors on Independent Labor Ticket." *Labor Notes*, December 4, 2013. http://labornotes.org/2013/12/ohioans-elect-two-dozen-city-councilors-independent-labor-ticket.

Bromwich, David. "Symptoms of the Bush-Obama Presidency." Nationof Change. Last modified August 19, 2011. www.nationofchange.org/symptoms-bush-obama-presidency-1313765152.

Brookes, Julian. "Must Read: Obama's Lousy Environmental Record." *Rolling Stone*, June 13, 2011. www.rollingstone.com/politics/news/must-read-obamas-lousy-environmental-record-20110613.

Chicago Teachers Union. "Resolution for the Chicago Teachers Union to Launch an Independent Political Organization (IPO)." Last modified January 8, 2014. www.ctunet.com/delegates/text/RESOLUTION-FOR-THE-CHICAGO-TEACHERS-UNION-TO-LAUNCH-AN-IPO-revissed-1-8-2014.pdf.

Coates, Andy. "Two-thirds of Americans Support Medicare-for-all." *Physicians for a National Health Program Blog*. Last modified December 9, 2009. http://pnhp.org/blog/2009/12/09/two-thirds-support-3/.

Cooke, Shamus. "Bad Romance: Labor, Obama and the Democrats." *Counterpunch*, www.counterpunch.org/2013/03/07/bad-romance-labor-obama-and-the-democrats/.

Corn, David. "Nader: Is There Life after Crucifixion?" *The Nation*, December 4, 2000. www.thenation.com/article/nader-there-life-after-crucifixion.

Dao, James. "Democrats Hear Thunder on Left, and Try to Steal Some of Nader's." *New York Times*, October 25, 2000. www.nytimes.com/2000/10/25/us/2000-campaign-green-party-democrats-hear-thunder-left-try-steal-some-nader-s.html.

Drusch, Andrea. "Poll: Afghan War Opposition Peaks." *Politico*, February 19, 2014. www.politico.com/story/2014/02/war-in-afghanistan-poll-103658.html.

Dudzic, Mark, and Katherine Isaac, "Labor Party Time? Not Yet." Labor Party. Last modified December, 2012. www.thelaborparty.org/d_lp_time.htm.

Eichler, Alexander. "Young People More Likely to Favor Socialism than Capitalism: Pew." *Huffington Post*, December 29, 2011. www.huffingtonpost.com/2011/12/29/young-people-socialism_n_1175218.html.

Ferguson, Thomas. *Golden Rule: The Investment Theory of Party Competition and the Logic of Money-Driven Political Systems*. University of Chicago: Chicago, 1995.

Ferguson, Thomas, and Joel Rogers. *Right Turn: The Decline of the Democrats and the Future of American Politics*. New York: Hill and Wang, 1986.

Feuer, Alan. "Occupy Sandy: A Movement Moves to Relief." *New York Times*, November 9, 2012. www.nytimes.com/2012/11/11/nyregion/where-fema-fell-short-occupy-sandy-was-there.html?pagewanted=all&_r=0.

Frontline. "The Untouchables: Transcript." PBS. Last modified January 22, 2013. www.pbs.org/wgbh/pages/frontline/business-economy-financial-crisis/untouchables/transcript-37/.

Greenberg Quinlan Rosner Research. "The Underdog Race for New York City Mayor: Bill de Blasio." Accessed November 8, 2014. www.gqrr.com/casestudies/new-york-city-mayor.

Greenhouse, Steven. "Wage Strikes Planned at Fast Food Outlets." *New York Times*, December 1, 2013. www.nytimes.com/2013/12/02/business/economy/wage-strikes-planned-at-fast-food-outlets-in-100-cities.html.

Green Party of California. "California Green Party Protests Exclusion of Green Candidates from Debates, Including Saturday's Gubernatorial 'Yawnfest.'" Green Party of the United States. Last modified October 10, 2006. www.gp.org/press/states/ca/ca_2006_10_10.shtml.

Green Party of the United States. "All Candidates for Office." Accessed April 20, 2014. www.gp.org/elections/candidates/index.php.

———. "Green Party Officeholders, U.S.: Green Party Mayors in the U.S. 1990-Present." Accessed November 8, 2014. www.gp.org/elections/Green-Mayors/index.shtml.

Hacker, Jacob S., and Paul Pierson. *Winner-Take-All Politics: How Washington Made the Rich Richer—And Turned Its Back on the Middle Class*. New York: Simon and Schuster, 2010.

Hayden, Tom. "You Can Make Democrats the Party of the People Again." Progressive Democrats of America. Accessed June 7, 2014. http://salsa3.salsalabs.com/o/1987/t/0/blastContent.jsp?email_blast_KEY=1277181.

Jaffe, Sarah. "Will Cuomo Keep His Promises? The Working Families Party Went Out on a Limb When It Endorsed the Conservative Democrat." *In These Times*, June 2, 2014. http://inthesetimes.com/article/16767/will_cuomo_keep_his_promises.

Janofsky, Michael. "The 2000 Campaign: The Green Party; Nader, Nominated by the Greens, Attacks Politics as Usual." *New York Times*, June 26, 2000. www.nytimes.com/2000/06/26/us/2000-campaign-green-party-nader-nominated-greens-attacks-politics-usual.html.

Johnson, Kirk. "A Rare Elected Voice for Socialism Pledges to Be Heard in Seattle." *New York Times*, December 28, 2013. www.nytimes.com/2013/12/29/us/a-rare-elected-voice-for-socialism-pledges-to-be-heard-in-seattle.html?_r=1&hp&adxnnl=1&adxnnlx=1388294386-51XtwhkQDcOqFYmc4gdd0w&.

Jones, Jeffrey M. "In U.S., Perceived Need for Third Party Reaches New High." Gallup Politics. Last modified Oct. 11, 2013. www.gallup.com/poll/165392/perceivedneed-third-party-reaches-new-high.aspx.

Katch, Danny. "How's He Doin'? Bill de Blasio after Six Months." *Truthout*, July 26, 2014. http://truth-out.org/news/item/25143-hows-he-doin-bill-de-blasio-after-six-months.

Kennedy, Liz. "Citizens Actually United: The Bi-Partisan Opposition to Corporate Political Spending and Support for Common Sense Solutions." Demos. Last modified October 25, 2012. www.demos.org/publication/citizens-actually-united-bi-partisan-opposition-corporate-political-spending-and-support.

Klein, Naomi. "Capitalism vs. the Climate." *The Nation*, November 28, 2011. www. thenation.com/article/164497/capitalism-vs-climate#.

Lewis, John. *Walking With the Wind: A Memoir of the Movement*. New York: Simon and Schuster, 1998.

Lichtenstein, Nelson. "From Corporatism to Collective Bargaining: Organized Labor and the Eclipse of Social Democracy in the Postwar Era." In *The Rise and Fall of the New Deal Order, 1930–1980*, edited by Steve Fraser and Gary Gerstle, 122–52. Princeton: Princeton University Press, 1989.

Lochhead, Carolyn. "Gay Marriage: Did Issue Help Re-elect Bush?" *SFGate*, November 4, 2004. www.sfgate.com/news/article/GAY-MARRIAGE-Did-issue-help-re-elect-Bush-2677003.php#page-1.

Lockman, Josh. "Jesse Jackson Urges Yalies to Support Gore-Lieberman." *YH Online*, October 27, 2000. www.yaleherald.com/archive/xxx/2000.10.27/news/p5jackson2. html#interview.

Lotke, Eric, Robert Gerson, Paul Waldman, and Andrew Seifter. *The Progressive Majority: Why a Conservative America Is a Myth*. Washington, DC: Campaign for America's Future and Media Matters for America, 2007. Accessed June 12, 2014. http://cloudfront. mediamatters.org/static/pdf/progressive_majority.pdf.

Meyerson, Harold. "The Left, Viewed From Space." *American Prospect*, March 3, 2014. http://prospect.org/article/left-viewed-space.

Moore, Ty. "City Council Socialism." *Jacobin*, December 15, 2013. www.jacobinmag. com/2013/12/city-council-socialism/.

Nader, Ralph. *Crashing the Party: Taking on Corporate Government in an Age of Surrender*. New York: Thomas Dunne Books, 2002.

———. "The Democrats Can't Defend the Country from the Retrograde GOP." *Huffington Post*, October 18, 2013. www.huffingtonpost.com/ralph-nader/democrats-congress_b_4123609.

Newfield, Jack. "Let This Election Be a Lesson to You." *New York Post*, November 9, 2000. http://nypost.com/2000/11/09/let-this-election-be-a-lesson-to-you/.

Newport, Frank. "Majority in U.S. Want Wealth More Evenly Distributed, and 52% Support Heavy Taxes on the Rich to Redistribute Wealth." Gallup Politics. Last modified April 17, 2013. www.gallup.com/poll/161927/majority-wealth-evenly-distributed.aspx.

Nichols, John. "Democrat? Green? Independent? The 'Run Bernie Run' Jockeying." *John Nichols* (blog). *The Nation*, May 12, 2014. www.thenation.com/blog/179798/democrat-green-independent-run-bernie-run-jockeying.

Nieves, Evelyn. "A Party Crasher's Lone Regret: That He Didn't Get More Votes." *New York Times*, February 18, 2001. www.nytimes.com/2001/02/18/weekinreview/conversation-ralph-nader-party-crasher-s-lone-regret-that-he-didn-t-get-more. html.

On the Issues. "Al Gore on Labor." Accessed June 24, 2014. www.ontheissues.org/Celeb/Al_Gore_Jobs.htm#Labor.

Orvetti, P. J. "D.C.'s 'Second Party'?" 4 NBC Washington, October 2, 2010. www.nbc washington.com/news/politics/DCs-Second-Party-105727308.html.

Packer, George. "Bill de Blasio's Vision." *New Yorker*, August 12, 2013. www.newyorker. com/news/daily-comment/bill-de-blasios-vision.

Paul, Ari. "The Rise and Fall of the Working Families Party." *Jacobin*, November 15, 2013. www.jacobinmag.com/2013/11/the-rise-and-fall-of-the-working-families-party/.

Pew Research Center for People and the Press. "A Closer Look at the Parties in 2012: GOP Makes Big Gains Among White Working Class Voters." Last modified August 23, 2012. www.people-press.org/2012/08/23/a-closer-look-at-the-parties-in-2012/.

———. "Little Change in Public's Response to 'Capitalism,' 'Socialism.'" Last modified December 28, 2011. www.people-press.org/2011/12/28/little-change-in-publics-response-to-capitalism-socialism/?src=prc-number.

———. "Nonvoters: Who They Are, What They Think." Last modified November 1, 2012. www.people-press.org/2012/11/01/nonvoters-who-they-are-what-they-think/.

———. "Obama Better Liked, Romney Ahead on the Economy: GOP Holds Early Turnout Edge But Little Enthusiasm for Romney." Last modified June 21, 2012. www.people-press.org/files/legacy-pdf/06–21–12%20Voter%20Attitudes.pdf.

Porter, Eduardo. "The Spreading Surge of Corporate Crime." *New York Times*, July 10, 2012. www.nytimes.com/2012/07/11/business/economy/the-spreading-scourge-of-corporate-corruption.html?r=0.

Progressive Democrats of America. "Encourage Senator Bernie Sanders to Run for President as a Democrat in 2016." Accessed June 19, 2014. www.credomobilize.com/petitions/encourage-senator-bernie-sanders-to-run-for-president-in-2016-as-a-democrat.

Ralston Reports. "Making Inequality Worse." Last modified December 4, 2013. http://cdn.ralstonreports.com/sites/default/files/ObamaCaretoAFL_FINAL.pdf.

Rasmussen Reports. "40% Favor Single-Payer Health Care, 44% Oppose." Last modified December 17, 2012. www.rasmussenreports.com/public_content/politics/current_events/healthcare/december_2012/40_favor_single_payer_health_care_system_44_oppose.

Reed, Adolph. "Nothing Left: The Long, Slow Surrender of American Liberals." *Harper's*, March, 2014. Accessed June 18 2014. http://harpers.org/archive/2014/03/nothing-left-2/.

Rogers, Joel. "Industrial Conflict and the Coming of the New Deal: The Triumph of Multinational Liberalism in America." In *The Rise and Fall of the New Deal Order*, edited by Steven Fraser and Gary Gerstle, 3–31. Princeton: Princeton University Press, 1989.

Salon Staff. "The Nader Letters." *Salon*, November 6, 2000. www.salon.com/2000/11/06/letters_7/.

Selfa, Lance. *The Democrats: A Critical History*. Chicago: Haymarket, 2008.

Sifry, Micah L. *Spoiling for a Fight: Third-Party Politics in America*. New York: Routledge, 2012.

Silverleib, Alan. "Analysis: Obama's New Democratic Majority." CNN Politics. Last modified November 7, 2012. www.cnn.com/2012/11/07/politics/exit-polls-analysis/.

Stoller, Matt. "The Progressive Case against Obama." *Salon*, www.salon.com/2012/10/27/the_progressive_case_against_obama/.

Teixiera, Ruy. "Public Opinion Snapshot: Cut Military Spending, Tax the Rich." Center for American Progress. Last modified February 27, 2012. http://americanprogress.org/issues/public-opinion/news/2012/02/27/11047/public-opinion-snapshot-cut-military-spending-tax-the-rich/.

———. "Public Opinion Snapshot: Public Still Backs Government Role in Health Care." Center for American Progress. Last modified August 6, 2012. http://americanprogress.org/issues/public-opinion/news/2012/08/06/11977/public-opinion-snapshot-public-still-backs-government-role-in-health-care/.

———. "Public Opinion Snapshot: Yes the Rich are Different. They Have Too Much Power." Center for American Progress. Last modified January 17, 2012.

http://americanprogress.org/issues/public-opinion/news/2012/01/17/10963/
public-opinion-snapshot-yes-the-rich-are-different-they-have-too-much-power/.

Townsend, Chris. "Capitol Hill Shop Steward: Let's Ask Al Gore—Which Side Are You
On?" UE Web. Accessed June 24, 2014. www.ranknfile-ue.org/cap_st13.html.

Uetricht, Micah. "Strike for America: The CTU and the Democrats." *Jacobin*, June 7, 2014.
www.jacobinmag.com/2012/12/ctu-and-dems/.

———. *Strike For America: Chicago Teachers against Austerity*. Brooklyn: Verso, 2014.

Vote Sawant. "Endorsements for Seattle City Council." Accessed June 26, 2014. www.
votesawant.org/endorsements.

Weisman, Jonathan. "Lines of Resistance on Fiscal Deal." *New York Times*, January 1, 2013.
www.nytimes.com/2013/01/02/us/politics/a-new-breed-of-republicans-resists-
the-fiscal-deal.html?r=0.

Zeese, Kevin, and Margaret Flowers. "Trans-Pacific Partnership: 'Will Not Obey'; Building a Global Resistance Movement." *Truthout*, November 2013. http://truth-out.
org/opinion/item/19843-trans-pacific-partnership-we-will-not-obey-building-a-
global-resistance-movement-to-transnational-corporate-power.

EPILOGUE

Questions and Answers about Progressive Third Party Empowerment

Jonathan H. Martin

Are there solid grounds for feeling hopeful and even inspired about the future of progressive third parties in the United States, and by extension, about the potential for shifting the country in a more constructive direction? The chapters in this collection have suggested that there are, and they have aimed to clarify the specific pathways to left third party empowerment. Yet they also may have left readers with important questions that need to be addressed in order to create a satisfying sense of closure or direction. Below I present and respond to what I suspect are the most common of these questions. Essentially, the dialogue reinforces, integrates, assesses, and supplements key points made throughout this book. The answers refer to pertinent contributors but ultimately represent the perspective of this editor-contributor. My conclusions are not intended to be definitive; rather, they are meant to be a stimulus for readers' own concluding reflections.

Updates

Q: **Has the U.S. left third party movement continued to make progress since the events described in prior chapters?**

A: Arguably, yes. Relevant gains and claims of progress as of this writing have included the following:

- The struggle for a $15-an-hour minimum wage, which achieved its first inspiring breakthrough in Seattle with the help of socialist city council member Kshama Sawant, has continued to grow. Grassroots activities, in which low-wage workers themselves have been prominently involved, have included protests, petitions, strikes, and ballot initiatives.[1] By early 2015, there were 20 "15 Now" chapters in a total of 18 states.[2] Following the June 2014 passage of a $15-an-hour minimum wage law in Seattle, similar measures were approved in San Francisco and Los Angeles within a year.[3]

- Kshama Sawant claims to have made important advances on other fronts in her first year in office—working with her organization Socialist Alternative and with community activists. She helped establish Indigenous People's Day in Seattle, stop a plan to dramatically raise rents on subsidized housing in the city, and amend the mayor's budget to include a variety of progressive initiatives.[4]

- The Green Party of the United States (GPUS) maintains that the 2014 elections were a success for the party. It points out that it won scores of local races around the country (as it often has done in elections since 2000). In California, it apparently won nearly half of the races it entered. Perhaps the most significant Green advance in a statewide race occurred in New York State, where Green gubernatorial candidate Howie Hawkins received nearly triple the number of votes that he had gotten for the same office four years earlier. The GPUS also notes that in 2014 it won ballot status in several more states than it did in 2010, the previous midterm election.[5] As a result, the party in 2016 may be positioned to participate more extensively in state and federal elections than it did in 2012. Jill Stein, Green presidential candidate in 2012 and for 2016, suggested that growing public discontent about certain key issues and how they are addressed by the two major parties (particularly the Democratic Party) could enable Greens to make a breakthrough in the 2016 presidential election.[6]

- In her two terms as the Green mayor of Richmond, California (2007–2014), Gayle McLaughlin led a variety of successful efforts to improve life in the city. Via her initiatives and actions, the city approved a minimum wage of $13 an hour; secured an agreement from the Chevron Corporation to pay an extra $114 million in municipal taxes; blocked approval for construction of a large casino; substantially reduced violent crime via an intervention program utilizing former offenders; and implemented a variety of significant environmental improvements. McLaughlin also advanced a novel proposal to use eminent domain to protect homeowners from foreclosure.[7] While she was legally barred from seeking a third mayoral term, she was elected to the city council in 2014, along with two other city council candidates supported by the Richmond Progressive Alliance. All three conservative city council candidates backed by Chevron were defeated. As a result, the progressive majority on the city council was strengthened. A progressive Democratic city council member endorsed by McLaughlin won the mayoral race against a Chevron-backed opponent.[8]

- Greens in Portland, Maine, have sustained and perhaps slightly strengthened their presence in government in recent years. Ben Chipman, the Portland

Green who won a state representative seat as an independent in 2010, was reelected in 2012 and 2014. He is known for promoting various progressive initiatives in the Maine State House.[9] John Eder, the former Green state representative in Portland, won a seat on the city's school committee in 2014. While Eder is one of only three Greens on the nine-member committee, he is likely to be a particularly active member. Following the 2014 election, there still were two Greens on the nine-member Portland City Council. [10]

- The Vermont Progressive Party (VPP) played an instrumental role in the 2011 passage of a law that required Vermont to develop plans for the implementation of a single-payer health care system (the first in the country). In 2010, when Governor Peter Shumlin was the Democratic gubernatorial nominee, he had agreed to support a shift to single-payer. He did so in exchange for the VPP's pledge not to run a gubernatorial candidate against him—and thereby potentially split the left-leaning vote enough to make him lose to his Republican opponent.[11] This deal also may have been facilitated by memories of the 2002 race for lieutenant governor in Vermont. Then, a VPP candidate who got 25 percent of the vote arguably did cause Shumlin, the Democrat, to lose to a Republican.[12]

- The VPP has made other progress. In 2012, its first statewide official (auditor of accounts Doug Hoffer, cross-nominated by the Democrats) was elected. In 2014, the VPP gained 2 seats (for a total of 7) in the Vermont House and kept all 3 seats in the Vermont Senate—resulting in the largest VPP presence to date in the state legislature.[13] In recent years, VPP state representatives and senators have been instrumental in advancing legislation not only for single-payer health care but also for campaign finance reform, equal health benefits for same-sex marriage partners, the regulation of genetically modified foods, decriminalization of marijuana, and other progressive goals.[14] In March 2015, the VPP recaptured from the Democrats the working plurality of seats on the city council in Burlington, Vermont. In so doing, it arguably became a major player in city politics again, a status that it seemingly had not had since it lost the mayor's office to the Democrats in 2012.[15]

- Senator Bernie Sanders (I-VT) was reelected in 2012. He continues to be a particularly strong progressive populist voice in Congress.[16] In March 2014, Sanders began openly considering whether to run for president, either as an independent or a Democrat.[17] Subsequently, the enthusiastic response at his exploratory speaking events around the nation seemed to suggest that there is a substantial reservoir of grassroots support for a compelling left-wing presidential candidate.[18] In April 2015, Sanders announced that he would run as a Democrat.[19] Whether this represents an opportunity for the Left as a whole or the progressive third party movement in particular is debatable. As this book goes to press, it remains to be seen whether Sanders will transform or merely bolster a largely centrist, corporate-dominated Democratic Party, and whether his Democratic candidacy ultimately will function to foster or to dampen left electoral politics outside of the major parties.

- Labor leaders in Lorain County, Ohio, who ran their own local candidates in 2013, some of whom won, are reported to still be committed to recruiting independent, pro-labor candidates. For the November 2015 election, one of the most prominent of these leaders endorsed a sympathetic independent challenger to the conservative Democratic mayor of the city of Lorain.[20]

- The Working Families Party (WFP) claims that it is continuing to make electoral progress at different levels and in various places.[21] For example, the party maintained that its grassroots organizing contributed to the victories of endorsed Democratic candidates for governor in Pennsylvania and Connecticut in 2014. Both of these candidates arguably were fiscally conservative centrists, but the WFP embraced them because of their support for certain key proworker reforms.[22] Likewise, on the heels of substantial election victories by WFP-Democrats in New York City in recent years, the party stressed how it was breaking through in other locales; sympathetic Democrats whom it endorsed and assisted in 2014 won new municipal seats in Washington, DC; Newark, New Jersey; and Richmond, California.[23] At the same time, the WFP actually credited itself for being willing to promote its own (non-Democratic) candidates in four New York state senate races in 2014—something that the party rarely does at that level.[24] It also celebrated the fact that in February 2015 in Bridgeport, Connecticut, it won a state legislative (state senate) race *for the first time with a candidate running only on the WFP ballot line*.[25] Before this occurred, the WFP already had secured a couple of its own municipal seats in Bridgeport and a few upstate in Hartford.[26] Additionally, in May 2015 the second WFP-only statehouse candidate won—this time in a special election for a Brooklyn seat in the New York State Assembly, the lower chamber of the New York State Legislature.[27]

- The Working Families Party also claims that its relationships with sympathetic politicians, its lobbying work, and its grassroots activism continue to help produce progressive policy victories at the state and municipal level.[28] According to the party, examples of such achievements just in mid-2014 through early 2015 included a minimum wage increase in Maryland;[29] new living wage rules in New York City and Philadelphia that cover additional workers;[30] the passage of paid sick days legislation in several cities;[31] and the banning of fracking (an environmentally destructive method of natural gas extraction) in New York State.[32]

- In 2014 in Chicago, United Working Families (UWF), an independent political organization that may develop into a significant new local party of the left was officially formed. Its founders were the Chicago Teachers Union (CTU), the SEIU Healthcare Illinois Indiana Union, and two progressive community groups. UWF was heavily involved in recruiting and supporting municipal candidates challenging the entrenched, increasingly conservative Democratic machine in the 2015 elections.[33] Several UWF-endorsed candidates won, despite strong opposition.[34] Although UWF is not formally associated with the Working Families Party, the two organizations have similar political backing and goals, and they have collaborated closely.[35]

- Progressive Dane, a left third party in Dane County, Wisconsin (encompassing Madison and surrounding towns), has gained electoral ground in recent years. In 2010 it held 3 out of 20 common council seats in Madison,[36] and by 2015, it occupied 7 seats. During this same period, its candidates began to win municipal offices, including a mayoral seat, in the Madison suburbs. Meanwhile, the party continued to claim roughly half of the city's school board membership and a significant minority of county board positions. Some of Progressive Dane's electoral success may be partly attributable to its left-leaning locale. However, an active program of organizing on key local issues and the ability to regularly recruit viable candidates strongly committed to the party (despite their often being cross-endorsed) also may play an important role.[37]

- In May 2015, a conference entitled "The Future of Left/Independent Electoral Action in the United States" was held in Chicago. It was the first national gathering of diverse third party and independent left activists in many years.[38] The stated purpose was to facilitate communication and collaboration among these activists at the conference and beyond. This author, who attended the event along with about 200 other people, observed that many conference-goers seemed pleasantly surprised by what appeared to be a rare spirit of unity among diverse elements of the third party/independent left.[39] Also notable were occasional references by certain attendees to the hope that the seed had been planted for the emergence of a new progressive third party network or even some sort of overarching new party of the left. Last, there seemed to be a consensus that post-conference communication should be fostered and that a follow-up gathering should be held in 2016. Soon thereafter, the conference website (Leftelect.org) started to be reoriented accordingly under its new title, the "Future of Left and Independent Politics Network."

Q: Are there any important ways in which left third parties appear to have lost ground recently?

A: Yes. Along with the above accomplishments and assertions of progress, there also have been a couple of striking setbacks, specifically involving betrayals by Democratic governors. The first of these happened to the Working Families Party. As noted by Daniel Cantor, in the summer of 2014 New York governor Andrew Cuomo (a conservative Democrat) pledged to help the WFP achieve some of its political goals in exchange for its endorsement in the upcoming gubernatorial election. Specifically, Cuomo promised to campaign hard for a Democratic takeover of the New York State Senate in November, and then to help the WFP achieve key parts of its progressive agenda afterward. However, immediately after this agreement Cuomo began to back away from his legislative pledges. During the campaign itself, he failed to use millions of dollars in his campaign account that could have helped promote Democratic candidates for the state senate. He also spent millions more to create a fake third party to draw votes away from the Working Families Party, and he even seemed to publically denigrate the WFP. In the end, Cuomo himself was reelected. But the Republicans strengthened their control of the state senate, and the prospects for advancing WFP initiatives in New York State in the near future seem to have dimmed significantly.[40]

A second dramatic setback for a left third party that involved an about-face by a Democratic governor occurred in Vermont in December 2014. At that time, Governor Shumlin reneged on his pledge to pursue the implementation of the single-payer health care system in the state—a promise that had been secured in large part by the Vermont Progressive Party, as described above. Shumlin claimed that the increase in taxes needed to fund single-payer was unacceptable.[41] The VPP responded on its website:

Governor Peter Shumlin . . . broke five years of campaign promises to Vermonters that he would not rest until we had single payer healthcare. . . . The Vermont Progressive Party did not run Progressive challengers against Governor Shumlin in the last three cycles, in large part because of his unwavering promise to lead on single payer. While we are outraged by Shumlin's broken promises, we are not terribly surprised. Progressives have long raised the same challenges Shumlin is now using as his excuses for why we can't move ahead on single payer. We have long pushed for discussions about how we can equitably fund our new system, and live up to our promise of healthcare as a human right. But rather than work through these issues or scale back the project, Shumlin decided to scrap it entirely (and with it, many Vermonters' hopes of a just and accessible healthcare system). Governor Shumlin only seems concerned about the projected future economic burden to businesses, not the burden that working people are bearing right now. . . . Vermont Progressives have built the strongest third political party in the country over the last 30 years, largely due to our unwavering commitment to reforming healthcare and economic justice. Our current elected legislators remain committed to finding a path forward. We are not backing down, despite this crisis of leadership. . . . Looking ahead, the Progressive Party will continue to find candidates to run for statewide and legislative office in 2016 who are unwavering in their commitment to comprehensive, universal health care.[42]

Ingredients of Electoral Success

Q: Are the local left third party electoral breakthroughs described in this book replicable in other places?

A: Each of these advances was facilitated by some potent combination of favorable political conditions. Such circumstances certainly don't exist everywhere in the United States all the time, but they likely can be found in various places in the country much of the time. A key challenge is being able to recognize and exploit them where and when they do occur, or perhaps try to create them when possible. In chapters by Ramy Khalil, Mike Feinstein, Patrick Quinlan, Terry Bouricius, and me, we have seen that on the local level, conditions favorable to a progressive third party election breakthrough tend to include several of the following elements:

- an open seat race with a weak opponent or an opponent backed by a major party machine that has grown complacent—or a race with an incumbent opponent who ignores common constituent concerns or doesn't campaign very actively;
- a two-way race, or no viable opponents from a second major party;
- a hardworking left third party candidate who is well known, well liked, and relatively well connected to the community;
- certain salient local problems that negatively impact significant segments of the electorate and remain poorly addressed by those in power;
- a simple populist message from the progressive third party candidate (addressing local problems in a way that creates a strong bond with ordinary voters);
- one or more energized, receptive left-leaning community organizations;
- a significant core of highly motivated and skilled party activists in the district, as well as a larger group of strong sympathizers;
- a significant pool of potentially sympathetic new voters or habitual nonvoters in the district (who may be inspired and mobilized to vote for the progressive third party candidate);
- receptive local media and interest groups that may endorse or help publicize the candidacy;
- a previous win or good showing in the district (or a nearby or similar district)—either by a candidate affiliated with the progressive third party or by some likeminded outsider candidate; and
- a district that is relatively small (in terms of size and population) and in which, accordingly, campaign spending is comparatively low and door-knocking can be more effective.

The complete list above may roughly be thought of as an ideal-type environment for a local left third party win. However, it shouldn't be viewed as a required formula or checklist. The successful local campaigns discussed in this book include those that were missing some items or parts of items mentioned here. For example, both Gayle McLaughlin and Kshama Sawant were elected to citywide municipal seats (mayor and at-large city council, respectively), rather than seats representing smaller urban districts. Also, Sawant was not well known prior to running for office.[43] Of course, progressive political change historically has not been restricted only to those places that have the most favorable conditions or the "ideal" leaders. In fact, it often has come sooner or later to some fairly inhospitable locations or via some unlikely heroes, in part through the sheer power of successful examples elsewhere and the initiative of various courageous, farsighted activists.

Yet, it could be useful to identify those conditions above that *most commonly* are present in local progressive third party victories. My own chapter that highlights the consistent role of candidate community connectedness in state legislative wins makes an initial contribution to that effort. More such systematic analysis of lower level left third party campaigns, focusing also on what typically fosters victories in municipal and county races, would help complete the picture.

Q: What is the most serious obstacle that progressive third parties and their candidates must overcome?

A: It is difficult to identify one obstacle that is generally the most serious across different electoral contexts. The various impediments identified in this book tend to reinforce one another as part of an integrated, dynamic system (that discriminates against minor parties and the Left to the advantage of major parties and ruling elites). Strategically, it may be more productive to focus on which barriers are the weakest. One of the more significant yet fragile obstacles may be the widespread public belief that third parties, especially those on the left, can't win. Victories or good showings by left third party candidates (particularly at the local level, where it is much easier to do well) may be decisive in puncturing this myth. More such outcomes therefore may be critical to building essential public support for the progressive third party movement.

Q: Doesn't the extreme financial advantage of the major parties make it impossible for progressive third party candidates to do well?

A: Not always. Money can be very helpful for running an effective campaign, but it isn't the only thing that determines election outcomes. At lower electoral levels, other factors can be equally if not more important. Various chapters in this book have highlighted how other campaign assets at the local level (such as strong organization, a compelling message, and an appealing candidate with solid community connections) can be used to overcome a significant financial disadvantage. In higher level races, as suggested by Sayeed Iftekhar Ahmed, having a lot less money than major party opponents may not necessarily prevent a well-known and well-organized progressive third party candidate from at least making a good showing—as long as the amount of campaign funds is not abysmally low. As discussed below, a good showing can function as an important step toward the longer term progress of a left third party.

Q: **Various chapters in this book stress how important it is for progressive third parties to run strong candidates in order to make electoral breakthroughs. From where do such candidates come?**

A: As illustrated throughout this book, strong progressive third party candidates often seem to emerge from favorable electoral contexts. At the local level, they may be more likely to step forward in situations where the opportunities to win as an outsider obviously start to seem more promising. These potential candidates, who commonly have a significant record of community leadership and accomplishment, typically may be strategically pragmatic. Consequently, they often may not seriously consider running on behalf of a progressive third party until they see signs that a successful campaign is possible—that there is a large enough base of support, that there may be the means to reach the necessary number of potentially sympathetic voters, and that the main opponent is sufficiently vulnerable. Without these positive omens, it can be difficult for a minor party of the left to attract good local candidates. However, steps can be taken to create a more fertile local recruitment environment, such as organizing to expand the party's grassroots base.[44]

As for getting strong candidates to run for statewide and federal office, a promising electoral context also would appear to be critical. As suggested by Terry Bouricius, gaining a substantial political foothold at the local level first, as the Vermont Progressives did, would seem to be vital for recruiting minimally viable statewide candidates. Significant local victories can attract such candidates by signaling to them that a statewide win or good showing might be possible. If the party amasses enough local power to become respected statewide, its local politicians and even some party organizers can indeed gain enough legitimacy to become serious competitors for statewide office, as occurred in Vermont. Following from such local success, it even may be possible for an especially renowned and capable politician from the party to step forward as a candidate for federal office—if it seems like there is a good chance of winning. This roughly describes how Bernie Sanders came to run successfully for Congress after having served multiple terms as the popular Progressive-affiliated mayor of the largest city in Vermont.

Of course, it is conceivable that a well-known, politically skilled progressive without the political experience described above would decide to run for higher office on behalf of a left third party, or as an independent. Yet such a candidate probably would have to be some rare public figure like Ralph Nader—one who strongly prioritizes the long-range building of alternatives to the two major parties and thus, does not focus mostly on short-term electoral results.

Q: **Aren't candidates who are explicitly associated with the Left viewed by the electorate as being too radical or too far outside the American "mainstream"?**

A: Not necessarily. Bernie Sanders, a self-described socialist, is highly popular among a wide cross-section of Vermonters. Some of his strongest support comes from rural voters, who traditionally tend to be viewed as more "conservative."[45] As mentioned by Bouricius, Sanders's longstanding appeal is largely based on the perception that he stands up for "the little guy."

Perhaps many ordinary Americans are less averse to left-wing ideology than is commonly thought. As noted by Ramy Khalil, John Halle, and Thomas Harrison, recent polls actually show that a substantial portion of the public, and particularly the young, says that it favors "socialism" over "capitalism." It may be that the increasing historical distance of the Cold War has made it easier for many Americans to seriously consider left alternatives to capitalism, or it could be that the recent financial crisis/recession has eroded the legitimacy of the economic system. Moreover, the Occupy movement seems to have succeeded in making a rudimentary radical critique of class inequality (concerning the "1 percent versus the 99 percent") more publically acceptable and even normal today. In sum, having an explicitly left-wing message and identity may not be such a political liability anymore. Among certain large sectors of the American public, it may even be an asset. This may help explain why even a revolutionary socialist like Kshama Sawant can get elected to a municipal body in a large U.S. city nowadays.

Still, as argued by Khalil and Ahmed, a progressive third party may be more successful electorally if it presents more radical ideas in ways that are popularly accessible. Seemingly, taking a left populist approach—focusing on the abuse of ordinary people by economic elites and their political allies—is a particularly compelling way to reach many Americans. As historian Eric Leif Davin notes, "This protest tradition, one that champions the common people against the rich and powerful, has always been America's dominant ideology of dissent."[46]

Q: **A couple of the chapters discuss the need for progressive third parties to compete for power in the arena of culture. For the sake of making electoral breakthroughs, what should such a strategy emphasize—educating Americans and changing their beliefs, or appealing to some of their existing knowledge, values, and attitudes?**

A: Arguably, it should involve more of the latter, at least for now. To illustrate, we first may consider how this might apply to the Green Party. As explained by Ahmed, many Green Party activists tend to see themselves as trying to educate Americans into accepting new Green values and a corresponding Green policy agenda (that includes much detail). Yet he also suggests that the party may do better in elections if it pitches its ideas to the public in a simpler way that is more consistent with core aspects of the prevailing popular ideology. One might speculate that such a framing could focus on commonly accepted American notions like opportunity, fairness, justice, and the common good. It also could stress very clear, concise statements of corresponding stands on issues, rather than the more sophisticated concepts and policy positions widely embraced by many Greens. Ralph Nader's 2000 Green campaign seemed to represent some movement in the direction of such accessibility, though of course, this alone couldn't enable Nader to get more than a small percentage of votes at the presidential level. Whether he may have changed many people's views, as Harrison suggests, rather than just articulated them well, is unclear. But according to Patrick Quinlan and Theresa Amato, Nader did inspire certain exceptional Green candidates at the local level, such as John Eder and Gayle McLaughlin. They excelled at communicating with the public and repeatedly won elections.

This book has offered other support for the view that progressive third party electoral breakthroughs are more the result of effectively channeling the existing popular consciousness than changing it. As mentioned above in relation to Bernie Sanders, Bouricius found that Vermont Progressives have won elections, in part, by communicating to ordinary voters in their own populist language. My own research on statehouse campaigns suggested that progressive third party candidates are more capable of winning elections if they reflect the predominant culture of their districts.

Of course, left third parties that win races may do more than just proficiently mirror some aspect of popular political attitudes. Demonstrating that they can win may itself transform some citizens profoundly—from believing that there is no viable alternative to the major parties to actively supporting the progressive third party movement. Such an attitudinal shift can foster further election victories, still greater recruitment of party activists, and so on. If such a cycle continues to unfold, it even may fuel public interest in left third parties' more radical values and visions. As the political means for actualizing such ideas appears to grow, the ideas themselves may start to seem less utopian and more worthy of serious consideration.

Q: **For the sake of broad popular appeal and participation, does it matter exactly how a progressive third party identifies itself?**

A: It may matter, but how much is unclear. It could be that the membership and leadership of certain contemporary left third parties have been constrained to some extent by these parties' names and their corresponding cultures. For example, many Americans may tend to think of the Green Party as the party of environmentalists and counterculture types, as implied by Ahmed. Likewise, the now dormant Labor Party may have been seen by those it reached in its organizing work and issue campaigns largely as a party of left-leaning blue-collar unionists. And the Vermont Progressive Party may be perceived by many Vermonters as the party of self-identified progressives, who typically are well-educated middle-class leftists. There would appear to be a strong element of truth to the above sort of perceptions, when one considers who these parties' founders and core activists mostly have been. Yet, all three parties have embraced policies that have represented much broader constituencies. All three in practice have championed the interests of a similar wide range of subordinate groups in American society. This apparent gap between identity and platform raises the following important question: How much more effective could these parties be if they were able to broaden their identity as much as their platform? (The same question could be applied to still other left third parties.[47]) In certain cases, such a broadening could necessitate a very difficult internal cultural shift, as also observed by Ahmed in relation to the Green Party. But what if a *new* third party of the left was able to assume a name (and corresponding identity) with a much wider sociological frame and appeal—something like the "99 Percent Party"? Could it become more diverse and popular than existing progressive third parties? Perhaps, but in order to really know, one might have to do relevant research (via surveys or focus groups), or actually try to create such a party on a small scale.

Defining Electoral Success

Q: **How well does a progressive third party candidate need to do in order to help his or her party advance politically—as opposed to just registering a protest or educating individual voters about issues?**

A: Winning, of course, is preferable, if one can do so. It provides an opportunity to directly shape public policy and discourse, and to strongly inspire other candidates who may be capable of winning. But just a good showing at the ballot box may be productive in its own way. It may be used to create a foundation for a future winnable race by the same candidate, motivate similar candidates to run, attract new party activists and funds, secure official status and future ballot access for the party, or help build popular and governmental support for particular policies.

However, what constitutes a good showing is somewhat subjective, as well as relative to the type of race and prevailing expectations for the candidate. For a local minor party candidate, a good showing could mean that one was able to come close to winning (such as within 10 percentage points) or to get what most experienced political observers would see as a respectable portion of votes (certainly more than 20 percent and probably over 30 percent in many races). For a statewide or federal race, it minimally could mean getting enough of the vote to obtain post-election party status and ballot access, which is between 1 and 5 percent in many states. A more significant good showing at this level might involve doing better than any non-left third party candidates on the ballot or most other past left third party candidates for the same office. As discussed by Ahmed, prominent examples of such results are those of Socialist, Eugene Debs (third place and 5.99 percent), and Green, Ralph Nader (third place and 2.74 percent) in their respective presidential runs in 1912 and 2000. Last, one could make the case that an unambiguously good showing for higher office requires something much more impressive and threatening to the major parties, like getting a vote percentage that is well into the double digits. Progressive Robert La Follette did this (with his 16.62 percent total) in his 1924 presidential bid. Campaigns that get a larger share of the vote may compel many activists, the public at large, and the powerful to take them and their parties more seriously, of course. By contrast, campaigns that get a relatively miniscule portion of the vote may tend to do the opposite, especially if they are a recurrent feature of a political party.

Q: **What does it take for a progressive third party candidate to make a good showing?**

A: At the local level, as shown in various chapters, having a high-intensity, well-organized campaign generally would seem to be essential. This would involve a lot of personal contact with voters, normally fortified with many helpers and a large supply of campaign literature. Having a basic pool of funds sufficient to run such a campaign also would seem to be important, the specific amount of which could vary, depending on the characteristics of the district. Strong community connections, which appear to be necessary for winning, also could be very useful for making a good showing. Possibly, a local candidate who is very well known and liked in a district could make a good showing without being hardworking, well organized, or sufficiently funded—though any such candidate probably would be squandering an opportunity to actually win.

In campaigns for higher office, as maintained by Ahmed in relation to presidential races, having a well-known candidate as well as being better organized and better funded (relative to the norm for minor party candidates at that level) would appear to be critical for making a good showing. Having an energetic candidate and campaign organization also would seem to be necessary.

Evaluating and Refining Strategy

Q: **In some chapters in this book it is suggested that progressive third parties will be more effective if they avoid running perceived "spoiler" candidates, while in other chapters the opposite is proposed. Which position is more compelling?**

A: Both perspectives may be valid in different contexts, especially if one approaches the spoiler problem from a standpoint that is more pragmatic than philosophical. Democratic political principles certainly are relevant to the selection of progressive electoral strategies, as argued by Theresa Amato. But the emphasis of this book is on *what can work* strategically— what it actually takes to create electoral breakthroughs as a left third party.

Pragmatically, when trying to win local elections in the short term, it generally may be more constructive for progressive third parties to prioritize running candidates where the fear of spoiling does not exist—in two-way races (as suggested by Khalil, Quinlan, and Bouricius). Such races tend to be more winnable, since people aren't afraid that voting for the left third party candidate unintentionally can contribute to the election of a major party candidate who is the "greater evil." And, as already mentioned, winning local races can be a critical way of legitimizing the progressive third party movement and fostering more substantial breakthroughs later. At the same time, the limited influence of lower level offices means that occasionally risking spoiling a more winnable three-way race at that level may not be such an irrational gamble; the consequences of losing there don't tend to be so great.

By contrast, in races for offices at the highest level (such as governor, president, and member of Congress), winning currently does not tend to be a realistic possibility, and there almost always are two major party candidates. As a result, for such races, pragmatism would demand a serious cost-benefit assessment before launching a left third party campaign. In this context, it may be a mistake to merely dismiss the alleged risk of contributing to the election of a conservative Republican on the ballot, since much of the left-leaning electorate seems to take that risk very seriously and to perceive the stakes as being high. Yet, if the prospective progressive third party candidate is strong enough, the possible long-term benefits of using the candidacy to build party leverage or organization may outweigh the potential short-term costs of being seen as a "spoiler." As described earlier, the events that enabled the Vermont Progressive Party to help pass a 2011 law facilitating the creation of a statewide single-payer health care system seemed to vindicate the party's decision to run someone in a prior statewide election who turned out to be a perceived spoiler candidate. (Even though the enactment of single payer in Vermont subsequently was sidelined by the governor, the fact that the new system came close to being implemented can be seen as an important step toward mobilizing support for progressive health care reform in the state and elsewhere in the future.) Whether the decision by the Green Party to run alleged spoiler Ralph Nader for president in 2000 has been justified overall by subsequent political developments is perhaps more debatable. However, a strong case to that effect has been made directly by Harrison and especially Amato, as well as indirectly by Ahmed.

Q: **How does one choose between the other contrasting electoral strategies advanced in this book (such as running lower level versus higher level campaigns; building progressive third parties from the top down versus the bottom up; and creating a progressive version of the Tea Party versus a truly independent left third party)?**

A: Again, from an organizational standpoint it may not always be necessary to choose between strategies in an absolute sense. Some apparently contradictory strategies above may be complementary at times, either simultaneously or sequentially. For instance, an established left third party sometimes may be able to run lower level *and* higher level campaigns that don't conflict with one another. If the candidates associated with both are strong, they may reinforce one another. Additionally, for those trying to build a new progressive party, it could make sense to primarily take a grassroots (bottom-oriented) approach at first, with a focus on appealing to ordinary people though electoral campaigns and other popularly accessible forms of activism. Support from prominent left-leaning organizations (at the top) could actively be sought later—after the party had demonstrated its ability to attract public interest and win elections.

Yet, it also is important to acknowledge that some clear-cut strategic choices do need to be made. Realistically, small political parties do have to decide where to concentrate limited time, energy, and resources. Thus, prioritizing particular strategies is unavoidable. Moreover, some of them may not be smoothly combined because of basic political contradictions or incompatibilities. For instance, this may apply to Daniel Cantor's proposal to create a left-wing Tea Party that promotes progressive Democrats and Thomas Harrison's proposal to construct an independent left party that promotes its own candidates. It may be difficult to produce a workable balanced blend of both these strategies. There may be strong pressures from influential party supporters to decisively go in one direction or the other—especially in more consequential elections at the statewide and national level. Additionally, in the vast majority of states, candidates are not allowed to represent multiple parties on the ballot, so this prevents minor parties there from running "fusion" (Democrat/minor party) candidates.[48]

When comparing apparently conflicting strategies, it is worth carefully considering whether different ones as framed really have what it takes to produce the desired political results. In so doing, one may have to face some sticky problems. For example, consider the challenge facing a nationwide Tea Party of the left under the auspices of the Working Families Party. It supposedly would aim to elect left-leaning Democrats and ensure that they follow through on their promises to promote a progressive agenda.[49] Yet, more conservative Democrats and their wealthy core funders appear to have such a potent grip on the Democratic Party as a whole that the chances of pushing it decisively to the left from within seem dubious at best.[50] Moreover, the WFP has shown itself to be inconsistent in its support of progressives. Already, as suggested by its critics in this book, the party is known for routinely supporting certain corporate Democrats, sometimes even when more left-leaning alternatives are available. A predictable result has been the pursuit of conservative policies by these same Democrats. For example, this occurred with New York governor Andrew Cuomo after the 2010 elections (as highlighted by Harrison as well as Mark Dudzic and Katherine Isaac). And as noted earlier, Cuomo betrayed the WFP yet again during the 2014 general election campaign—despite Cantor's enthusiasm about the governor's prior promise to help the party in exchange for its endorsement. A deeper part of the problem with the Working Families Party may be that it gets much of its financial backing and influence from unions that want to maintain relationships with Democrats in power and the Democratic Party in general—seemingly at almost any cost.[51]

Of course, skillfully exhorting key unions and other leading progressive groups to abandon the Democrats and found their own completely independent party (as done by Harrison) probably won't work on its own. Most of these organizations apparently feel that it is necessary to ignore this longstanding advice from left third party advocates. This may be due to a perceived need to try to block the most aggressive right-wing Republican policies and defend the immediate interests of their membership (as argued by Dudzic and Isaac), or because the leadership of certain progressive groups has been co-opted or corrupted by those in power (as suggested by Halle). As a result, it is also questionable whether most major left-liberal organizations can be convinced to invest even a small percentage of their valuable resources toward building a new progressive third party (as proposed by Dudzic and Isaac), even if it makes long-term political sense.

Effective ways of addressing the above types of problems need to be found in order for their corresponding strategies to become more workable. Perhaps, as previously suggested, complementary strategies should be considered—such as a more bottom-up approach to party building that isn't primarily or immediately dependent on the approval of compromised elites (whether within the Democratic Party or at the top of progressive organizations). Various contributors to this book do advocate or contemplate a more independent, bottom-up method, which could help bridge the strategic gap. One such approach, alluded to by Dudzic and Isaac, would entail trying to first build a critical mass of left third party support within the progressive activist base. If sufficiently organized and mobilized, this mass might be able to exert pivotal pressure on its leaders to support a left-wing third party, at least to some extent. A parallel effort—consistent with the observations of Khalil, Quinlan, Bouricius, and Halle—would involve demonstrating the grassroots electoral viability and appeal of progressive third parties more clearly. This would require recruiting and running some particularly strong local candidates, building new mini-movements around them, gaining some key local endorsements, winning certain high-profile municipal or state legislative races, and maybe even producing a viable candidate for statewide or federal office on occasion. Perhaps this type of success could start to change the minds of some leading progressives who refuse to back left third parties, primarily because of their perceived inability to win.[52]

In fact, there is no reason that both of the above bottom-up strategies shouldn't be attempted simultaneously by different factions of left third party supporters. It would seem that advancement on either front could help stimulate gains on the other. If over time and after some significant local electoral and organizing successes the leaders of major progressive groups still didn't start to come aboard, there might be enough accumulated popular interest and political momentum to create a minimally viable national or regional left third party without them. Such a party wouldn't have access to certain significant resources held by these groups (viewed as a fatal problem by Dudzic and Isaac, as well as Harrison). Yet, it might have gained enough legitimacy to raise much more of its own money and attract many more activists than one might think. A left third party with the populist clarity of a Bernie Sanders, the movement energy of Kshama Sawant and her supporters, and the creativity and resonance of an Occupy movement could have that capacity—if it started to capture the popular imagination with a string of electrifying local victories and some inspiring public displays of righteous indignation at the unjust status quo.

Of course, independent new bottom-up efforts do have their own particular pitfalls. Importantly, they almost always are hampered at first by a lack of money, staff, coordination, stability, and credibility. This is why progressive third party groups should carefully choose where and when they launch their own grassroots-oriented projects. Selecting the most favorable local organizing contexts, where the opportunities for breakthroughs with ripple effects are greatest, is critical to maximizing the impact of limited assets.

Still, from an individual standpoint, if one really wants to make a political difference as an activist, one shouldn't expend too much time and energy in pursuit of the project with the "right" strategy. Each approach described in this book arguably has its own notable advantages and problems. Choosing and pursuing a strategy that seems "good enough," or at least better than the rest in a specific time and place, should be acceptable. If one makes a bad judgment, it probably won't take long until events make that apparent. Then it will be possible to change course. Certainly, it would better to have activists experimenting with different strategies and demonstrating to each other what does and does not work than to have them continually studying and debating the alternatives.

Q: How can left third parties avoid being steered into one of the following two classic strategic traps: (1) becoming so preoccupied with promoting an alternative political vision that they can't or won't do what is necessary to do well in elections (extreme idealism), or (2) becoming so concerned with winning elections that they back away from some of their core progressive commitments (extreme pragmatism)?

A: Throughout this book and chapter, certain strategies have been highlighted that may help left third parties to stay away from these snares. If a party publically asserts its preference for such strategies, activists who support them may be better able to maintain the upper hand and keep the party on course. Getting derailed by extreme idealists may be avoided if the party openly commits itself to routinely running more winnable races, developing viable candidacies, and appealing to ordinary people. Conversely, getting led astray by extreme pragmatists may be averted if the party explicitly articulates its key progressive principles, distinguishes itself from both major parties, and emphasizes the need for party leaders and politicians to be responsive and accountable to party membership. A party that can't or won't take the above types of steps may be dominated by ideologues or opportunists. If that in fact is the case, strategically more moderate members may have to decide whether they want to challenge and possibly replace party leaders, join a different party, or create a new one.

Longevity and Impact

Q: What enables progressive third party politicians to remain in office for many years?

A: Different chapters in this book highlight examples of certain left third party officials who were able to do this successfully and others who were ousted by major party opponents within one or two election cycles. Various factors that seem to be positively associated with political longevity include being a hardworking, accessible, and very well-known politician; amassing a record of notable policy accomplishments while in office; holding a higher profile office that strongly reinforces name recognition; being willing and able to continue to conduct strong grassroots election campaigns; having relatively weak major party organization and opponents in the district; and having politically dissimilar major party opponents. A systematic comparison of relevant cases at different ends of the longevity spectrum would be needed to definitively determine which configuration of factors are most strongly associated with left third party politicians staying in office for longer periods.

Q: **If progressive third party candidates get elected only to a small minority of seats in a legislative body, can they really make a political difference?**

A: Yes. Just having a small presence within a school committee, city council, or statehouse or in Congress can put significant pressure on major party politicians in the majority to be more responsive to progressive concerns (or risk losing more seats to the left third party).[53] At the very least, a small progressive third party minority within a legislative body can use its official authority to make government decision-making more transparent to the public—an important step toward greater democracy. Also, winning some seats in local government may enable a left third party to establish enough popular recognition and credibility to win more seats later—and perhaps to eventually achieve a local majority. Depending on the political context, such an accumulation of power may occur in a dramatic surge, or it may take many years of protracted, ebbing and flowing struggle.[54]

Q: **Suppose a progressive third party is able to get its candidates elected in a particular place but is unable to hold onto most of their seats over time. Does that negate the value of the original breakthroughs?**

A: Not necessarily. Having shown that victory is possible in a certain place, a progressive third party may continue to inspire its candidates to run for office there or elsewhere far into the future—long after the party's initial electoral surge has been stemmed or even reversed by the major party in power.[55] Moreover, even when a major party is eventually able to contain or defeat a rising left third party in a locale, it may have to run candidates who are more progressive in order to do so. This ultimately may foster better government policies in that area than those that would have prevailed if the minor party surge had never occurred.[56]

Q: **The stories and visions of political change discussed in this book tend to depict progressive third party empowerment as a very gradual process in the United States as a whole. This seems far too slow relative to the severity of the problems facing the country and world. What might enable the process to proceed much more quickly?**

A: Theoretically, more substantial gains by the progressive third party movement could occur if certain powerful, respected groups or individuals publicly joined, supported, and represented a left third party. This scenario is consistent with Harrison's call for leading progressive groups to defect from the Democrats; Ralph Nader's fictional vision of elite-led progressive change in his book *Only the Super-Rich Can Save Us!*; and a longstanding hope among American leftists that Bernie Sanders will run for president as an independent or minor party candidate. The key question of course is whether such heroics from the top are a realistic possibility or just an unobtainable fantasy driven by wishful thinking. Major progressive groups, wealthy left-liberals, and Sanders all seem highly resistant to taking the lead for the independent/third party left on a national level—despite occasional threats, gestures, or implications to the contrary.[57] They may think that such a move will be politically ineffective or counterproductive in the short term. One can't totally discount the possibility that they will change their minds. But it doesn't seem likely for the foreseeable future—unless they are inspired by some new, vivid left-independent or left third party victories, or by the rise of a more viable new party of the left.

Of course, a dramatic national crisis that the Democratic and Republican parties don't address sufficiently could create the impetus for a left third party to gain power more rapidly in the United States. This especially could be the case if the crisis generates a vigorous popular movement for progressive change. Given the failure of the U.S. government to implement strong financial and environmental reforms, another economic crash or a sudden intensification of ecological problems in the near future is a distinct possibility. Probably, the more organized and electorally credible that progressive third parties start to become now, the better able they may be to channel the next major crisis into substantial electoral gains.

At the same time, it is possible that an innovative, especially potent new approach by a progressive third party could enable it to proliferate more quickly in the United States, prior to an extraordinary new crisis. After all, polls cited elsewhere in this book do indicate that the majority of the American public already is receptive to third parties and progressive policies. While crises and the movements they spawn eventually may jolt many people into becoming more aware of the commonality and urgency of such aspirations, an exceptionally well-crafted and well-organized initiative by left third party activists might be able to ignite this consciousness in the meantime. In modern U.S. history, there have been some political movements (for example, the civil rights and women's movements) that caught fire in the country in the absence of a preceding crisis. In such cases, activists took bold actions, large and small, that inspired and mobilized many others. It may have taken certain social conditions to make this possible. Yet, with all the persistent discontent in the United States concerning the unfairness of the economy and the corruption of the political system, underlying conditions may be ripe for a new eruption of popular activism that challenges the duopoly.

In 2011 the Occupy movement fueled a significant flare-up of antisystemic consciousness in the United States. This was facilitated in part by an earlier economic crash and a severe recession, certain effects of which still linger as of this writing. Could left third party activists explicitly build on Occupy's accomplishment and add to it a coherent strategy for gaining political power? In so doing, could they help catalyze and guide a new progressive populist surge throughout the country—even before another major economic downturn occurs? It may be hard to imagine exactly how that could happen. Yet, in the past it also may have been difficult to envision how a relatively small number of committed activists could have launched other movements that eventually bloomed enough to change American society. Some thematic and tactical experimentation outside the already well-established progressive third parties might show what if any new approach could help trigger another, more partisan version of Occupy. A hypothetical example of this, mentioned earlier, would be an attempt to create an actual "99 Percent Party."

First Steps

Q: **What should I do if I want to get involved in progressive third party politics? Where can I find pertinent information, and how can I become active or supportive in a meaningful way?**

A: Decide which if any of the progressive third parties mentioned in this book appeals to you. Go to its website to see if it is active in your area. Determine whether there are any relevant events that you can attend to become acquainted with the organization. Consider whether it has a compelling strategic orientation, or at least one that has the potential to be effective. If you like what you see, choose the level of involvement that best suits your current situation and interest. That could mean becoming a member, making a donation, attending local chapter meetings or events, joining a working committee or electoral campaign, or even becoming a candidate. If there are no appealing progressive third parties in your area, consider starting a small community group that explores the possibility of establishing a local chapter of an existing party, or even a completely new party. If it is a new party, then try to connect early on with any similar such efforts in your state or region, or in the United States as a whole. Readers outside the United States may contact and possibly offer some sort of assistance to American progressive third parties, though they should be careful to abide by any relevant legal restrictions. They also may join or found left-wing parties in their own countries or regions. For readers anywhere who would like to connect with each other for the purpose of building political parties on the left, an interactive website associated with the title of this book may be available.

Ultimately, the process of empowering progressive political parties and using them to change our society and world for the better is a collective act. Yet that act is made possible by the vision and initiative of each individual who participates, each of whom thereby advances democracy.

Notes

1 For example, see Boston.com, "Boston Fast Food Workers"; Aubrey, "Across the Country Workers Rally"; Ausick, "Walmart Workers Seek $15 an Hour"; and Watson, "$15 Wins in Boston."

2 15 Now, "15 Now Chapters."

3 O'Connor, "San Francisco Votes $15"; and Medina and Sheiber, "Los Angeles Lifts Minimum Wage."

4 Sawant, "Kshama Sawant."

5 Green Party of the United States, "Green Party Highlights from Election Day 2014"; and Green Party of the United States, "Summary 2014." The U.S. Green Party reports that Greens ran in 273 races and won 41 (or 15 percent) of them across the country in 2014, including 32 victories out of 66 races in California alone. This apparently does not include all of the technically non-partisan local races in which Greens were candidates. The highest-level win in the nation was the reelection of Bruce Delgado, the mayor of Marina, California (in Monterey County). Of 131 total listed Green officeholders in the United States in 2014, 53 of them were in California (Green Party of the United States, "Current Green Officeholders").

6 Katz, "Jill Stein Says Americans Are Ready."

7 City of Richmond, California, "Mayor's Biography"; and Rogers, "Richmond Mayor Savors Successes."

8 Team Richmond, "Voters Tell Chevron 'No Sale!'"

9 Patrick Quinlan, e-mail message to author, November 28, 2014.

10 Ibid.

11 Worthen, "As Vermont Goes."

12 Early, *Save Our Unions*, 263.

13 Vermont Progressive Party, "Vermont Progressive Party Makes Gains."

14 For details on such legislative efforts, see Vermont Progressive Party, "Legislative Updates" and "In the Media."

15 Heintz and Hallenbeck, "Progressives Overtake Democrats on Council." After the 2015 election, 6 members of the newly downsized 12-member city council were aligned with the Progressives—including 4 self-identified Progressives and 2 Progressive-leaning independents. Five council members were Democrat-affiliated. On the prior 14-member council, 5 members were in the Progressive faction and 7 were on the Democratic side.

16 See Sanders, "Bernie Sanders."

17 Nichols, "Bernie Sanders: 'I Am Prepared to Run.'"

18 Sullivan, "Bernie Sanders, Weighing Presidential Run."

19 Rappeport, "Bernie Sanders Enters Presidential Race."

20 Bostick, "Lorain Labor Defends Independence"; and Goodenow, "Carrion to Seek Mayor's Post."

21 See Working Families Party, "Victories."

22 Working Families Party, "Winning with Wolf in Pennsylvania"; and "Thank You!"

23 Working Families Party, "DC Wins 1st Member!"; "Ras Baraka Will Be Mayor!"; and "Where We Won Big."

24 Working Families Party, "Working Families Party Independent Candidates." The WFP explained, "We frequently cross-endorse candidates from another party because we believe they are the best candidate in the race. . . . But in some elections, there simply aren't candidates who share our values. In those cases we run our own candidates on

our own ballot line. It gives voters the choice of a candidate that will stand up for them. That is the case this year with four Working Families candidates running for State Senate."

25 Working Families Party, "Ed Gomes Just Made History!"; and Lockhart and Ocasio, "Working Families Claims Victory." Notably, the WFP candidate barely lost a vote for Democratic cross-endorsement.

26 Ibid.

27 Yee, "Working Families Candidate Wins"; and Working Families Party, "Diana Richardson Elected on WFP Line." In this four-way race, the WFP candidate did not receive cross-endorsement from the Democratic Party, and there was no Democratic candidate on the ballot. The Democratic nominee failed to file ballot access papers before the deadline.

28 See Working Families Party, "Victories."

29 Working Families Party, "Maryland's Minimum Wage Increase Begins."

30 Working Families Party, "Living Wage Victory in NYC"; and "Philly Wins Higher Wages!"

31 Working Families Party, "Have the Sniffles? Stay Home"; "Four Cities. One Week"; and "VICTORY: Paid Sick Days!"

32 Working Families Party, "Fracking Banned in New York State!"

33 Uetricht, "Meet Rahm Emanuel's Other Challenger."

34 Uetricht, "Four More Years."

35 Uetricht, "Meet Rahm Emanuel's Other Challenger."

36 Gillespie, *Challengers to Duopoly*, 213–14.

37 Progressive Dane, "Past Elections"; and "And the Results Are In"; Marsha Rummel, Progressive Dane Alder (Madison, WI), e-mail messages to author, May 20–21, 2015; Progressive Dane, "What is Progressive Dane?"; and "Our Endorsed Candidates."

38 Attendees and presenters came from various parties or proto-parties discussed in this book, including the Green Party, the Vermont Progressive Party, Socialist Alternative, United Working Families, and Progressive Dane. There also was participation from other relevant lower profile groups, such as the Peace and Freedom Party (of California), the Justice Party (which is attempting to form a new national progressive party), and a few lesser known yet active socialist organizations.

39 The only obvious dispute at the conference concerned whether or not to support Bernie Sanders's 2016 Democratic presidential candidacy. The key point of contention was whether Sanders would be able to take advantage of the Democratic primary to fuel active public interest in left politics, or whether he eventually would function mainly to corral progressives into backing a more conservative Democratic nominee. Audience reaction to relevant commentary suggested that the large majority of conference-goers had the latter expectation.

40 Louis, "Why Empire State Turned Red"; Jaffe, "Will Cuomo Keep His Promises?"; and Kaplan, "Cuomo, Backed by Working Families Party."

41 Shumlin. "'Time Not Right' for Single-Payer."

42 Daybell, "Shumlin's Decision a Betrayal." The author of this statement is the vice chairman of the VPP.

43 City of Seattle, "Kshama Sawant Biography"; and Rosenthal, "Conlin Making Issue of Sawant's Registration." Sawant had lived in Seattle since 2006, just several years before becoming a political candidate. During that time, she worked as an adjunct economics professor, joined Socialist Alternative, and became an Occupy movement activist.

44 For suggestions on how to recruit strong progressive third party candidates, especially at the local level, see Green Party of the United States, "Green Party Candidate Recruiting Manual." Base-building toward that end may be fostered by recruiting new party members and volunteers; registering new party voters; sponsoring well-attended events; actively supporting efforts by likeminded progressive groups; and perhaps running certain candidates who are weaker yet still able to conduct high intensity, well-organized campaigns.

45 Sifry, *Spoiling for a Fight*, 58–59.

46 Davin, *Radicals in Power*.

47 Consider how many people might feel left out of the groups that seem to be represented by the names "Socialist Alternative" or "Working Families Party"—even though much of the actual program of the organizations so labeled may appeal to a very wide segment of the American public.

48 In several states where candidates can represent more than one party, the Working Families Party has its own ballot line for the Democrats it backs. In other words, one can vote for such Democrats on either a Democratic or WFP line. Similarly, the Vermont Progressive Party runs certain candidates who are identified on the ballot not only as Progressives but also as Democrats. However, in the above cases candidates who represent two parties often primarily affiliate with one.

49 In addition to Chapter 10, see Meyerson, "Dan Cantor's Machine."

50 Hacker and Pierson, *Winner-Take-All Politics*.

51 Jaffe, "Will Cuomo Keep His Promises?"

52 For a contemporary illustration of how a left third party can gain support from progressive organizations, in addition to the examples provided in this book, see Early, "Building a Labor Base." Early explains how the Vermont Progressive Party has been able to garner significant backing from organized labor in Vermont in recent years. He credits the VPP's electoral achievements and its strong participation in grassroots labor activism.

53 A striking example of such influence by a left third party legislative minority is the passage of the $15-an-hour minimum wage in Seattle in 2014—just months after its key advocate on the city council, Socialist Alternative's Kshama Sawant, was elected. An additional conspicuous confirmation of the same possibility comes from a Democratic leader of the state legislature in Vermont. In a conversation in 2009, he privately admitted to me that the Vermont Progressive Party (with only a handful of statehouse politicians) had become the Democrats' progressive "conscience" in recent years.

54 For relevant illustration of how progressive power in local government has been built over time and exercised, in addition to the pertinent accounts in this book, see Davin, *Radicals in Power*.

55 Such ripples of past progressive third party surges can be seen in Portland, Maine, and in Vermont. As described in the chapter by Patrick Quinlan and at the beginning of this chapter, Greens won additional offices in Portland after their initial wave of success receded in 2006. In Vermont, Progressives had been a dominant or at least equal partisan force on the Burlington City Council from their initial surge of 1980s until the Democrats regained the upper hand in the early 2000s. During the past decade and until their comeback in 2015, Progressives mostly had become a subordinate faction on the city council. Moreover, in 2012 the Progressives lost the mayor's office to the Democrats for the first time since Bernie Sanders was elected in 1981, and they failed to recapture it in the 2015 election (Guma, "Mayor's Race in Burlington"; and note

15).Yet during the above years in which Progressive power waned in Burlington City Hall, it firmly and stably established itself in the Vermont State House via consistent winning of several state legislative seats in different parts of Vermont.This was a ripple of success inspired by the Progressives' original surge in Burlington.The same might be said of Bernie Sanders's ascension from mayor of Burlington to congressman to U.S. senator over the course of a couple of decades.

56 During the interviews for my research on statehouse campaigns, various key political observers in Portland, Maine, and Burlington,Vermont, suggested that an enduring leftward shift of Democratic candidates and politicians in their city had been stimulated by the past success of the local progressive third party (the Greens and the Progressives, respectively). These observers included certain prominent local Democrats and journalists.

57 Concerning Sanders's longtime resistance to becoming a progressive third party leader, see Sifry, *Spoiling for a Fight*, 292. Sanders has expressed a clear reluctance to run for president outside of the major parties. He has mentioned how difficult it would be to create a nationwide campaign structure as an independent. See Sanders, "Sanders on Meet the Press."

Bibliography

15 Now. "15 Now Chapters." Accessed April 4, 2015. http://15now.org/get-involved/in-your-area/.

Aubrey, Allison. "Across the Country, Fast-Food Workers Rally for $15-an-hour Pay." *The Salt*. National Public Radio (blog), September 4, 2014. www.npr.org/blogs/thesalt/2014/09/04/345825903/across-the-country-fast-food-workers-rally-for-15-an-hour-pay.

Ausick, Paul. "Walmart Workers Now Seek $15 an Hour, Fulltime Work." 24/7 Wall St. Last modified October 16, 2014. http://247wallst.com/retail/2014/10/16/walmart-workers-now-seek-15-an-hour-full-time-work/.

Bostick, Bruce. "Lorain, Ohio Labor Defends Political Independence." *Labor Notes* (blog), November 17, 2014. http://labornotes.org/blogs/2014/11/lorain-ohio-labor-defends-political-independence.

Boston.com. "Boston Fast Workers Join in Global Protest." *Boston Globe*, May 15, 2014. www.bostonglobe.com/business/2014/05/15/fast-food-workers-strike-ripples-around-world/nvs9Z2WiLxxsbLswRxDU2L/story.html.

City of Richmond, California. "Mayor's Biography." Accessed December 1, 2014. http://ca-richmond2.civicplus.com/index.aspx?nid=399.

City of Seattle. "Kshama Sawant, Position 2: Biography." Seattle.gov. Accessed June 9, 2015. www.seattle.gov/council/sawant/bio.htm.

Davin, Eric Leif. *Radicals in Power:The New Left Experience in Office*. Lanham, MD: Lexington Books, 2012.

Daybell, Morgan. "Shumlin's Decision to Scrap Single Payer a Betrayal of Vermont's Working Families." Vermont Progressive Party. Last modified December 18, 2014. www.progressiveparty.org/blog/2014/shumlins-decision-scrap-single-payer-betrayal-vermonts-working-families.

Early, Steve. "Building a Labor Base for Third Party Campaigning: Union Member Recruitment by Vermont Progressives." *Social Policy*, Summer, 2014.

———. *Save Our Unions: Dispatches from a Movement in Distress*. New York: Monthly Review Press, 2013.

Gillespie, David J. *Challengers to Duopoly: Why Third Parties Matter in American Two-Party Politics*. Columbia: University of South Carolina Press, 2012.

Goodenow, Evan. "Carrion to Seek Lorain Mayor's Post (Updated)." *Chronicle Online*, May 4, 2014. http://chronicle.northcoastnow.com/2015/05/04/carrion-seek-lorain-mayors-post/.

Green Party of the United States. "Current Green Officeholders." Accessed April 3, 2015. http://www.gp.org/officeholders.

———. "Green Party Candidate Recruiting Manual, 1st Edition 2004." Manual presented at the Green National Convention, Milwaukee, WI, June 2004. http://gp.org/committees/campaign/manual/recruiting.pdf.

———. "Green Party Highlights from Election Day 2014." Last modified November 10, 2014. http://gp.org/press/pr-national.php?ID=749.

———. "Summary of 2014." Accessed April 3, 2015. http://gp.org/elections/candidates/index.php.

Guma, Greg. "Mayor's Race Heats Up in Burlington." VTDigger.org. Last modified October 6, 2011. http://vtdigger.org/2011/10/06/mayor%E2%80%99s-race-heats-up-in-burlington/.

Hacker, Jacob S., and Paul Pierson. *Winner-Take-All Politics: How Washington Made the Rich Richer—And Turned Its Back on the Middle Class*. New York: Simon & Schuster, 2010.

Heintz, Paul, and Terri Hallenbeck. "Progressives Overtake Democrats on Burlington City Council." *Off Message: Vermont's Politics and News Blog. Seven Days*, March 3, 2015. www.sevendaysvt.com/OffMessage/archives/2015/03/03/progressives-overtake-democrats-on-burlington-city-council.

Jaffe, Sarah. "Will Cuomo Keep His Promises? The Working Families Party Went Out on a Limb When It Endorsed the Conservative Democrat." *In These Times*, June 2, 2014. http://inthesetimes.com/article/16767/will_cuomo_keep_his_promises.

Kaplan, Thomas. "Cuomo, Backed by Working Families Party, May Chip Away at Its Clout at the Polls." *New York Times*, October 31, 2014. www.nytimes.com/2014/11/01/nyregion/cuomo-backed-by-working-families-party-may-chip-away-at-its-clout-at-the-polls.html?_r=0.

Katz, Emily Tess. "Jill Stein, Former Green Party Nominee, Says Americans Are Ready for a Third-Party President." *Huffington Post*, April 6, 2015. www.huffingtonpost.com/2015/04/06/jill-stein-green-party-president_n_7011176.html.

Lockhart, Brian, and Keila Torres Ocasio. "Working Families Party Claims Big Victory." *Connecticut Post*, February 28, 2015. www.ctpost.com/local/article/Working-Families-Party-claims-big-victory-6108415.php.

Louis, Errol. "Why Empire State Building Turned Red." CNN Opinion. Last modified November 6, 2014. www.cnn.com/2014/11/05/opinion/louis-new-york-cuomo/.

Medina, Jennifer, and Noam Sheiber. "Los Angeles Lifts Its Minimum Wage to $15 Per Hour." *New York Times*, May 19, 2015. www.nytimes.com/2015/05/20/us/los-angeles-expected-to-raise-minimum-wage-to-15-an-hour.html?_r=1.

Meyerson, Harold. "Dan Cantor's Machine." *The American Prospect*, January 6, 2014. http://prospect.org/article/dan-cantors-machine.

Nader, Ralph. *Only the Super-Rich Can Save Us!* New York: Seven Stories, 2011.

Nichols, John. "Bernie Sanders: 'I Am Prepared to Run for President of the United States.'" *Truthout*. Last modified March 7, 2014. www.truthout.org/news/item/22316-bernie-sanders-i-am-prepared-to-run-for-president-of-the-united-states.

O'Connor, Lydia. "San Francisco Votes to Raise Minimum Wage to $15." *Huffington Post*, November 5, 2014. www.huffingtonpost.com/2014/10/28/san-francisco-minimum-wage_n_6064922.html.

Progressive Dane. "And the Results Are In (Mostly): Some Sad Losses Here, But Overall a Great Night for Progressives around Dane County." Last modified April 7, 2015. www.facebook.com/progressivedane/posts/10153165277769898.

———. "Our Endorsed Candidates." Accessed May 21, 2015. www.prodane.org/endorsements2015.

———. "Past Elections." Accessed May 20, 2015. www.prodane.org/past_elections.

———. "What Is Progressive Dane?" Accessed May 20, 2015. http://www.prodane.org/.

Rappeport, Alan. "Bernie Sanders, Long-Serving Independent, Enters Presidential Race as a Democrat." New York Times, April 29, 2015. www.nytimes.com/2015/04/30/us/politics/bernie-sanders-campaign-for-president.html?_r=0.

Rogers, Robert. "Richmond Mayor Gayle McLaughlin Savors Successes as She Steps Down." San Jose Mercury News, December 16, 2014. www.mercurynews.com/my-town/ci_27149927/richmond-mayor-gayle-mclaughlin-savors-successes-she-steps.

Rosenthal, Brian M. "Richard Conlin Making Issue of Kshama Sawant's Registration." Politics Northwest (blog). *Seattle Times*, October 8, 2013. http://blogs.seattletimes.com/politicsnorthwest/2013/10/08/richard-conlin-making-issue-of-kshama-sawants-voter-registration/.

Sanders, Bernie. "Bernie Sanders: United States Senator for Vermont." Accessed March 18, 2015. www.sanders.senate.gov/.

———. "Sanders on Meet the Press." Youtube video, 5:33. Posted September 14, 2014, www.youtube.com/watch?v=XcaSYclEKQg.

Sawant, Kshama. "Kshama Sawant: One Year in Office." Socialist Alternative. Last Modified February 10, 2015. www.socialistalternative.org/2015/02/10/kshama-sawant-year-office/#prettyPhoto.

Shumlin, Peter. "Gov. Shumlin Says 'The Time is Not Right' for Single-Payer Health Care." *Burlington Free Press* video, 11:37. December 17, 2014. www.burlingtonfreepress.com/videos/news/local/vermont/2014/12/17/20562287/.

Sifry, Micah. *Spoiling for a Fight: Third-Party Politics in America.* New York: Routledge, 2003.

Sullivan, Sean. "Bernie Sanders, Weighing Presidential Run, Calls for 'Political Revolution.'" *Washington Post*, April 2, 2015. www.washingtonpost.com/blogs/post-politics/wp/2015/04/02/bernie-sanders-weighing-presidential-run-calls-for-political-revolution/.

Team Richmond. "Voters Tell Chevron 'No Sale!': Team Richmond Prevails in Richmond City Council Election." Richmond Progressive Alliance. Accessed December 1, 2014. www.teamrichmond.net/.

Uetricht, Micah. "Four More Years: Rahm Emanuel's Win in the Chicago Mayoral Election Doesn't Spell the Defeat of the City's Grassroots Movements." *Jacobin*, April 18, 2015. www.jacobinmag.com/2015/04/chicago-mayoral-election-rahm-chuy/.

———. "Meet Rahm Emanuel's Other Election Day Challenger." *The Nation*, April 6, 2015. www.thenation.com/article/203673/meet-rahm-emanuels-other-election-day-challenger#.

Vermont Progressive Party. "In the Media." Accessed April 4, 2014. www.progressiveparty.org/media.

———. "Legislative Updates." Accessed April 4, 2014. www.progressiveparty.org/legislative.

———. "Vermont Progressive Party Makes Gains Despite National, Statewide Political Climate." VTDigger.org. Last modified November 10, 2014. http://vtdigger.org/2014/11/12/vermont-progressive-party-makes-modest-gains-despite-national-statewide-political-climate/.

Watson, Bryan. "$15 Wins in Roxbury, Boston." 15now.org. Last modified November 29, 2014. http://15now.org/2014/11/15-wins-in-roxbury-boston/.

Working Families Party. "DC Wins 1st Working Families Backed Council Member!" Last modified November 6, 2014. http://workingfamilies.org/2014/11/dc-wins-1st-working-families-backed-council-member.

———."Diana Richardson Becomes First Legislator Elected Only on WFP Line." Last modified May 5, 2015. http://workingfamilies.org/2015/05/diana-richardson-becomes-first-legislator-elected-solely-wfp-line/.

———."Ed Gomes Just Made History!" Last modified February 25, 2015. http://workingfamilies.org/2015/02/ed-gomes-just-made-history/.

———. "Four Cities. One Week." Last modified September 10, 2014. http://workingfamilies.org/2014/09/four-cities-one-week/.

———."Fracking Banned in New York State!" Last modified December 17, 2014. http://workingfamilies.org/2014/12/fracking-ban-new-york-state/.

———."Have the Sniffles? Stay Home." Last modified August 4, 2014. http://workingfamilies.org/2014/08/sniffles-stay-home/.

———. "Living Wage Victory in NYC: This Is Big." Last modified September 30, 2014. http://workingfamilies.org/2014/09/living-wage-victory-nyc-big/.

———. "Maryland's Minimum Wage Increase Begins." Last modified January 14, 2015. http://workingfamilies.org/2015/01/marylands-minimum-wage-increase-begins/.

———. "Philly Wins Higher Wages at the Ballot Box!" Last modified May 23, 2014. http://workingfamilies.org/2014/05/philly-wins-higher-wages-ballot-box/.

———."Ras Baraka Will Be Newark's Next Mayor!" Last modified May 14, 2014. http://workingfamilies.org/2014/05/ras-baraka-wins-mayor-newark/.

———. "Thank You!" Last modified November 5, 2014. http://workingfamilies.org/2014/11/thank/.

———."Victories." Accessed April 4, 2015. http://workingfamilies.org/victories/.

———."VICTORY: Paid Sick Days Passes in Philly!" Last modified February 12, 2015. http://workingfamilies.org/2015/02/victory-paid-sick-days-passes-philly/.

———. "Where We Won Big, and How We Did It." Last modified November 11, 2014. http://workingfamilies.org/2014/11/won-big/.

———. "Winning with Wolf in Pennsylvania!" http://workingfamilies.org/2014/11/winning-wolf-pennsylvania/.

———. "Working Families Party Independent Candidates Challenge the Status Quo." Last modified November 3, 2014. http://workingfamilies.org/2014/11/working-families-party-independent-candidates-challenge-status-quo/.

Worthen, Molly. "As Vermont Goes, So Goes the Nation?" New York Times, April 5, 2014. www.nytimes.com/2014/04/06/opinion/sunday/as-vermont-goes-so-goes-the-nation.html?emc=eta1&_r=1.

Yee, Vivian. "Working Families Candidate Diana Richardson Wins Brooklyn Assembly Post." New York Times, May 5, 2015. www.nytimes.com/2015/05/06/nyregion/working-families-candidate-diana-richardson-wins-brooklyn-assembly-post.html?_r=1.

INDEX